013

JACK LEON RUBY
aka Jack Leon Rubenstein
(White-Male)

36398

FBI-

POLICE DEPARTMENT. DALLAS, TEXAS

J. A. TANNER, CAPTAIN BUREAU OF IDEN

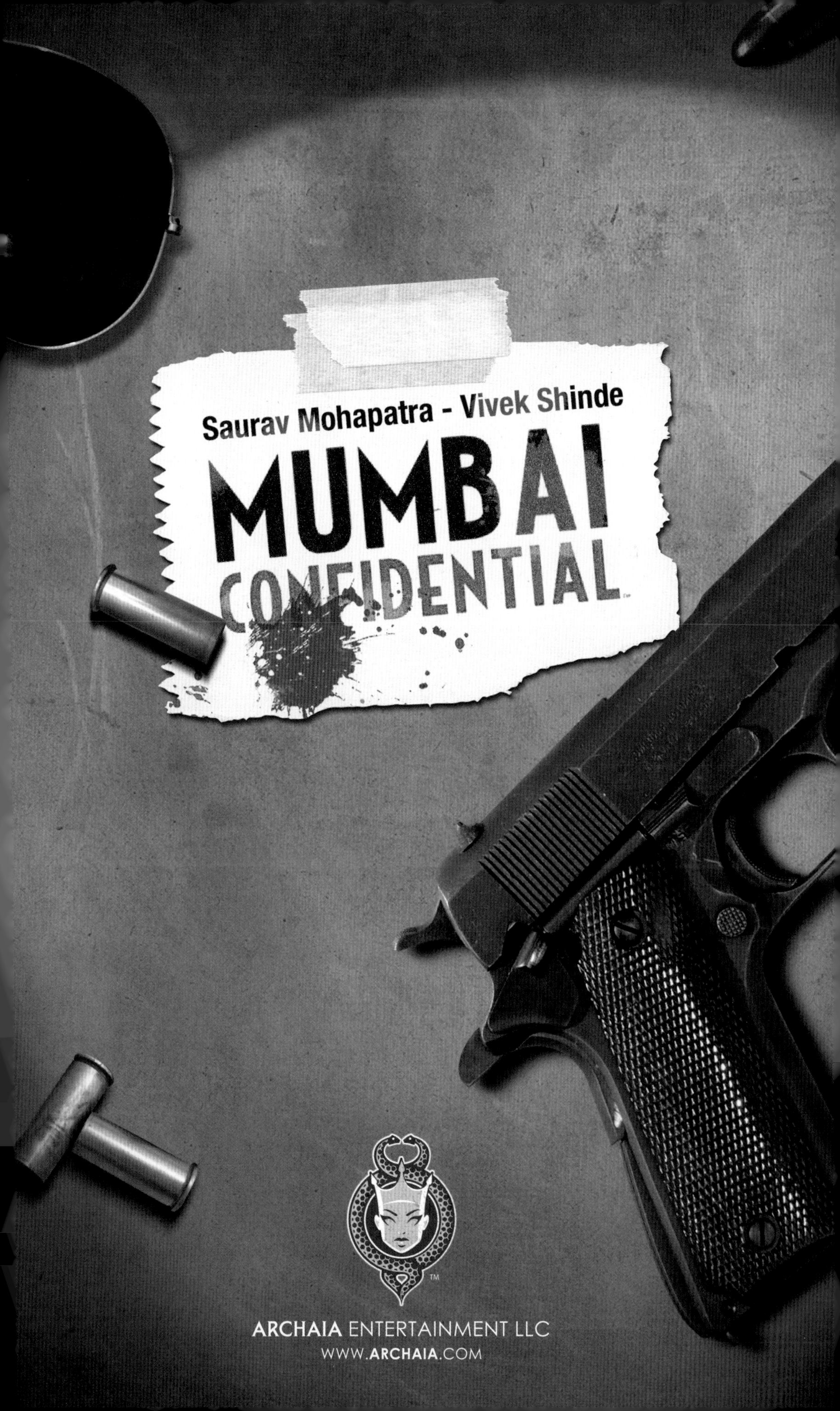
Saurav Mohapatra - Vivek Shinde
MUMBAI
CONFIDENTIAL
ARCHAIA ENTERTAINMENT LLC
WWW.ARCHAIA.COM

MUMBAI CONFIDENTIAL™

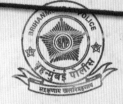

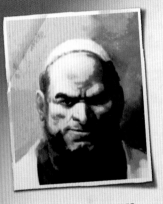

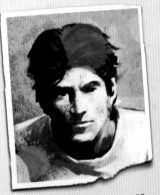

WRITTEN BY

SAURAV MOHAPATRA

ILLUSTRATED BY

VIVEK SHINDE

WANTED

Featuring additional art by
Sid Kotian, Saumin Patel,
Vinay Brahmania, and Devaki Neogi

Howling Monkey Studio, *Design*
Rebecca Taylor, *Editor*
Scott Newman, *Production Manager*

Archaia Entertainment
PJ Bickett, *Chairman*
Jack Cummins, *President & COO*
Mark Smylie, *CCO*
Mike Kennedy, *Publisher*
Stephen Christy, *Editor-in-Chief*
Mel Caylo, *Marketing Manager*

Published by Archaia
Archaia Entertainment LLC
1680 Vine Street, Suite 1010
Los Angeles, CA 90028
www.archaia.com

MUMBAI CONFIDENTIAL BOOK ONE: GOOD COP, BAD COP. Original Graphic Novel Hardcover. March 2013. FIRST PRINTING.

10 9 8 7 6 5 4 3 2 1

ISBN: 1-936393-65-4

ISBN-13: 978-1-936393-65-7

ARCHAIA™
NEW STORIES. NEW WORLDS.

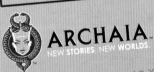

Printed in China.

Table of Contents

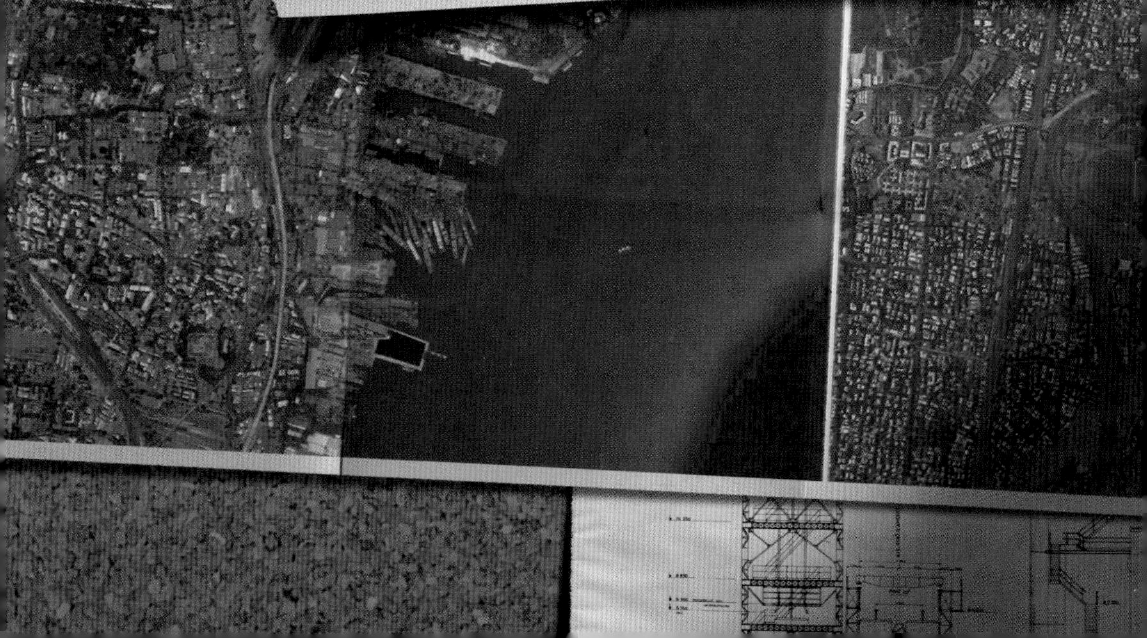

POLICE DEPARTMENT

Confidentially Speaking...

I could tell you how Saurav Mohapatra is a considerably better writer now than when I first met and edited him at the late, lamented Virgin Comics (and he was pretty good back then). I could tell you about how Vivek Shinde has grown as an artist since I first encountered his work. I could discuss the broader ramifications of globalization meeting comics head-on and the great wealth of Indian talent ready to make its mark in the American market. All of that is true, but it's besides the point. And the point is, and always will be, the story.

MUMBAI CONFIDENTIAL is a story universal in its nature and appeal, but entirely specific in its setting. Noir lives in the shadows of human nature. It explores the lurking, darker impulses and possibility for violence inherent in all of us. The setting takes what could be overly familiar to Western sensibilities and makes it fresh, exciting ... even exotic.

This is a story of good cops and bad cops, or more precisely, dirty cops and dirtier cops. But these crooked cops don't prowl the mean streets of New York City, or sun-bleached avenues of the City of Angels. Their beat is Mumbai, and I can't imagine a more fitting noir setting. The city is caught between the modern and the ancient. High-rise luxury towers nestle next to slums of corrugated tin. Mumbai offers triumph as well as tragedy, the best and worst of humanity on display all at once. It's a perfect place to tell this story.

As a creator, you learn that the most important stories are the ones only you can tell. The next chapter in the endless superhero drama? The next iteration of whatever licensed franchise needs propping up? There's always somebody to do those jobs, and there's nothing wrong with that.

But it's not the same as telling a story only you can tell, that you bring to life via your unique skills, experiences and passions. MUMBAI CONFIDENTIAL isn't a story I could tell. Not in this way, not set in this place, not with this style. This story exists because Saurav, Vivek, and their collaborators are the only ones who could breathe such life into it. I'm glad they did.

Ron Marz

December, 2012

Ron Marz is a veteran comics writer whose list of credits includes lengthy runs on GREEN LANTERN, SILVER SURFER, and WITCHBLADE, as well as the creator-owned series SHINKU, SAMURAI: HEAVEN AND EARTH, and DRAGON PRINCE.

I like my town with a little drop of poison.
Nobody knows they're lining up to go insane.
I'm all alone, I smoke my friends down to the filter,
But I feel much cleaner after it rains."

- "Little Drop of Poison"
TOM WAITS

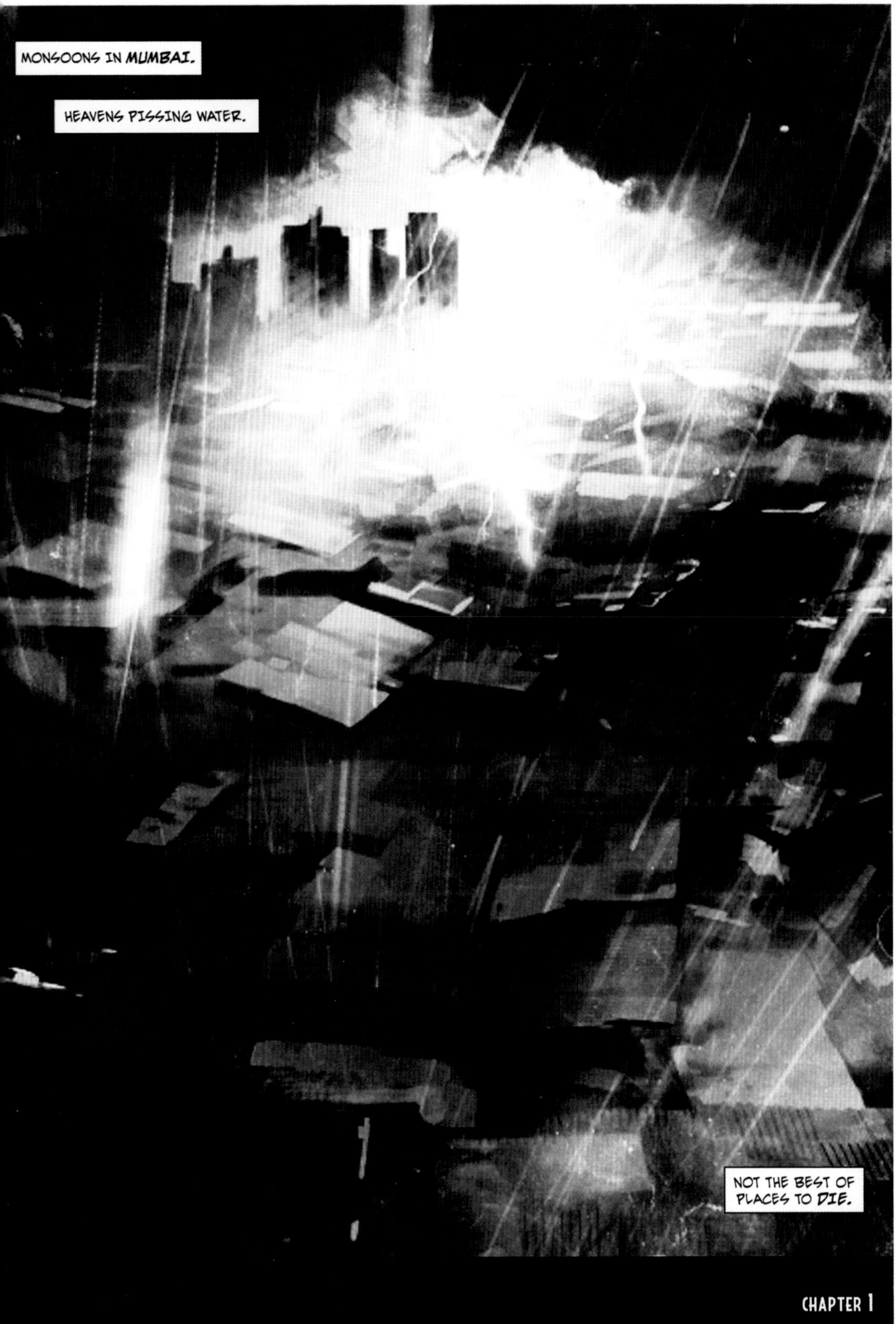
MONSOONS IN MUMBAI.
HEAVENS PISSING WATER.
NOT THE BEST OF PLACES TO DIE.

CHAPTER 1

ONCE UPON A MONSOON MIDNIGHT IN MUMBAI

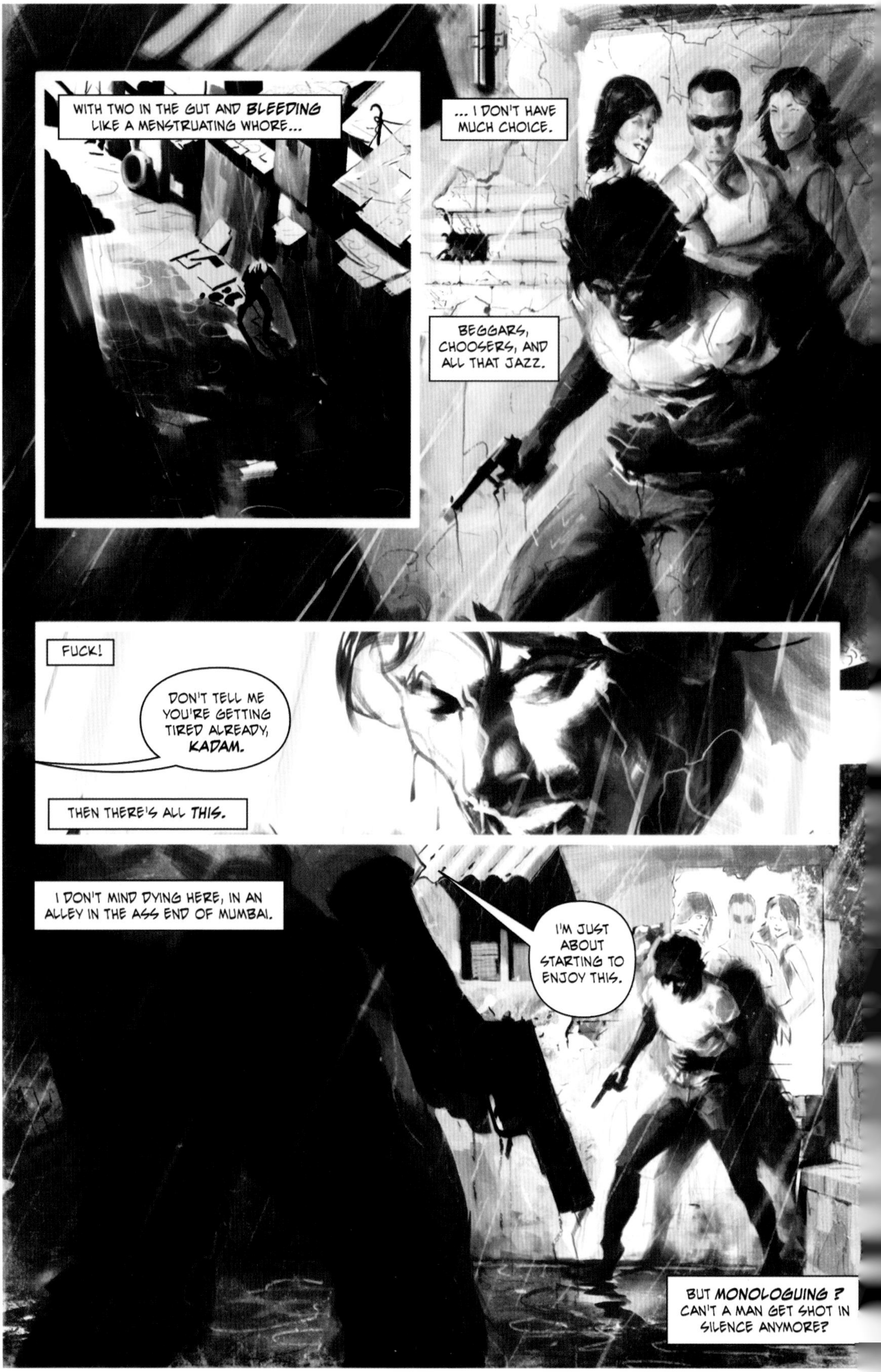
WITH TWO IN THE GUT AND BLEEDING LIKE A MENSTRUATING WHORE...
... I DON'T HAVE MUCH CHOICE.
BEGGARS, CHOOSERS, AND ALL THAT JAZZ.
FUCK!
DON'T TELL ME YOU'RE GETTING TIRED ALREADY, KADAM.
THEN THERE'S ALL THIS.
I DON'T MIND DYING HERE, IN AN ALLEY IN THE ASS END OF MUMBAI.
I'M JUST ABOUT STARTING TO ENJOY THIS.
BUT MONOLOGUING ? CAN'T A MAN GET SHOT IN SILENCE ANYMORE?

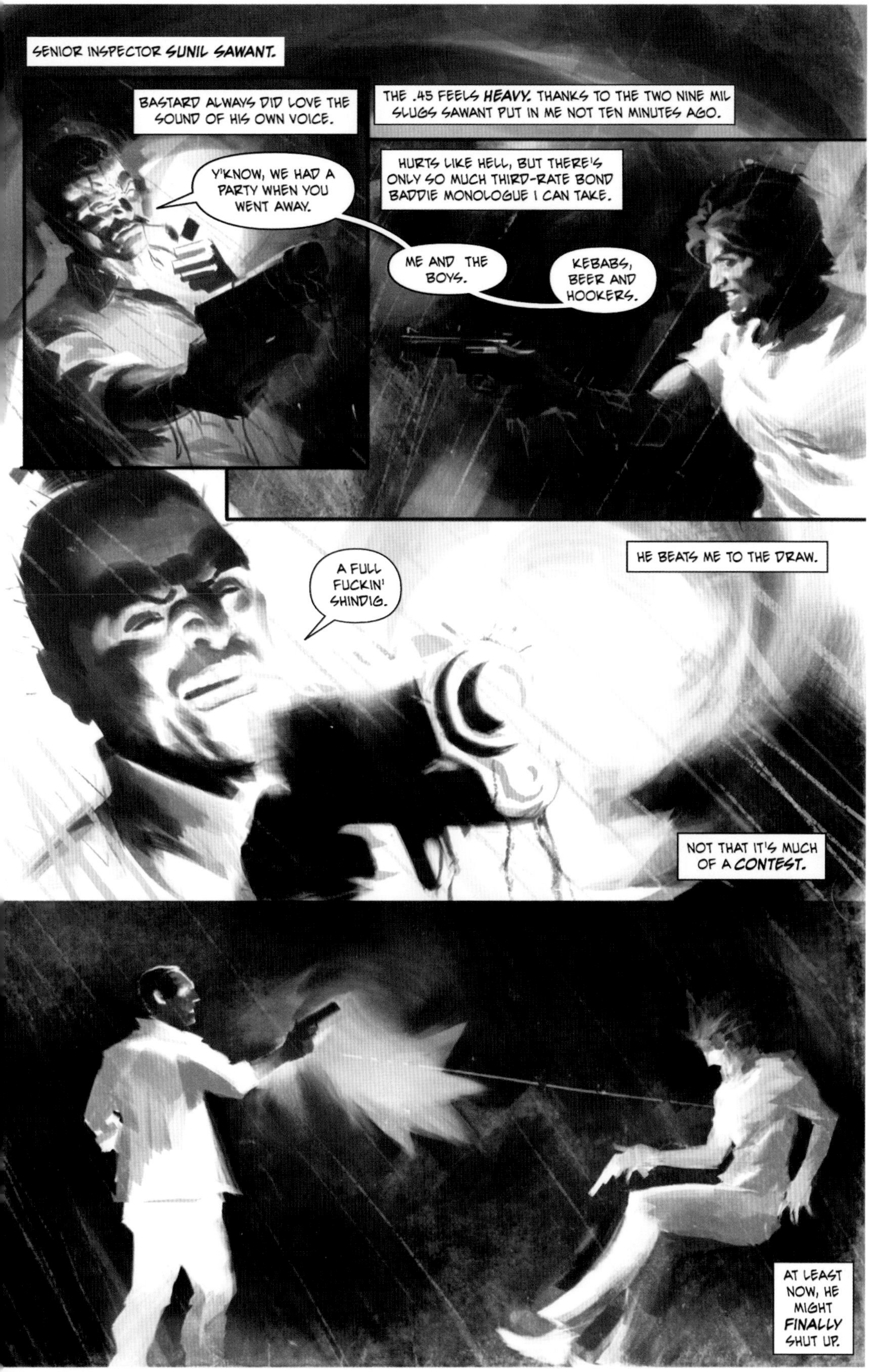
SENIOR INSPECTOR SUNIL SAWANT.
BASTARD ALWAYS DID LOVE THE SOUND OF HIS OWN VOICE.
THE .45 FEELS HEAVY. THANKS TO THE TWO NINE MIL SLUGS SAWANT PUT IN ME NOT TEN MINUTES AGO.
HURTS LIKE HELL, BUT THERE'S ONLY SO MUCH THIRD-RATE BOND BADDIE MONOLOGUE I CAN TAKE.
Y'KNOW, WE HAD A PARTY WHEN YOU WENT AWAY.
ME AND THE BOYS.
KEBABS, BEER AND HOOKERS.
A FULL FUCKIN' SHINDIG.
HE BEATS ME TO THE DRAW.
NOT THAT IT'S MUCH OF A CONTEST.
AT LEAST NOW, HE MIGHT FINALLY SHUT UP.

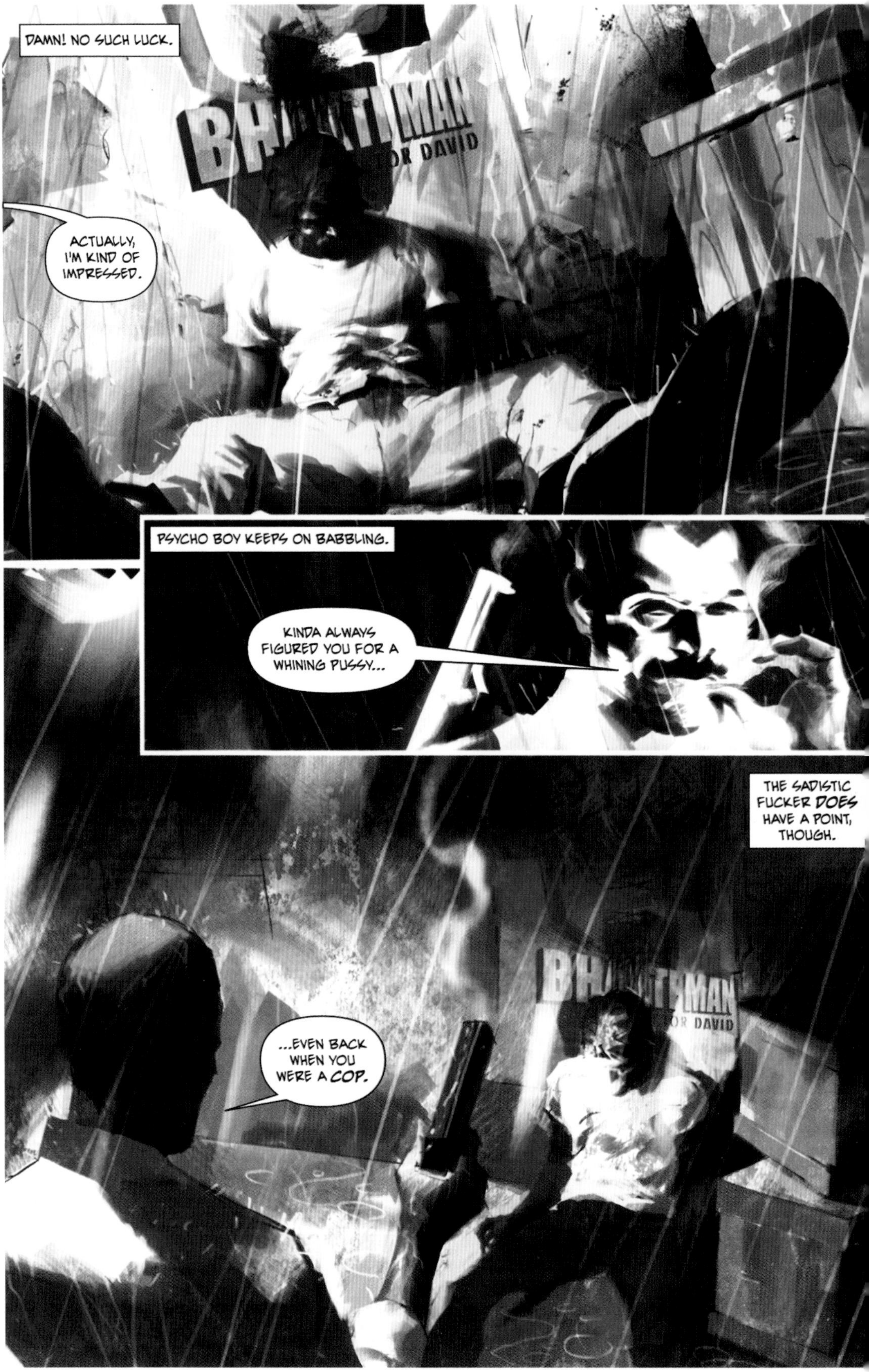
DAMN! NO SUCH LUCK.
ACTUALLY, I'M KIND OF IMPRESSED.
PSYCHO BOY KEEPS ON BABBLING.
KINDA ALWAYS FIGURED YOU FOR A WHINING PUSSY...
THE SADISTIC FUCKER DOES HAVE A POINT, THOUGH.
...EVEN BACK WHEN YOU WERE A COP.

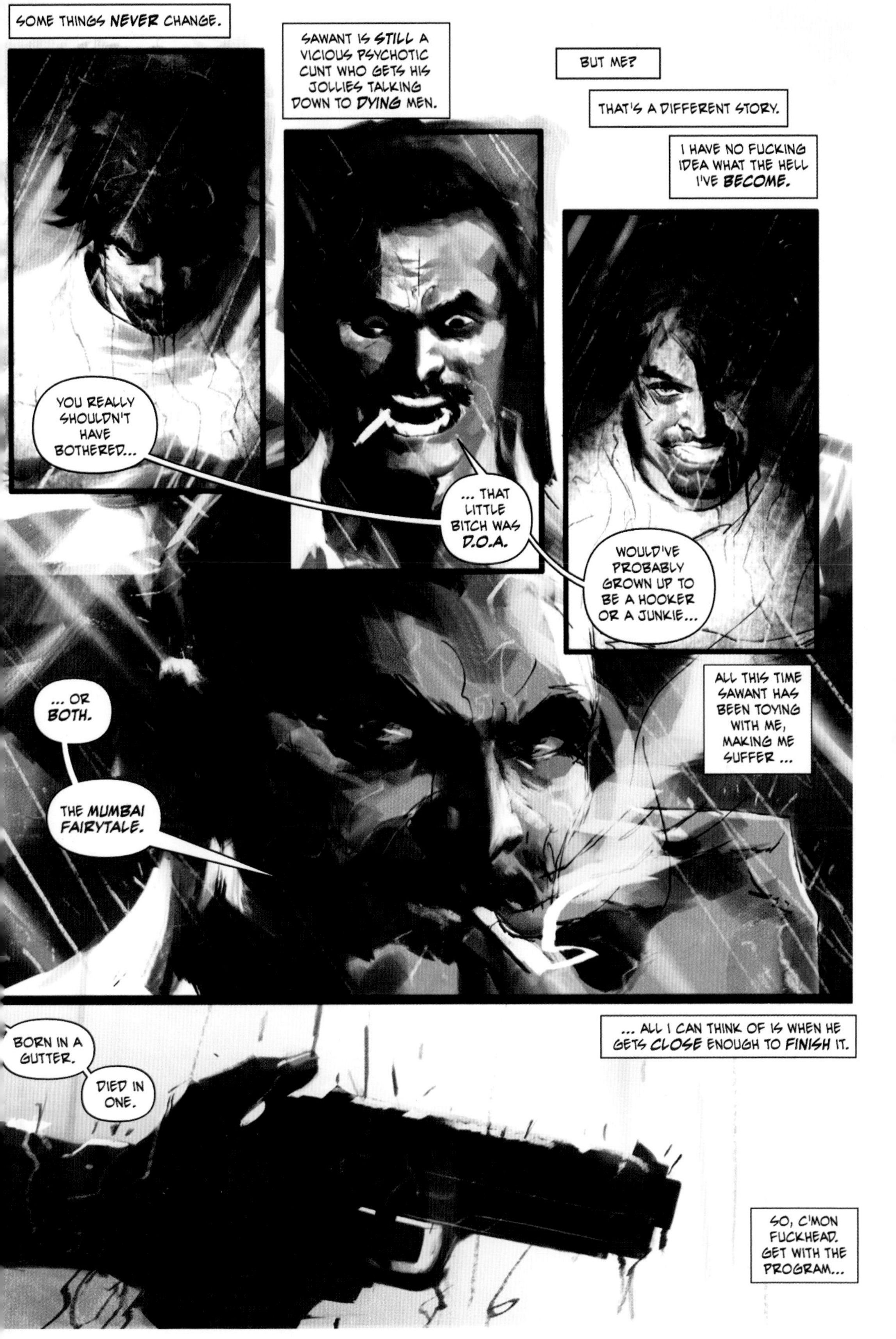
SOME THINGS NEVER CHANGE.
SAWANT IS STILL A VICIOUS PSYCHOTIC CUNT WHO GETS HIS JOLLIES TALKING DOWN TO DYING MEN.
BUT ME?
THAT'S A DIFFERENT STORY.
I HAVE NO FUCKING IDEA WHAT THE HELL I'VE BECOME.
YOU REALLY SHOULDN'T HAVE BOTHERED...
... THAT LITTLE BITCH WAS D.O.A.
WOULD'VE PROBABLY GROWN UP TO BE A HOOKER OR A JUNKIE...
... OR BOTH.
THE MUMBAI FAIRYTALE.
ALL THIS TIME SAWANT HAS BEEN TOYING WITH ME, MAKING ME SUFFER ...
BORN IN A GUTTER.
DIED IN ONE.
... ALL I CAN THINK OF IS WHEN HE GETS CLOSE ENOUGH TO FINISH IT.
SO, C'MON FUCKHEAD. GET WITH THE PROGRAM...

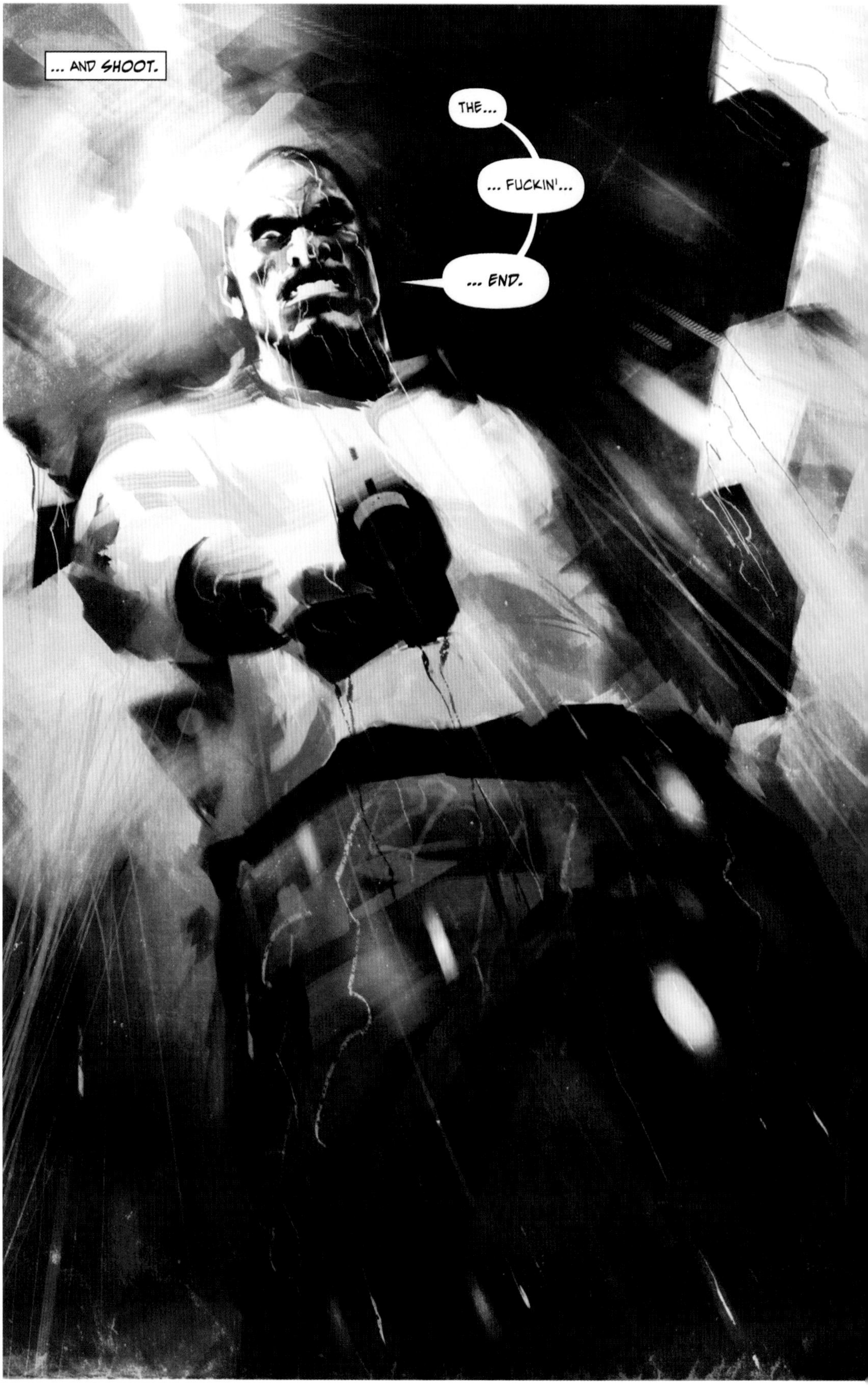
... AND SHOOT.
THE...
... FUCKIN'...
... END.

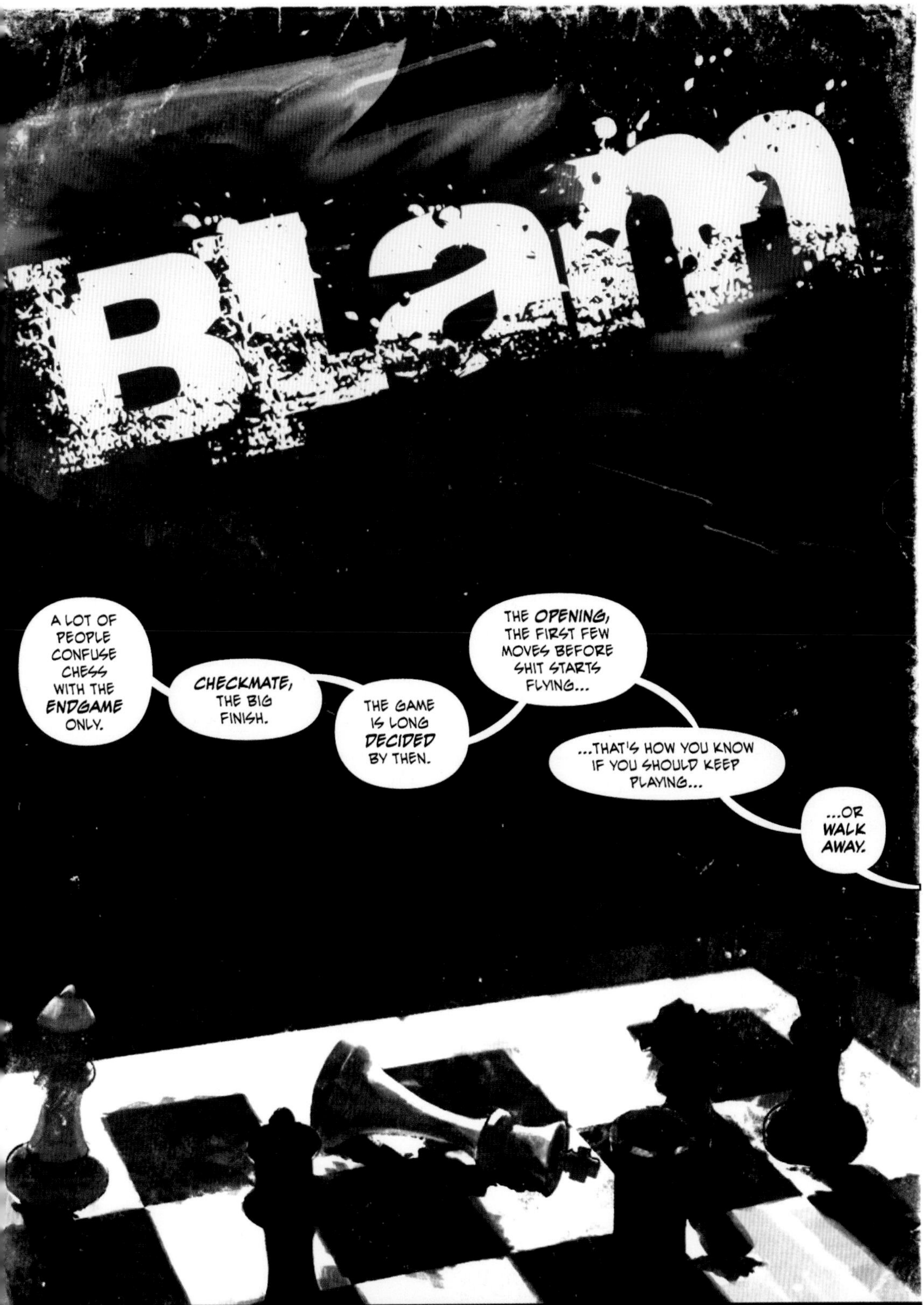
BLAM
A LOT OF PEOPLE CONFUSE CHESS WITH THE ENDGAME ONLY.
CHECKMATE, THE BIG FINISH.
THE GAME IS LONG DECIDED BY THEN.
THE OPENING, THE FIRST FEW MOVES BEFORE SHIT STARTS FLYING...
...THAT'S HOW YOU KNOW IF YOU SHOULD KEEP PLAYING...
...OR WALK AWAY.

CHAPTER 2

THE MOURNING MAN

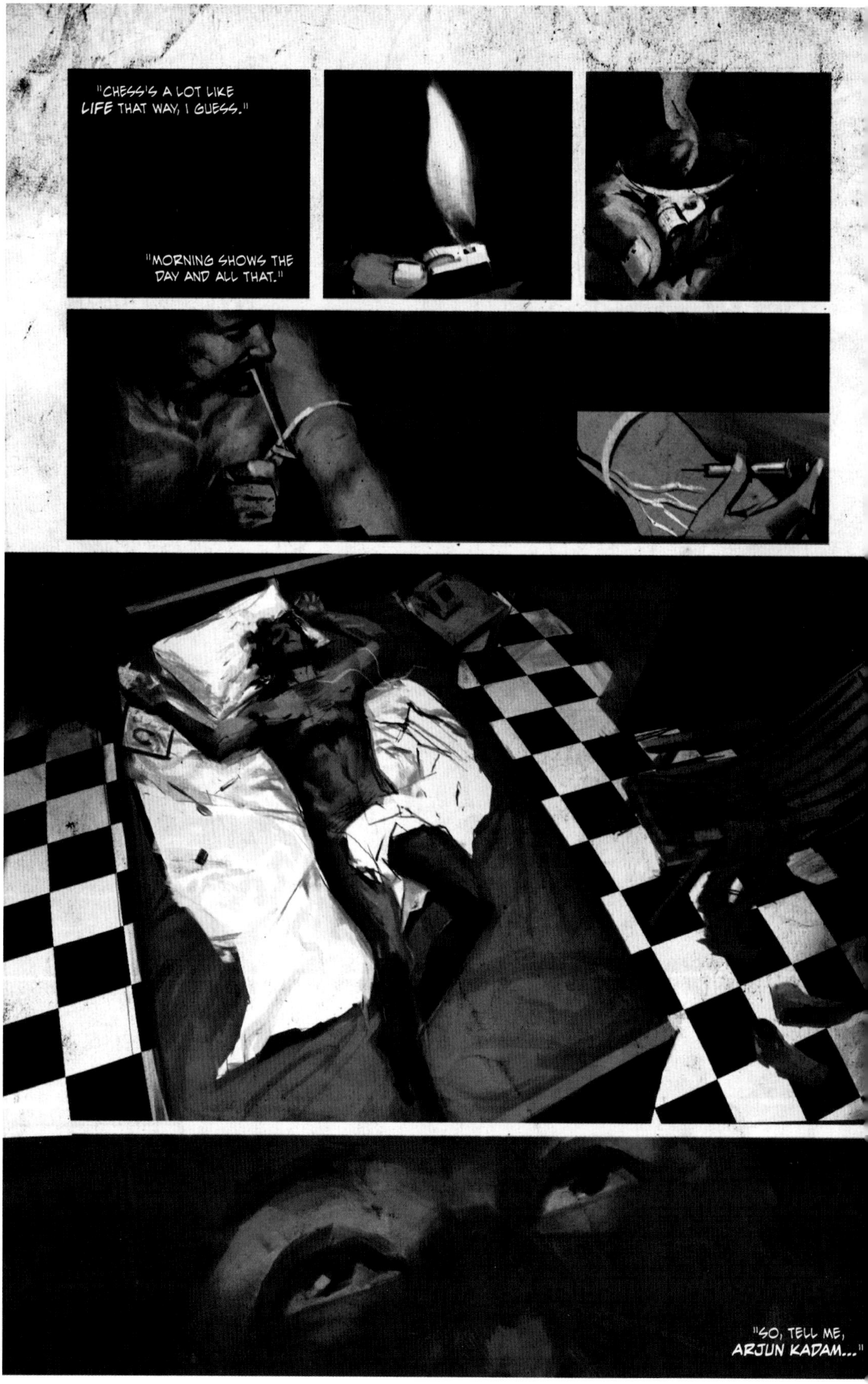
"CHESS'S A LOT LIKE LIFE THAT WAY, I GUESS."
"MORNING SHOWS THE DAY AND ALL THAT."
"SO, TELL ME, ARJUN KADAM..."

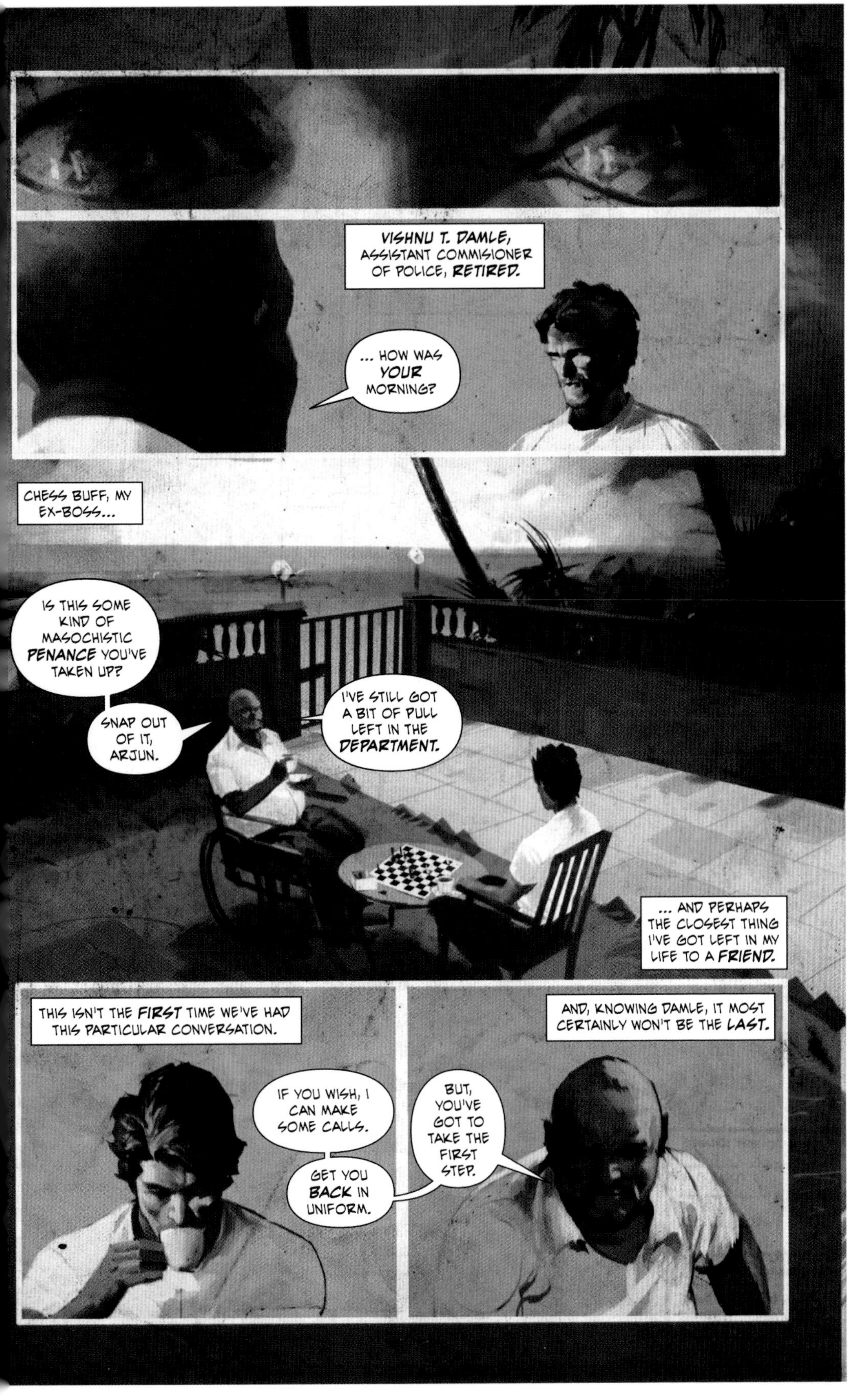
VISHNU T. DAMLE, ASSISTANT COMMISIONER OF POLICE, RETIRED.
... HOW WAS YOUR MORNING?
CHESS BUFF, MY EX-BOSS...
IS THIS SOME KIND OF MASOCHISTIC PENANCE YOU'VE TAKEN UP?
SNAP OUT OF IT, ARJUN.
I'VE STILL GOT A BIT OF PULL LEFT IN THE DEPARTMENT.
... AND PERHAPS THE CLOSEST THING I'VE GOT LEFT IN MY LIFE TO A FRIEND.
THIS ISN'T THE FIRST TIME WE'VE HAD THIS PARTICULAR CONVERSATION.
IF YOU WISH, I CAN MAKE SOME CALLS.
GET YOU BACK IN UNIFORM.
AND, KNOWING DAMLE, IT MOST CERTAINLY WON'T BE THE LAST.
BUT, YOU'VE GOT TO TAKE THE FIRST STEP.

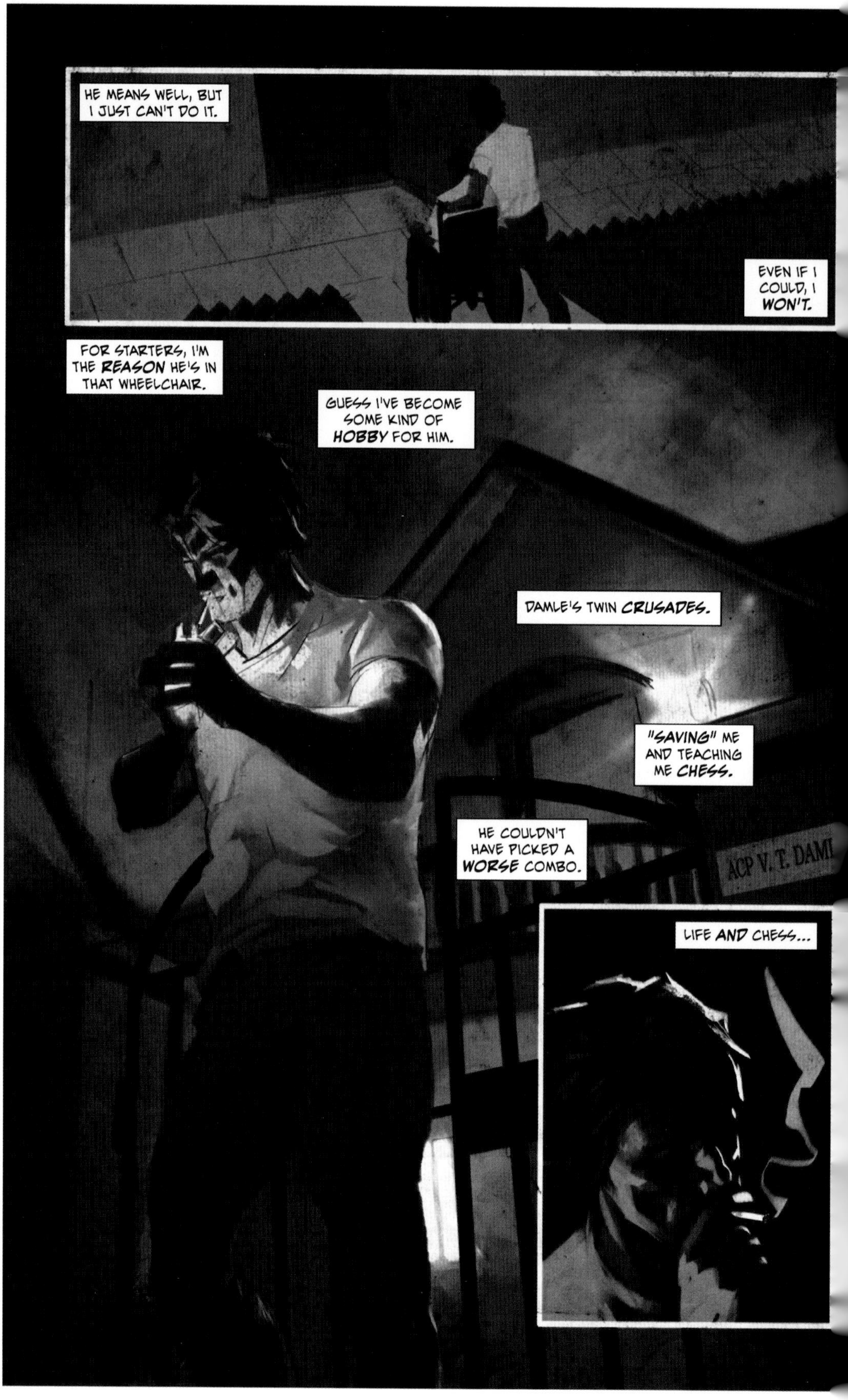
HE MEANS WELL, BUT I JUST CAN'T DO IT.
EVEN IF I COULD, I WON'T.
FOR STARTERS, I'M THE REASON HE'S IN THAT WHEELCHAIR.
GUESS I'VE BECOME SOME KIND OF HOBBY FOR HIM.
DAMLE'S TWIN CRUSADES.
"SAVING" ME AND TEACHING ME CHESS.
HE COULDN'T HAVE PICKED A WORSE COMBO.
ACP V. T. DAMI
LIFE AND CHESS...

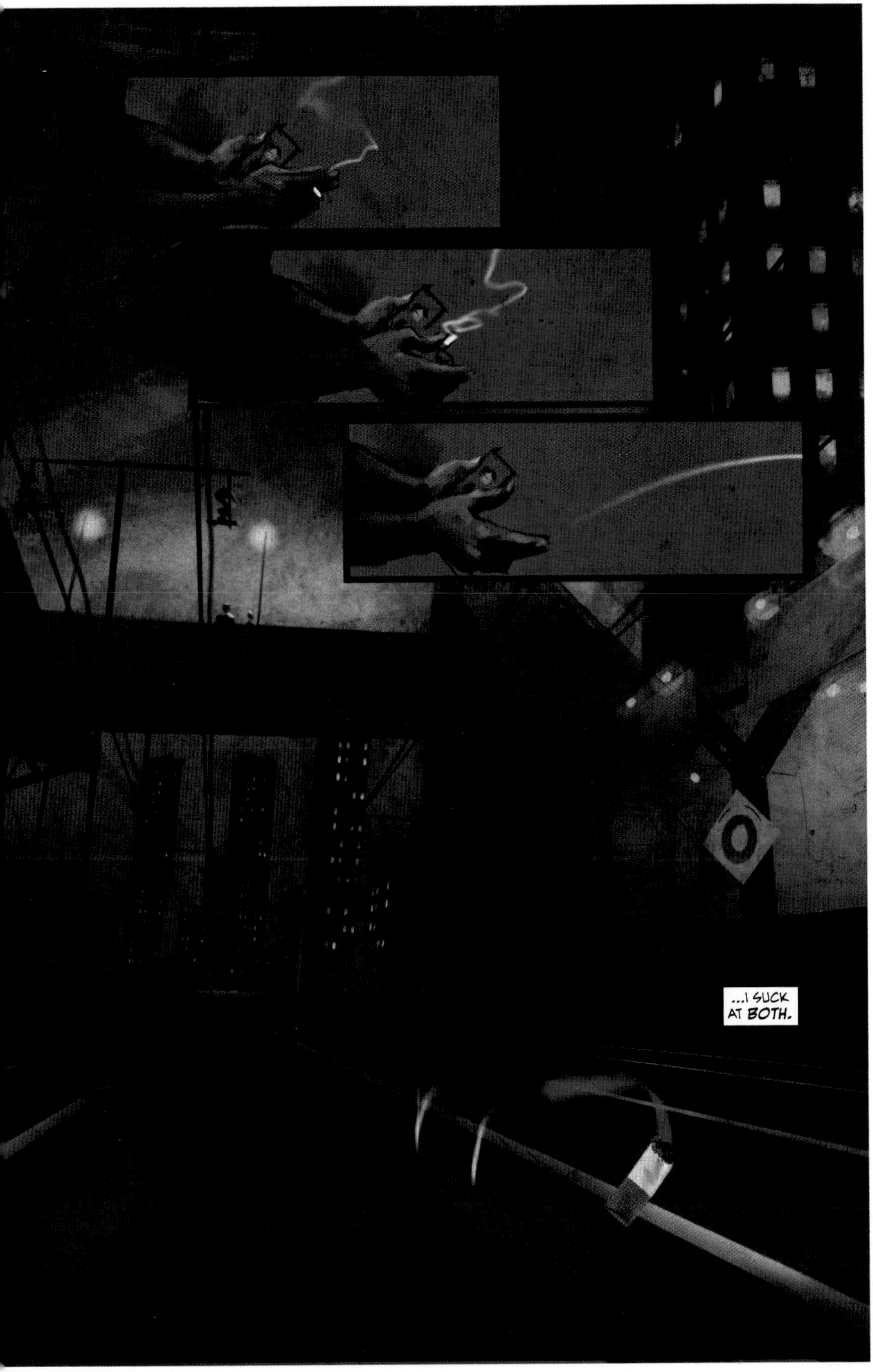
...I SUCK AT BOTH.

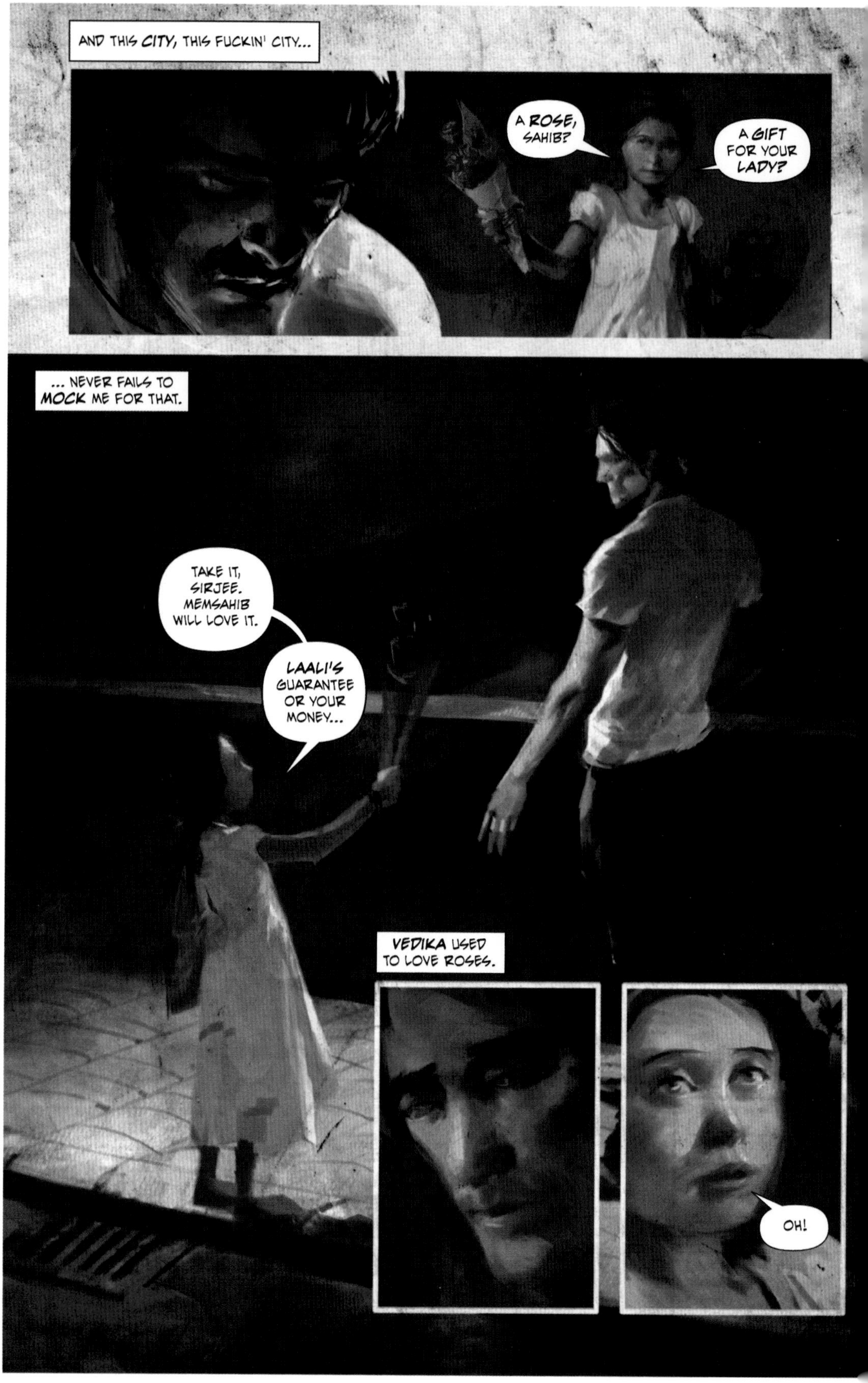
AND THIS CITY, THIS FUCKIN' CITY...
A ROSE, SAHIB?
A GIFT FOR YOUR LADY?
... NEVER FAILS TO MOCK ME FOR THAT.
TAKE IT, SIRJEE. MEMSAHIB WILL LOVE IT.
LAALI'S GUARANTEE OR YOUR MONEY...
VEDIKA USED TO LOVE ROSES.
OH!

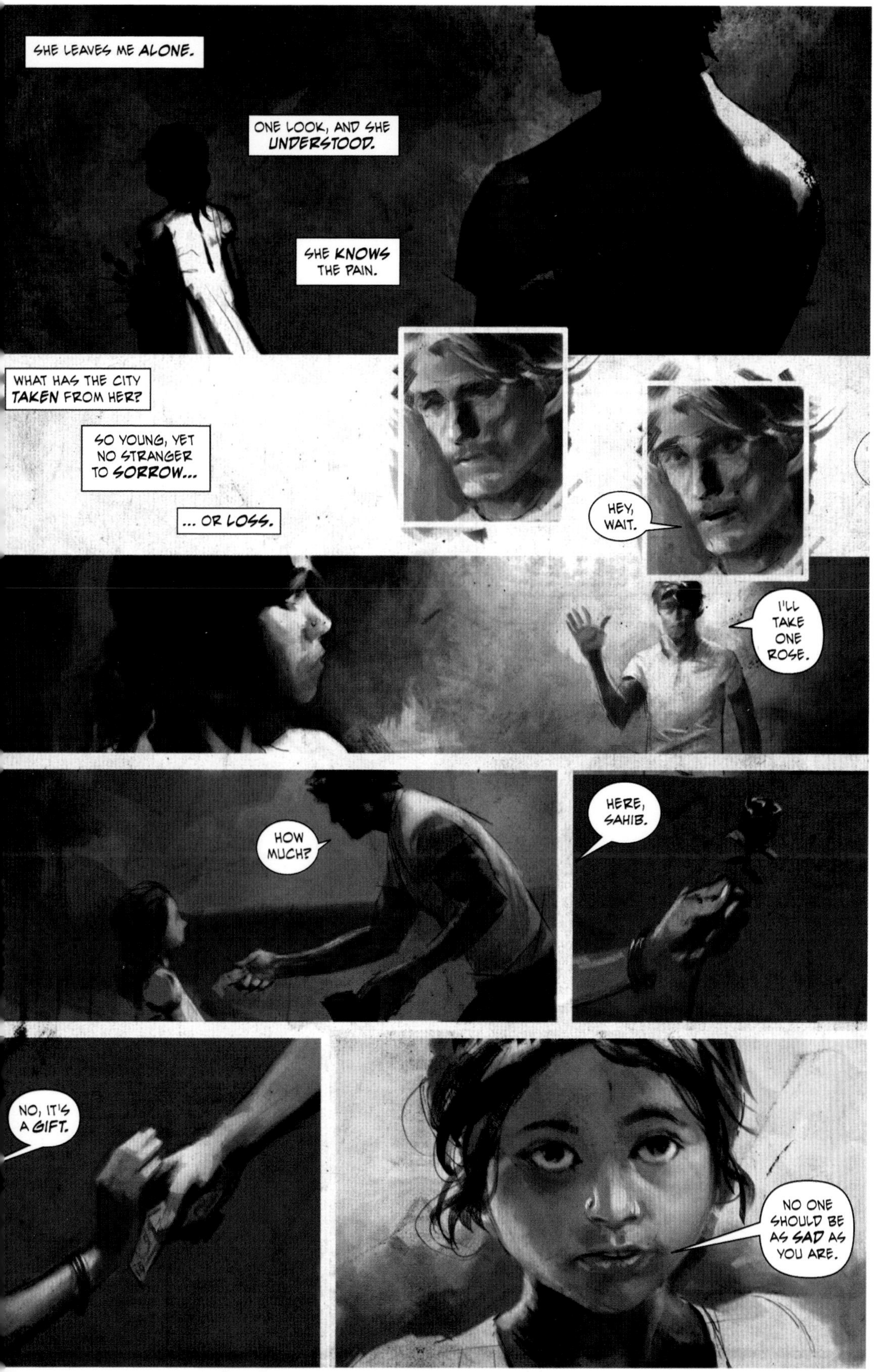
SHE LEAVES ME ALONE.
ONE LOOK, AND SHE UNDERSTOOD.
SHE KNOWS THE PAIN.
WHAT HAS THE CITY TAKEN FROM HER?
SO YOUNG, YET NO STRANGER TO SORROW...
... OR LOSS.
HEY, WAIT.
I'LL TAKE ONE ROSE.
HOW MUCH?
HERE, SAHIB.
NO, IT'S A GIFT.
NO ONE SHOULD BE AS SAD AS YOU ARE.

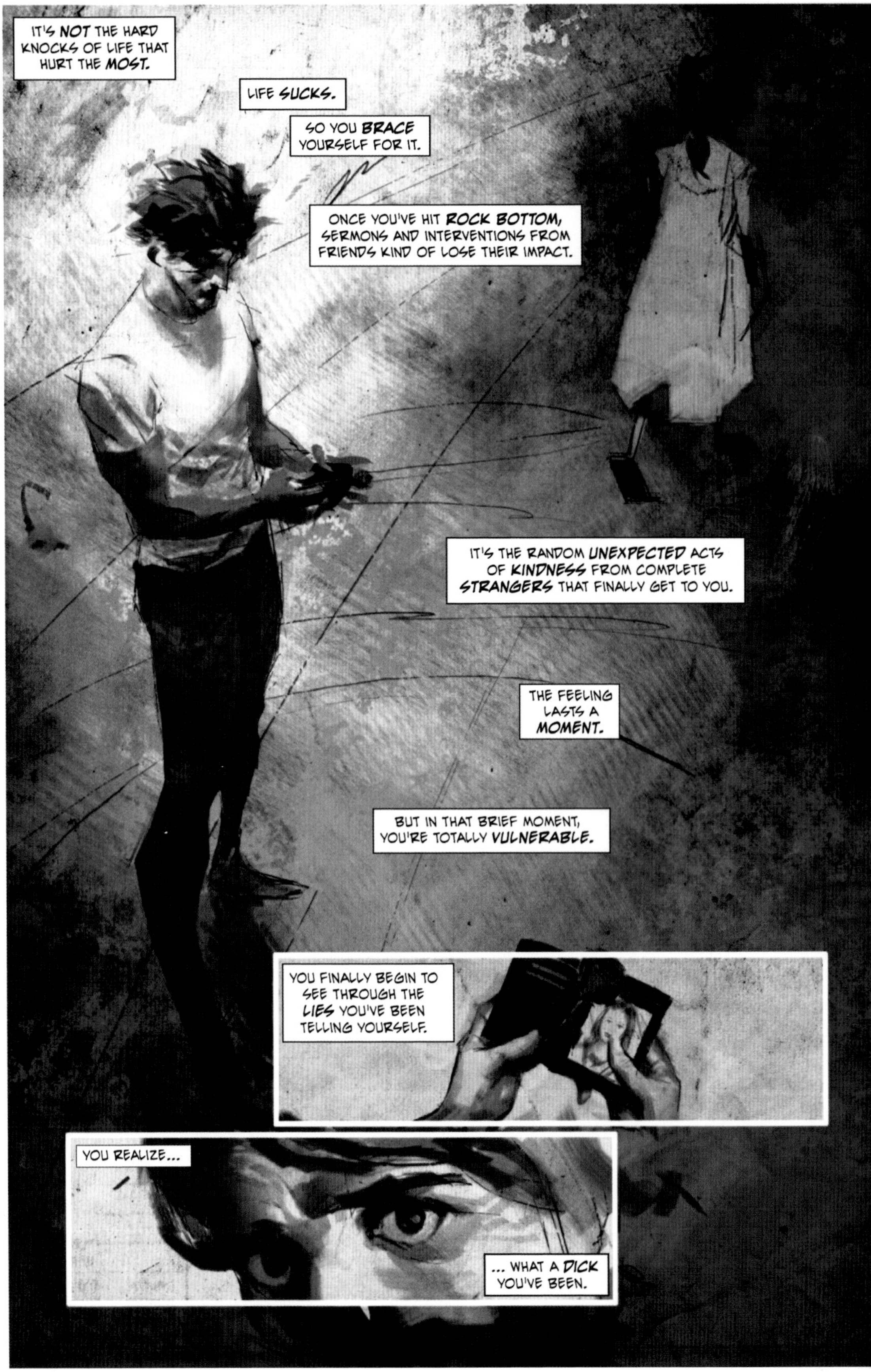
IT'S NOT THE HARD KNOCKS OF LIFE THAT HURT THE MOST.
LIFE SUCKS.
SO YOU BRACE YOURSELF FOR IT.
ONCE YOU'VE HIT ROCK BOTTOM, SERMONS AND INTERVENTIONS FROM FRIENDS KIND OF LOSE THEIR IMPACT.
IT'S THE RANDOM UNEXPECTED ACTS OF KINDNESS FROM COMPLETE STRANGERS THAT FINALLY GET TO YOU.
THE FEELING LASTS A MOMENT.
BUT IN THAT BRIEF MOMENT, YOU'RE TOTALLY VULNERABLE.
YOU FINALLY BEGIN TO SEE THROUGH THE LIES YOU'VE BEEN TELLING YOURSELF.
YOU REALIZE...
... WHAT A DICK YOU'VE BEEN.

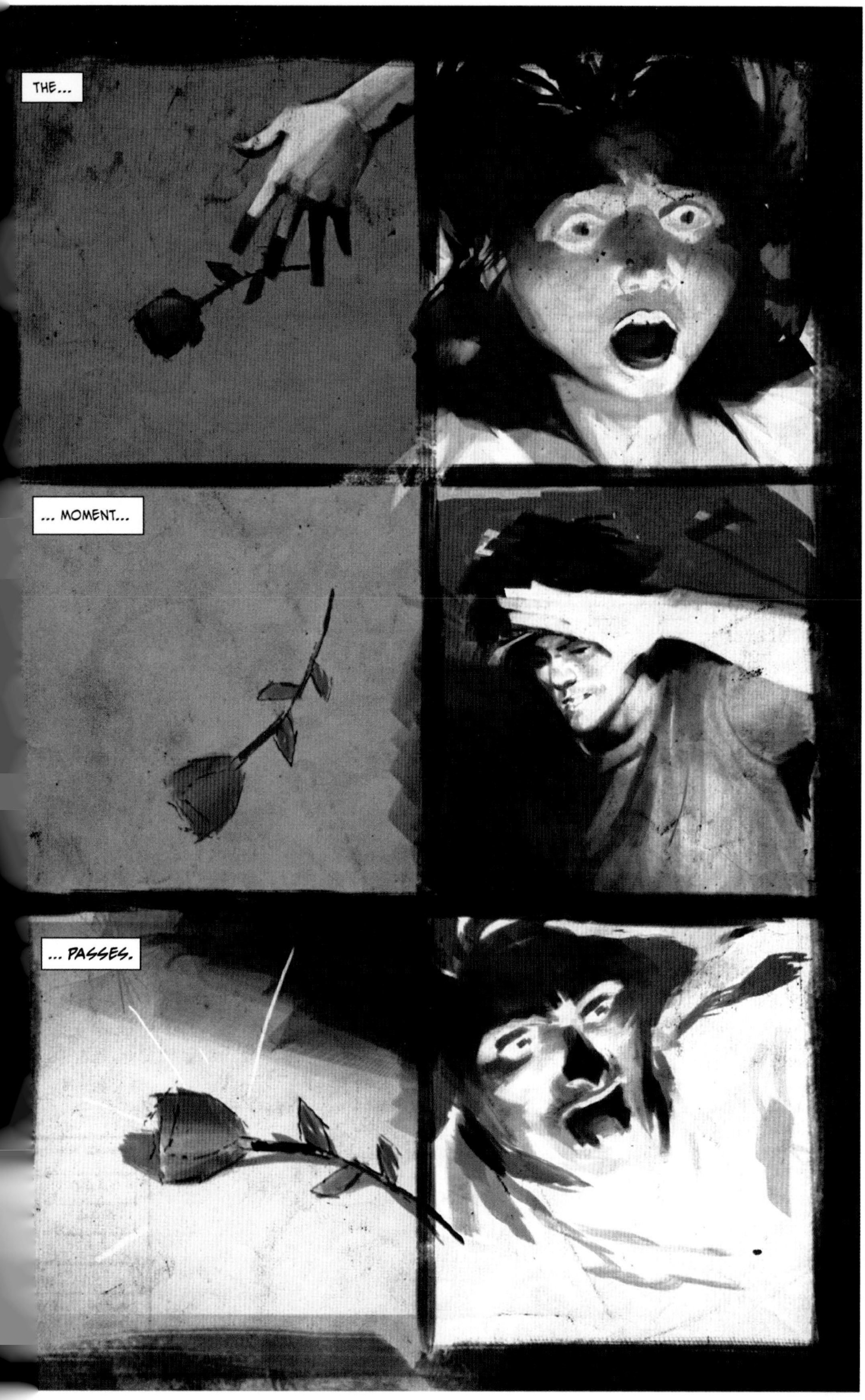
THE...
... MOMENT...
... PASSES.

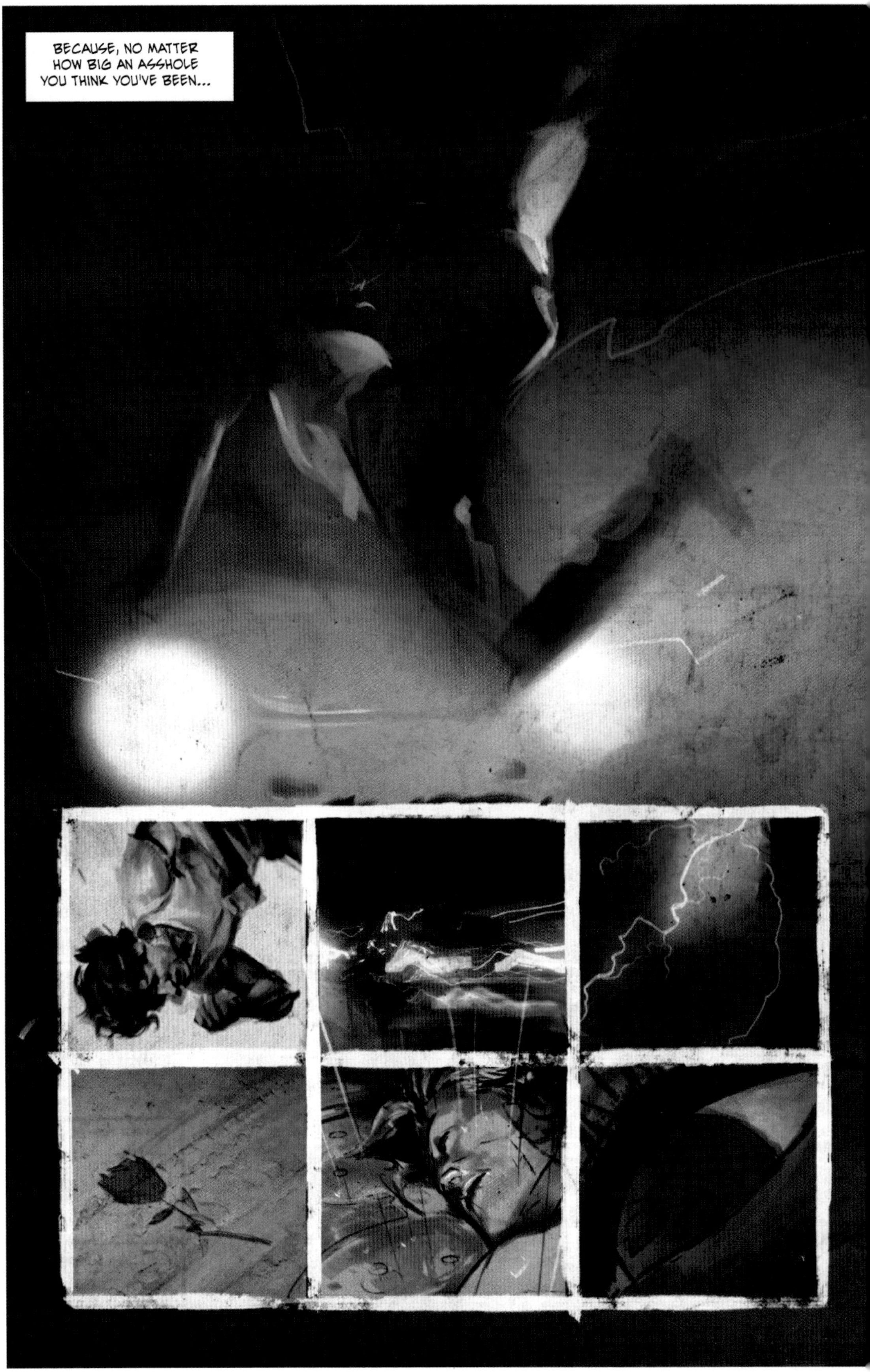
BECAUSE, NO MATTER HOW BIG AN ASSHOLE YOU THINK YOU'VE BEEN...

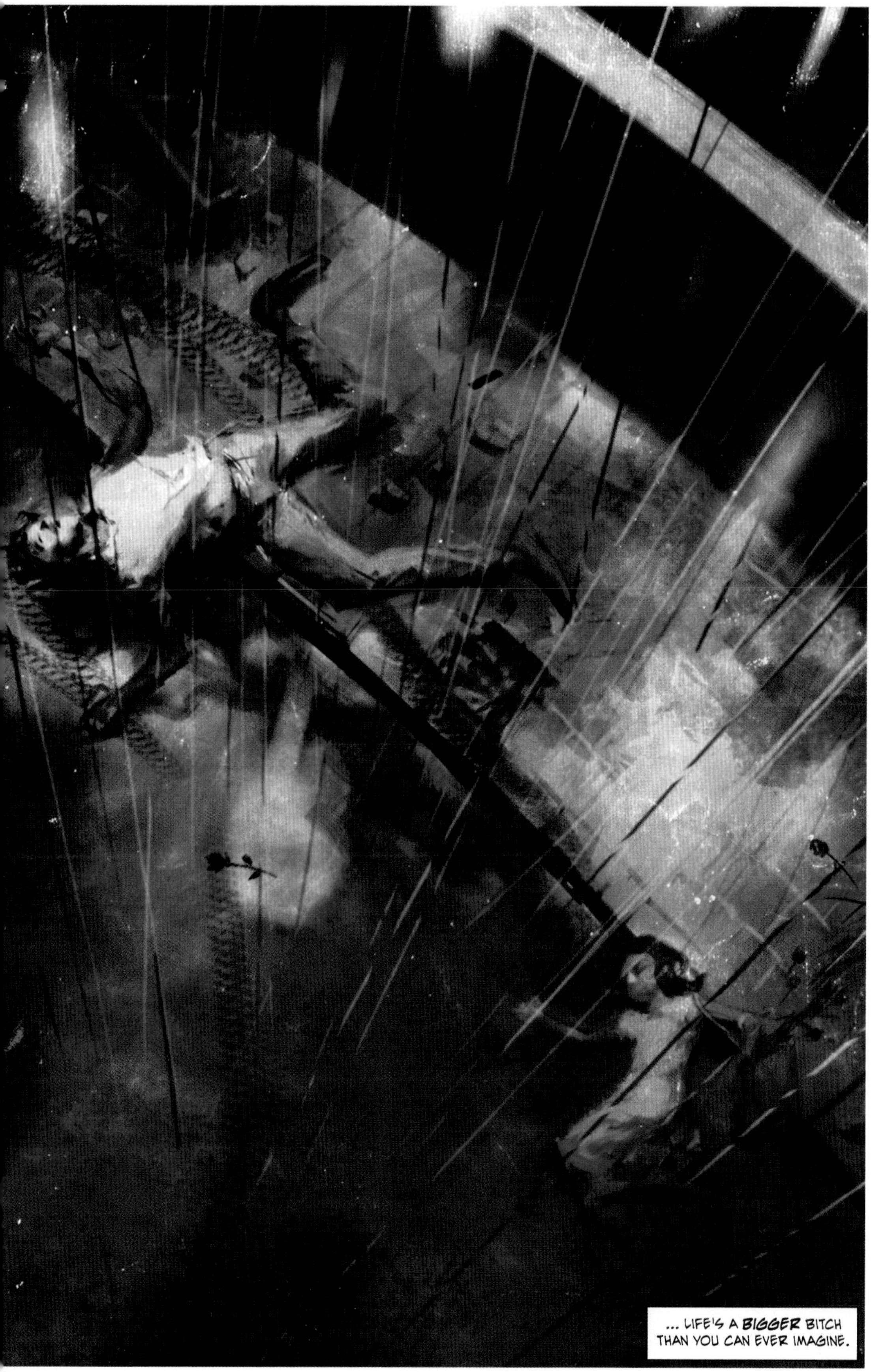
... LIFE'S A BIGGER BITCH THAN YOU CAN EVER IMAGINE.

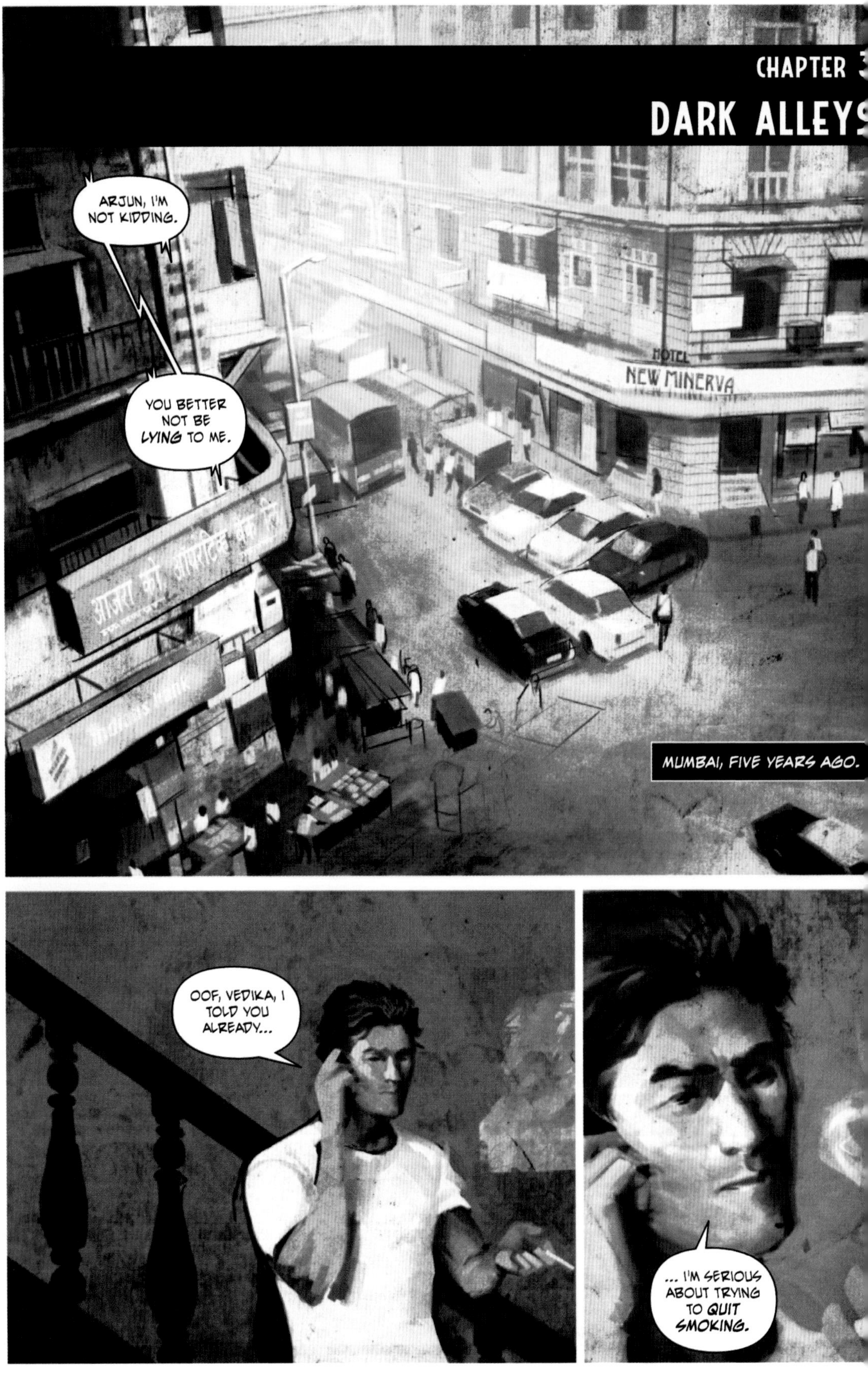
CHAPTER 3
DARK ALLEYS
ARJUN, I'M NOT KIDDING.
YOU BETTER NOT BE LYING TO ME.
HOTEL NEW MINERVA
MUMBAI, FIVE YEARS AGO.
OOF, VEDIKA, I TOLD YOU ALREADY...
... I'M SERIOUS ABOUT TRYING TO QUIT SMOKING.

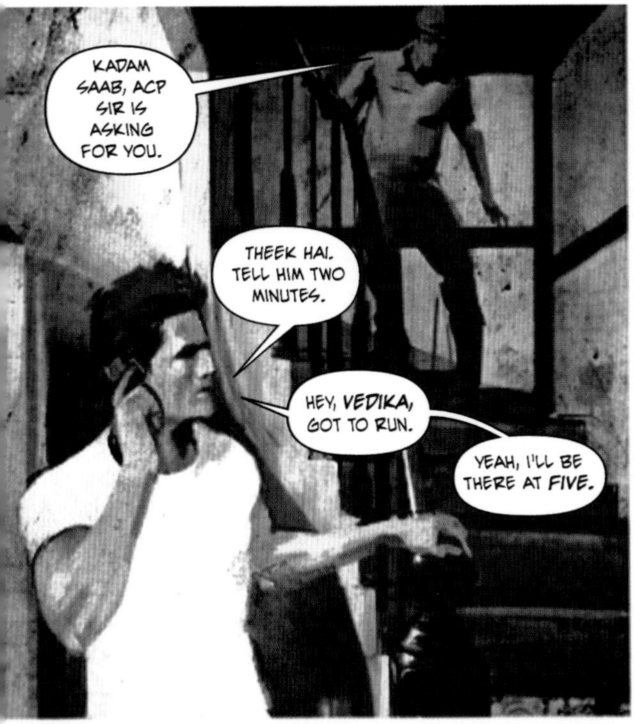
KADAM SAAB, ACP SIR IS ASKING FOR YOU.
THEEK HAI. TELL HIM TWO MINUTES.
HEY, VEDIKA, GOT TO RUN.
YEAH, I'LL BE THERE AT FIVE.

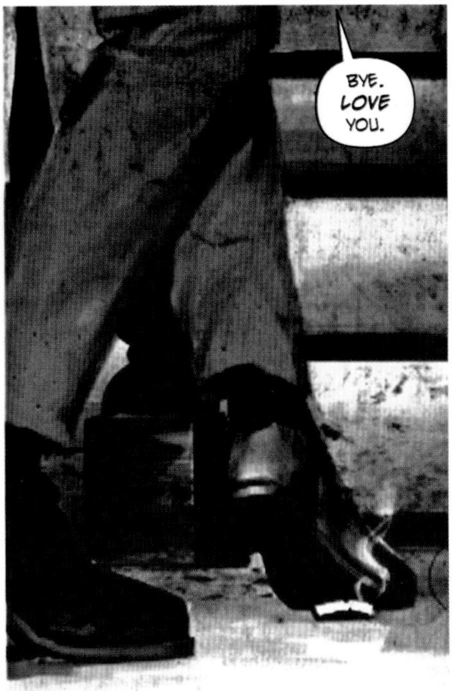
BYE. LOVE YOU.

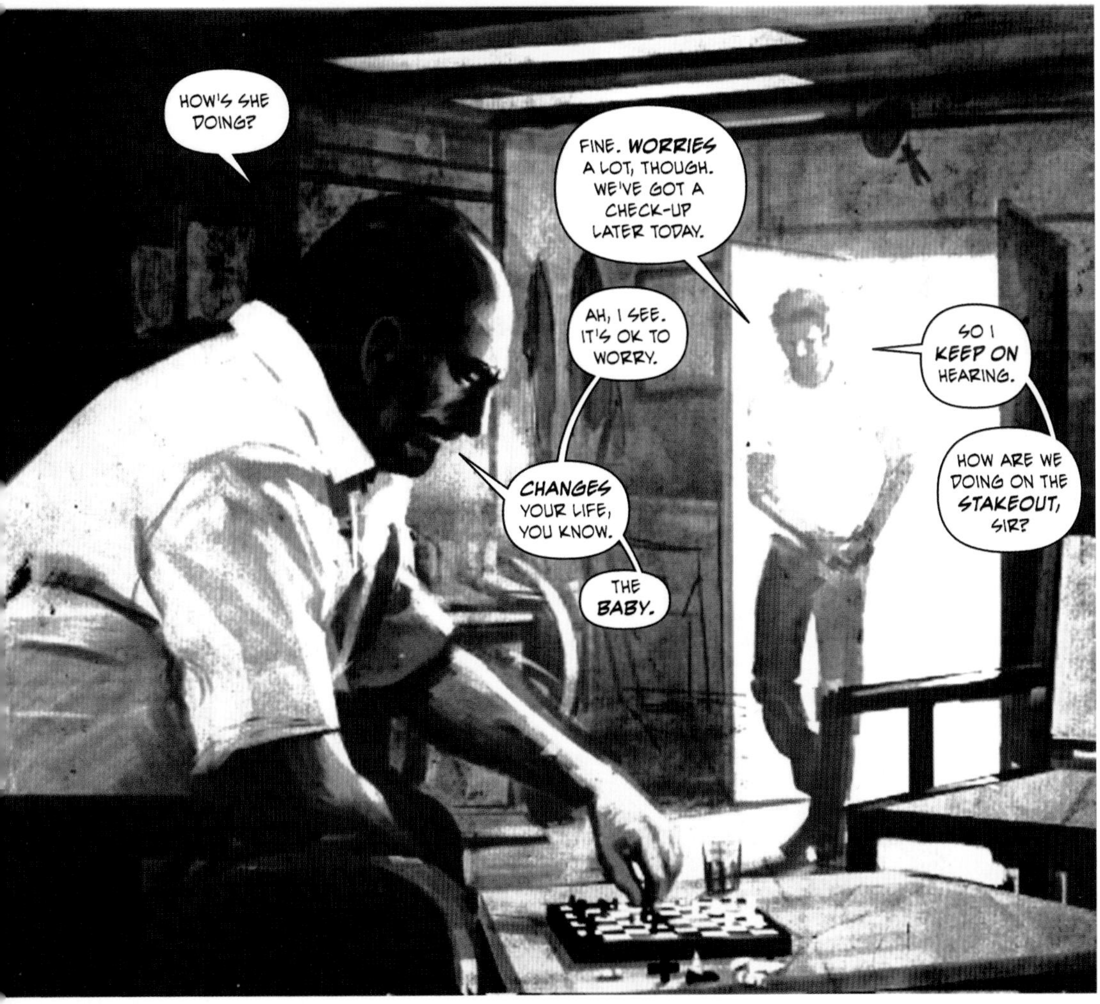
HOW'S SHE DOING?
FINE. WORRIES A LOT, THOUGH. WE'VE GOT A CHECK-UP LATER TODAY.
AH, I SEE. IT'S OK TO WORRY.
CHANGES YOUR LIFE, YOU KNOW.
THE BABY.
SO I KEEP ON HEARING.
HOW ARE WE DOING ON THE STAKEOUT, SIR?

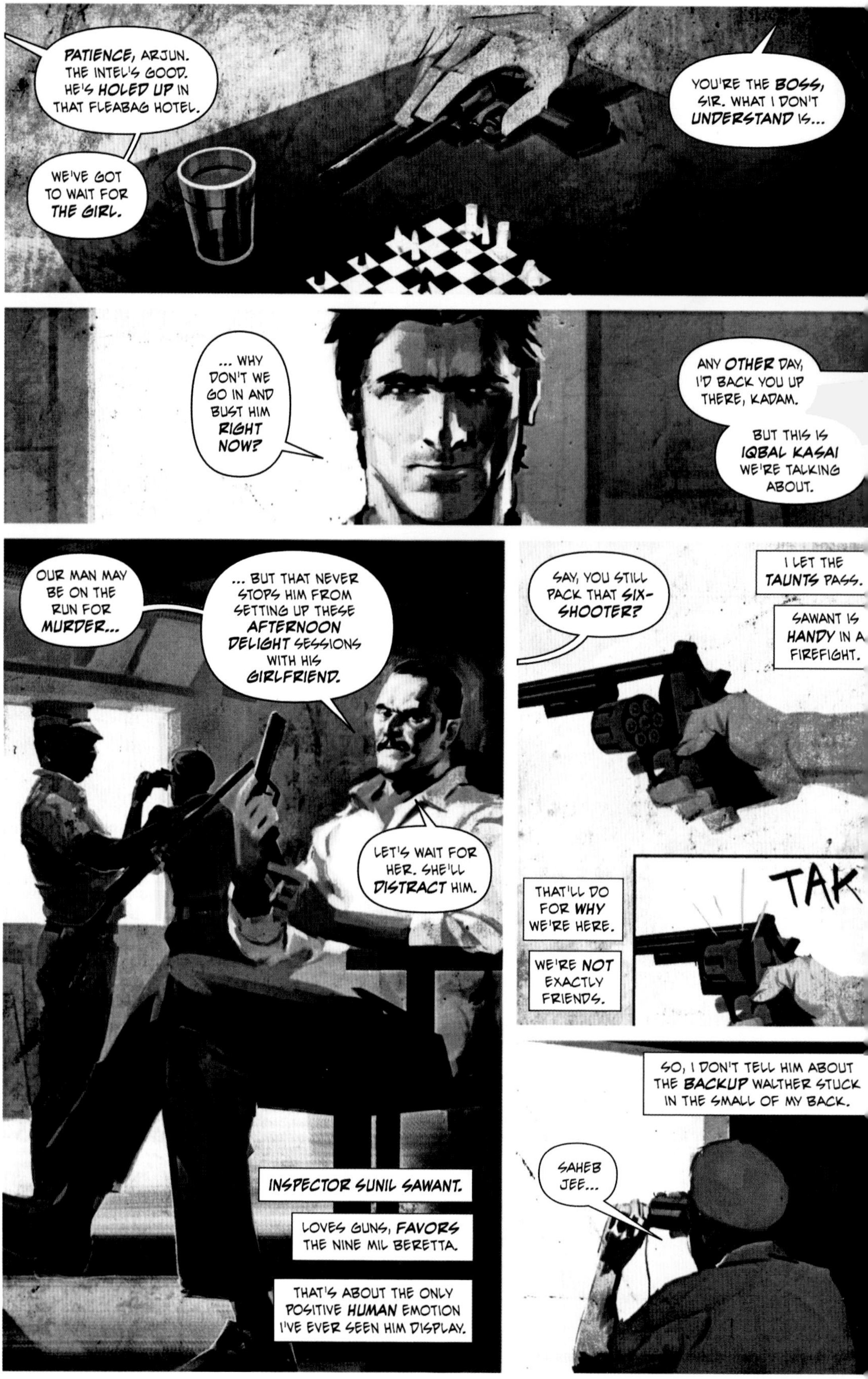
PATIENCE, ARJUN. THE INTEL'S GOOD. HE'S HOLED UP IN THAT FLEABAG HOTEL.
WE'VE GOT TO WAIT FOR THE GIRL.
YOU'RE THE BOSS, SIR. WHAT I DON'T UNDERSTAND IS...
... WHY DON'T WE GO IN AND BUST HIM RIGHT NOW?
ANY OTHER DAY, I'D BACK YOU UP THERE, KADAM.
BUT THIS IS IQBAL KASAI WE'RE TALKING ABOUT.
OUR MAN MAY BE ON THE RUN FOR MURDER...
... BUT THAT NEVER STOPS HIM FROM SETTING UP THESE AFTERNOON DELIGHT SESSIONS WITH HIS GIRLFRIEND.
LET'S WAIT FOR HER. SHE'LL DISTRACT HIM.
INSPECTOR SUNIL SAWANT.
LOVES GUNS, FAVORS THE NINE MIL BERETTA.
THAT'S ABOUT THE ONLY POSITIVE HUMAN EMOTION I'VE EVER SEEN HIM DISPLAY.
SAY, YOU STILL PACK THAT SIX-SHOOTER?
I LET THE TAUNTS PASS.
SAWANT IS HANDY IN A FIREFIGHT.
TAK
THAT'LL DO FOR WHY WE'RE HERE.
WE'RE NOT EXACTLY FRIENDS.
SO, I DON'T TELL HIM ABOUT THE BACKUP WALTHER STUCK IN THE SMALL OF MY BACK.
SAHEB JEE...

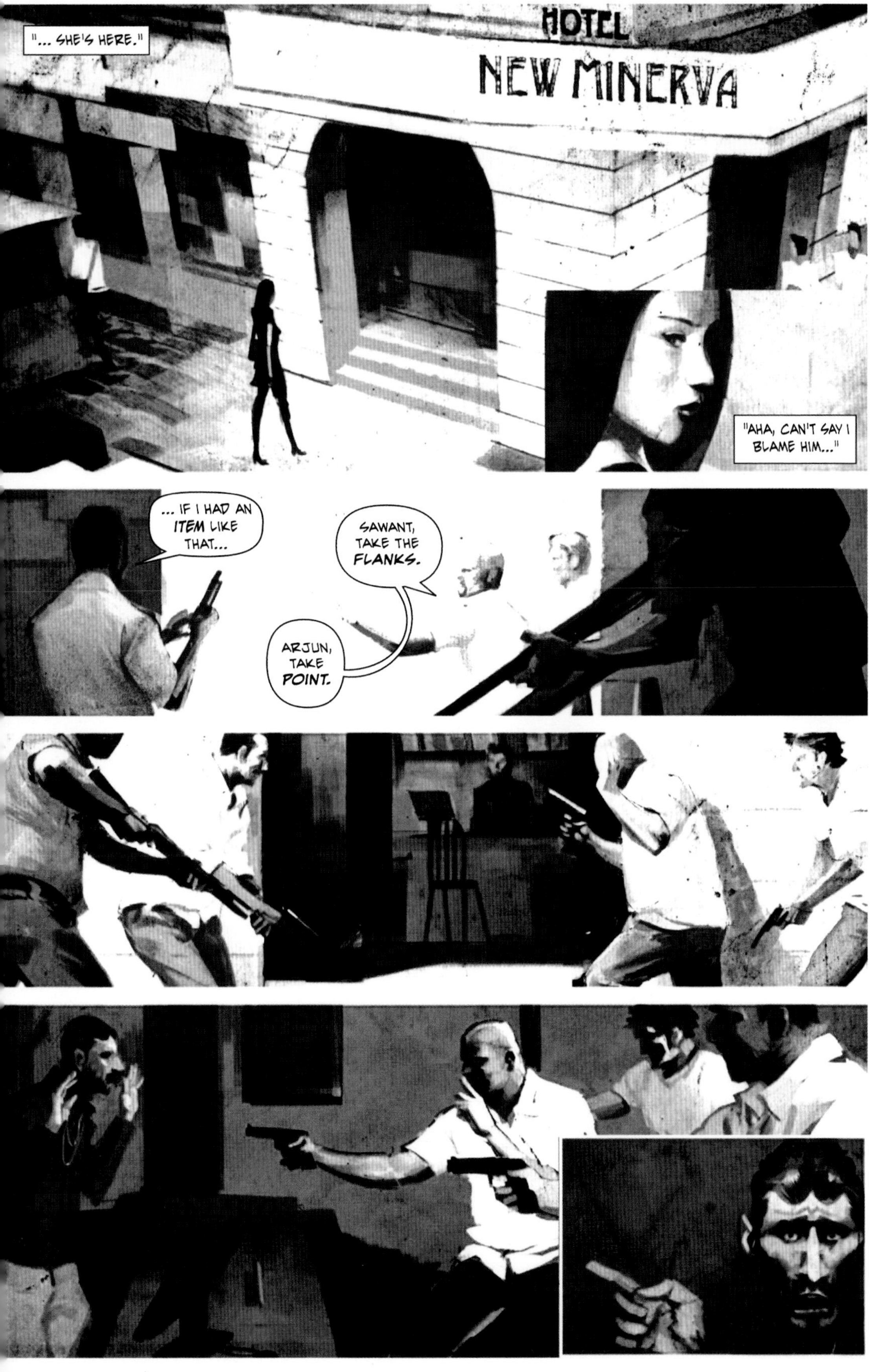
"... SHE'S HERE."
HOTEL
NEW MINERVA
"AHA, CAN'T SAY I BLAME HIM..."
... IF I HAD AN ITEM LIKE THAT...
SAWANT, TAKE THE FLANKS.
ARJUN, TAKE POINT.

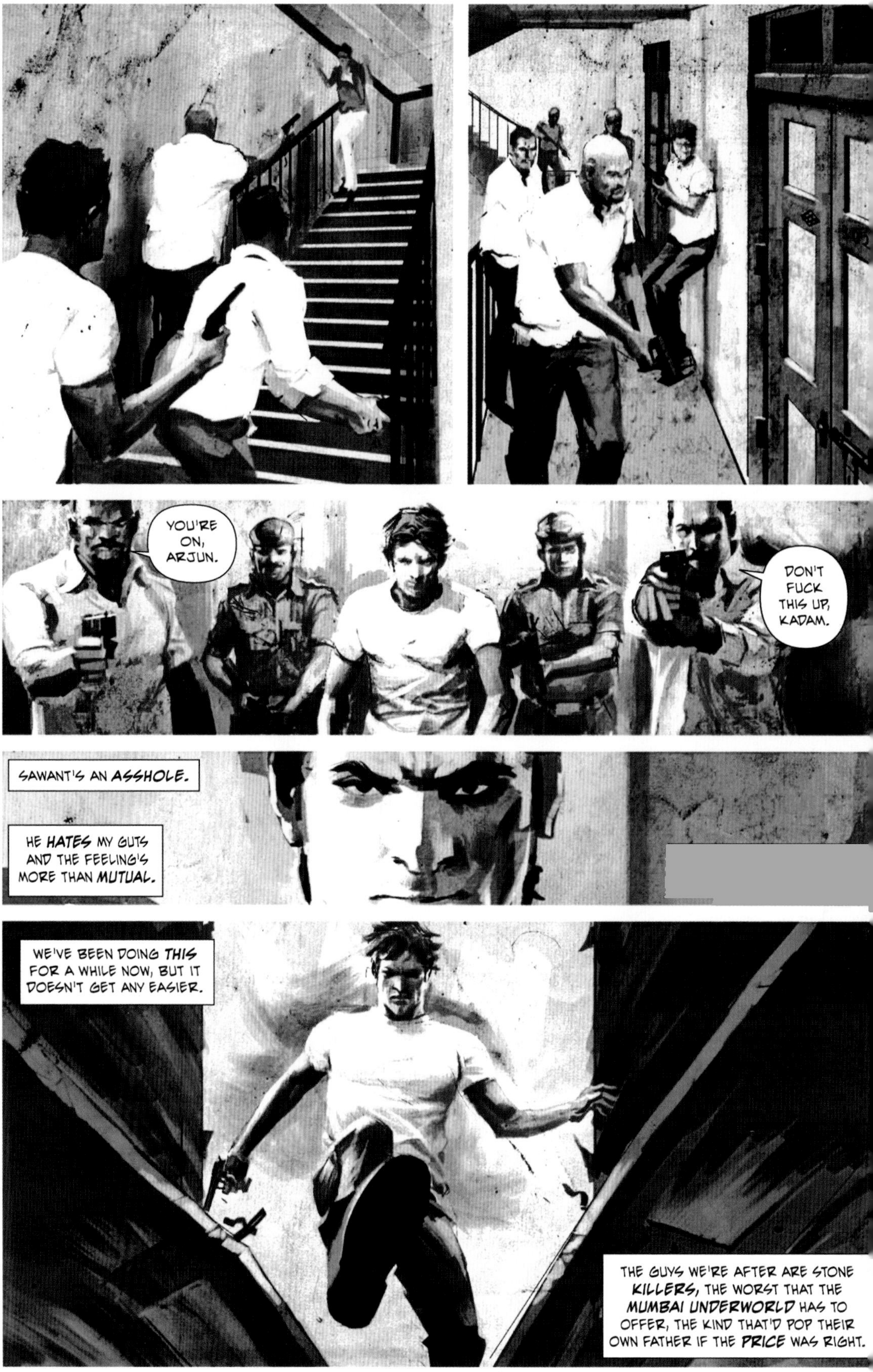
YOU'RE ON, ARJUN.
DON'T FUCK THIS UP, KADAM.
SAWANT'S AN ASSHOLE.
HE HATES MY GUTS AND THE FEELING'S MORE THAN MUTUAL.
WE'VE BEEN DOING THIS FOR A WHILE NOW, BUT IT DOESN'T GET ANY EASIER.
THE GUYS WE'RE AFTER ARE STONE KILLERS, THE WORST THAT THE MUMBAI UNDERWORLD HAS TO OFFER, THE KIND THAT'D POP THEIR OWN FATHER IF THE PRICE WAS RIGHT.

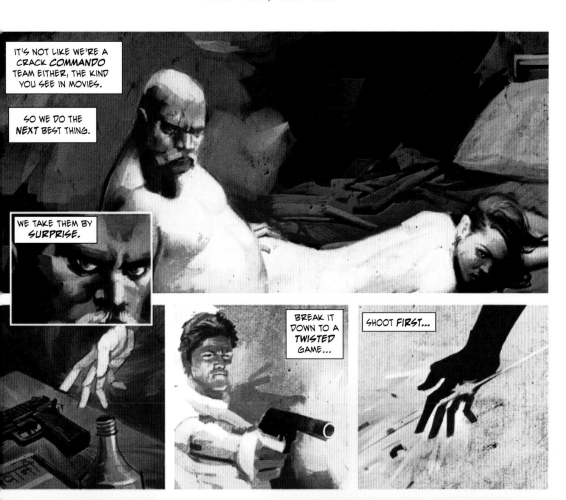

IT'S NOT LIKE WE'RE A CRACK *COMMANDO* TEAM EITHER, THE KIND YOU SEE IN MOVIES.

SO WE DO THE *NEXT* BEST THING.

WE TAKE THEM BY *SURPRISE.*

BREAK IT DOWN TO A *TWISTED* GAME...

SHOOT *FIRST*...

... AND *SCORE.*

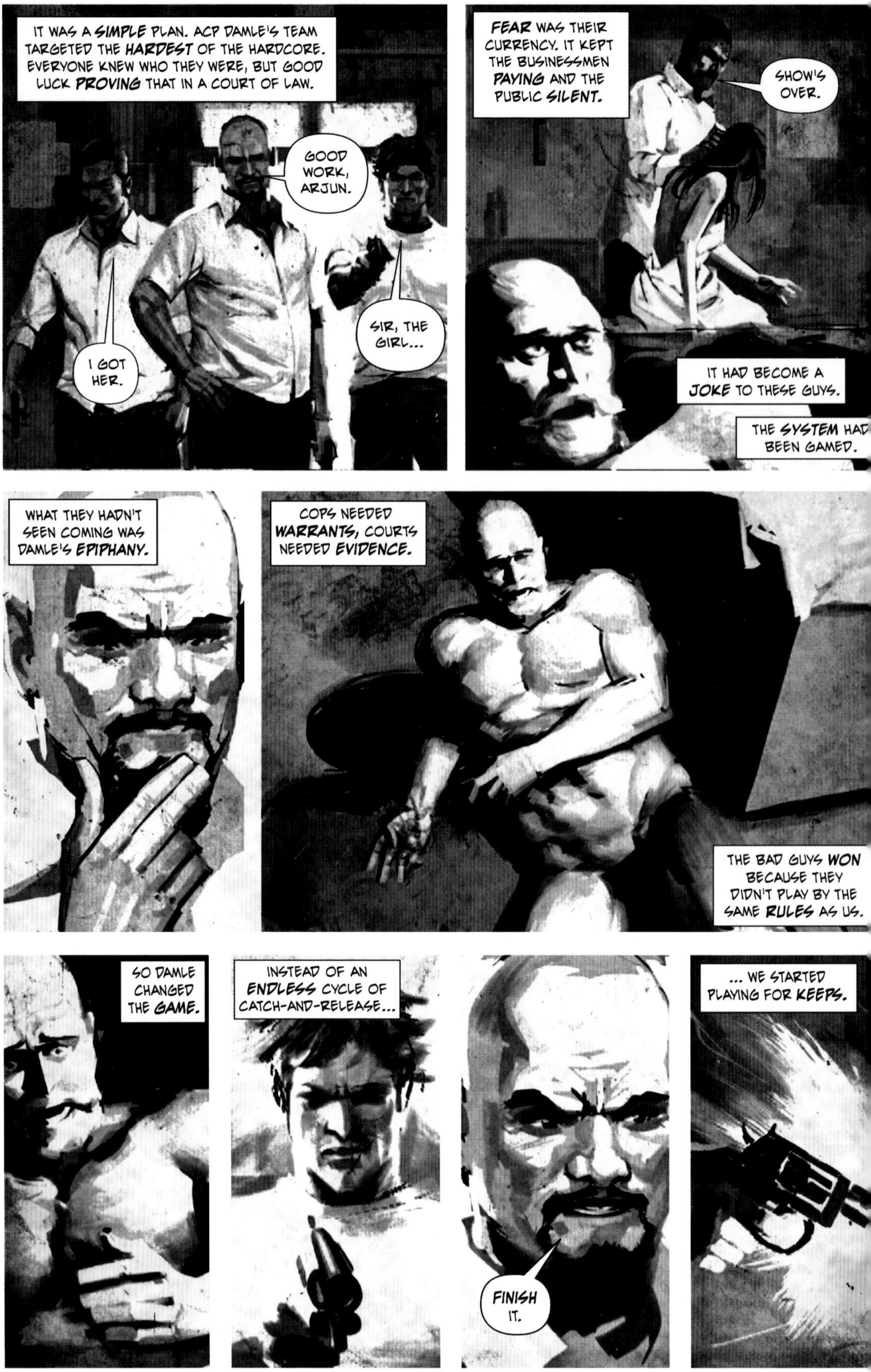
IT WAS A SIMPLE PLAN. ACP DAMLE'S TEAM TARGETED THE HARDEST OF THE HARDCORE. EVERYONE KNEW WHO THEY WERE, BUT GOOD LUCK PROVING THAT IN A COURT OF LAW.
GOOD WORK, ARJUN.
I GOT HER.
SIR, THE GIRL...
FEAR WAS THEIR CURRENCY. IT KEPT THE BUSINESSMEN PAYING AND THE PUBLIC SILENT.
SHOW'S OVER.
IT HAD BECOME A JOKE TO THESE GUYS.
THE SYSTEM HAD BEEN GAMED.
WHAT THEY HADN'T SEEN COMING WAS DAMLE'S EPIPHANY.
COPS NEEDED WARRANTS, COURTS NEEDED EVIDENCE.
THE BAD GUYS WON BECAUSE THEY DIDN'T PLAY BY THE SAME RULES AS US.
SO DAMLE CHANGED THE GAME.
INSTEAD OF AN ENDLESS CYCLE OF CATCH-AND-RELEASE...
FINISH IT.
... WE STARTED PLAYING FOR KEEPS.

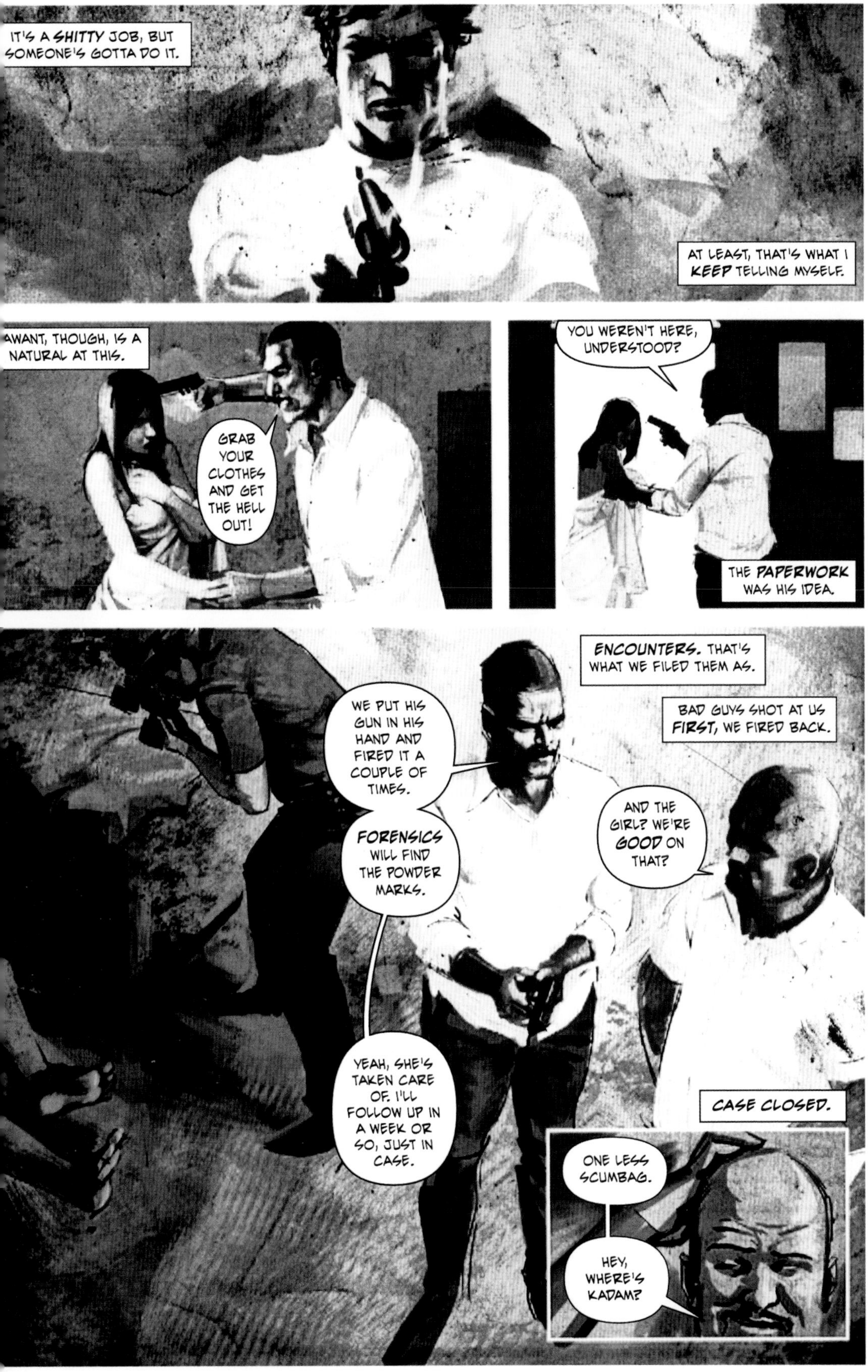
IT'S A SHITTY JOB, BUT SOMEONE'S GOTTA DO IT.
AT LEAST, THAT'S WHAT I KEEP TELLING MYSELF.
AWANT, THOUGH, IS A NATURAL AT THIS.
GRAB YOUR CLOTHES AND GET THE HELL OUT!
YOU WEREN'T HERE, UNDERSTOOD?
THE PAPERWORK WAS HIS IDEA.
ENCOUNTERS. THAT'S WHAT WE FILED THEM AS.
BAD GUYS SHOT AT US FIRST, WE FIRED BACK.
WE PUT HIS GUN IN HIS HAND AND FIRED IT A COUPLE OF TIMES.
FORENSICS WILL FIND THE POWDER MARKS.
AND THE GIRL? WE'RE GOOD ON THAT?
YEAH, SHE'S TAKEN CARE OF. I'LL FOLLOW UP IN A WEEK OR SO, JUST IN CASE.
CASE CLOSED.
ONE LESS SCUMBAG.
HEY, WHERE'S KADAM?

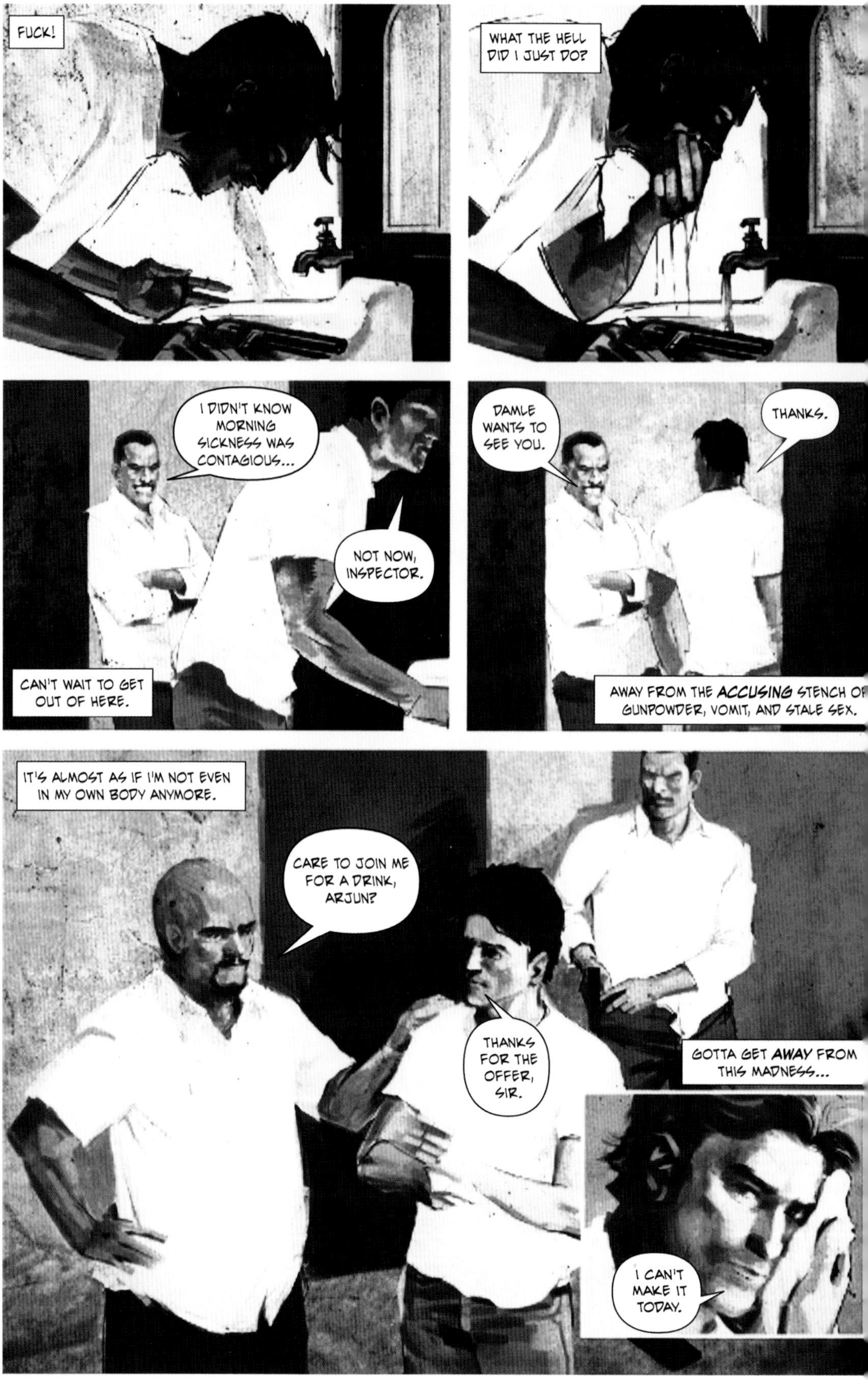
FUCK!
WHAT THE HELL DID I JUST DO?
I DIDN'T KNOW MORNING SICKNESS WAS CONTAGIOUS...
NOT NOW, INSPECTOR.
CAN'T WAIT TO GET OUT OF HERE.
DAMLE WANTS TO SEE YOU.
THANKS.
AWAY FROM THE ACCUSING STENCH OF GUNPOWDER, VOMIT, AND STALE SEX.
IT'S ALMOST AS IF I'M NOT EVEN IN MY OWN BODY ANYMORE.
CARE TO JOIN ME FOR A DRINK, ARJUN?
THANKS FOR THE OFFER, SIR.
GOTTA GET AWAY FROM THIS MADNESS...
I CAN'T MAKE IT TODAY.

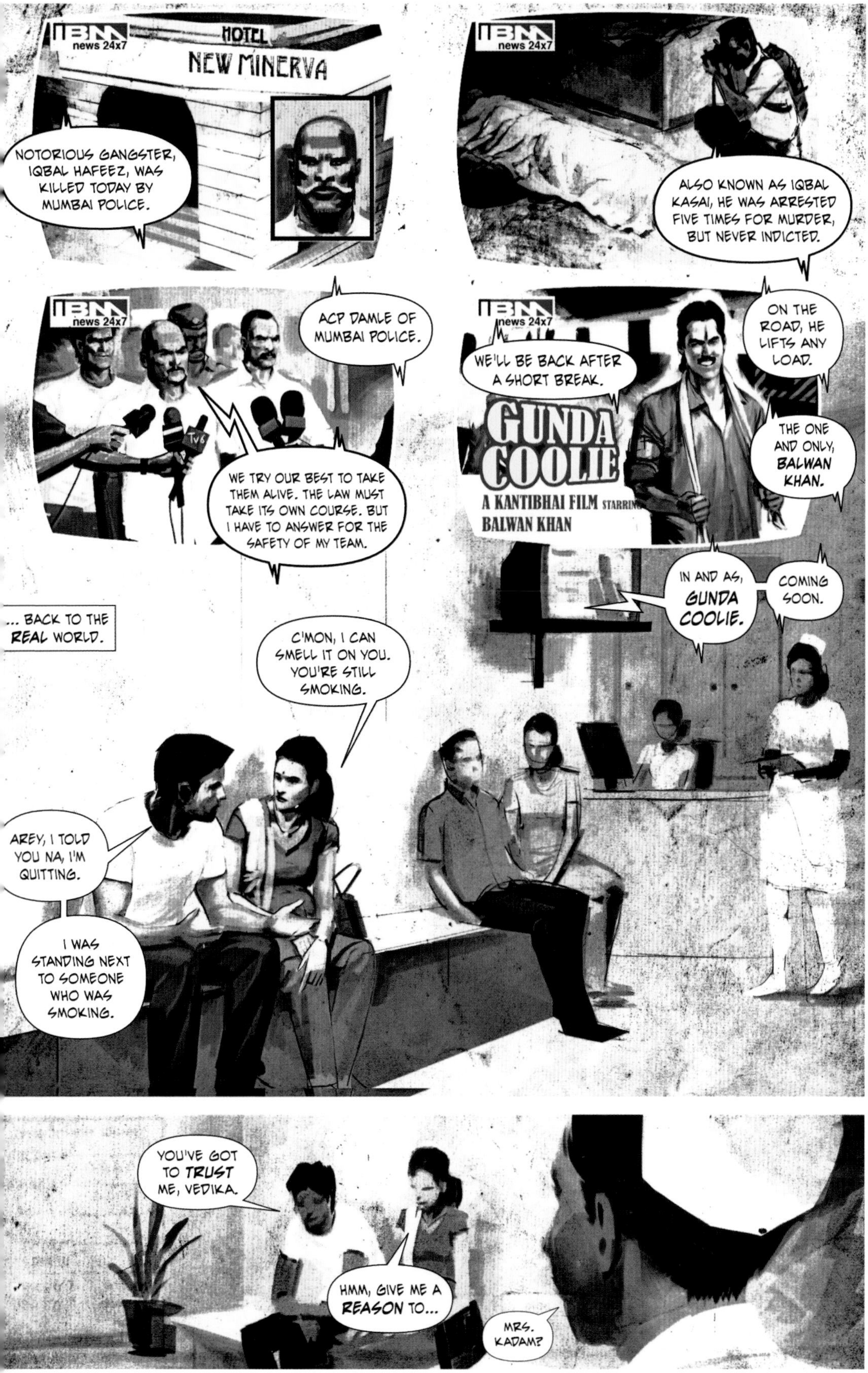

IBN news 24x7
HOTEL NEW MINERVA
NOTORIOUS GANGSTER, IQBAL HAFEEZ, WAS KILLED TODAY BY MUMBAI POLICE.
IBN news 24x7
ALSO KNOWN AS IQBAL KASAI, HE WAS ARRESTED FIVE TIMES FOR MURDER, BUT NEVER INDICTED.
IBN news 24x7
ACP DAMLE OF MUMBAI POLICE.
WE TRY OUR BEST TO TAKE THEM ALIVE. THE LAW MUST TAKE ITS OWN COURSE. BUT I HAVE TO ANSWER FOR THE SAFETY OF MY TEAM.
IBN news 24x7
WE'LL BE BACK AFTER A SHORT BREAK.
GUNDA COOLIE
A KANTIBHAI FILM STARRING BALWAN KHAN
ON THE ROAD, HE LIFTS ANY LOAD.
THE ONE AND ONLY, BALWAN KHAN.
IN AND AS, GUNDA COOLIE.
COMING SOON.
... BACK TO THE REAL WORLD.
C'MON, I CAN SMELL IT ON YOU. YOU'RE STILL SMOKING.
AREY, I TOLD YOU NA, I'M QUITTING.
I WAS STANDING NEXT TO SOMEONE WHO WAS SMOKING.
YOU'VE GOT TO TRUST ME, VEDIKA.
HMM, GIVE ME A REASON TO...
MRS. KADAM?

OKAY, I PROMISE I'LL QUIT... SOON.

MRS. KADAM, THE TEST RESULTS ARE BACK.

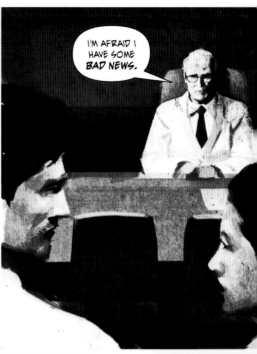

I'M AFRAID I HAVE SOME **BAD NEWS.**

THE BABY...?

THERE'S NO **EASY** WAY TO SAY THIS.

THERE ARE SOME SEVERE **COMPLICATIONS** WITH YOUR PREGNANCY.

THE DOCTOR RATTLES ON ABOUT "MALIGNANT TUMORS" AND "FALLOPIAN TUBES." I'M NOT REALLY LISTENING, OR IF I AM, MY MIND'S NOT PROCESSING IT.

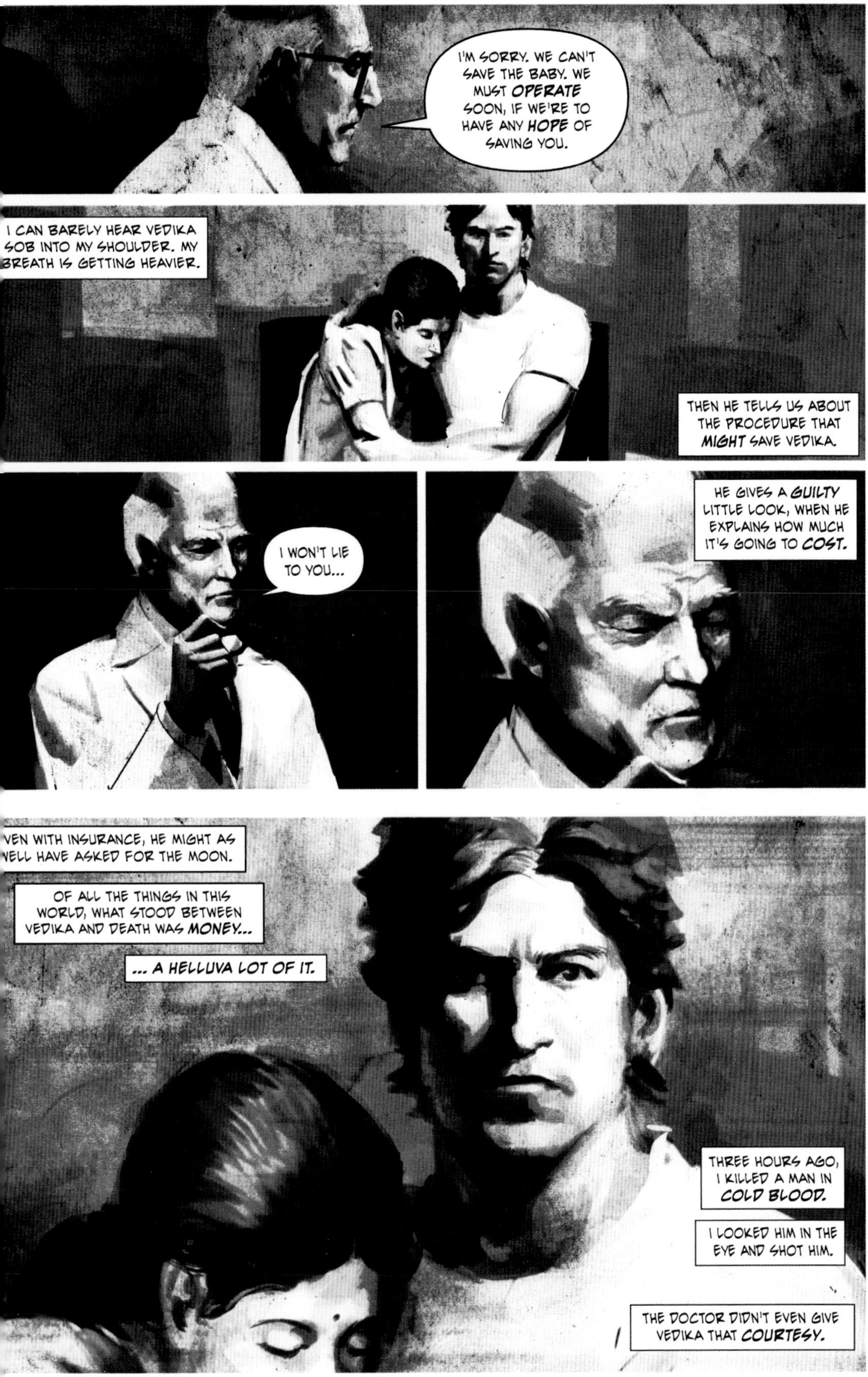
I'M SORRY. WE CAN'T SAVE THE BABY. WE MUST OPERATE SOON, IF WE'RE TO HAVE ANY HOPE OF SAVING YOU.
I CAN BARELY HEAR VEDIKA SOB INTO MY SHOULDER. MY BREATH IS GETTING HEAVIER.
THEN HE TELLS US ABOUT THE PROCEDURE THAT MIGHT SAVE VEDIKA.
I WON'T LIE TO YOU...
HE GIVES A GUILTY LITTLE LOOK, WHEN HE EXPLAINS HOW MUCH IT'S GOING TO COST.
VEN WITH INSURANCE, HE MIGHT AS VELL HAVE ASKED FOR THE MOON.
OF ALL THE THINGS IN THIS WORLD, WHAT STOOD BETWEEN VEDIKA AND DEATH WAS MONEY...
... A HELLUVA LOT OF IT.
THREE HOURS AGO, I KILLED A MAN IN COLD BLOOD.
I LOOKED HIM IN THE EYE AND SHOT HIM.
THE DOCTOR DIDN'T EVEN GIVE VEDIKA THAT COURTESY.

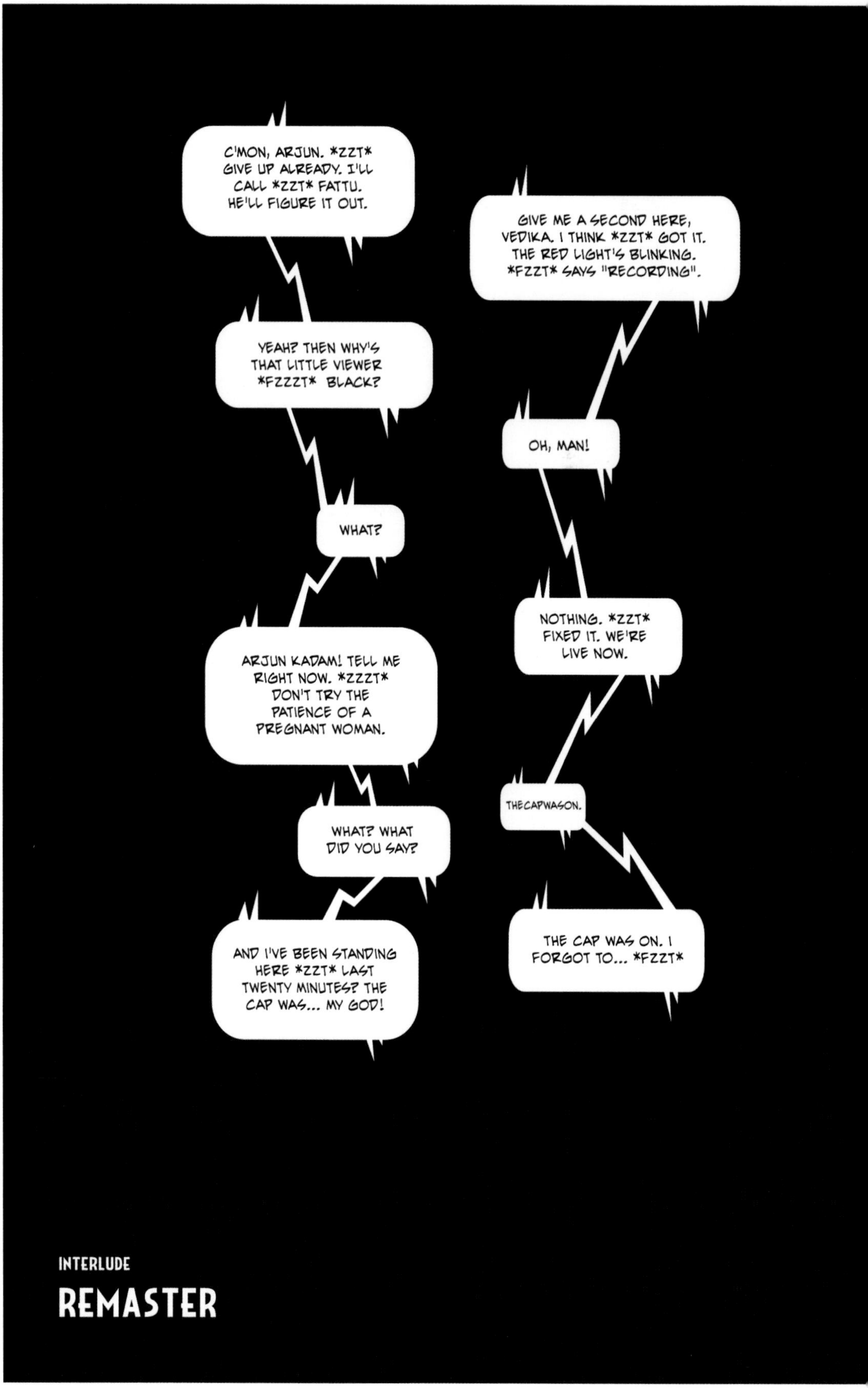
C'MON, ARJUN. *ZZT* GIVE UP ALREADY. I'LL CALL *ZZT* FATTU. HE'LL FIGURE IT OUT.
GIVE ME A SECOND HERE, VEDIKA. I THINK *ZZT* GOT IT. THE RED LIGHT'S BLINKING. *FZZT* SAYS "RECORDING".
YEAH? THEN WHY'S THAT LITTLE VIEWER *FZZZT* BLACK?
OH, MAN!
WHAT?
NOTHING. *ZZT* FIXED IT. WE'RE LIVE NOW.
ARJUN KADAM! TELL ME RIGHT NOW. *ZZZT* DON'T TRY THE PATIENCE OF A PREGNANT WOMAN.
THECAPWASON.
WHAT? WHAT DID YOU SAY?
THE CAP WAS ON. I FORGOT TO... *FZZT*
AND I'VE BEEN STANDING HERE *ZZT* LAST TWENTY MINUTES? THE CAP WAS... MY GOD!
INTERLUDE
REMASTER

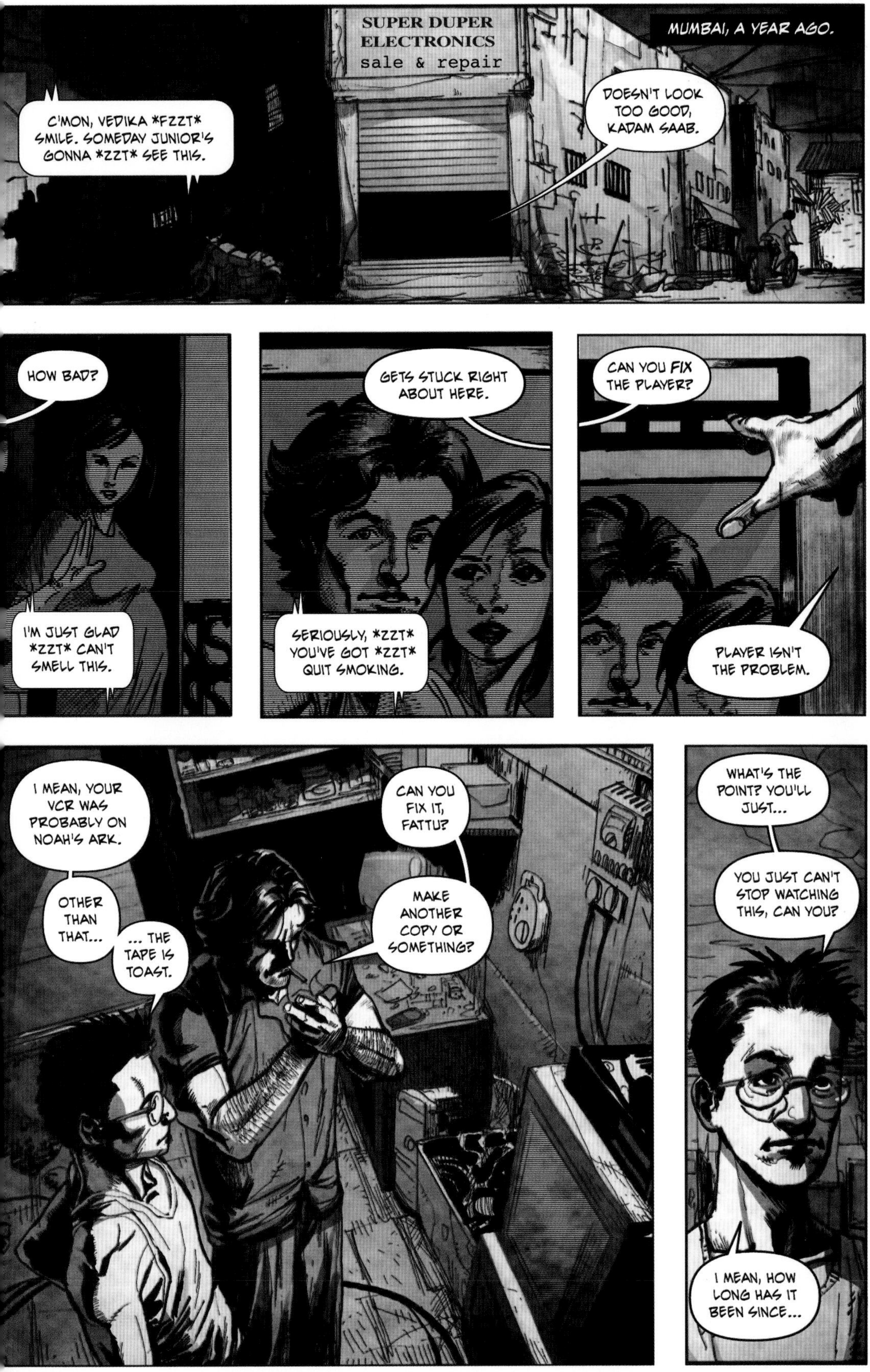
SUPER DUPER ELECTRONICS
sale & repair
MUMBAI, A YEAR AGO.
C'MON, VEDIKA *FZZT* SMILE. SOMEDAY JUNIOR'S GONNA *ZZT* SEE THIS.
DOESN'T LOOK TOO GOOD, KADAM SAAB.
HOW BAD?
I'M JUST GLAD *ZZT* CAN'T SMELL THIS.
GETS STUCK RIGHT ABOUT HERE.
SERIOUSLY, *ZZT* YOU'VE GOT *ZZT* QUIT SMOKING.
CAN YOU FIX THE PLAYER?
PLAYER ISN'T THE PROBLEM.
I MEAN, YOUR VCR WAS PROBABLY ON NOAH'S ARK.
OTHER THAN THAT...
... THE TAPE IS TOAST.
CAN YOU FIX IT, FATTU?
MAKE ANOTHER COPY OR SOMETHING?
WHAT'S THE POINT? YOU'LL JUST...
YOU JUST CAN'T STOP WATCHING THIS, CAN YOU?
I MEAN, HOW LONG HAS IT BEEN SINCE...

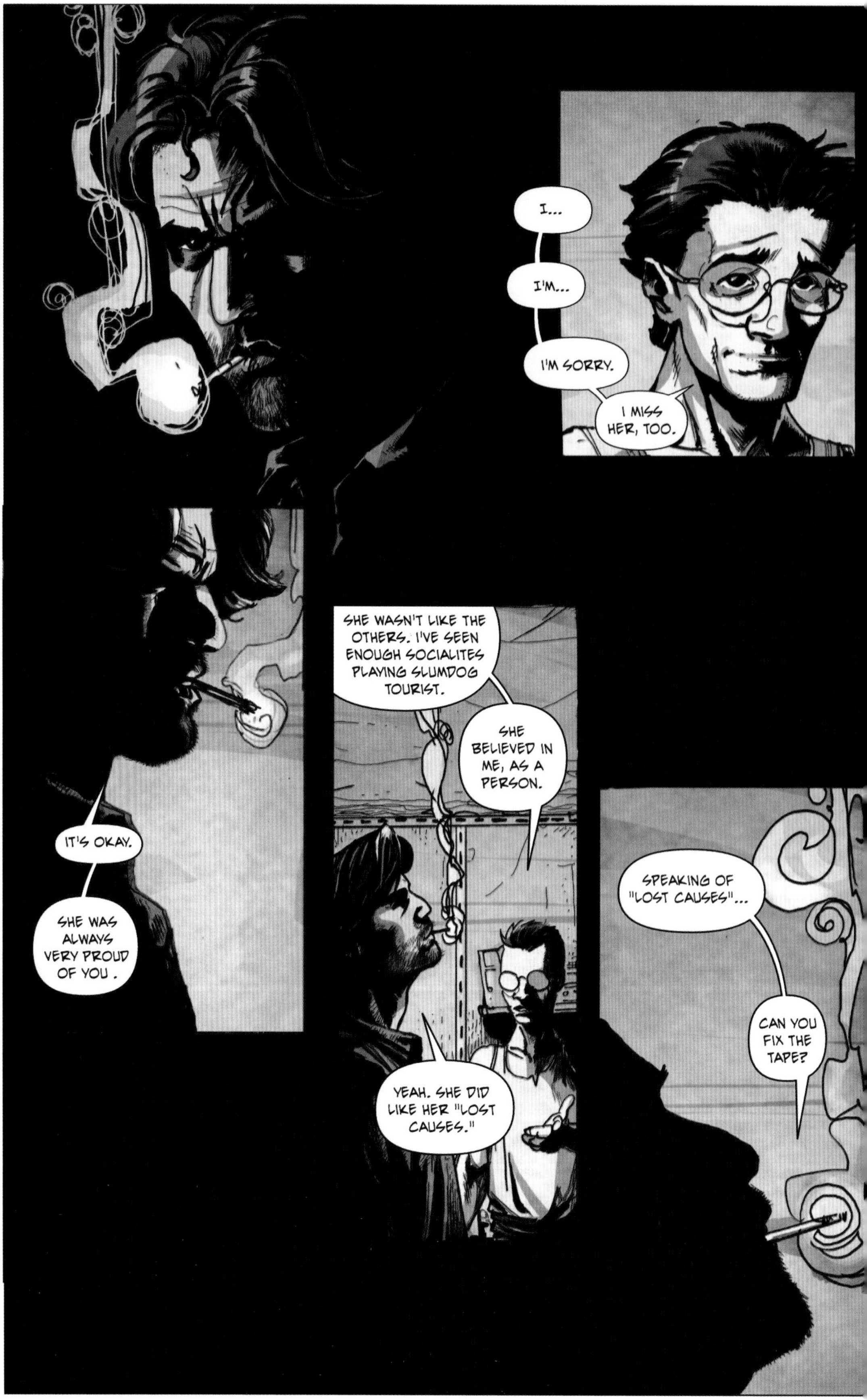
I...
I'M...
I'M SORRY.
I MISS HER, TOO.
IT'S OKAY.
SHE WAS ALWAYS VERY PROUD OF YOU .
SHE WASN'T LIKE THE OTHERS. I'VE SEEN ENOUGH SOCIALITES PLAYING SLUMDOG TOURIST.
SHE BELIEVED IN ME, AS A PERSON.
YEAH. SHE DID LIKE HER "LOST CAUSES."
SPEAKING OF "LOST CAUSES"...
CAN YOU FIX THE TAPE?

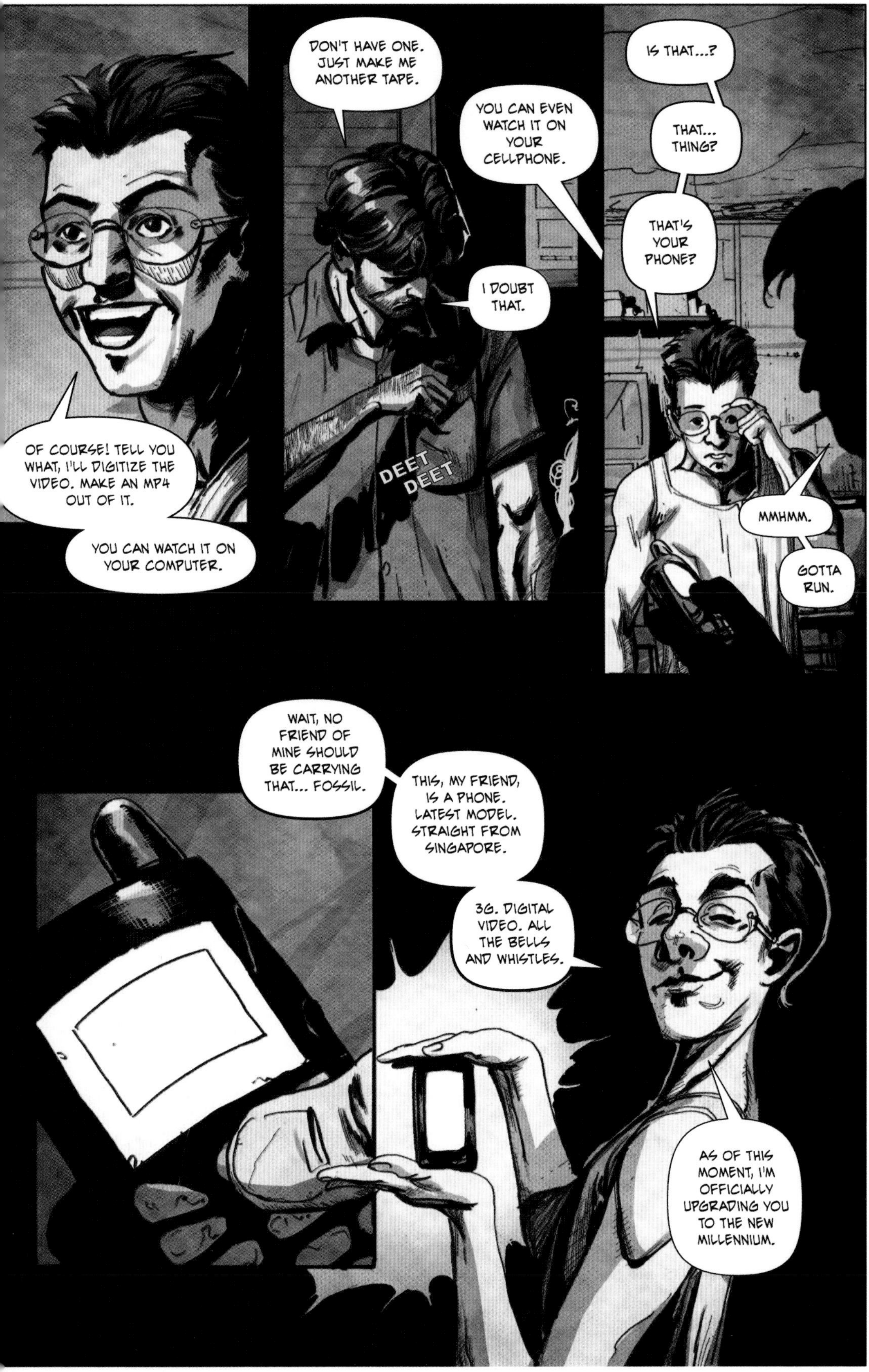
OF COURSE! TELL YOU WHAT, I'LL DIGITIZE THE VIDEO. MAKE AN MP4 OUT OF IT.
YOU CAN WATCH IT ON YOUR COMPUTER.
DON'T HAVE ONE. JUST MAKE ME ANOTHER TAPE.
YOU CAN EVEN WATCH IT ON YOUR CELLPHONE.
I DOUBT THAT.
DEET DEET
IS THAT...?
THAT... THING?
THAT'S YOUR PHONE?
MMHMM.
GOTTA RUN.
WAIT, NO FRIEND OF MINE SHOULD BE CARRYING THAT... FOSSIL.
THIS, MY FRIEND, IS A PHONE. LATEST MODEL. STRAIGHT FROM SINGAPORE.
3G. DIGITAL VIDEO. ALL THE BELLS AND WHISTLES.
AS OF THIS MOMENT, I'M OFFICIALLY UPGRADING YOU TO THE NEW MILLENNIUM.

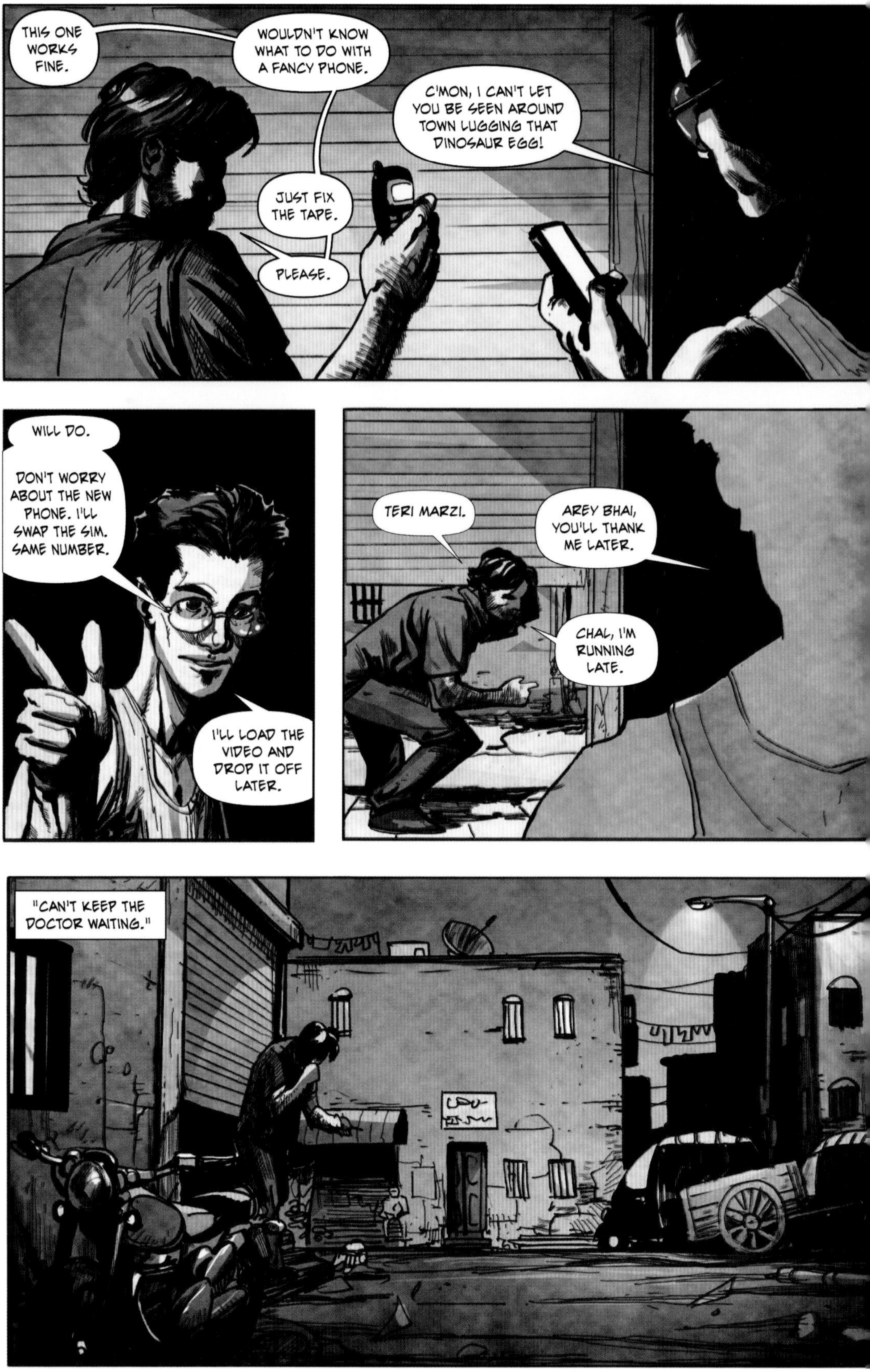
THIS ONE WORKS FINE.
WOULDN'T KNOW WHAT TO DO WITH A FANCY PHONE.
C'MON, I CAN'T LET YOU BE SEEN AROUND TOWN LUGGING THAT DINOSAUR EGG!
JUST FIX THE TAPE.
PLEASE.
WILL DO.
DON'T WORRY ABOUT THE NEW PHONE. I'LL SWAP THE SIM. SAME NUMBER.
I'LL LOAD THE VIDEO AND DROP IT OFF LATER.
TERI MARZI.
AREY BHAI, YOU'LL THANK ME LATER.
CHAL, I'M RUNNING LATE.
"CAN'T KEEP THE DOCTOR WAITING."

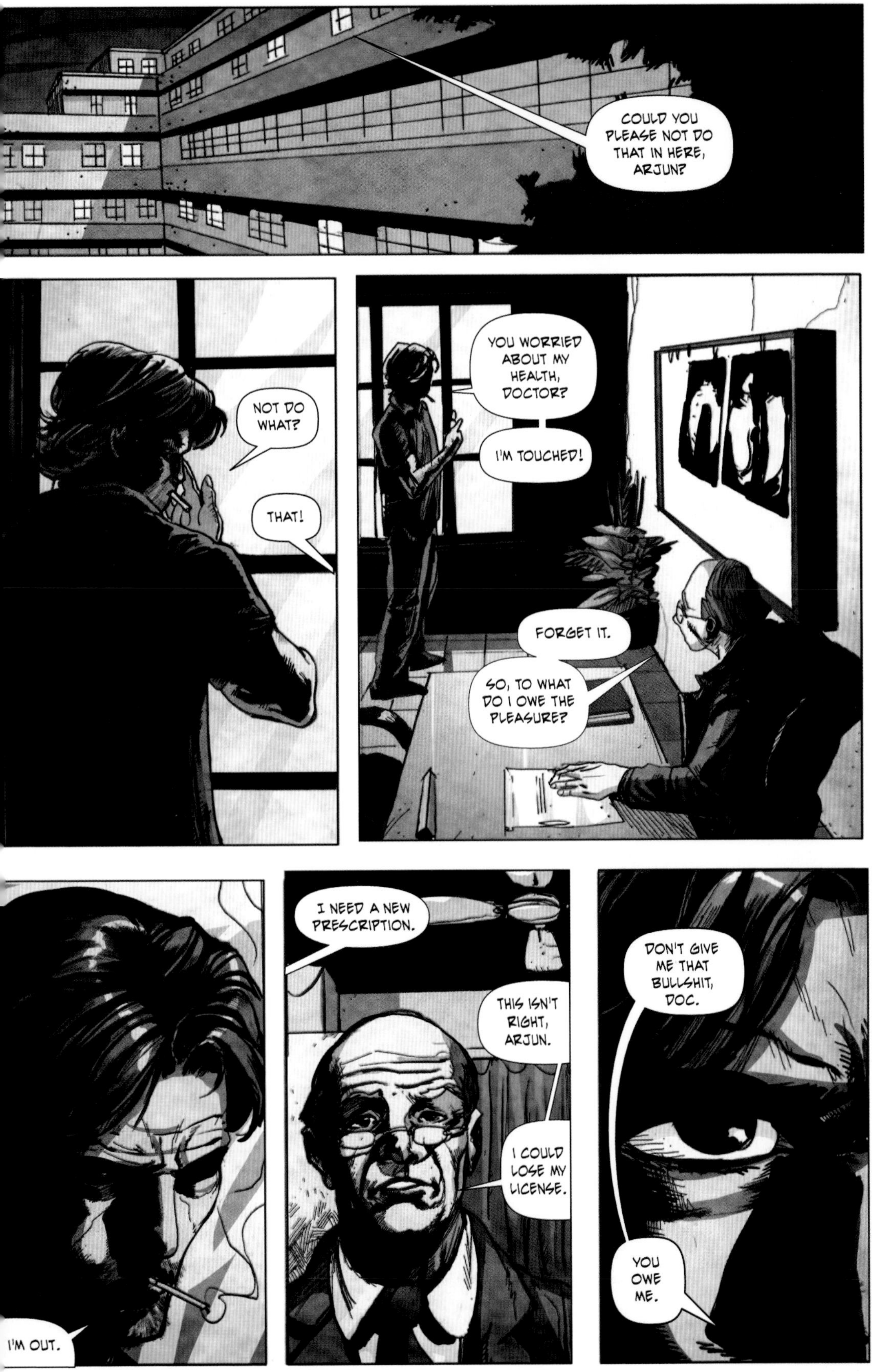
COULD YOU PLEASE NOT DO THAT IN HERE, ARJUN?
NOT DO WHAT?
THAT!
YOU WORRIED ABOUT MY HEALTH, DOCTOR?
I'M TOUCHED!
FORGET IT.
SO, TO WHAT DO I OWE THE PLEASURE?
I'M OUT.
I NEED A NEW PRESCRIPTION.
THIS ISN'T RIGHT, ARJUN.
I COULD LOSE MY LICENSE.
DON'T GIVE ME THAT BULLSHIT, DOC.
YOU OWE ME.

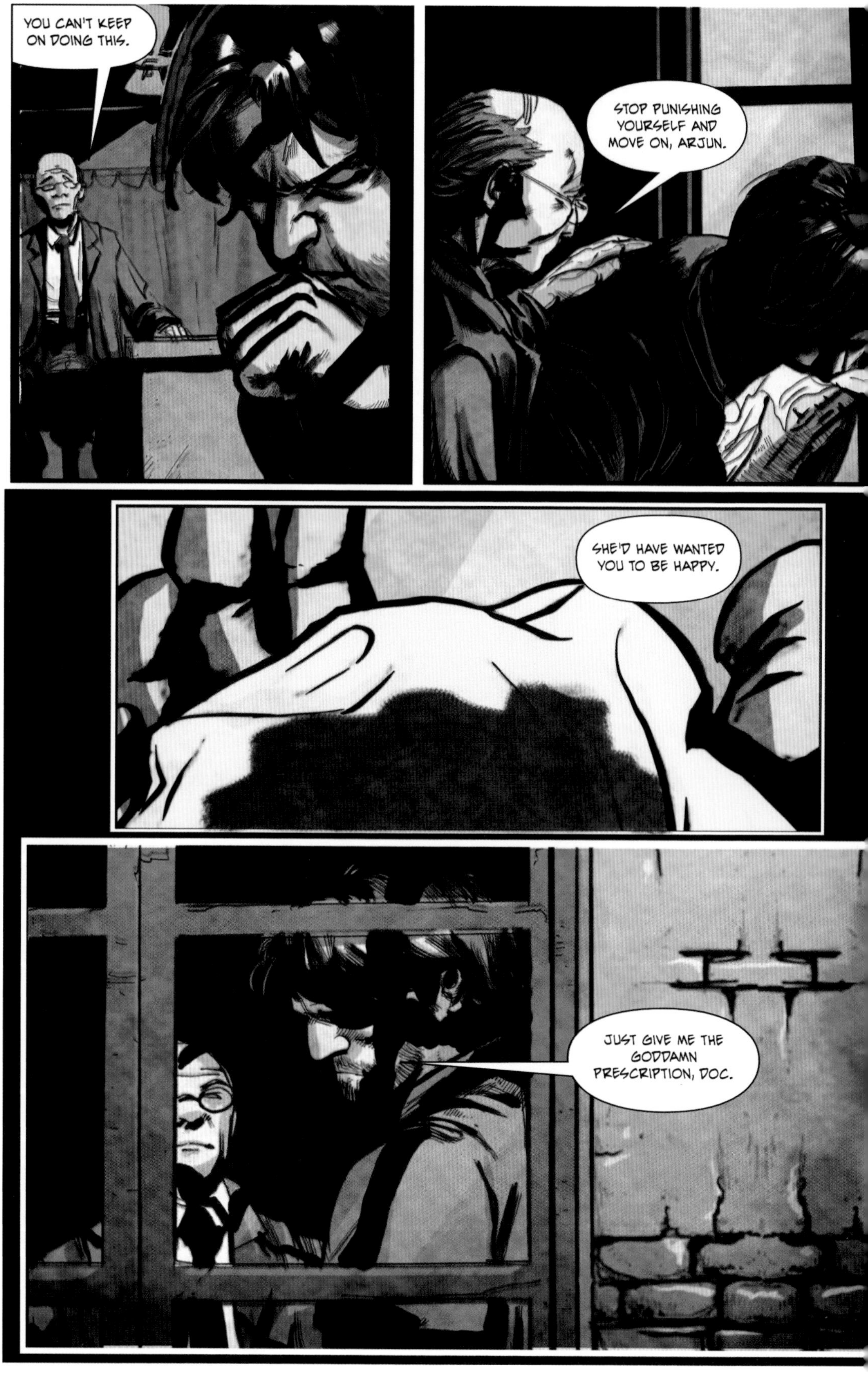
YOU CAN'T KEEP ON DOING THIS.
STOP PUNISHING YOURSELF AND MOVE ON, ARJUN.
SHE'D HAVE WANTED YOU TO BE HAPPY.
JUST GIVE ME THE GODDAMN PRESCRIPTION, DOC.

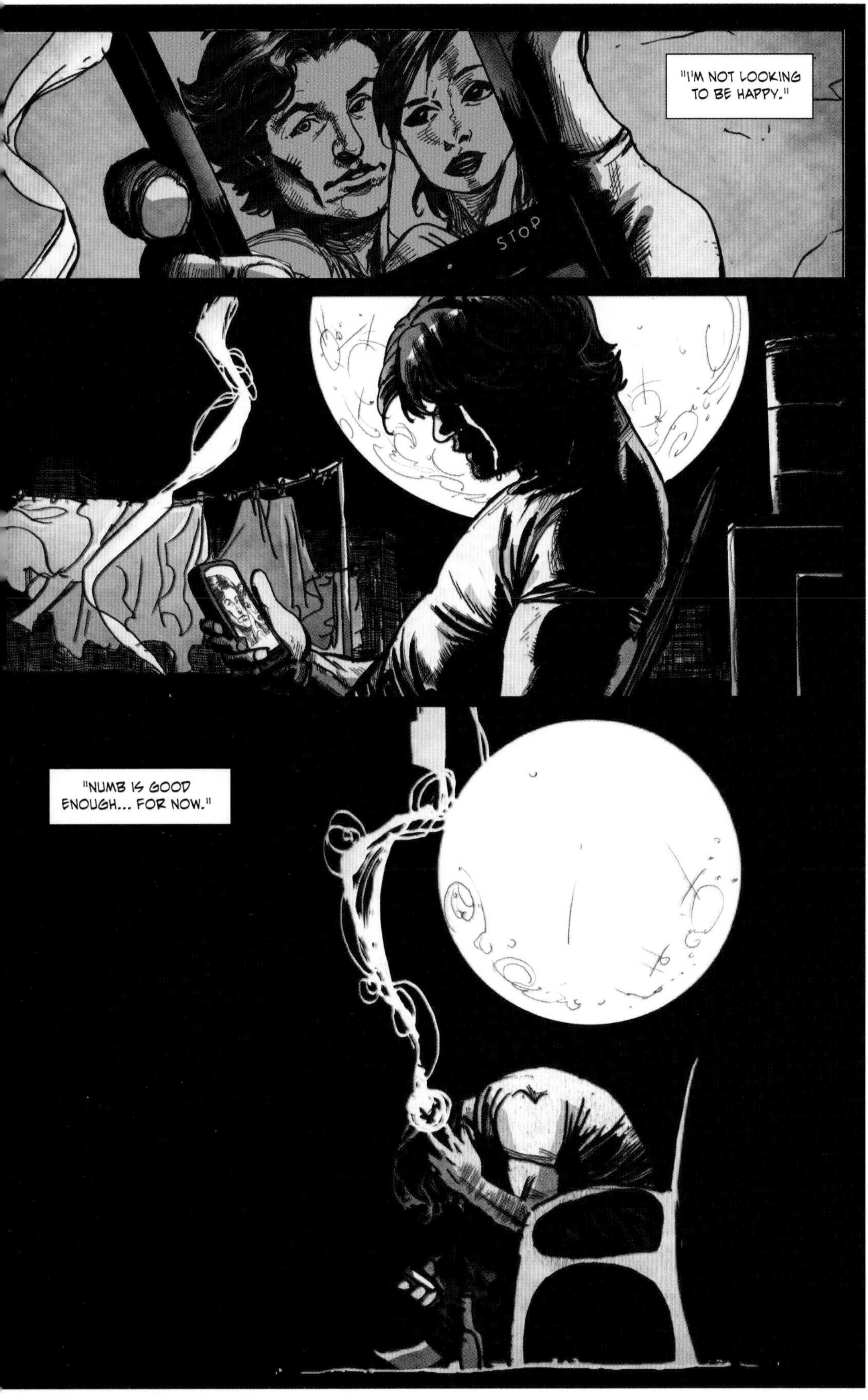
"I'M NOT LOOKING TO BE HAPPY."
STOP
"NUMB IS GOOD ENOUGH... FOR NOW."

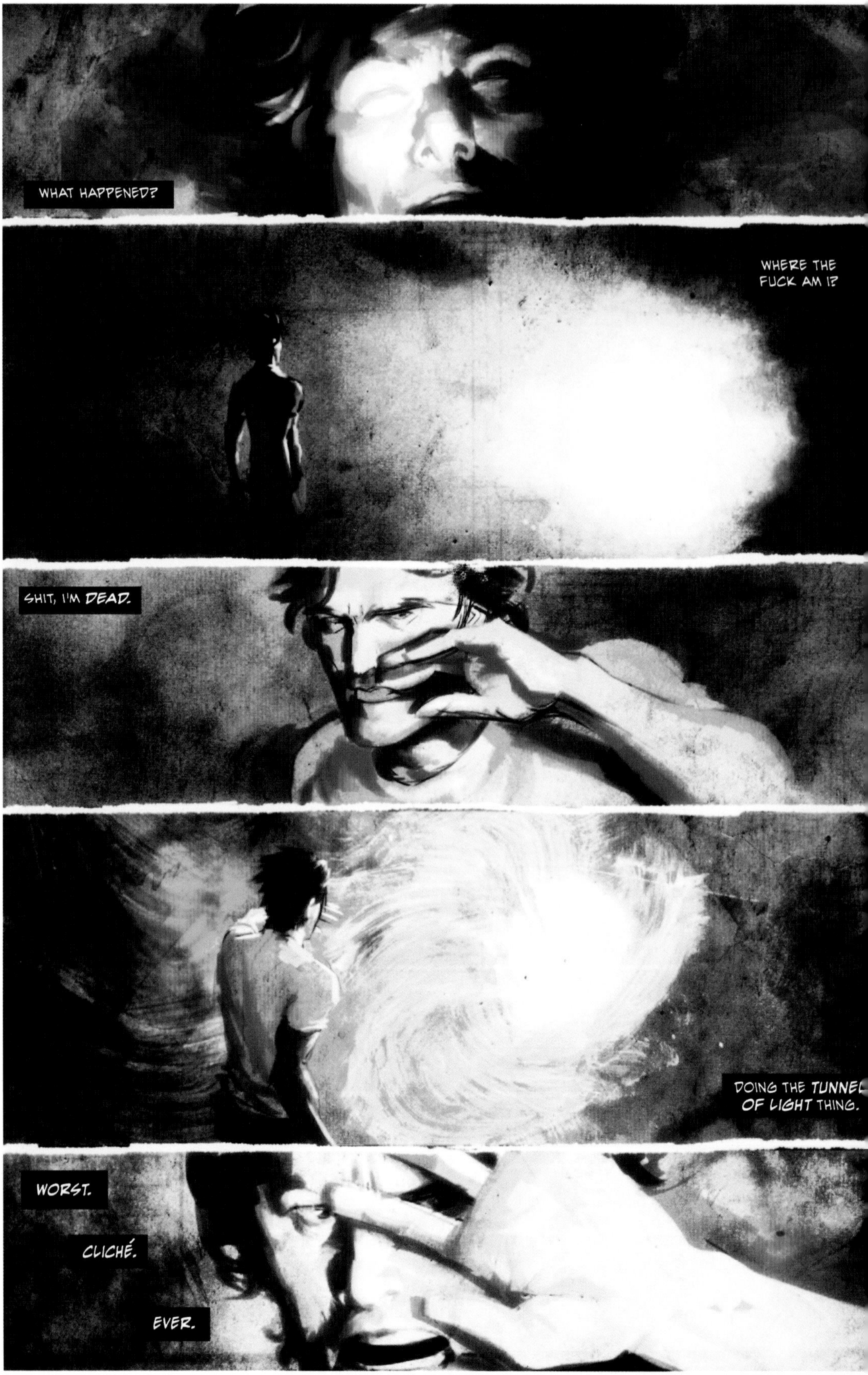
WHAT HAPPENED?
WHERE THE FUCK AM I?
SHIT, I'M DEAD.
DOING THE TUNNEL OF LIGHT THING.
WORST.
CLICHÉ.
EVER.

CHAPTER 4
GOOD MORNING, MR. KADAM

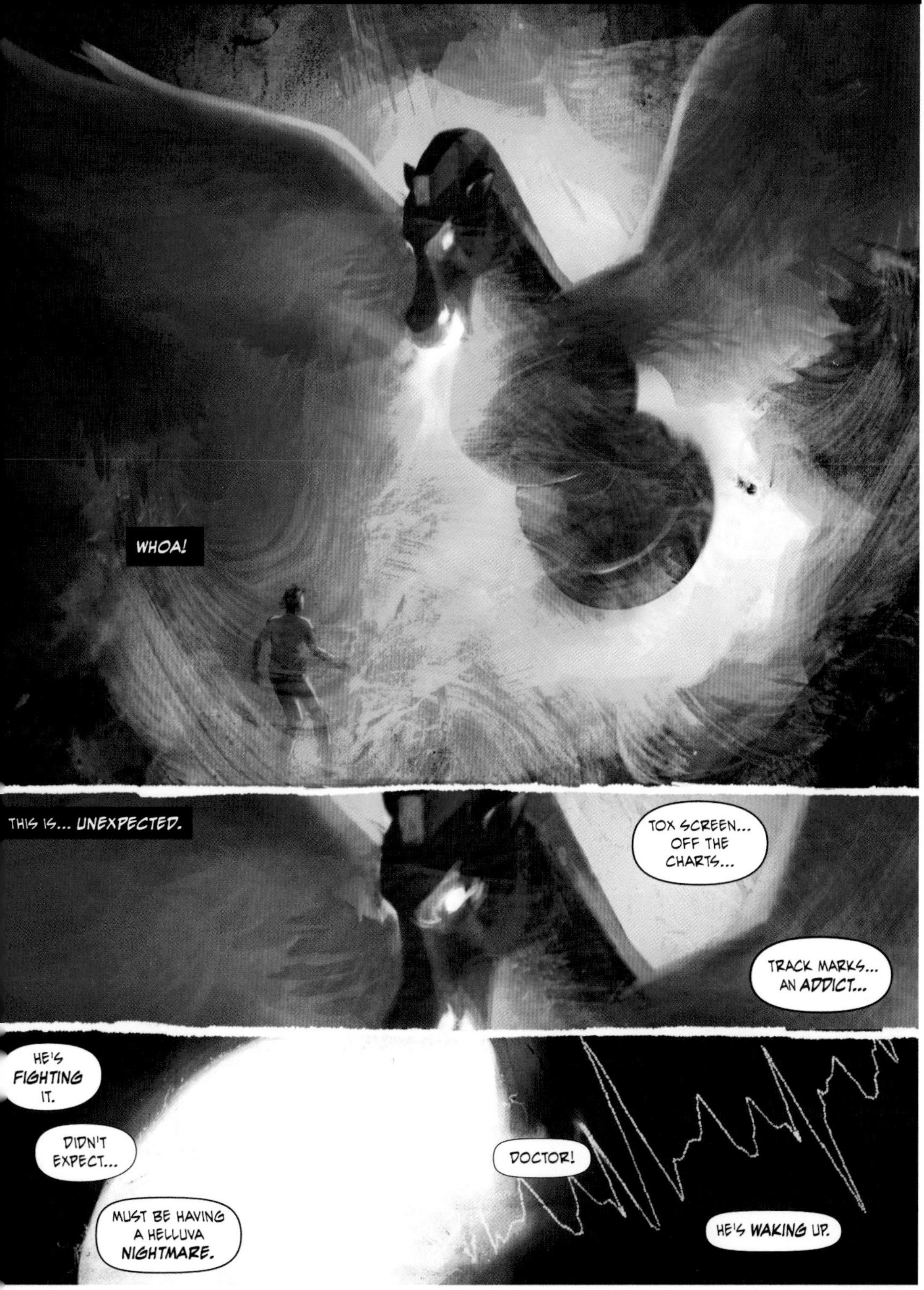
WHOA!
THIS IS... UNEXPECTED.
TOX SCREEN... OFF THE CHARTS...
TRACK MARKS... AN ADDICT...
HE'S FIGHTING IT.
DIDN'T EXPECT...
MUST BE HAVING A HELLUVA NIGHTMARE.
DOCTOR!
HE'S WAKING UP.

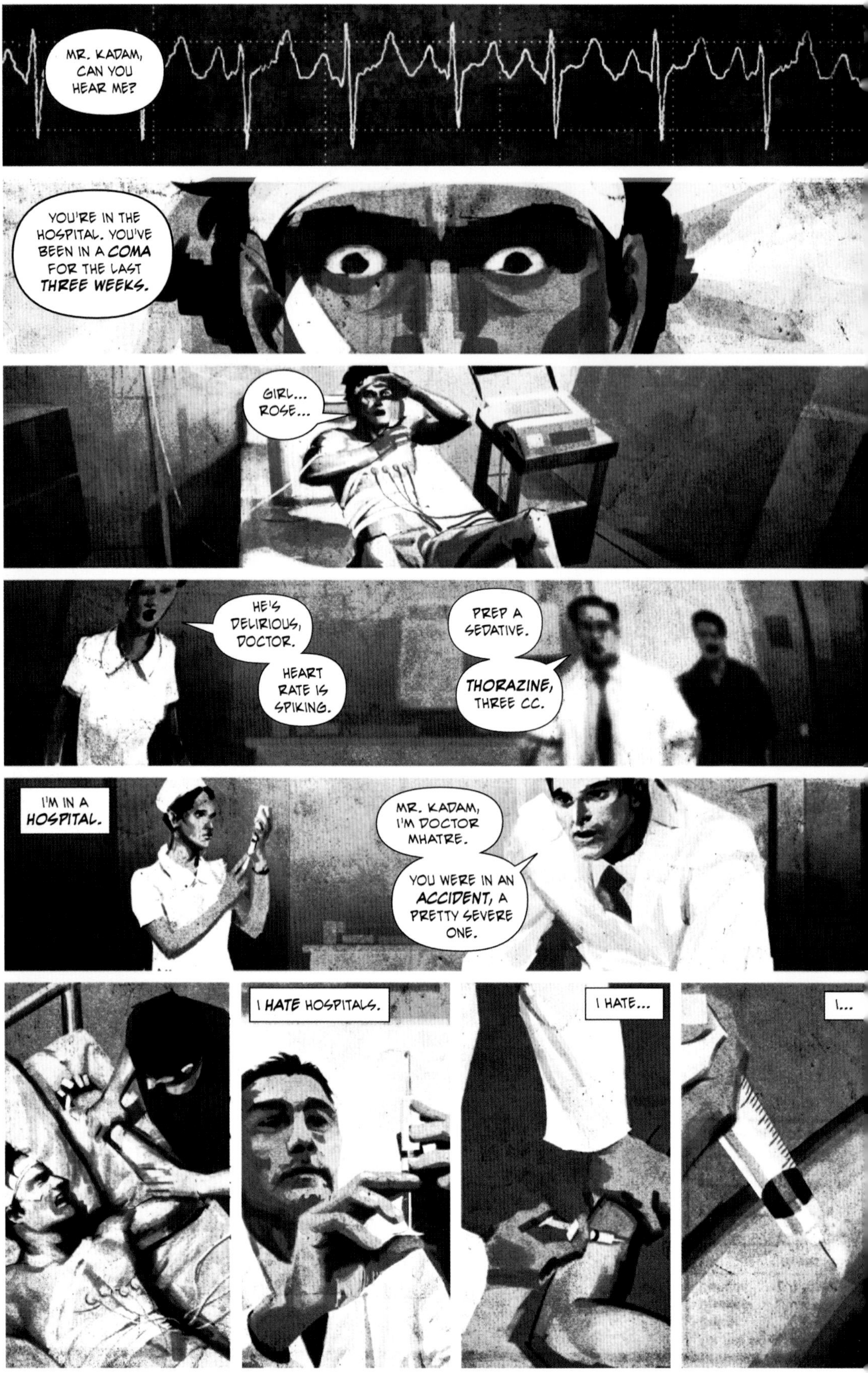
MR. KADAM, CAN YOU HEAR ME?
YOU'RE IN THE HOSPITAL. YOU'VE BEEN IN A COMA FOR THE LAST THREE WEEKS.
GIRL... ROSE...
HE'S DELIRIOUS, DOCTOR.
HEART RATE IS SPIKING.
PREP A SEDATIVE.
THORAZINE, THREE CC.
I'M IN A HOSPITAL.
MR. KADAM, I'M DOCTOR MHATRE.
YOU WERE IN AN ACCIDENT, A PRETTY SEVERE ONE.
I HATE HOSPITALS.
I HATE...
I...

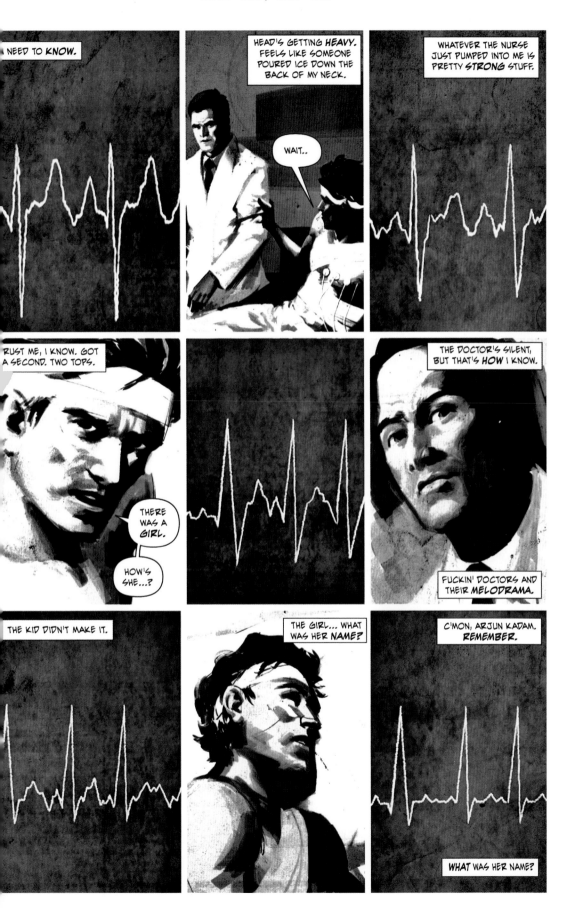

NEED TO **KNOW**.

HEAD'S GETTING **HEAVY**. FEELS LIKE SOMEONE POURED ICE DOWN THE BACK OF MY NECK.

WAIT..

WHATEVER THE NURSE JUST PUMPED INTO ME IS PRETTY **STRONG** STUFF.

RUST ME, I KNOW. GOT A SECOND. TWO TOPS.

THERE WAS A **GIRL**.

HOW'S SHE...?

THE DOCTOR'S **SILENT**, BUT THAT'S **HOW** I KNOW.

FUCKIN' DOCTORS AND THEIR **MELODRAMA**.

THE KID DIDN'T MAKE IT.

THE GIRL... WHAT WAS HER **NAME**?

C'MON, ARJUN KADAM. **REMEMBER**.

WHAT WAS HER NAME?

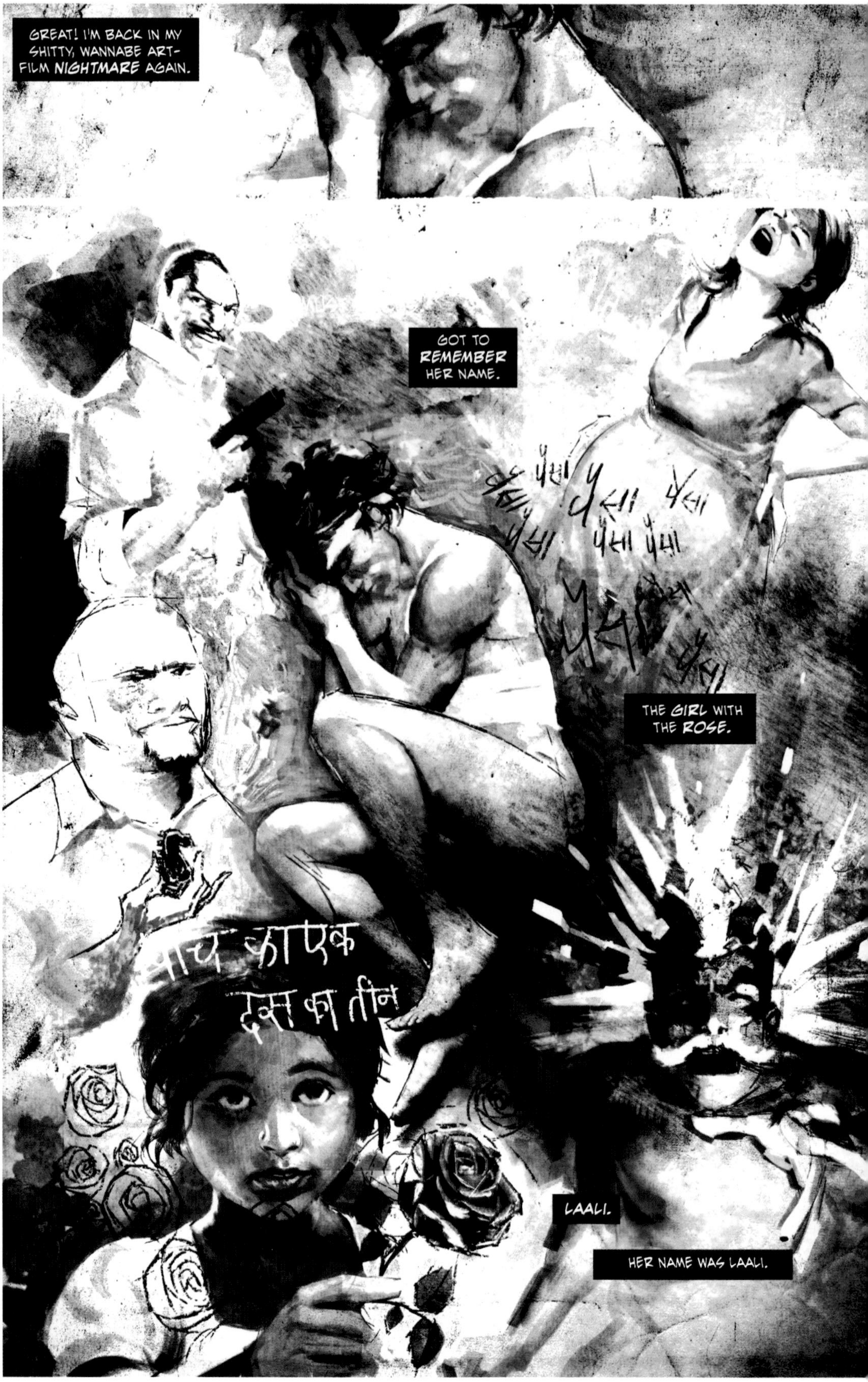
GREAT! I'M BACK IN MY SHITTY, WANNABE ART-FILM NIGHTMARE AGAIN.
GOT TO REMEMBER HER NAME.
THE GIRL WITH THE ROSE.
दस का तीन
LAALI.
HER NAME WAS LAALI.

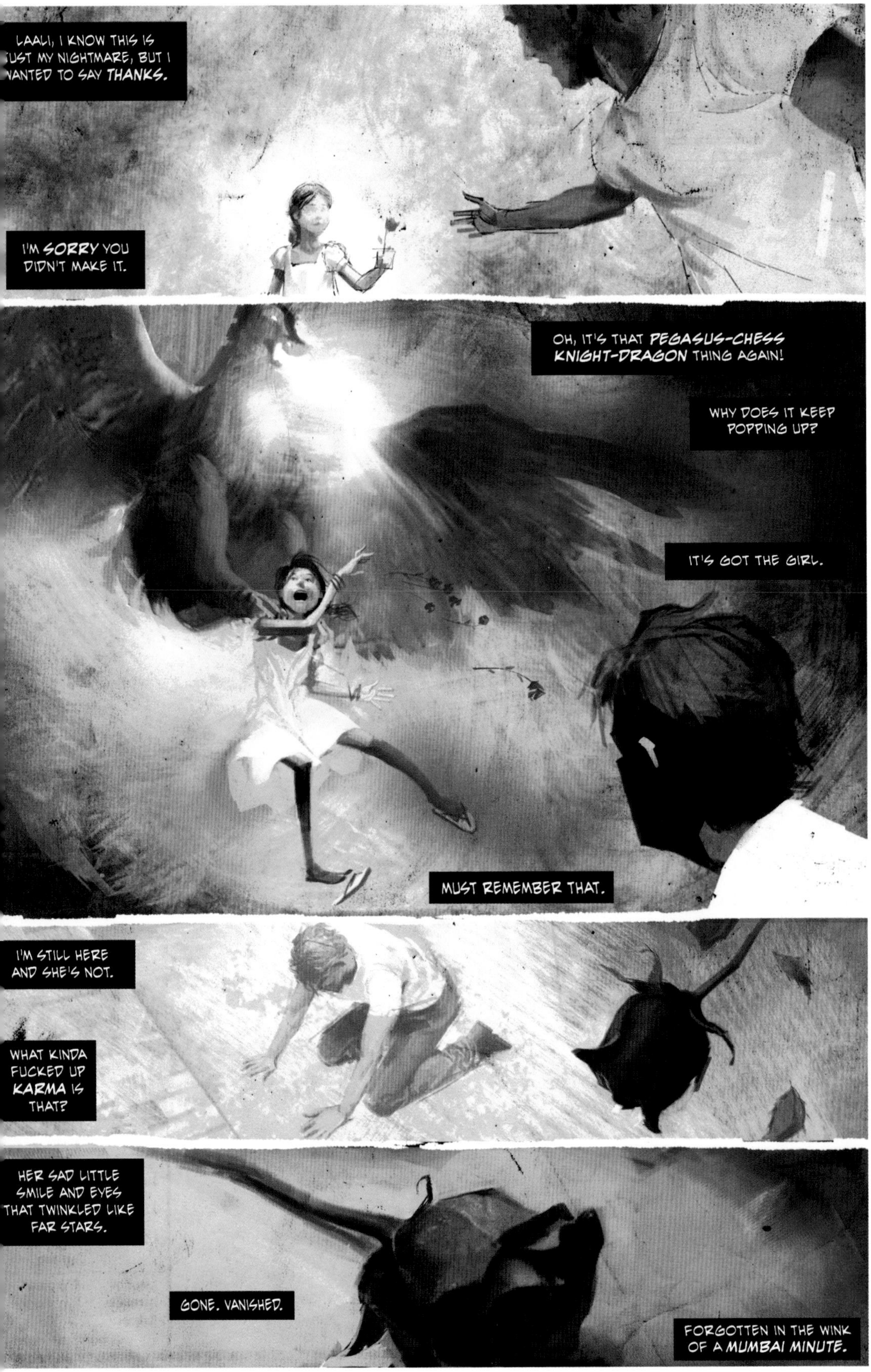
LAALI, I KNOW THIS IS JUST MY NIGHTMARE, BUT I WANTED TO SAY THANKS.
I'M SORRY YOU DIDN'T MAKE IT.
OH, IT'S THAT PEGASUS-CHESS KNIGHT-DRAGON THING AGAIN!
WHY DOES IT KEEP POPPING UP?
IT'S GOT THE GIRL.
MUST REMEMBER THAT.
I'M STILL HERE AND SHE'S NOT.
WHAT KINDA FUCKED UP KARMA IS THAT?
HER SAD LITTLE SMILE AND EYES THAT TWINKLED LIKE FAR STARS.
GONE. VANISHED.
FORGOTTEN IN THE WINK OF A MUMBAI MINUTE.

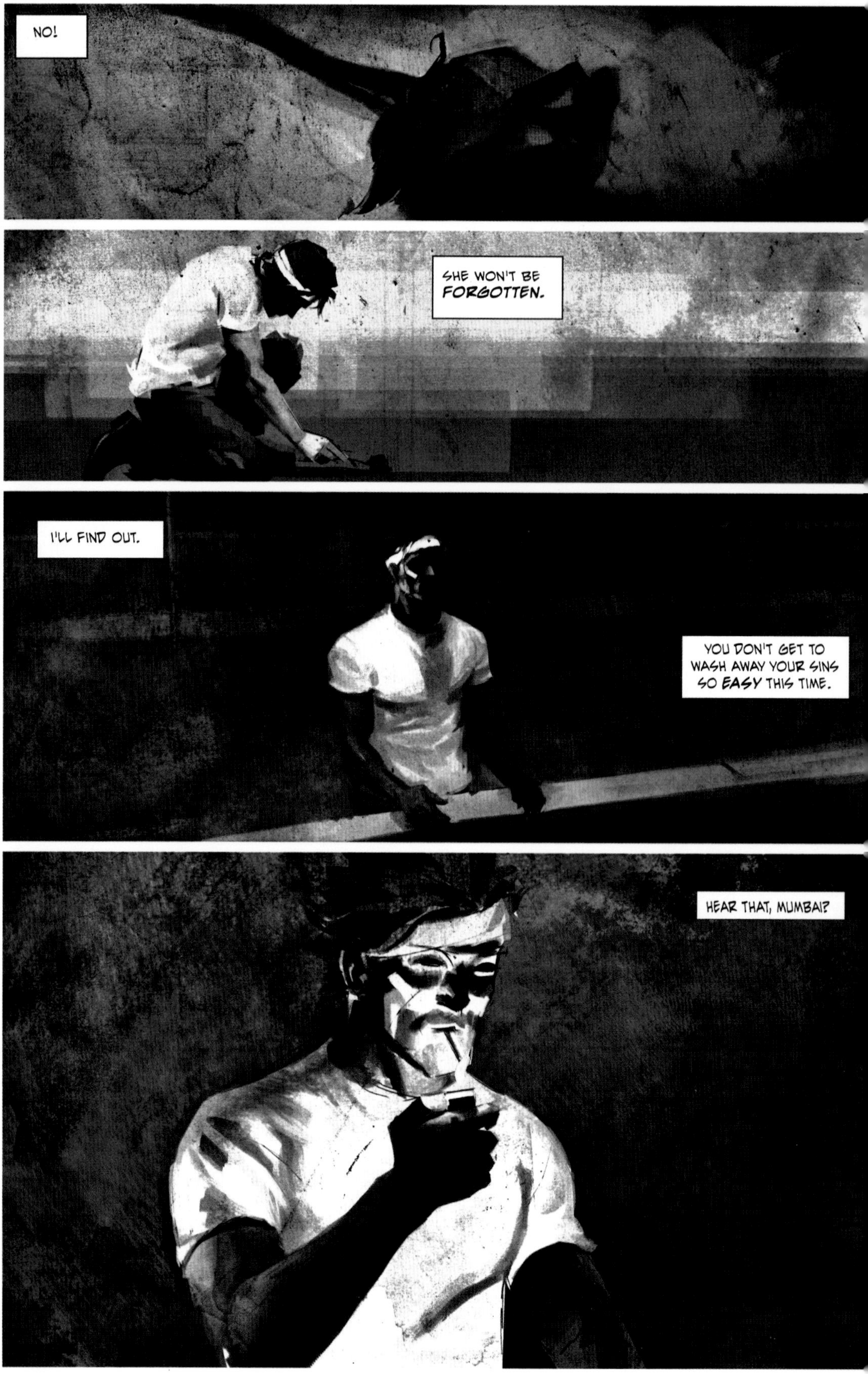
NO!
SHE WON'T BE FORGOTTEN.
I'LL FIND OUT.
YOU DON'T GET TO WASH AWAY YOUR SINS SO EASY THIS TIME.
HEAR THAT, MUMBAI?

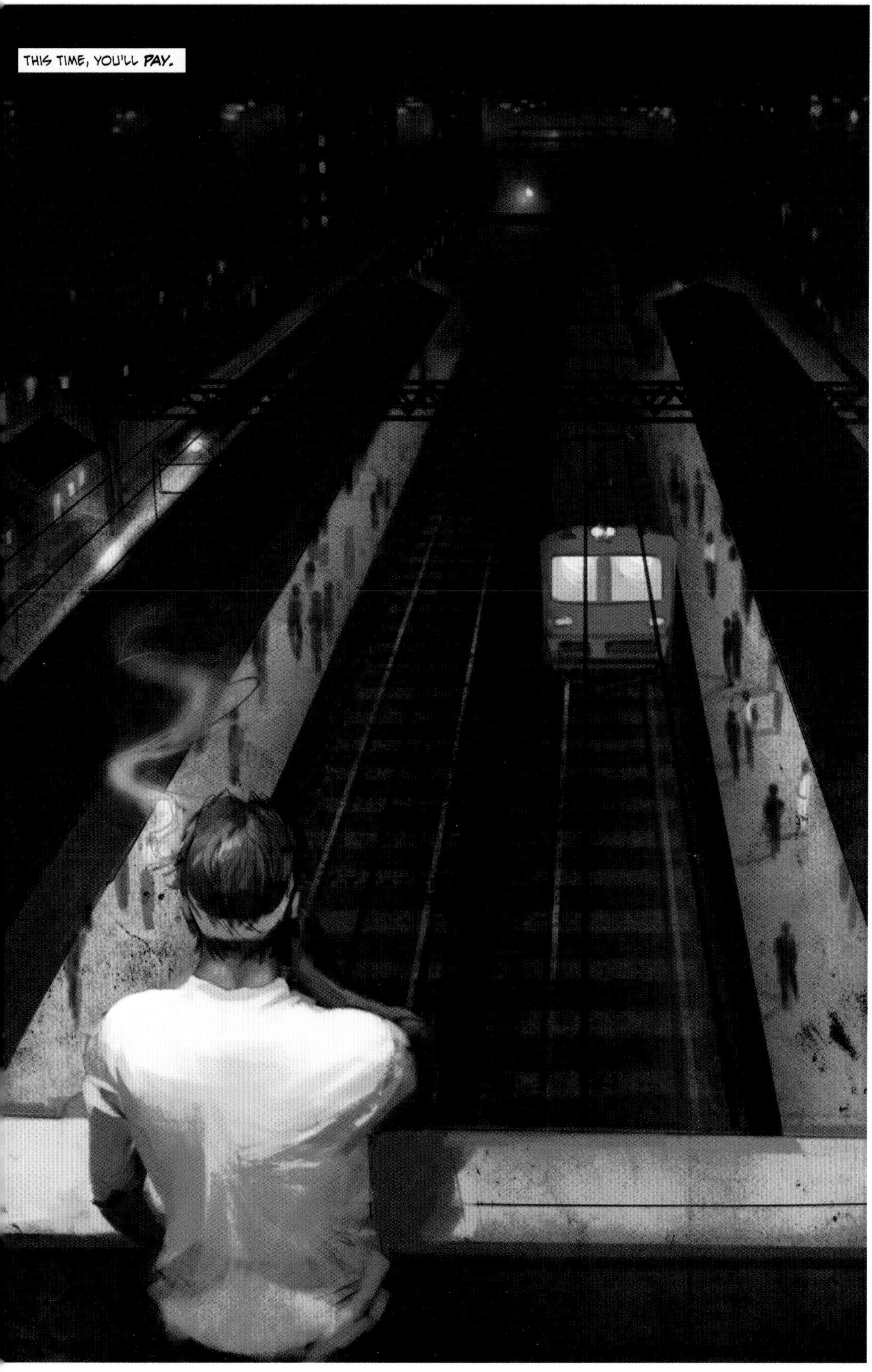
THIS TIME, YOU'LL PAY.

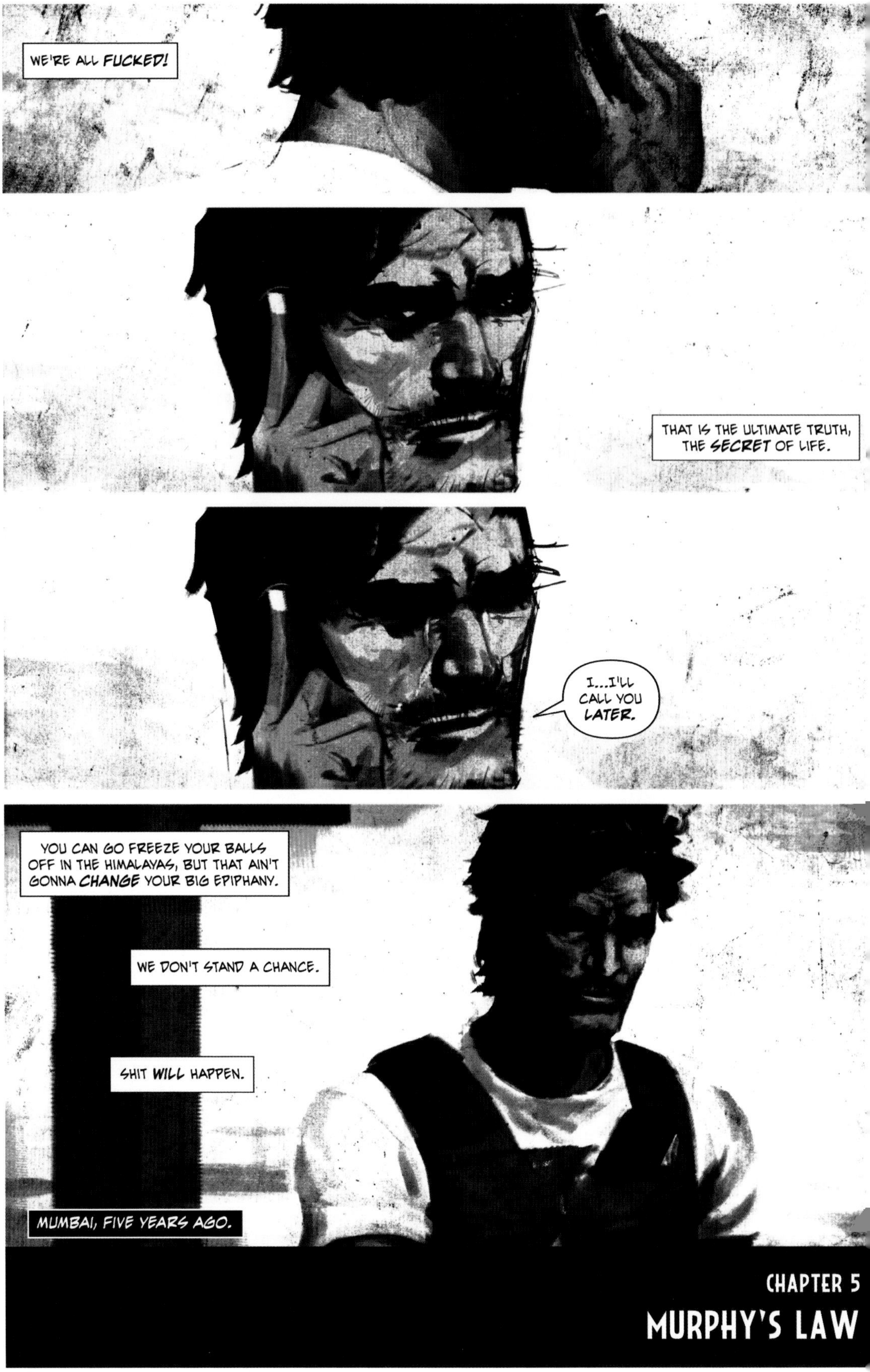
WE'RE ALL FUCKED!
THAT IS THE ULTIMATE TRUTH, THE SECRET OF LIFE.
I...I'LL CALL YOU LATER.
YOU CAN GO FREEZE YOUR BALLS OFF IN THE HIMALAYAS, BUT THAT AIN'T GONNA CHANGE YOUR BIG EPIPHANY.
WE DON'T STAND A CHANCE.
SHIT WILL HAPPEN.
MUMBAI, FIVE YEARS AGO.
CHAPTER 5
MURPHY'S LAW

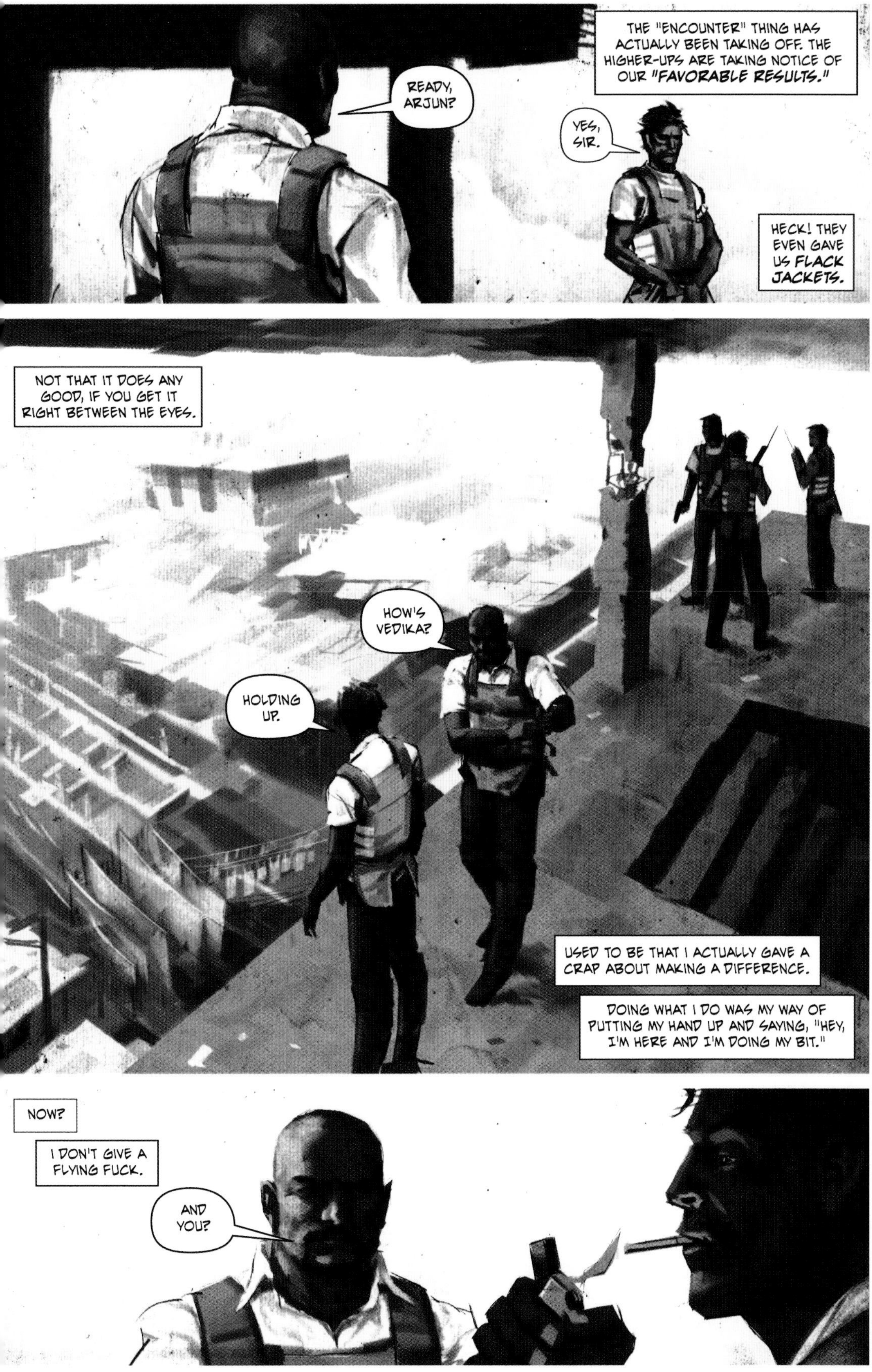
THE "ENCOUNTER" THING HAS ACTUALLY BEEN TAKING OFF. THE HIGHER-UPS ARE TAKING NOTICE OF OUR "FAVORABLE RESULTS."
READY, ARJUN?
YES, SIR.
HECK! THEY EVEN GAVE US FLACK JACKETS.
NOT THAT IT DOES ANY GOOD, IF YOU GET IT RIGHT BETWEEN THE EYES.
HOW'S VEDIKA?
HOLDING UP.
USED TO BE THAT I ACTUALLY GAVE A CRAP ABOUT MAKING A DIFFERENCE.
DOING WHAT I DO WAS MY WAY OF PUTTING MY HAND UP AND SAYING, "HEY, I'M HERE AND I'M DOING MY BIT."
NOW?
I DON'T GIVE A FLYING FUCK.
AND YOU?

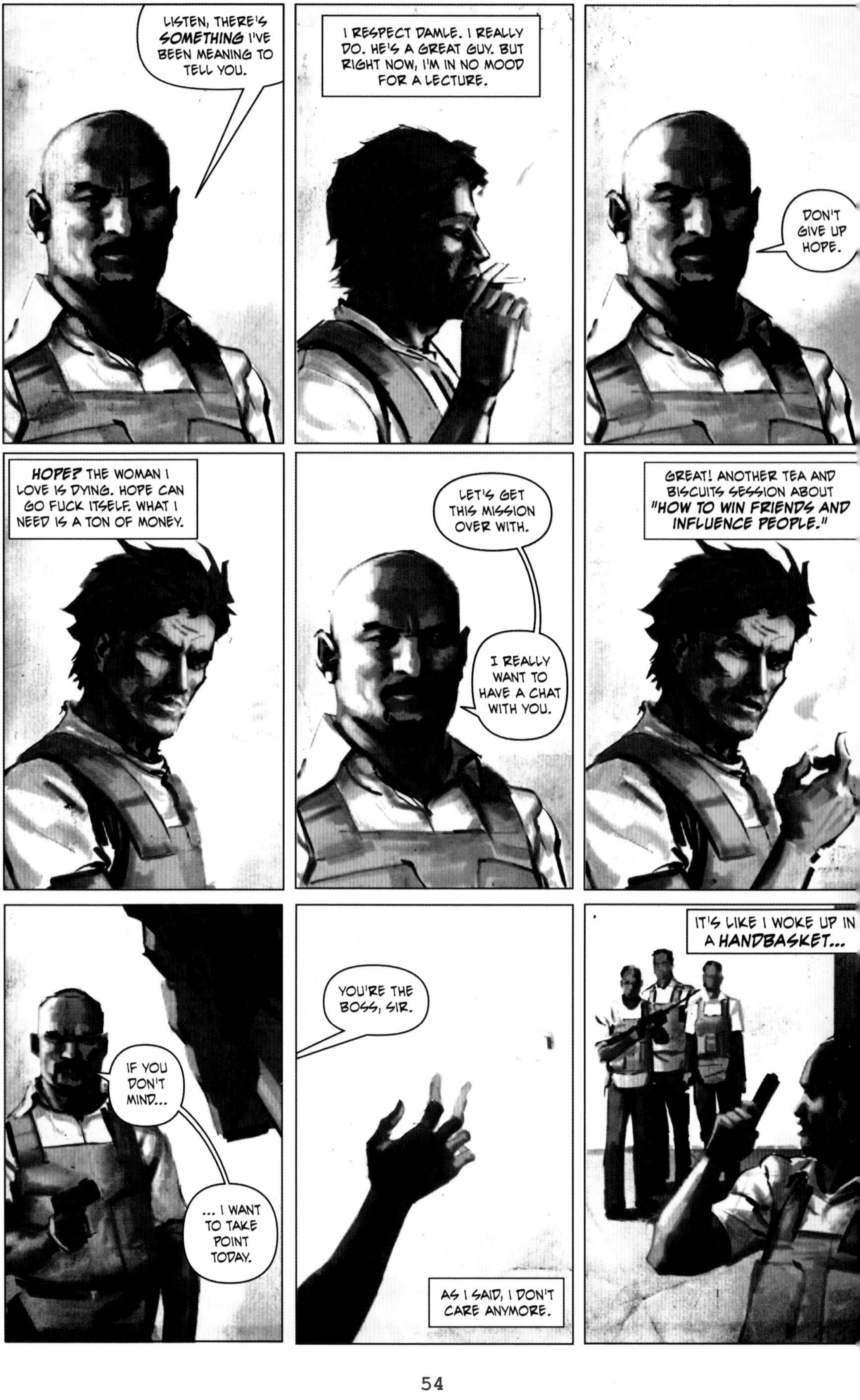
LISTEN, THERE'S SOMETHING I'VE BEEN MEANING TO TELL YOU.
I RESPECT DAMLE. I REALLY DO. HE'S A GREAT GUY. BUT RIGHT NOW, I'M IN NO MOOD FOR A LECTURE.
DON'T GIVE UP HOPE.
HOPE? THE WOMAN I LOVE IS DYING. HOPE CAN GO FUCK ITSELF. WHAT I NEED IS A TON OF MONEY.
LET'S GET THIS MISSION OVER WITH.
I REALLY WANT TO HAVE A CHAT WITH YOU.
GREAT! ANOTHER TEA AND BISCUITS SESSION ABOUT "HOW TO WIN FRIENDS AND INFLUENCE PEOPLE."
IF YOU DON'T MIND...
... I WANT TO TAKE POINT TODAY.
YOU'RE THE BOSS, SIR.
AS I SAID, I DON'T CARE ANYMORE.
IT'S LIKE I WOKE UP IN A HANDBASKET...

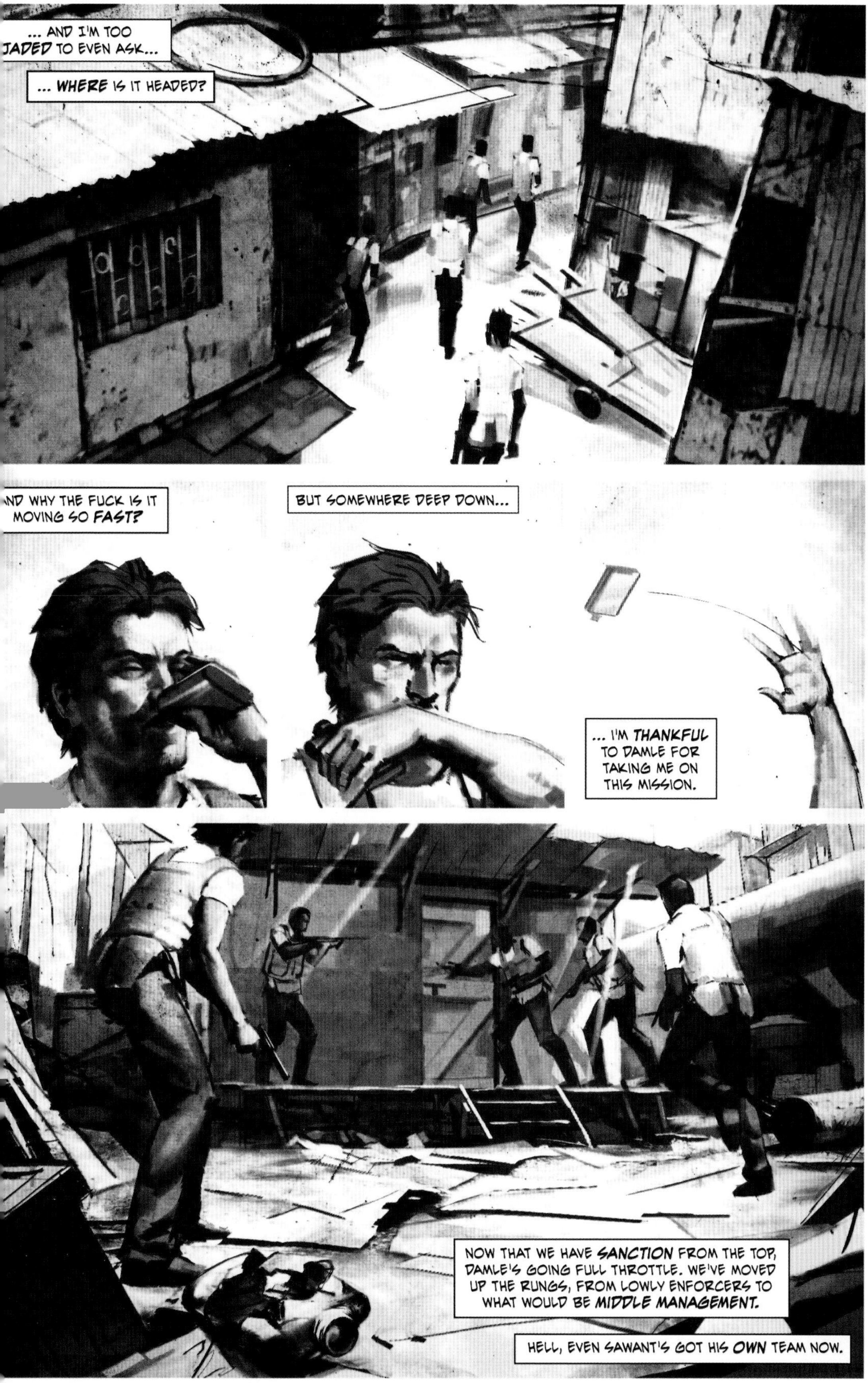
... AND I'M TOO JADED TO EVEN ASK...
... WHERE IS IT HEADED?
ND WHY THE FUCK IS IT MOVING SO FAST?
BUT SOMEWHERE DEEP DOWN...
... I'M THANKFUL TO DAMLE FOR TAKING ME ON THIS MISSION.
NOW THAT WE HAVE SANCTION FROM THE TOP, DAMLE'S GOING FULL THROTTLE. WE'VE MOVED UP THE RUNGS, FROM LOWLY ENFORCERS TO WHAT WOULD BE MIDDLE MANAGEMENT.
HELL, EVEN SAWANT'S GOT HIS OWN TEAM NOW.

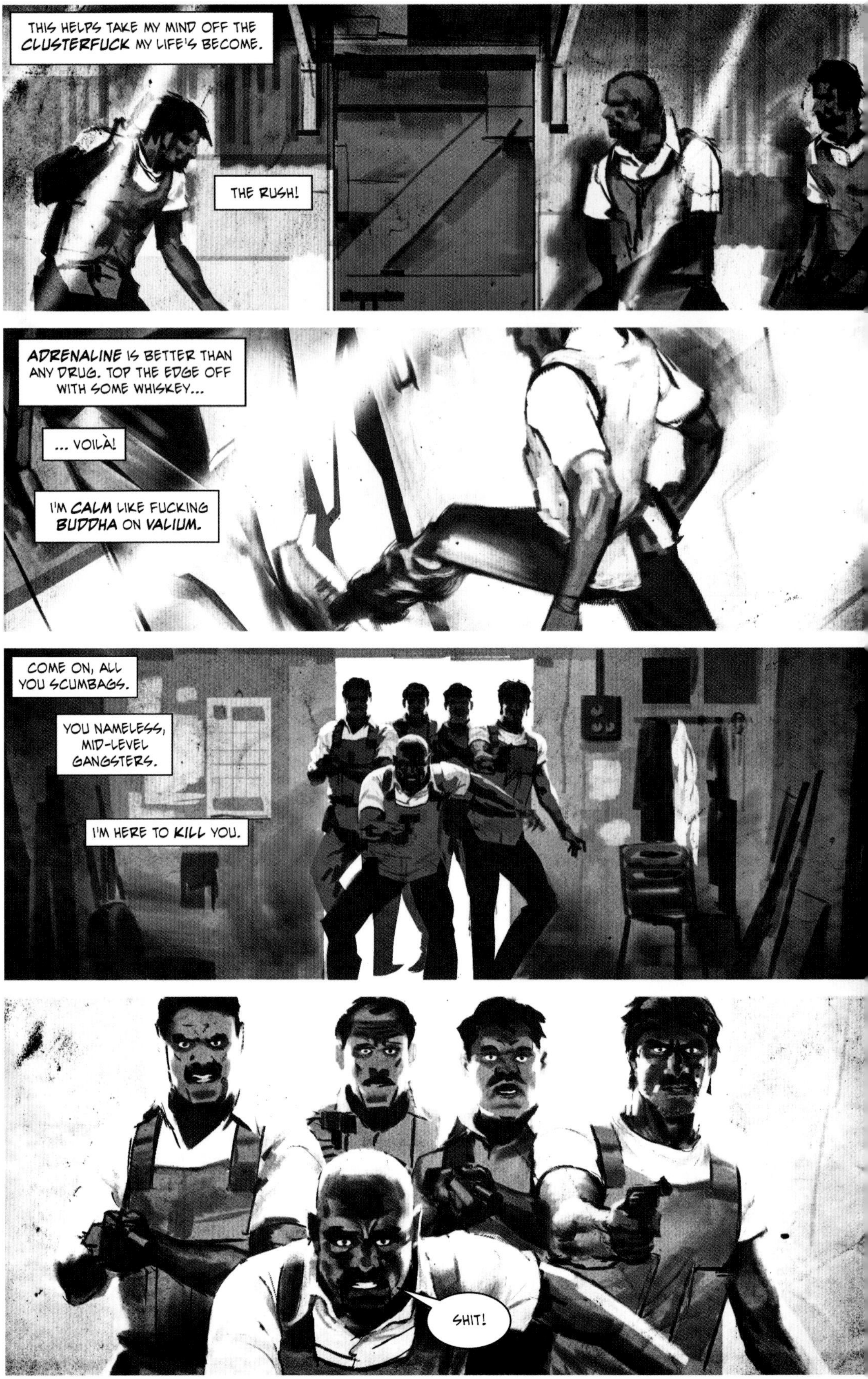
THIS HELPS TAKE MY MIND OFF THE CLUSTERFUCK MY LIFE'S BECOME.
THE RUSH!
ADRENALINE IS BETTER THAN ANY DRUG. TOP THE EDGE OFF WITH SOME WHISKEY...
... VOILÀ!
I'M CALM LIKE FUCKING BUDDHA ON VALIUM.
COME ON, ALL YOU SCUMBAGS.
YOU NAMELESS, MID-LEVEL GANGSTERS.
I'M HERE TO KILL YOU.
SHIT!

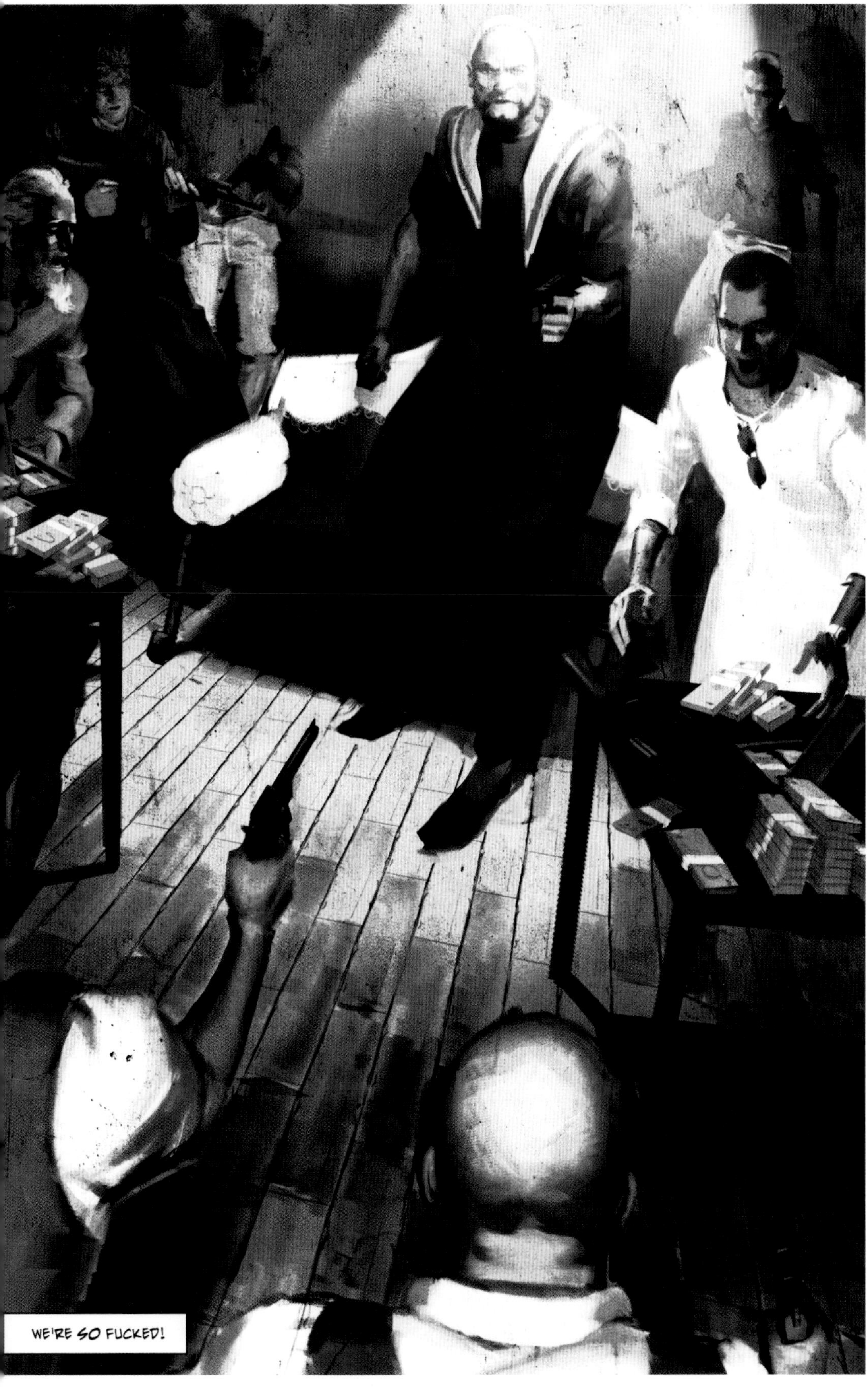
WE'RE SO FUCKED!

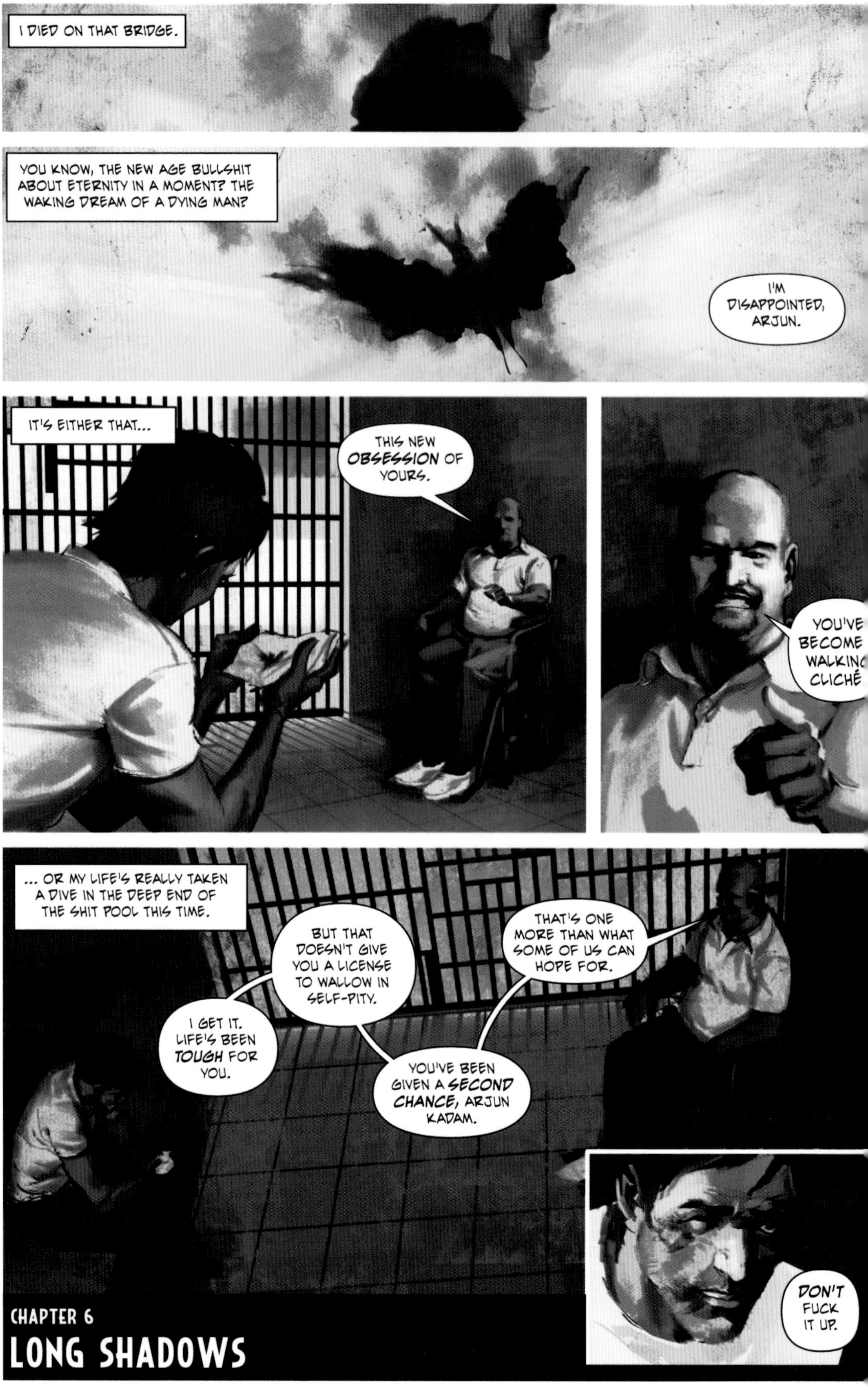
I DIED ON THAT BRIDGE.
YOU KNOW, THE NEW AGE BULLSHIT ABOUT ETERNITY IN A MOMENT? THE WAKING DREAM OF A DYING MAN?
I'M DISAPPOINTED, ARJUN.
IT'S EITHER THAT...
THIS NEW OBSESSION OF YOURS.
YOU'VE BECOME WALKING CLICHÉ
... OR MY LIFE'S REALLY TAKEN A DIVE IN THE DEEP END OF THE SHIT POOL THIS TIME.
I GET IT. LIFE'S BEEN TOUGH FOR YOU.
BUT THAT DOESN'T GIVE YOU A LICENSE TO WALLOW IN SELF-PITY.
YOU'VE BEEN GIVEN A SECOND CHANCE, ARJUN KADAM.
THAT'S ONE MORE THAN WHAT SOME OF US CAN HOPE FOR.
CHAPTER 6
LONG SHADOWS
DON'T FUCK IT UP.

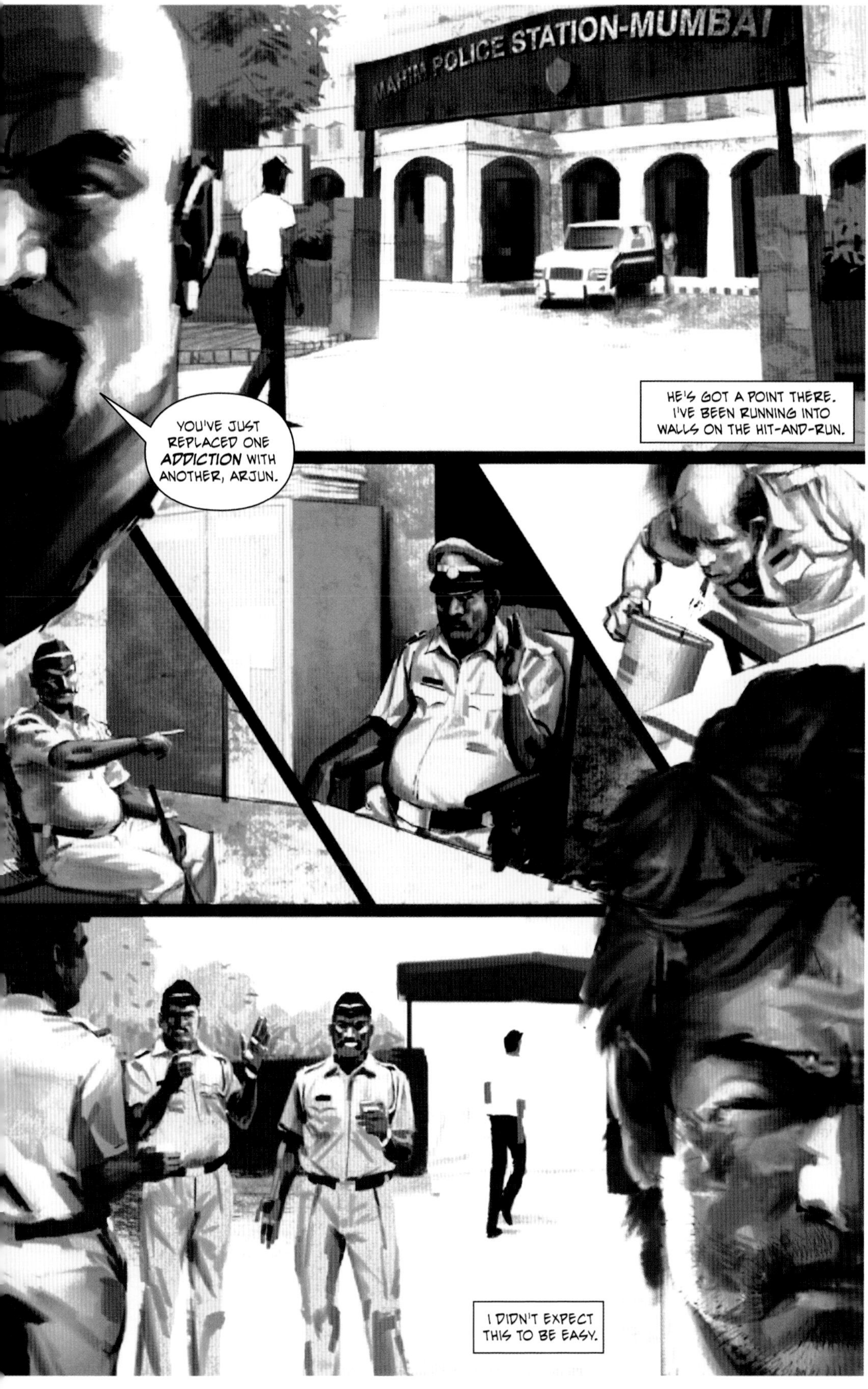
MAHIM POLICE STATION-MUMBAI
YOU'VE JUST REPLACED ONE ADDICTION WITH ANOTHER, ARJUN.
HE'S GOT A POINT THERE. I'VE BEEN RUNNING INTO WALLS ON THE HIT-AND-RUN.
I DIDN'T EXPECT THIS TO BE EASY.

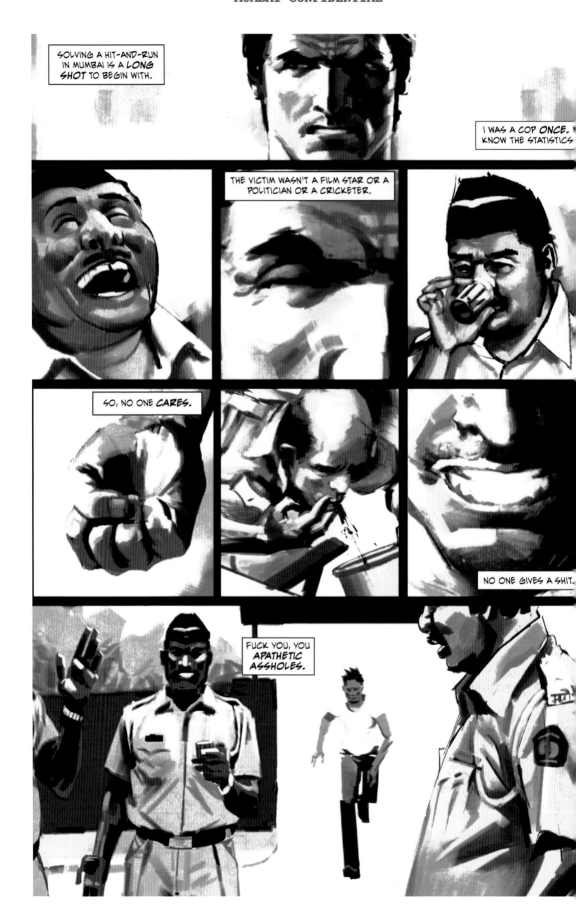

SOLVING A HIT-AND-RUN IN MUMBAI IS A *LONG SHOT* TO BEGIN WITH.

I WAS A COP *ONCE.* KNOW THE STATISTICS

THE VICTIM WASN'T A FILM STAR OR A POLITICIAN OR A CRICKETER.

SO, NO ONE *CARES.*

NO ONE GIVES A SHIT.

FUCK YOU, YOU *APATHETIC ASSHOLES.*

Welcome to
Skokie Public Library

Customer ID: **********1442

Items that you checked out

Title:
  Mumbai confidential / [written by Saurav
  Mohapatra ; illustrated by Vivek Shinde ;
  featuring additio
ID: 31232007038500
Due: Wednesday, June 20, 2018

Total items: 1
Account balance: $0.00
Wednesday, May 30, 2018 3:33 PM
Ready for pickup: 0

Renew online: www.skokielibrary.info
Renew by phone: (847) 673-2675

Thank you for using the Express Check
Out

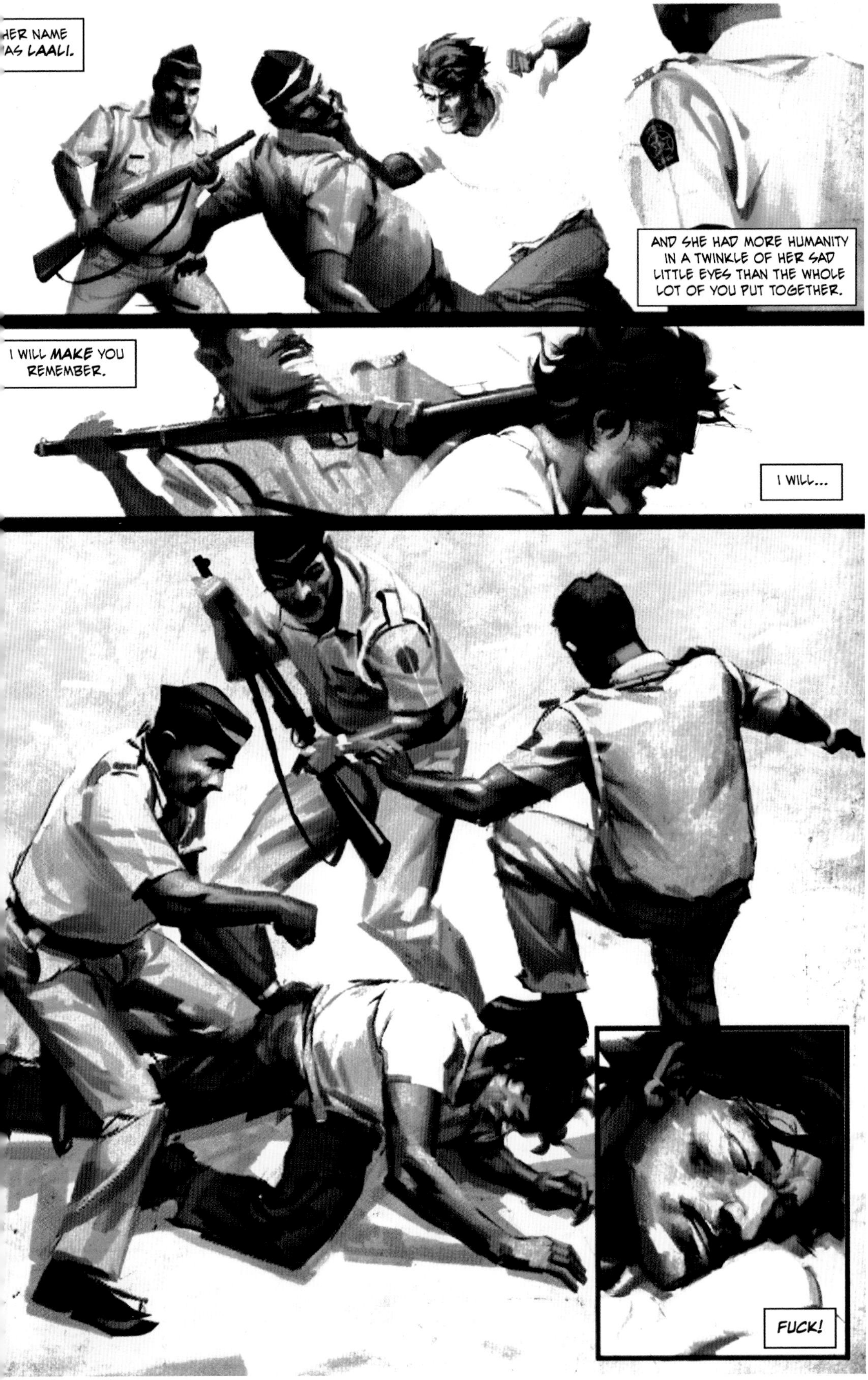
HER NAME
AS LAALI.
AND SHE HAD MORE HUMANITY IN A TWINKLE OF HER SAD LITTLE EYES THAN THE WHOLE LOT OF YOU PUT TOGETHER.
I WILL MAKE YOU REMEMBER.
I WILL...
FUCK!

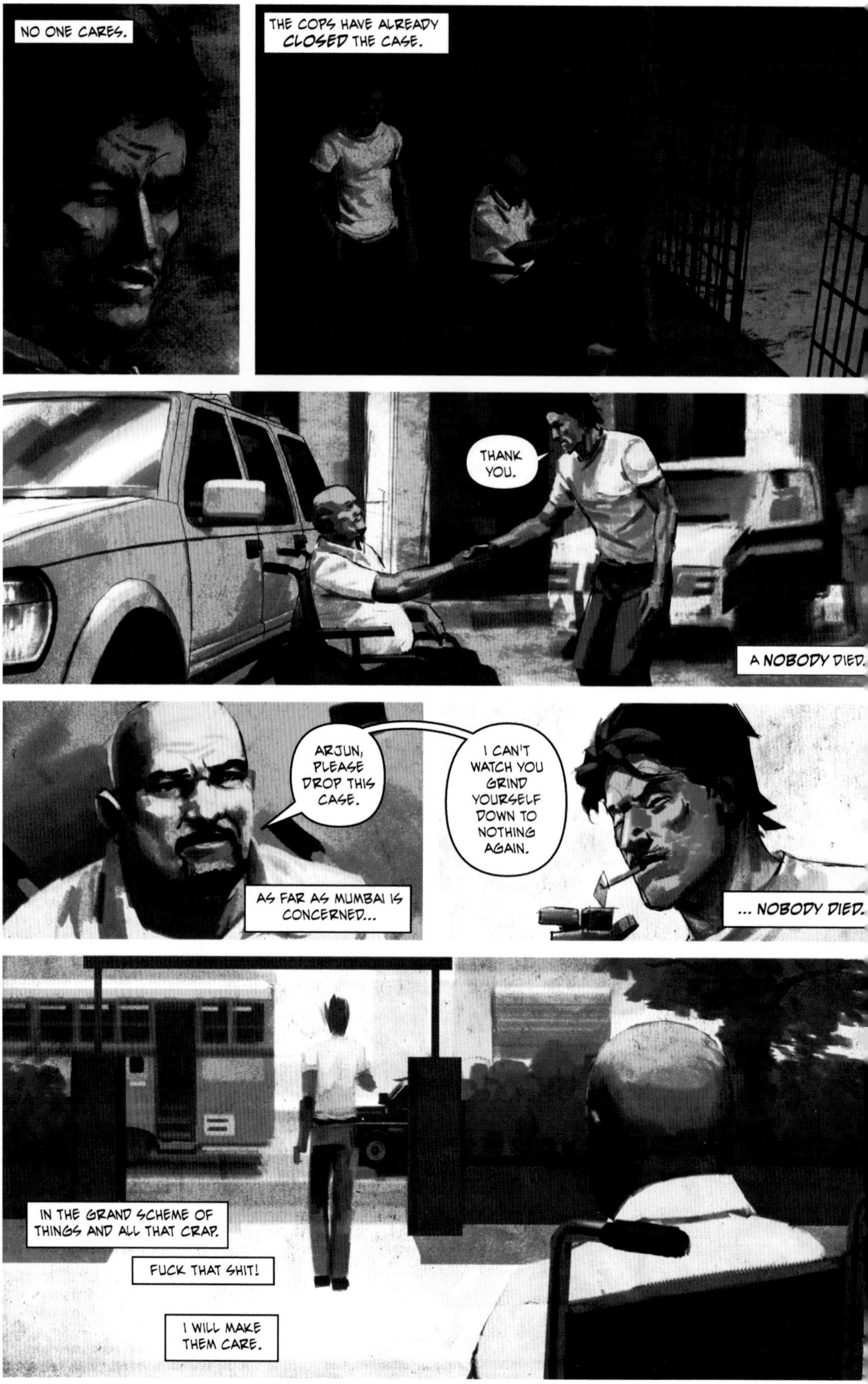
NO ONE CARES.
THE COPS HAVE ALREADY CLOSED THE CASE.
THANK YOU.
A NOBODY DIED.
ARJUN, PLEASE DROP THIS CASE.
I CAN'T WATCH YOU GRIND YOURSELF DOWN TO NOTHING AGAIN.
AS FAR AS MUMBAI IS CONCERNED...
... NOBODY DIED.
IN THE GRAND SCHEME OF THINGS AND ALL THAT CRAP.
FUCK THAT SHIT!
I WILL MAKE THEM CARE.

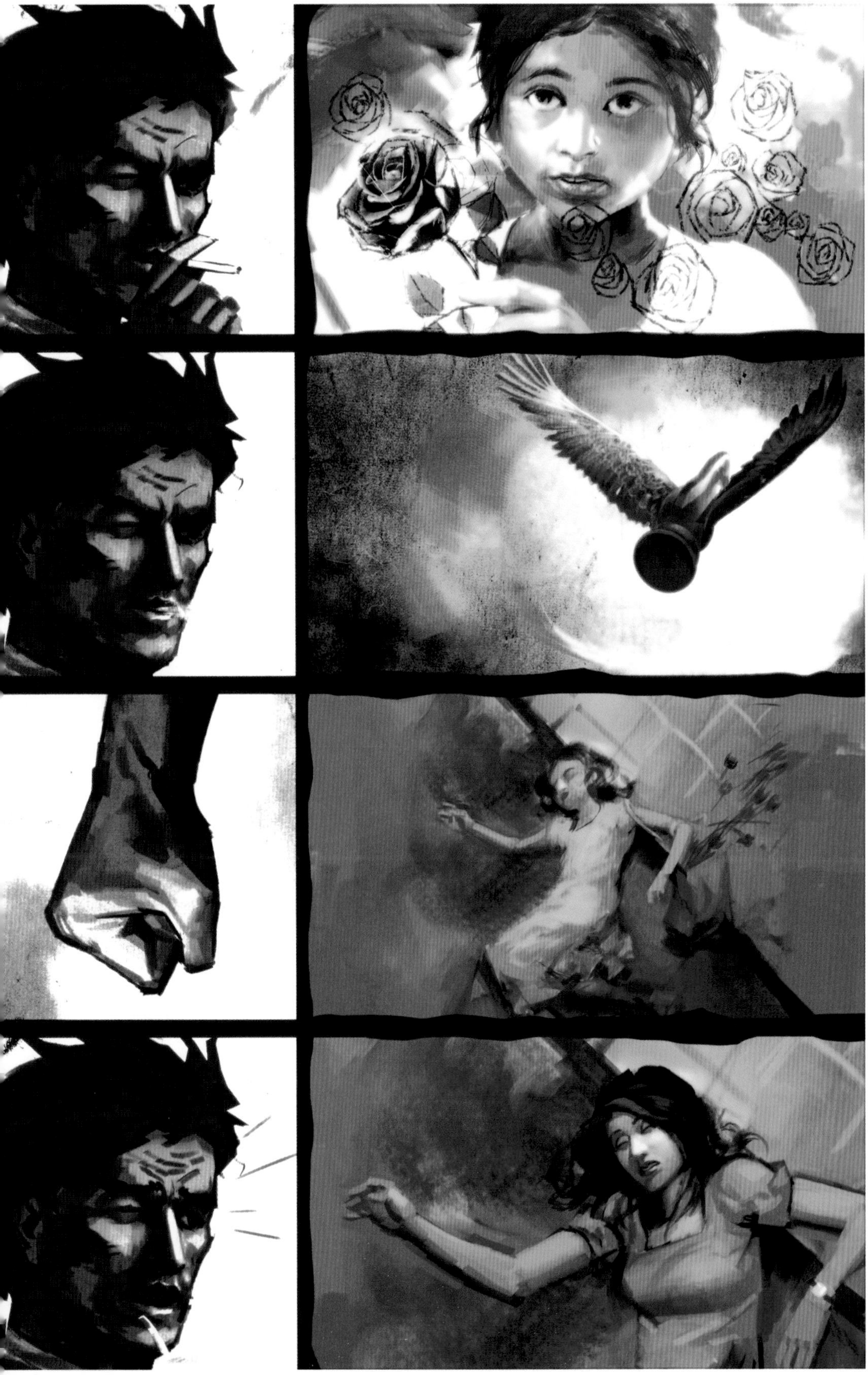

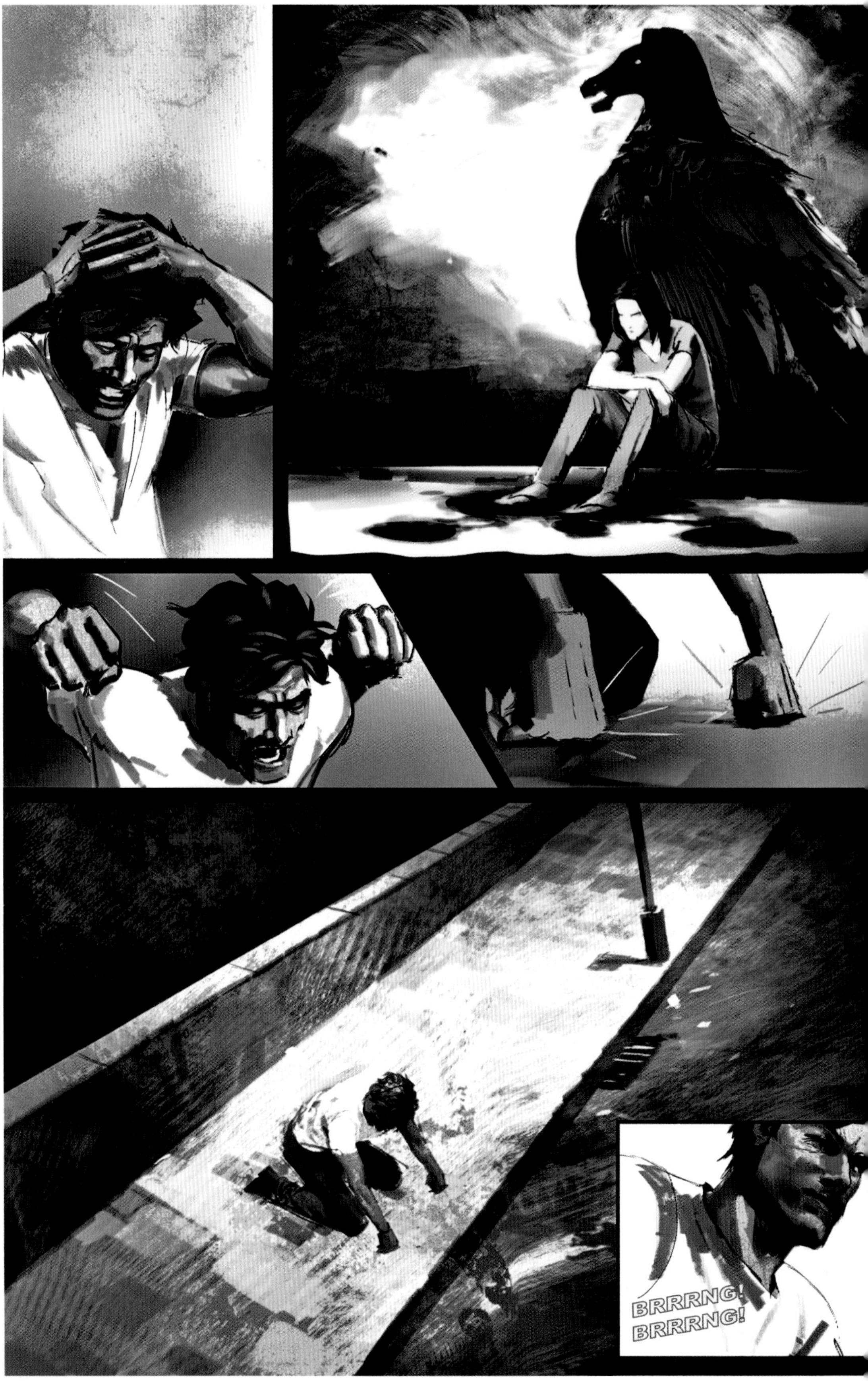
BRRRNG!
BRRRNG!

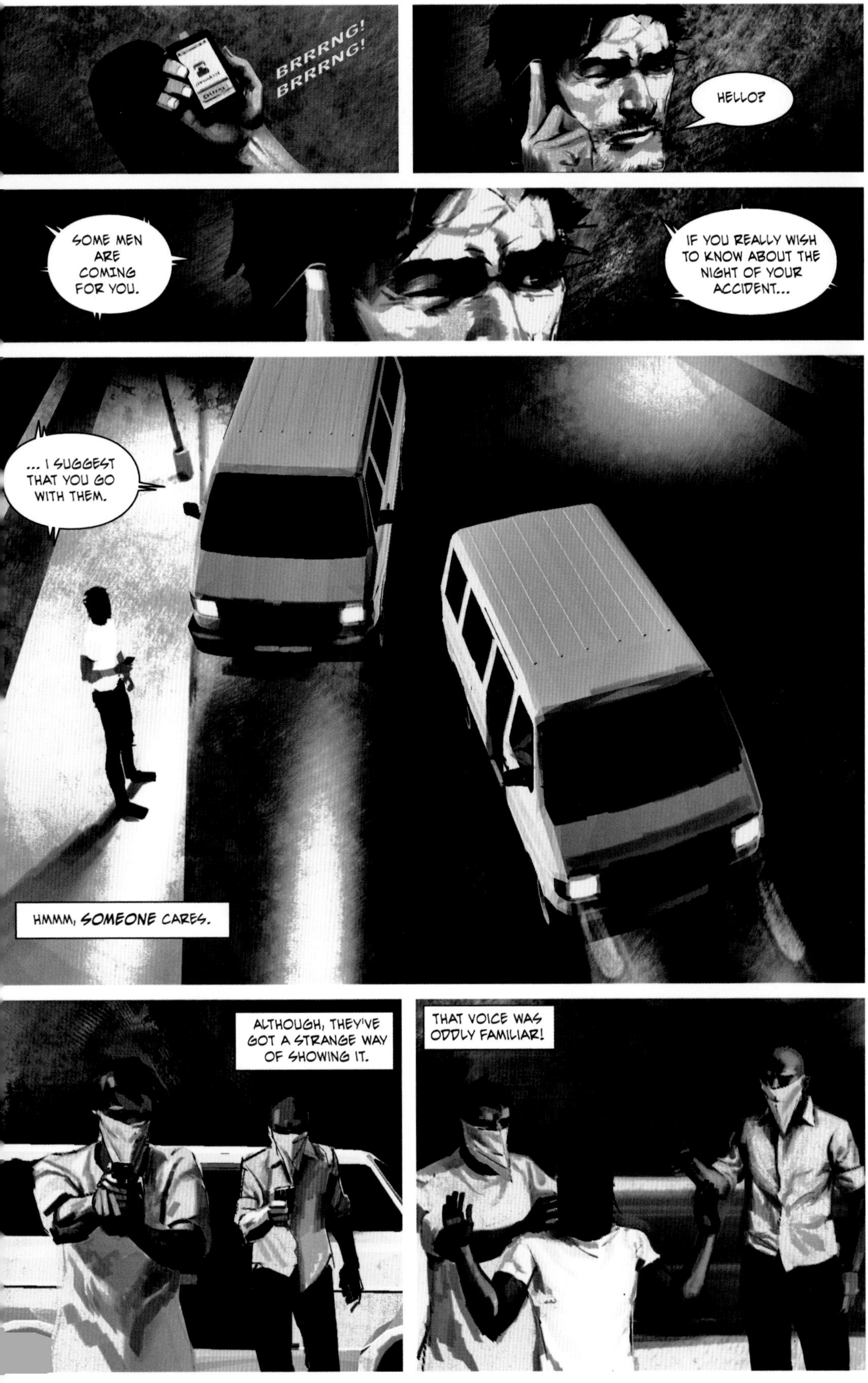
BRRRNG!
BRRRNG!
HELLO?
SOME MEN ARE COMING FOR YOU.
IF YOU REALLY WISH TO KNOW ABOUT THE NIGHT OF YOUR ACCIDENT...
... I SUGGEST THAT YOU GO WITH THEM.
HMMM, SOMEONE CARES.
ALTHOUGH, THEY'VE GOT A STRANGE WAY OF SHOWING IT.
THAT VOICE WAS ODDLY FAMILIAR!

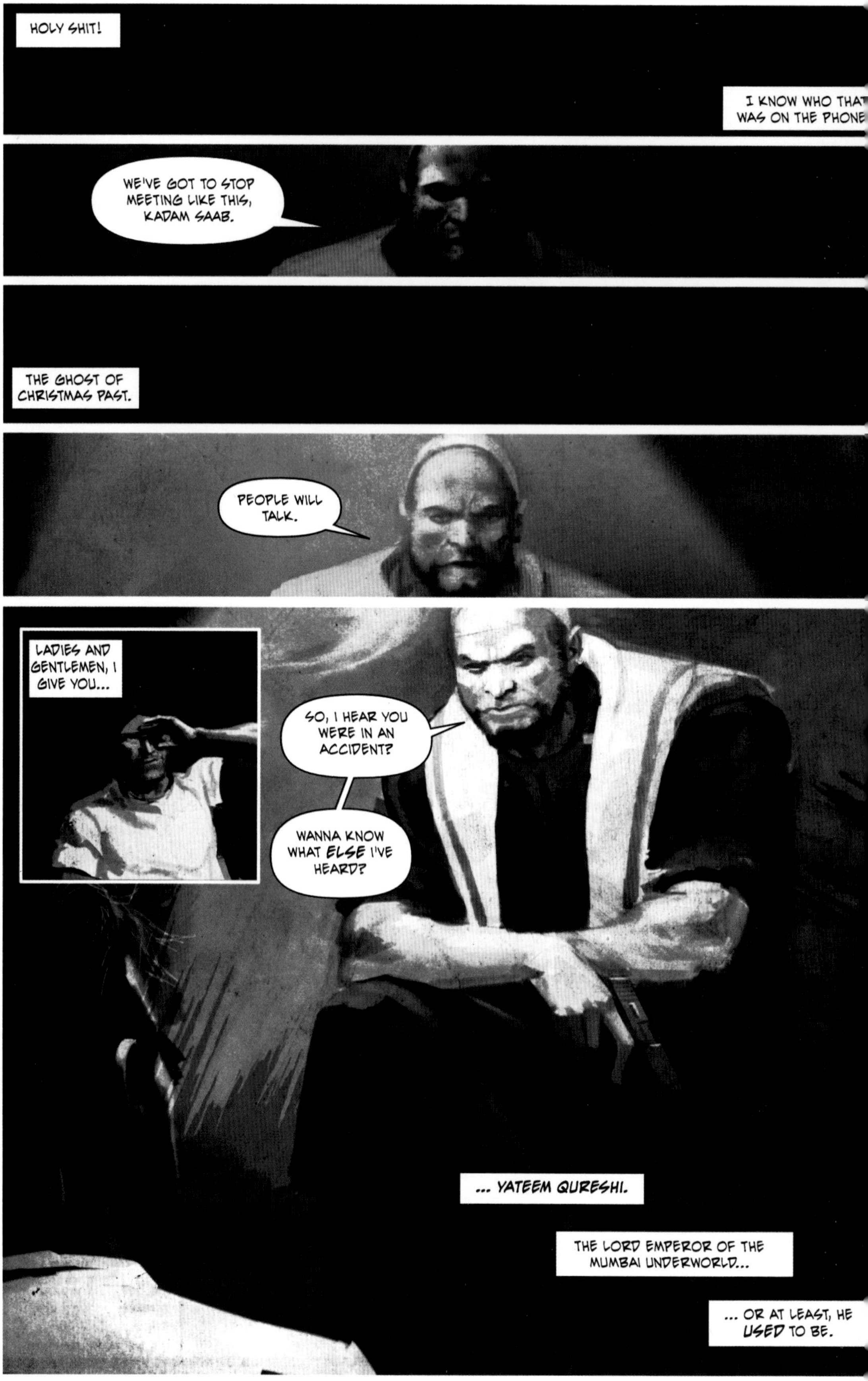
HOLY SHIT!
I KNOW WHO THAT WAS ON THE PHONE
WE'VE GOT TO STOP MEETING LIKE THIS, KADAM SAAB.
THE GHOST OF CHRISTMAS PAST.
PEOPLE WILL TALK.
LADIES AND GENTLEMEN, I GIVE YOU...
SO, I HEAR YOU WERE IN AN ACCIDENT?
WANNA KNOW WHAT ELSE I'VE HEARD?
... YATEEM QURESHI.
THE LORD EMPEROR OF THE MUMBAI UNDERWORLD...
... OR AT LEAST, HE USED TO BE.

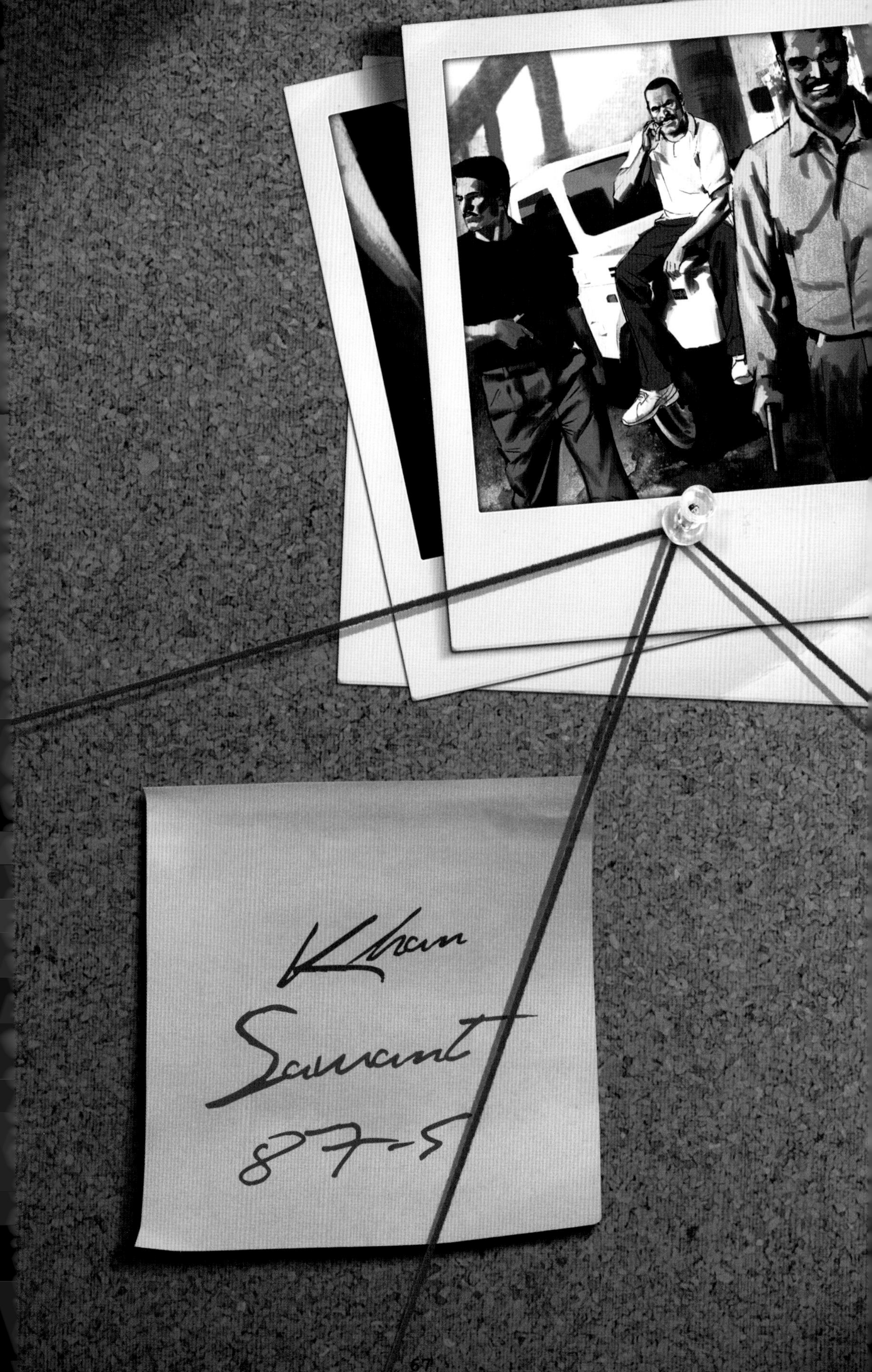
Khan
Sawant
87-5

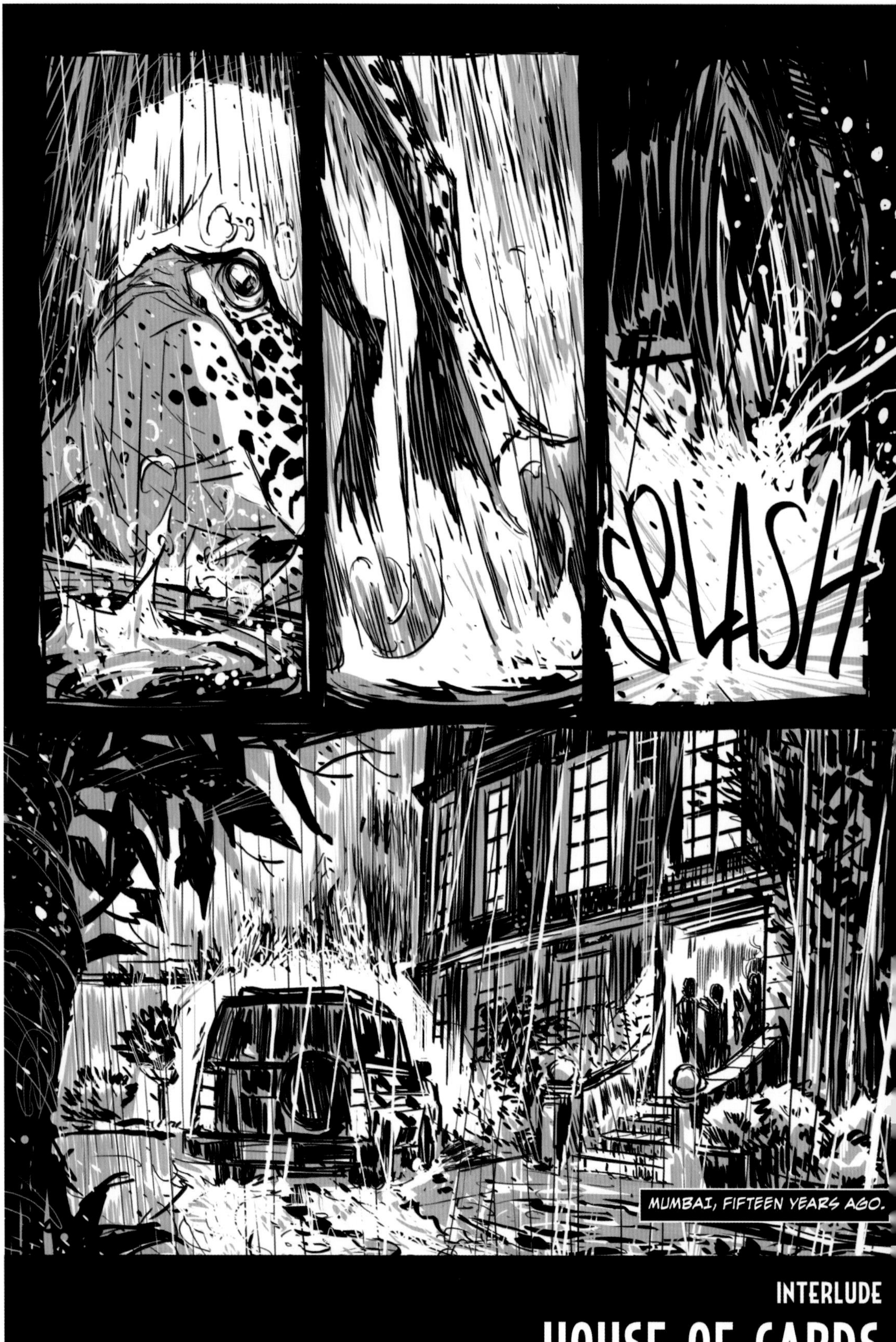
SPLASH
MUMBAI, FIFTEEN YEARS AGO.
INTERLUDE
HOUSE OF CARDS

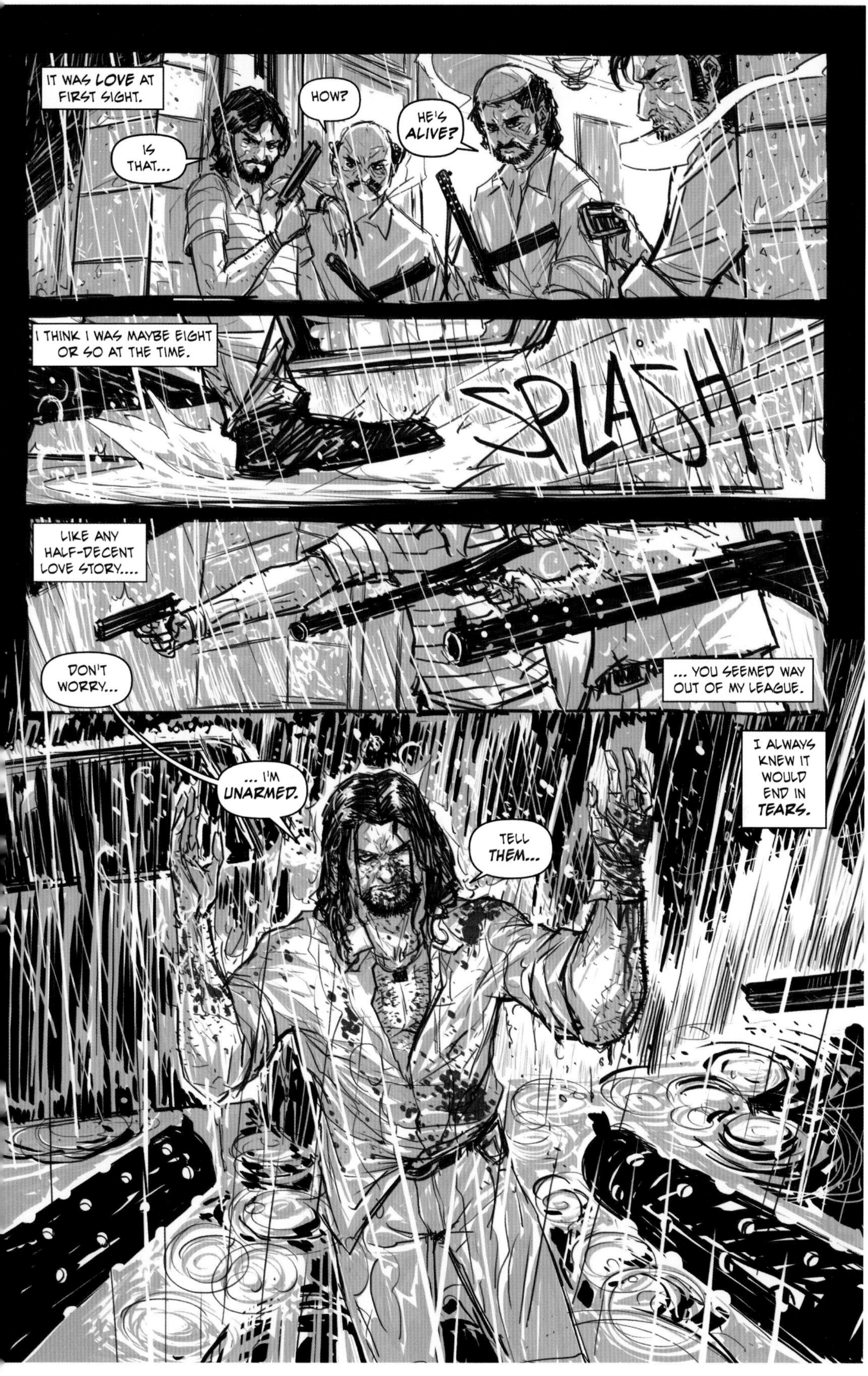
IT WAS LOVE AT FIRST SIGHT.
IS THAT...
HOW?
HE'S ALIVE?
I THINK I WAS MAYBE EIGHT OR SO AT THE TIME.
SPLASH
LIKE ANY HALF-DECENT LOVE STORY....
... YOU SEEMED WAY OUT OF MY LEAGUE.
DON'T WORRY...
... I'M UNARMED.
TELL THEM...
I ALWAYS KNEW IT WOULD END IN TEARS.

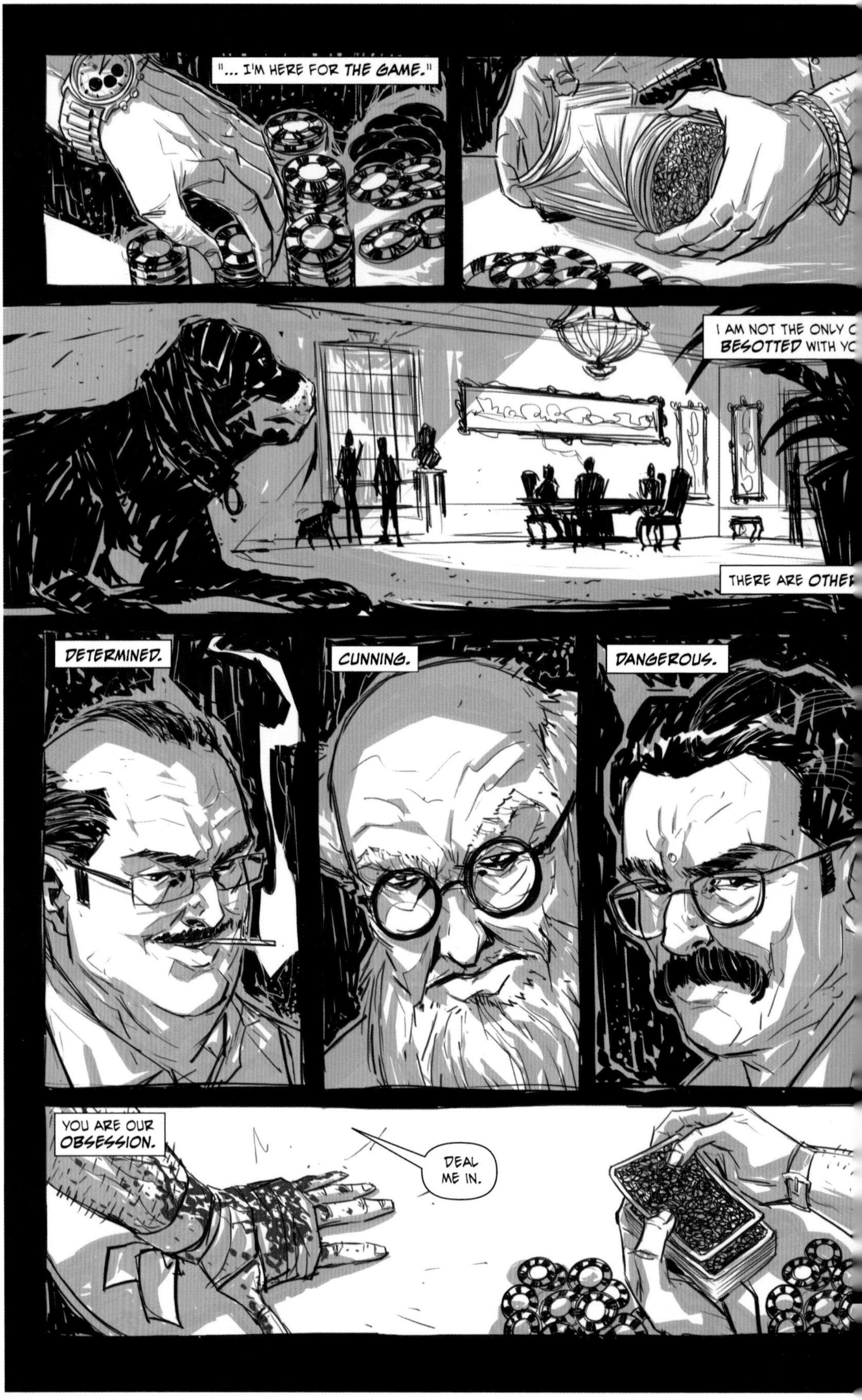
"... I'M HERE FOR THE GAME."
I AM NOT THE ONLY
BESOTTED WITH
THERE ARE
DETERMINED.
CUNNING.
DANGEROUS.
YOU ARE OUR OBSESSION.
DEAL ME IN.

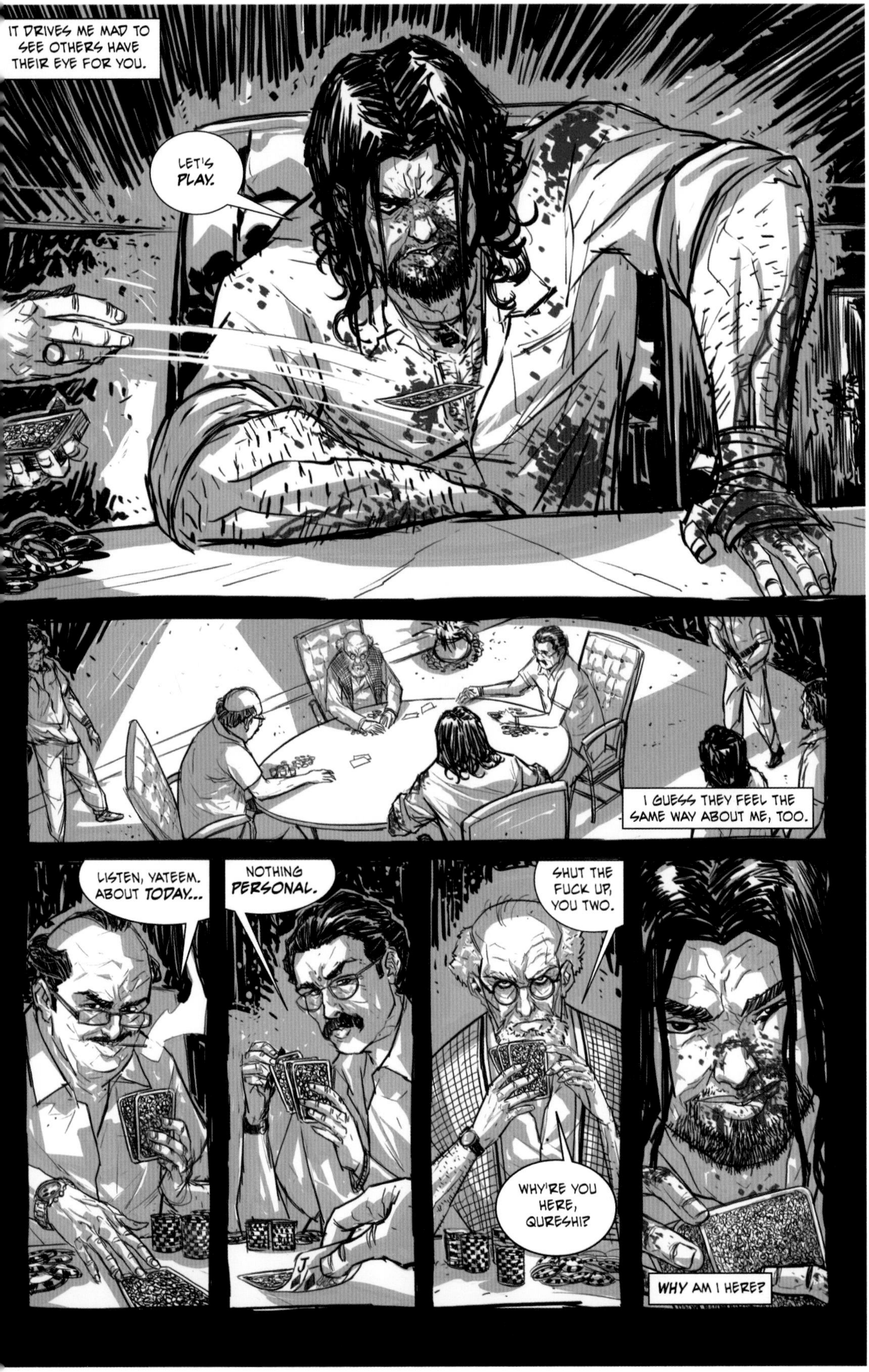
IT DRIVES ME MAD TO SEE OTHERS HAVE THEIR EYE FOR YOU.
LET'S PLAY.
I GUESS THEY FEEL THE SAME WAY ABOUT ME, TOO.
LISTEN, YATEEM. ABOUT TODAY...
NOTHING PERSONAL.
SHUT THE FUCK UP, YOU TWO.
WHY'RE YOU HERE, QURESHI?
WHY AM I HERE?

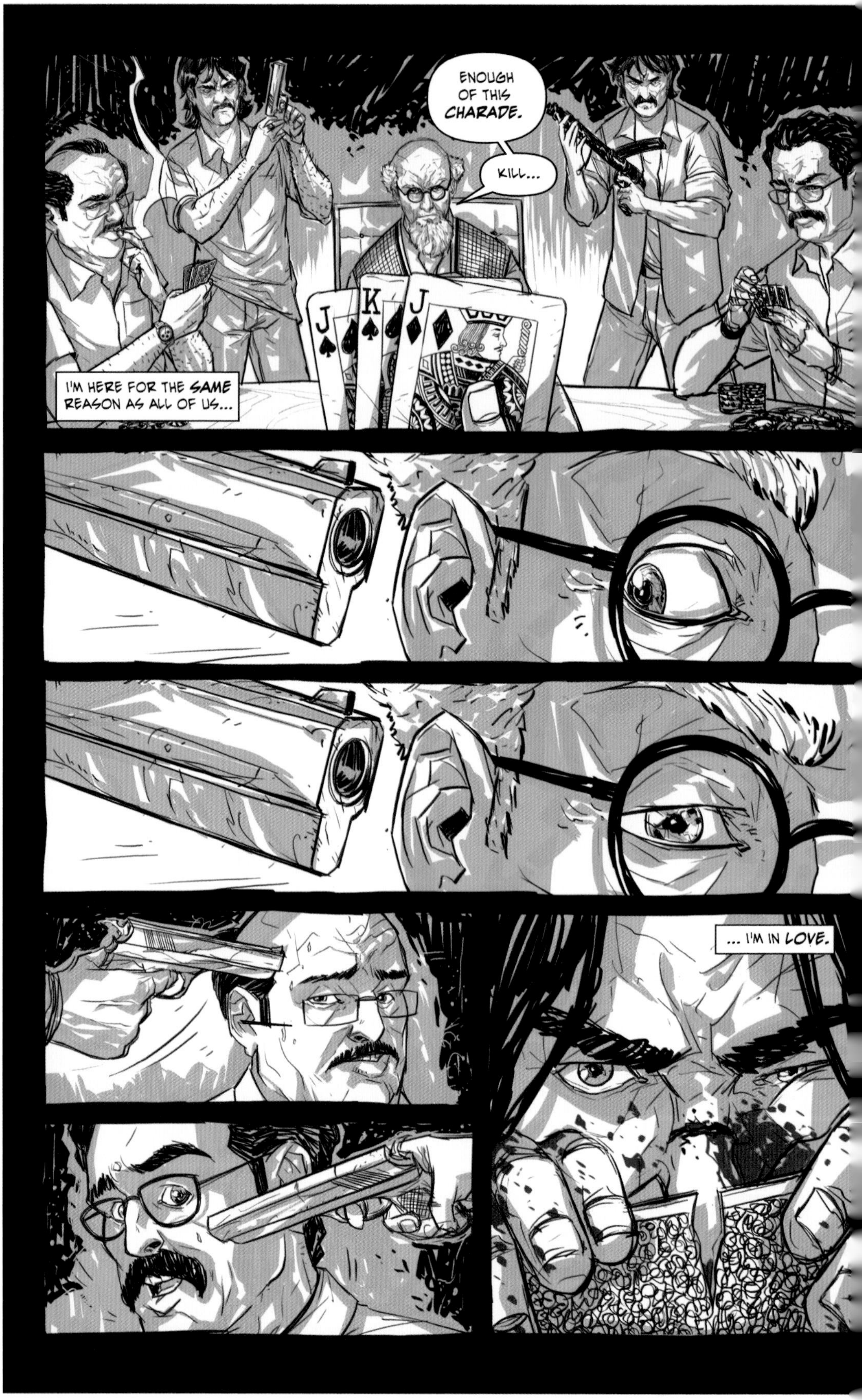
ENOUGH OF THIS CHARADE.
KILL...
I'M HERE FOR THE SAME REASON AS ALL OF US...
... I'M IN LOVE.

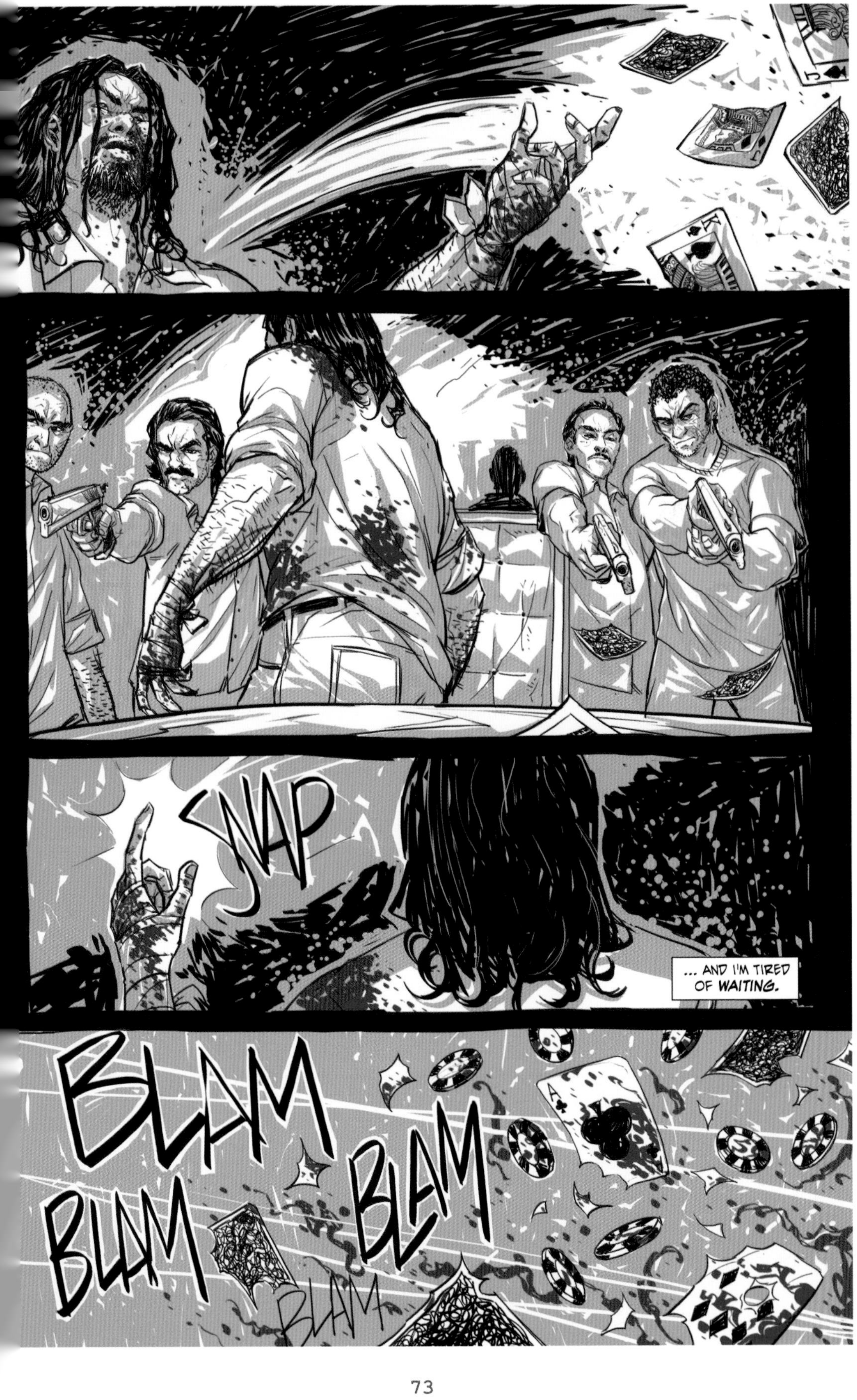
SNAP
... AND I'M TIRED OF WAITING.
BLAM
BLAM
BLAM
BLAM

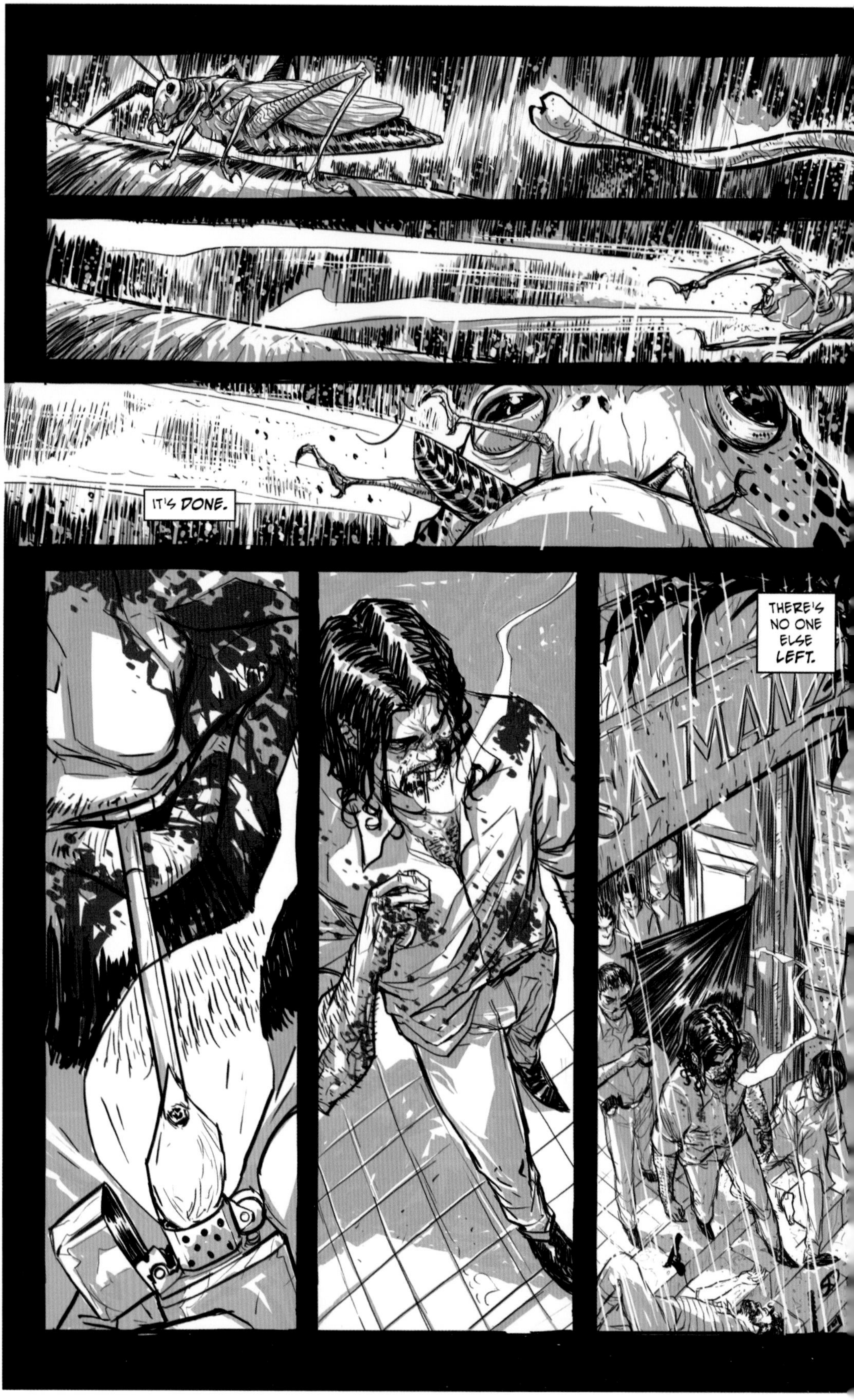
IT'S DONE.
THERE'S NO ONE ELSE LEFT.

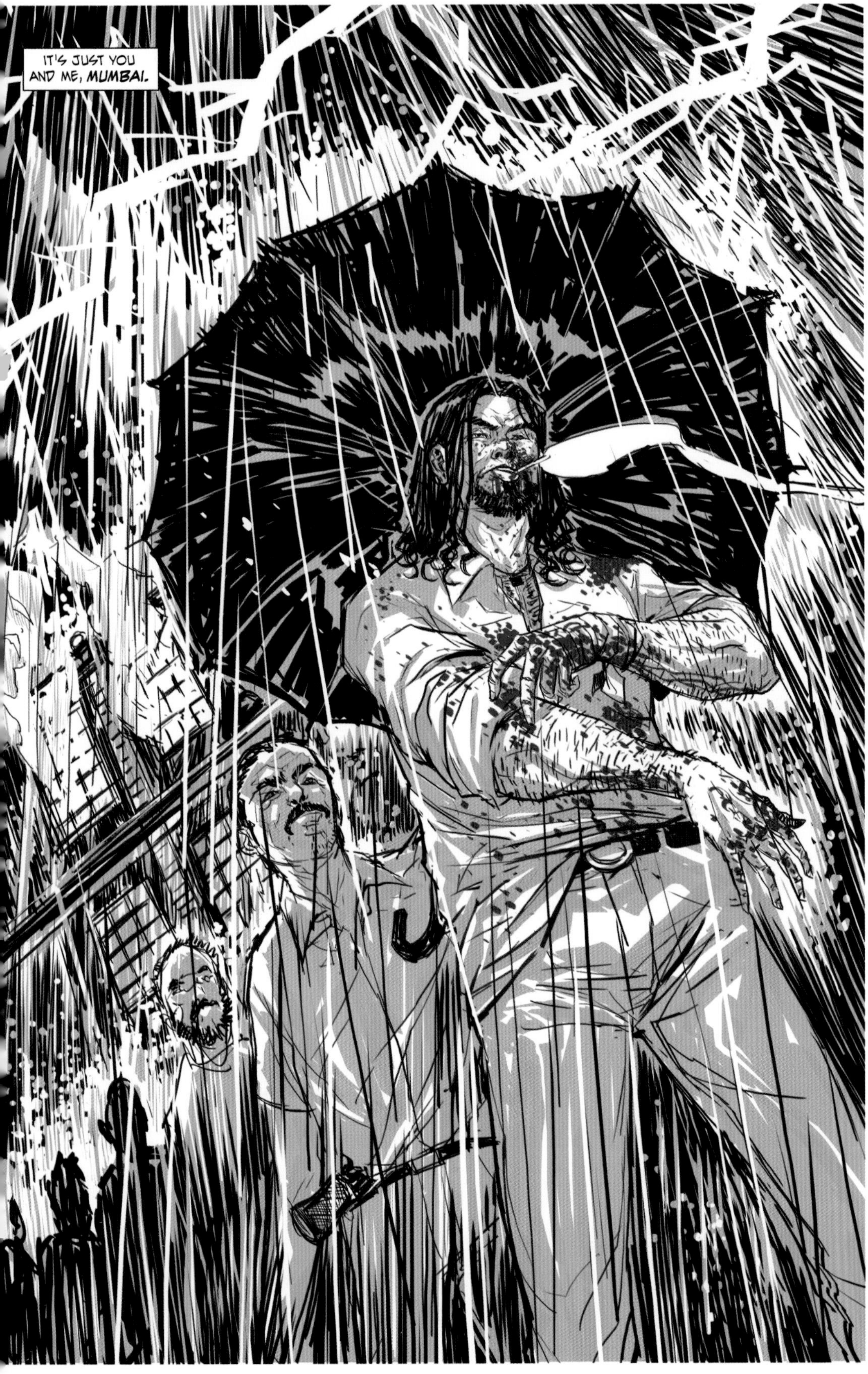
IT'S JUST YOU AND ME, MUMBAI.

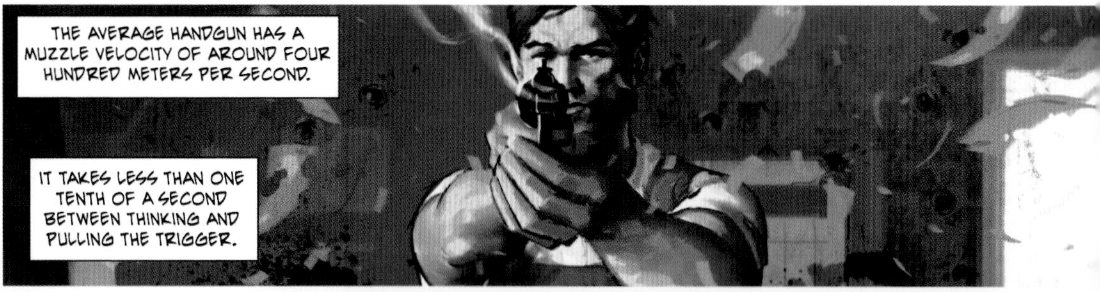
THE AVERAGE HANDGUN HAS A MUZZLE VELOCITY OF AROUND FOUR HUNDRED METERS PER SECOND.
IT TAKES LESS THAN ONE TENTH OF A SECOND BETWEEN THINKING AND PULLING THE TRIGGER.

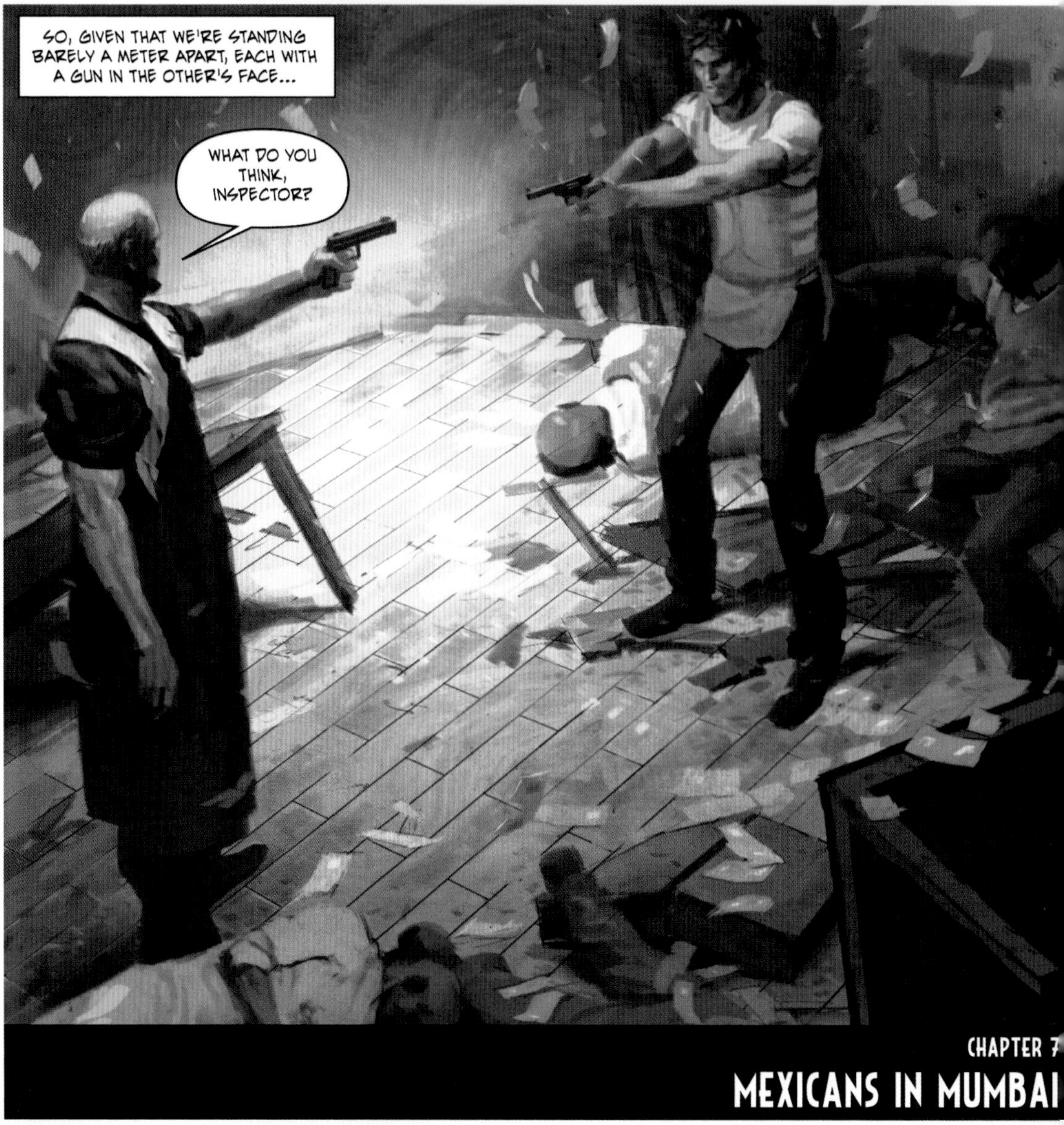
SO, GIVEN THAT WE'RE STANDING BARELY A METER APART, EACH WITH A GUN IN THE OTHER'S FACE...
WHAT DO YOU THINK, INSPECTOR?

CHAPTER 7

MEXICANS IN MUMBAI

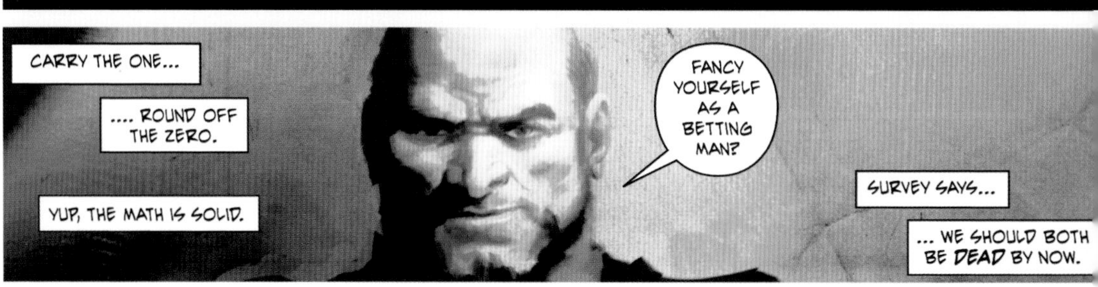
CARRY THE ONE...
.... ROUND OFF THE ZERO.
YUP, THE MATH IS SOLID.
FANCY YOURSELF AS A BETTING MAN?
SURVEY SAYS...
... WE SHOULD BOTH BE DEAD BY NOW.

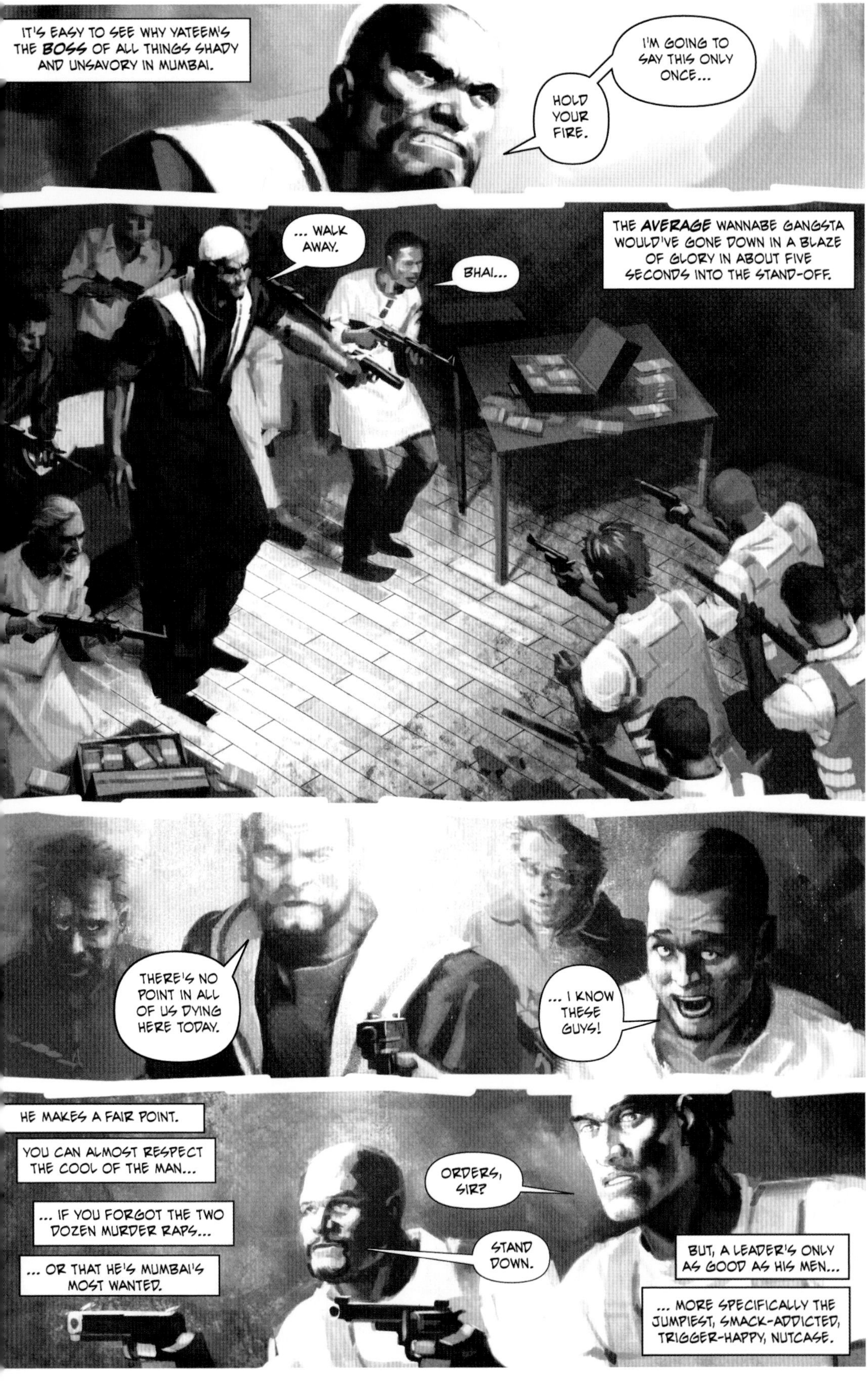
IT'S EASY TO SEE WHY YATEEM'S THE BOSS OF ALL THINGS SHADY AND UNSAVORY IN MUMBAI.
HOLD YOUR FIRE.
I'M GOING TO SAY THIS ONLY ONCE...
... WALK AWAY.
BHAI...
THE AVERAGE WANNABE GANGSTA WOULD'VE GONE DOWN IN A BLAZE OF GLORY IN ABOUT FIVE SECONDS INTO THE STAND-OFF.
THERE'S NO POINT IN ALL OF US DYING HERE TODAY.
... I KNOW THESE GUYS!
HE MAKES A FAIR POINT.
YOU CAN ALMOST RESPECT THE COOL OF THE MAN...
... IF YOU FORGOT THE TWO DOZEN MURDER RAPS...
... OR THAT HE'S MUMBAI'S MOST WANTED.
ORDERS, SIR?
STAND DOWN.
BUT, A LEADER'S ONLY AS GOOD AS HIS MEN...
... MORE SPECIFICALLY THE JUMPIEST, SMACK-ADDICTED, TRIGGER-HAPPY, NUTCASE.

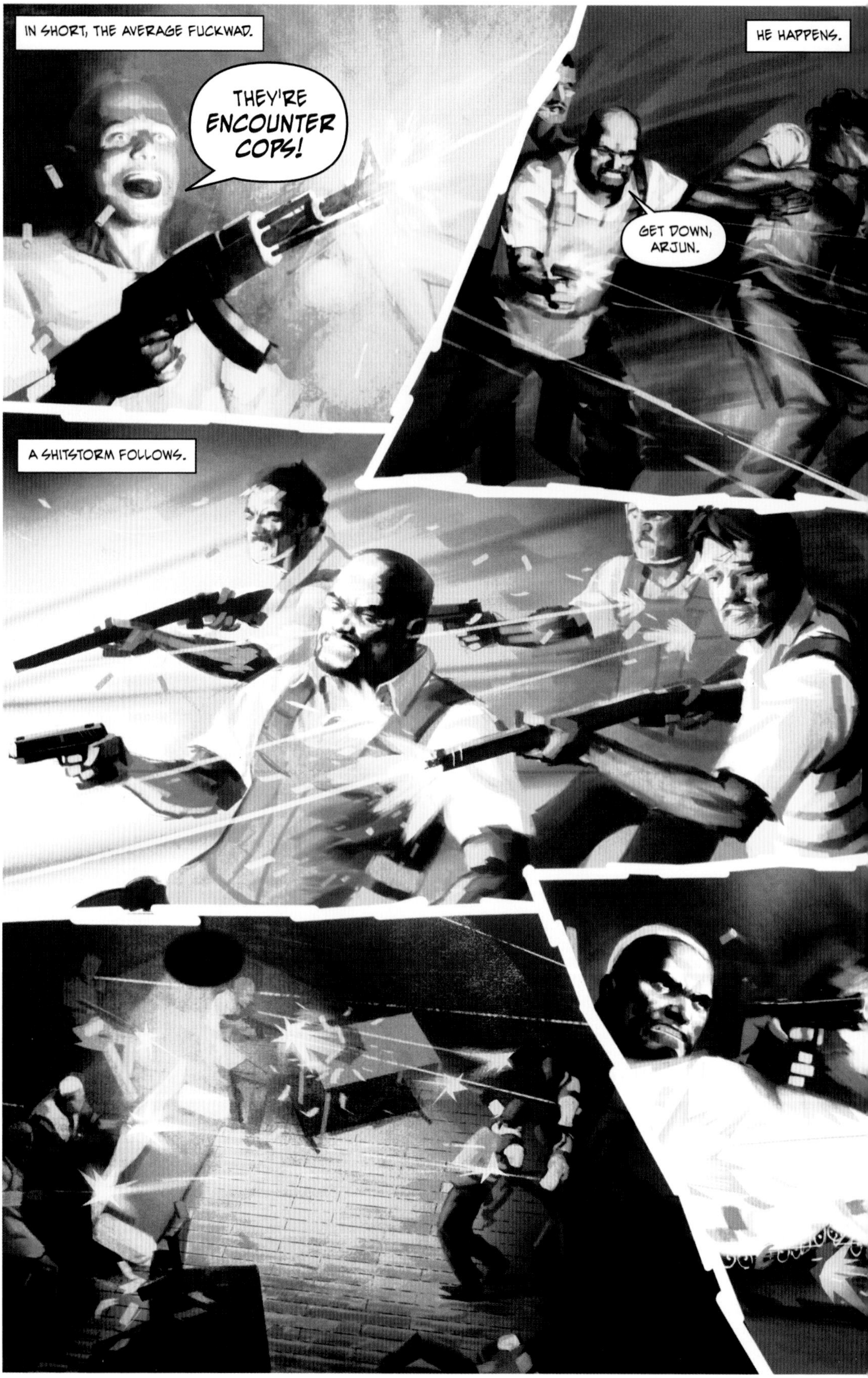
IN SHORT, THE AVERAGE FUCKWAD.
THEY'RE ENCOUNTER COPS!
HE HAPPENS.
GET DOWN, ARJUN.
A SHITSTORM FOLLOWS.

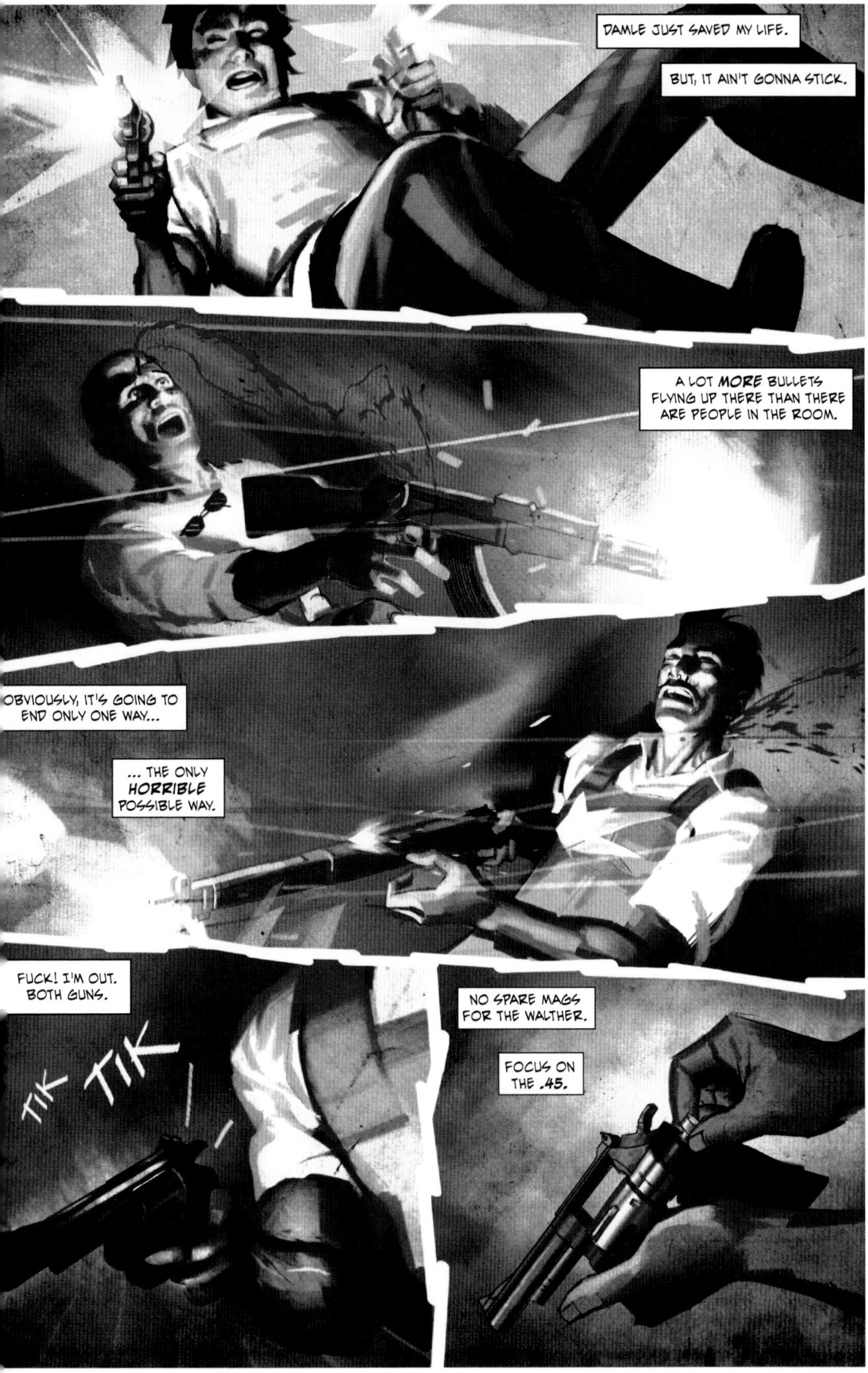
DAMLE JUST SAVED MY LIFE.
BUT, IT AIN'T GONNA STICK.
A LOT MORE BULLETS FLYING UP THERE THAN THERE ARE PEOPLE IN THE ROOM.
OBVIOUSLY, IT'S GOING TO END ONLY ONE WAY...
... THE ONLY HORRIBLE POSSIBLE WAY.
FUCK! I'M OUT. BOTH GUNS.
TIK TIK
NO SPARE MAGS FOR THE WALTHER.
FOCUS ON THE .45.

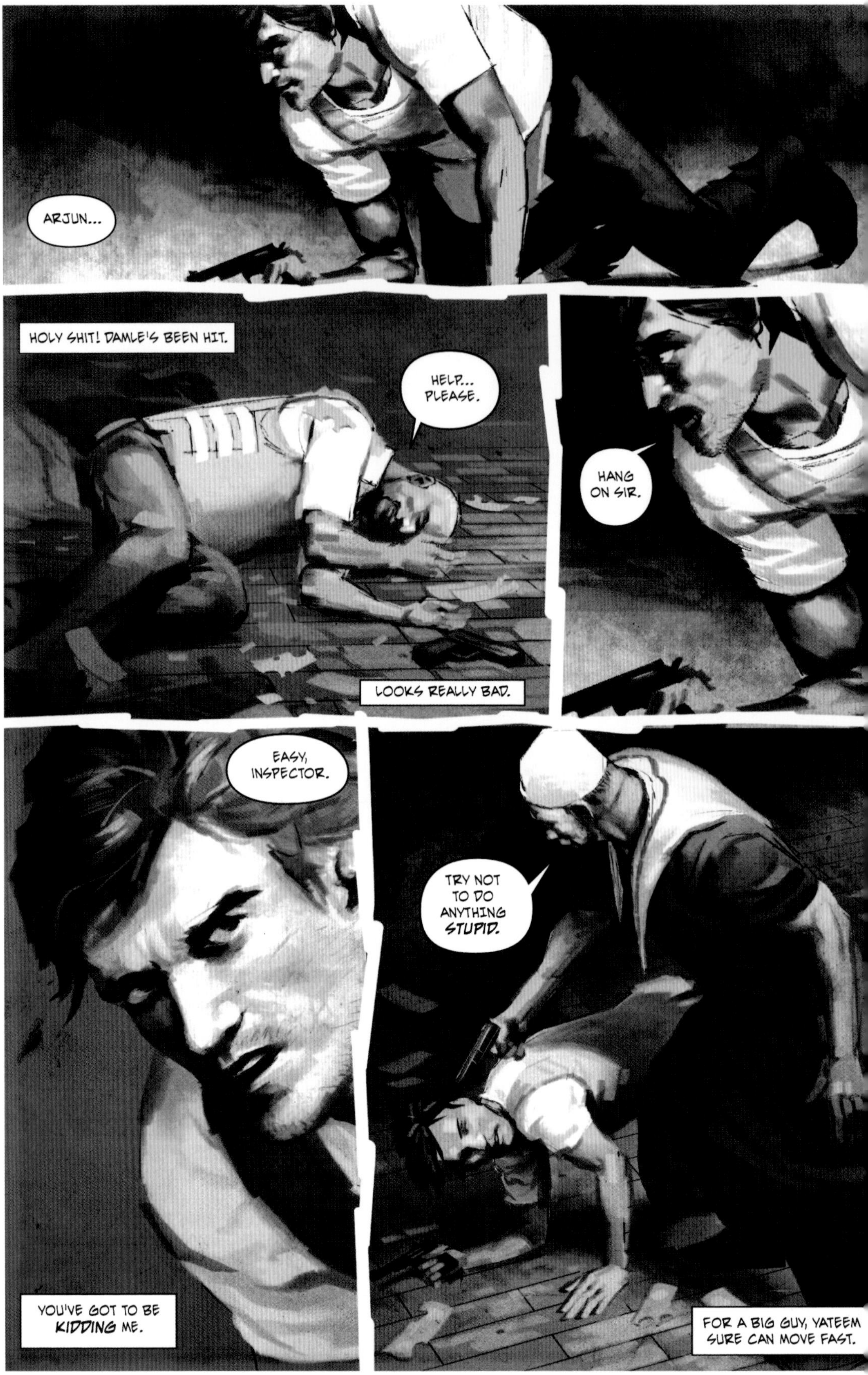
ARJUN...
HOLY SHIT! DAMLE'S BEEN HIT.
HELP... PLEASE.
LOOKS REALLY BAD.
HANG ON SIR.
EASY, INSPECTOR.
YOU'VE GOT TO BE KIDDING ME.
TRY NOT TO DO ANYTHING STUPID.
FOR A BIG GUY, YATEEM SURE CAN MOVE FAST.

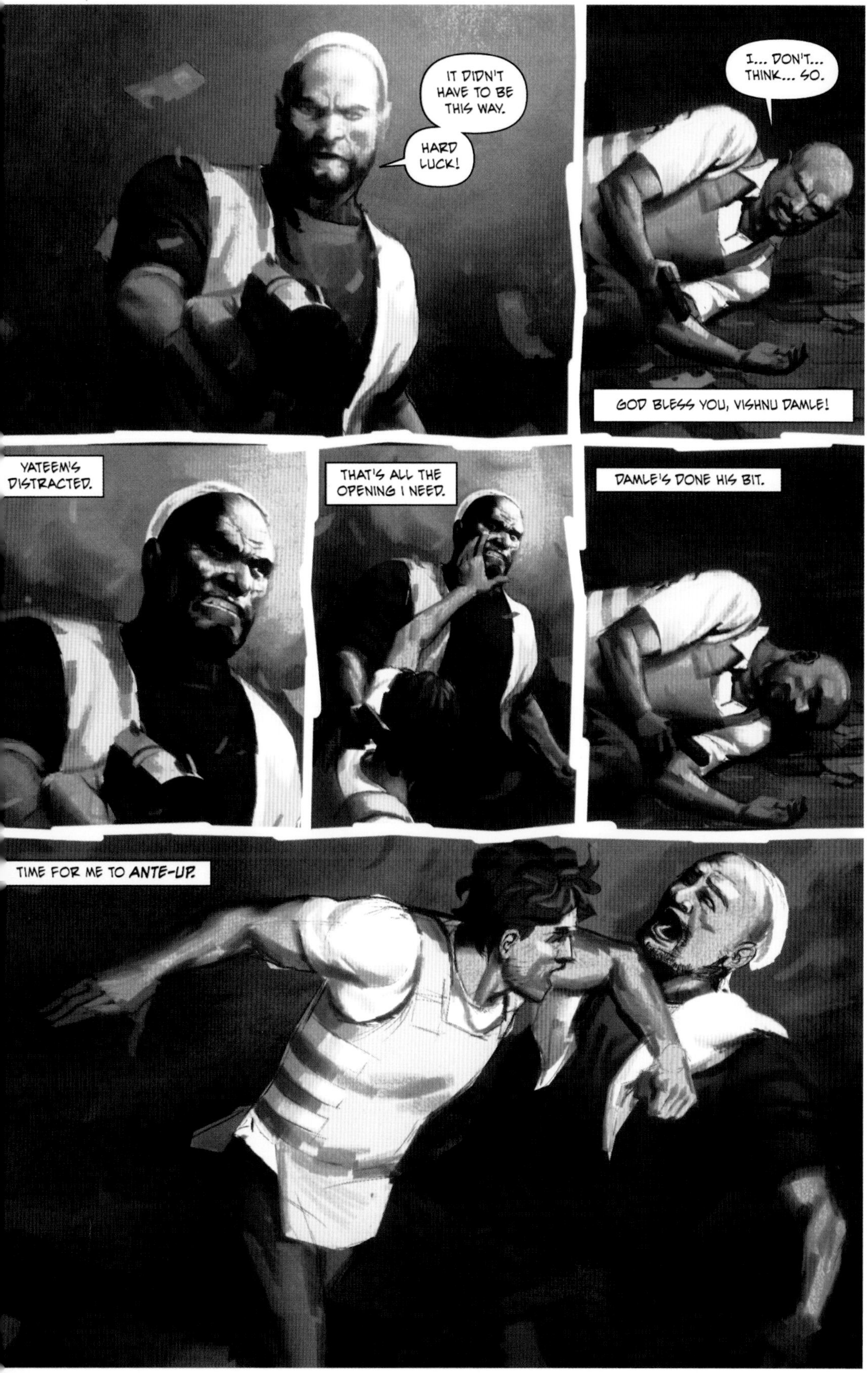
IT DIDN'T HAVE TO BE THIS WAY.
HARD LUCK!
I... DON'T... THINK... SO.
GOD BLESS YOU, VISHNU DAMLE!
YATEEM'S DISTRACTED.
THAT'S ALL THE OPENING I NEED.
DAMLE'S DONE HIS BIT.
TIME FOR ME TO ANTE-UP.

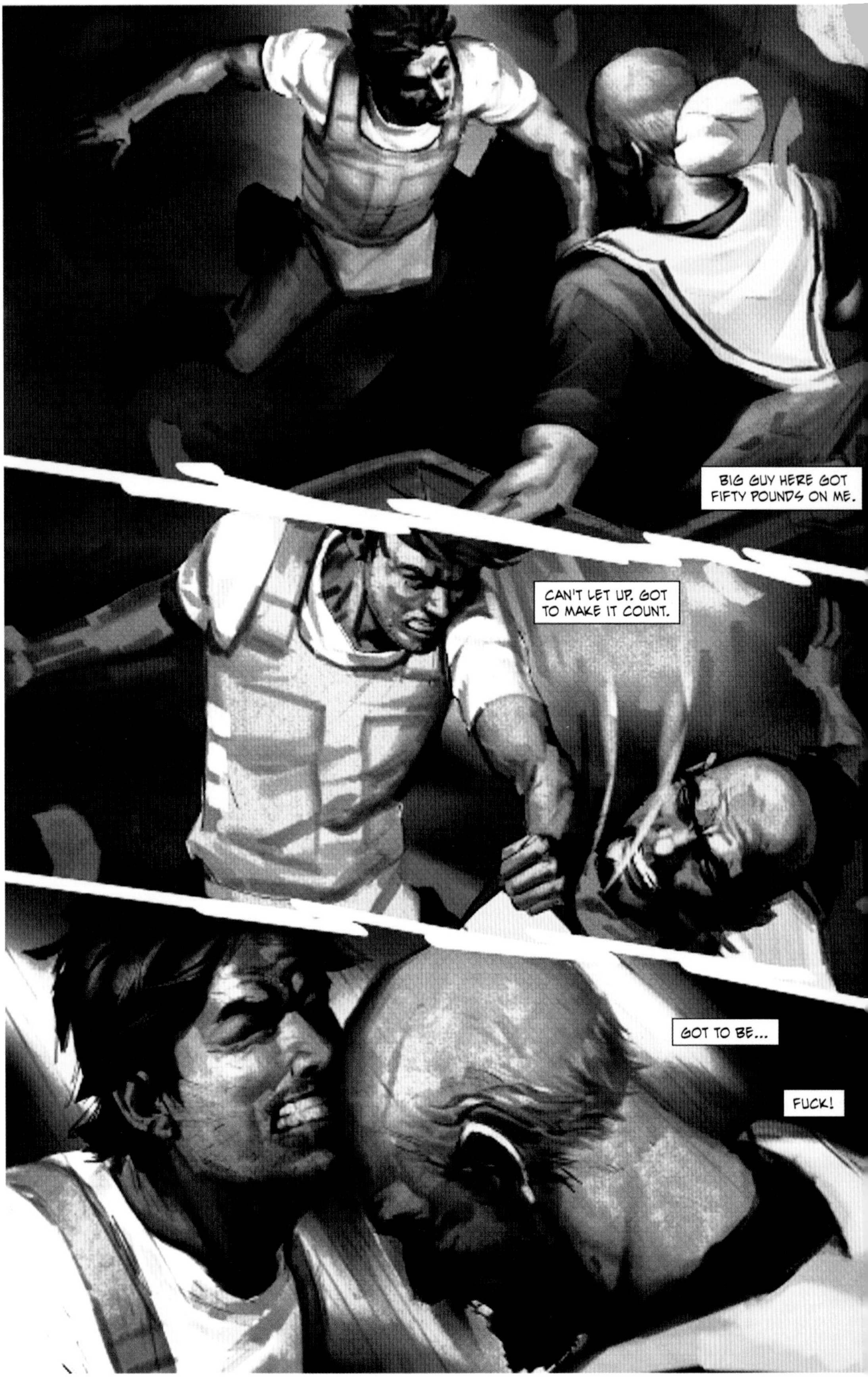
BIG GUY HERE GOT FIFTY POUNDS ON ME.
CAN'T LET UP. GOT TO MAKE IT COUNT.
GOT TO BE...
FUCK!

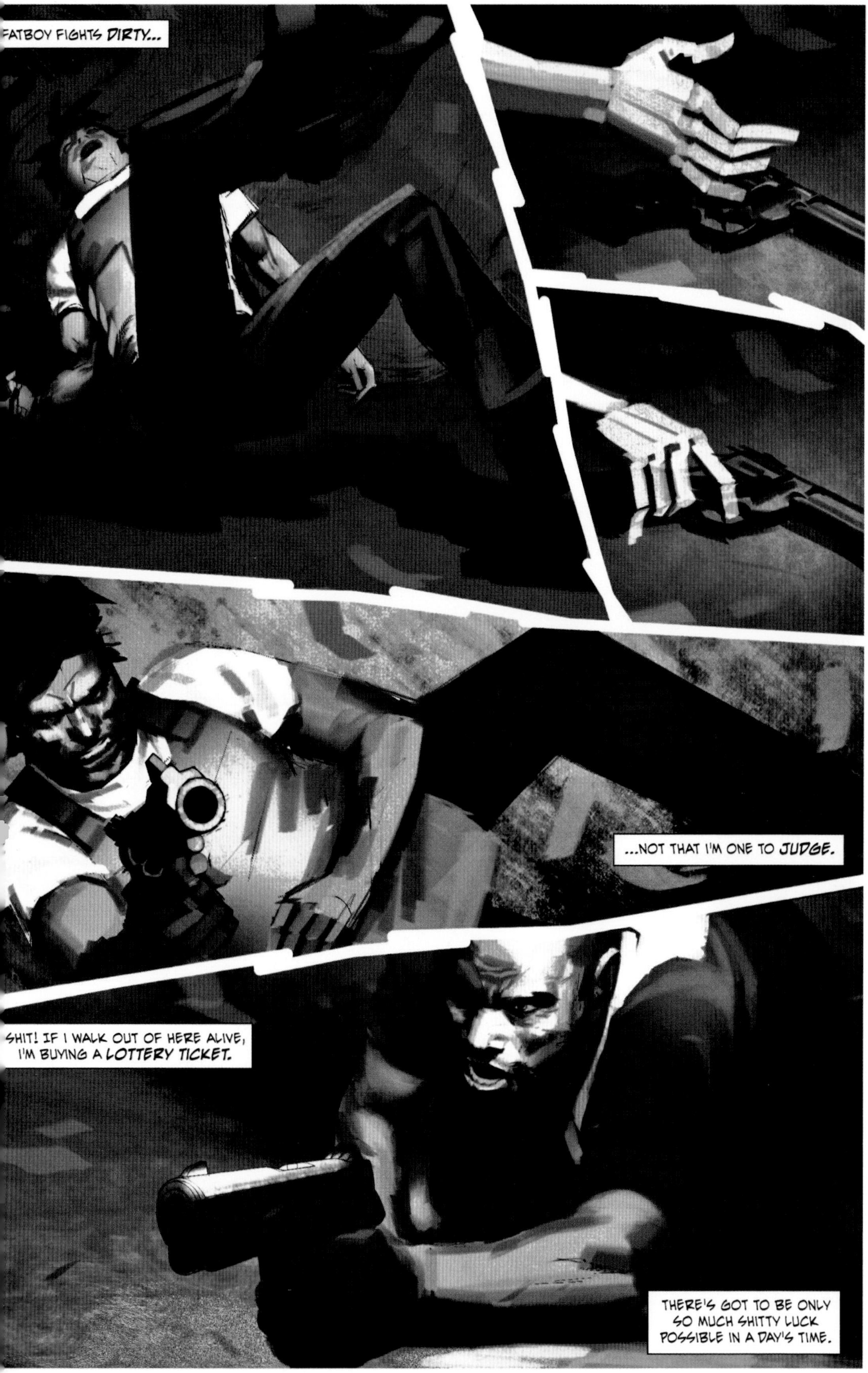
FATBOY FIGHTS DIRTY...
...NOT THAT I'M ONE TO JUDGE.
SHIT! IF I WALK OUT OF HERE ALIVE, I'M BUYING A LOTTERY TICKET.
THERE'S GOT TO BE ONLY SO MUCH SHITTY LUCK POSSIBLE IN A DAY'S TIME.

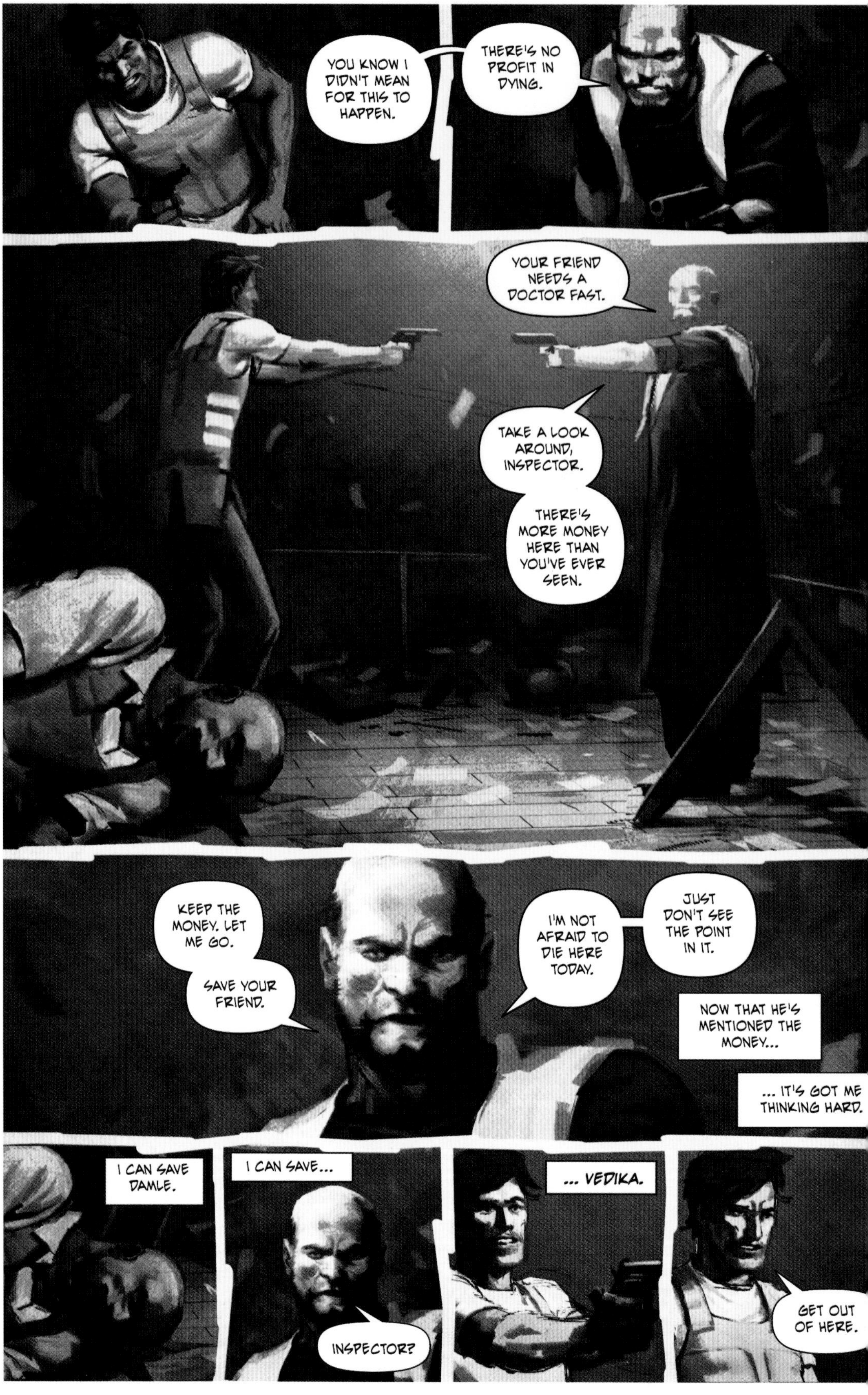
YOU KNOW I DIDN'T MEAN FOR THIS TO HAPPEN.
THERE'S NO PROFIT IN DYING.
YOUR FRIEND NEEDS A DOCTOR FAST.
TAKE A LOOK AROUND, INSPECTOR.
THERE'S MORE MONEY HERE THAN YOU'VE EVER SEEN.
KEEP THE MONEY. LET ME GO.
SAVE YOUR FRIEND.
I'M NOT AFRAID TO DIE HERE TODAY.
JUST DON'T SEE THE POINT IN IT.
NOW THAT HE'S MENTIONED THE MONEY...
... IT'S GOT ME THINKING HARD.
I CAN SAVE DAMLE.
I CAN SAVE...
INSPECTOR?
... VEDIKA.
GET OUT OF HERE.

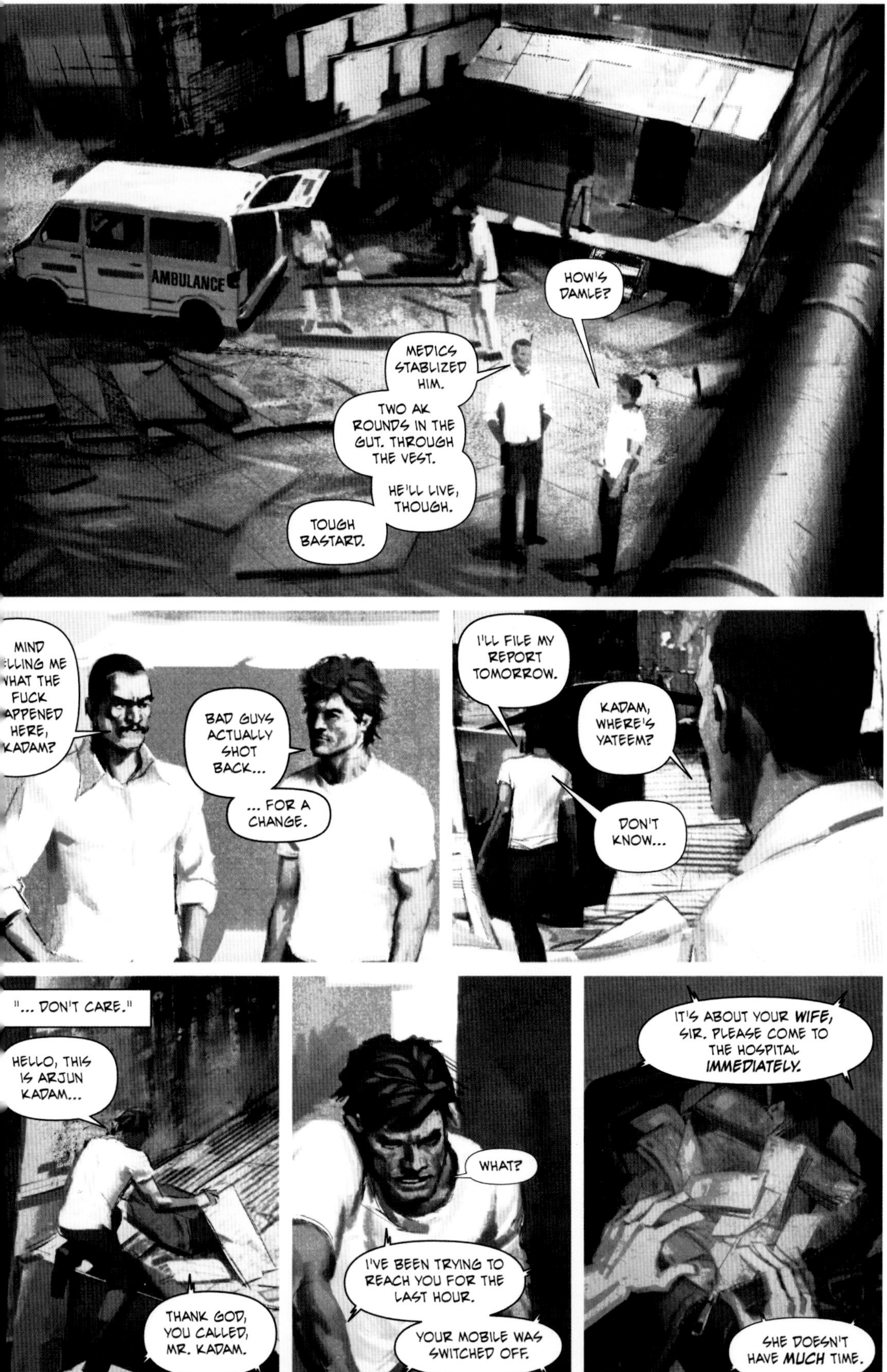
AMBULANCE
HOW'S DAMLE?
MEDICS STABLIZED HIM.
TWO AK ROUNDS IN THE GUT. THROUGH THE VEST.
HE'LL LIVE, THOUGH.
TOUGH BASTARD.
MIND ELLING ME VHAT THE FUCK APPENED HERE, KADAM?
BAD GUYS ACTUALLY SHOT BACK...
... FOR A CHANGE.
I'LL FILE MY REPORT TOMORROW.
KADAM, WHERE'S YATEEM?
DON'T KNOW...
"... DON'T CARE."
HELLO, THIS IS ARJUN KADAM...
THANK GOD, YOU CALLED, MR. KADAM.
WHAT?
I'VE BEEN TRYING TO REACH YOU FOR THE LAST HOUR.
YOUR MOBILE WAS SWITCHED OFF.
IT'S ABOUT YOUR WIFE, SIR. PLEASE COME TO THE HOSPITAL IMMEDIATELY.
SHE DOESN'T HAVE MUCH TIME.

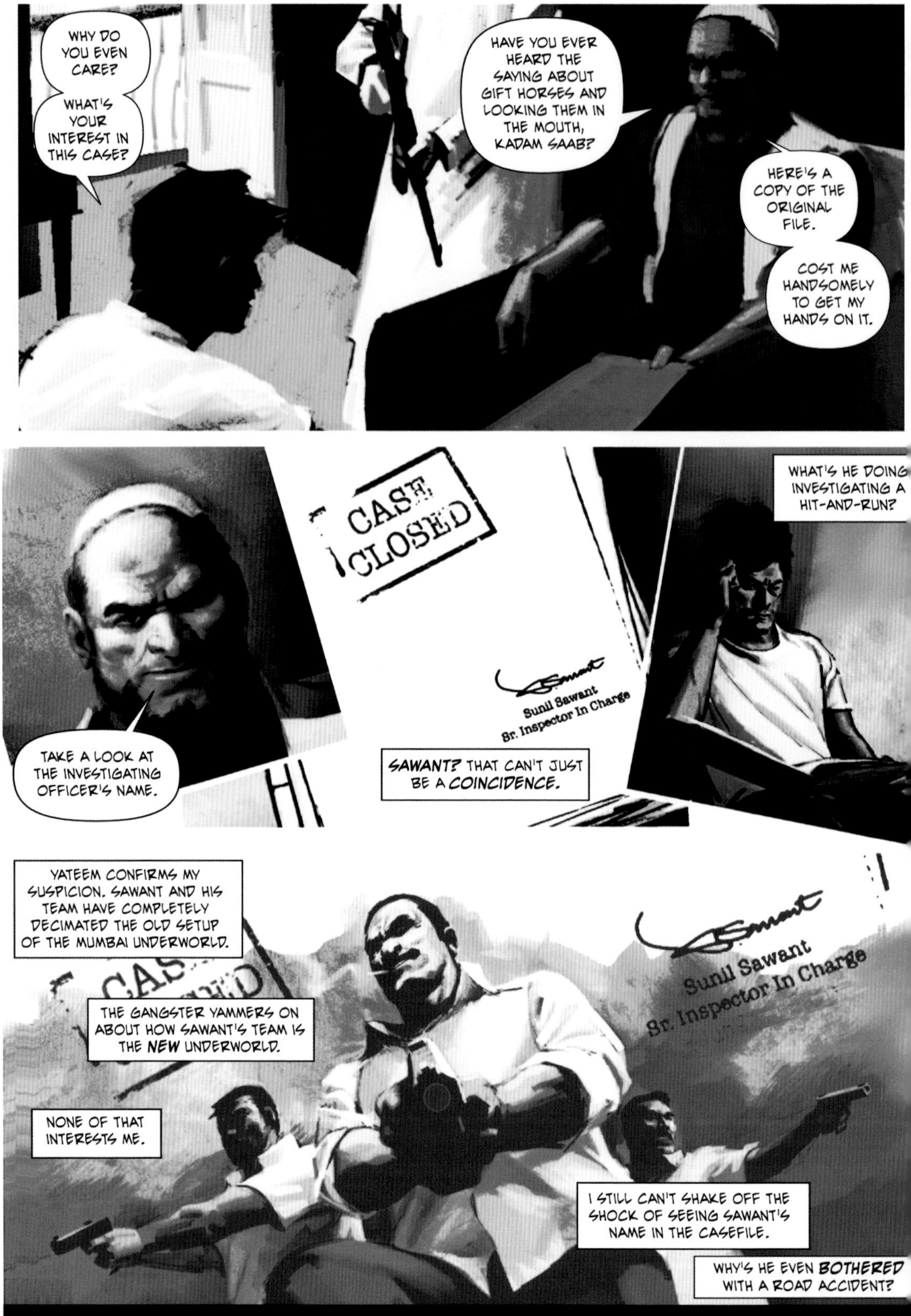
WHY DO YOU EVEN CARE?
WHAT'S YOUR INTEREST IN THIS CASE?
HAVE YOU EVER HEARD THE SAYING ABOUT GIFT HORSES AND LOOKING THEM IN THE MOUTH, KADAM SAAB?
HERE'S A COPY OF THE ORIGINAL FILE.
COST ME HANDSOMELY TO GET MY HANDS ON IT.
TAKE A LOOK AT THE INVESTIGATING OFFICER'S NAME.
CASE CLOSED
Sunil Sawant
Sr. Inspector In Charge
SAWANT? THAT CAN'T JUST BE A COINCIDENCE.
WHAT'S HE DOING INVESTIGATING A HIT-AND-RUN?
YATEEM CONFIRMS MY SUSPICION. SAWANT AND HIS TEAM HAVE COMPLETELY DECIMATED THE OLD SETUP OF THE MUMBAI UNDERWORLD.
Sunil Sawant
Sr. Inspector In Charge
THE GANGSTER YAMMERS ON ABOUT HOW SAWANT'S TEAM IS THE NEW UNDERWORLD.
NONE OF THAT INTERESTS ME.
I STILL CAN'T SHAKE OFF THE SHOCK OF SEEING SAWANT'S NAME IN THE CASEFILE.
WHY'S HE EVEN BOTHERED WITH A ROAD ACCIDENT?

CHAPTER 8
CHEAP DATE

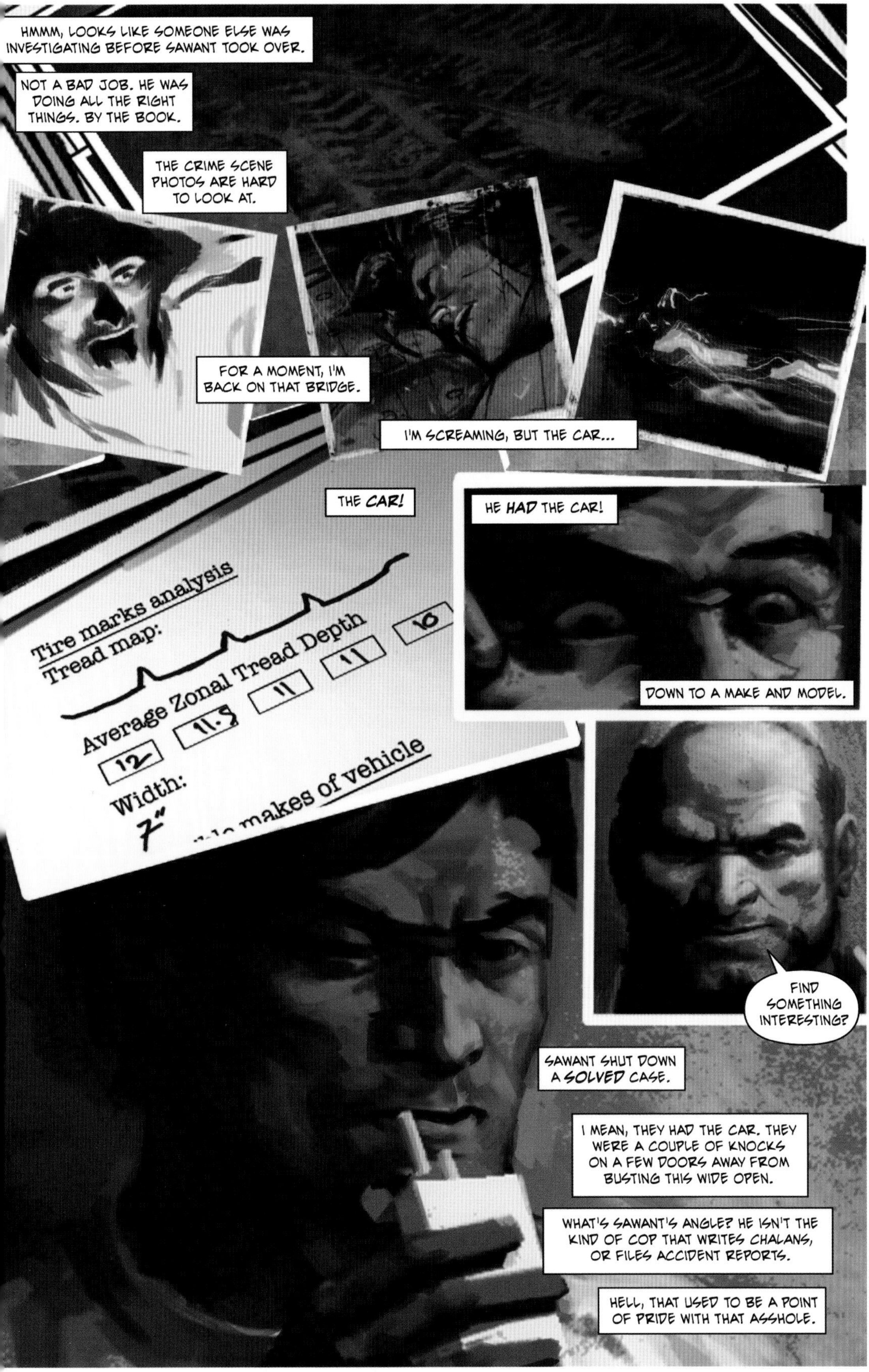
HMMM, LOOKS LIKE SOMEONE ELSE WAS INVESTIGATING BEFORE SAWANT TOOK OVER.
NOT A BAD JOB. HE WAS DOING ALL THE RIGHT THINGS. BY THE BOOK.
THE CRIME SCENE PHOTOS ARE HARD TO LOOK AT.
FOR A MOMENT, I'M BACK ON THAT BRIDGE.
I'M SCREAMING, BUT THE CAR...
THE CAR!
HE HAD THE CAR!
Tire marks analysis
Tread map:
Average Zonal Tread Depth
12
11.5
11
11
10
Width:
7"
makes of vehicle
DOWN TO A MAKE AND MODEL.
FIND SOMETHING INTERESTING?
SAWANT SHUT DOWN A SOLVED CASE.
I MEAN, THEY HAD THE CAR. THEY WERE A COUPLE OF KNOCKS ON A FEW DOORS AWAY FROM BUSTING THIS WIDE OPEN.
WHAT'S SAWANT'S ANGLE? HE ISN'T THE KIND OF COP THAT WRITES CHALANS, OR FILES ACCIDENT REPORTS.
HELL, THAT USED TO BE A POINT OF PRIDE WITH THAT ASSHOLE.

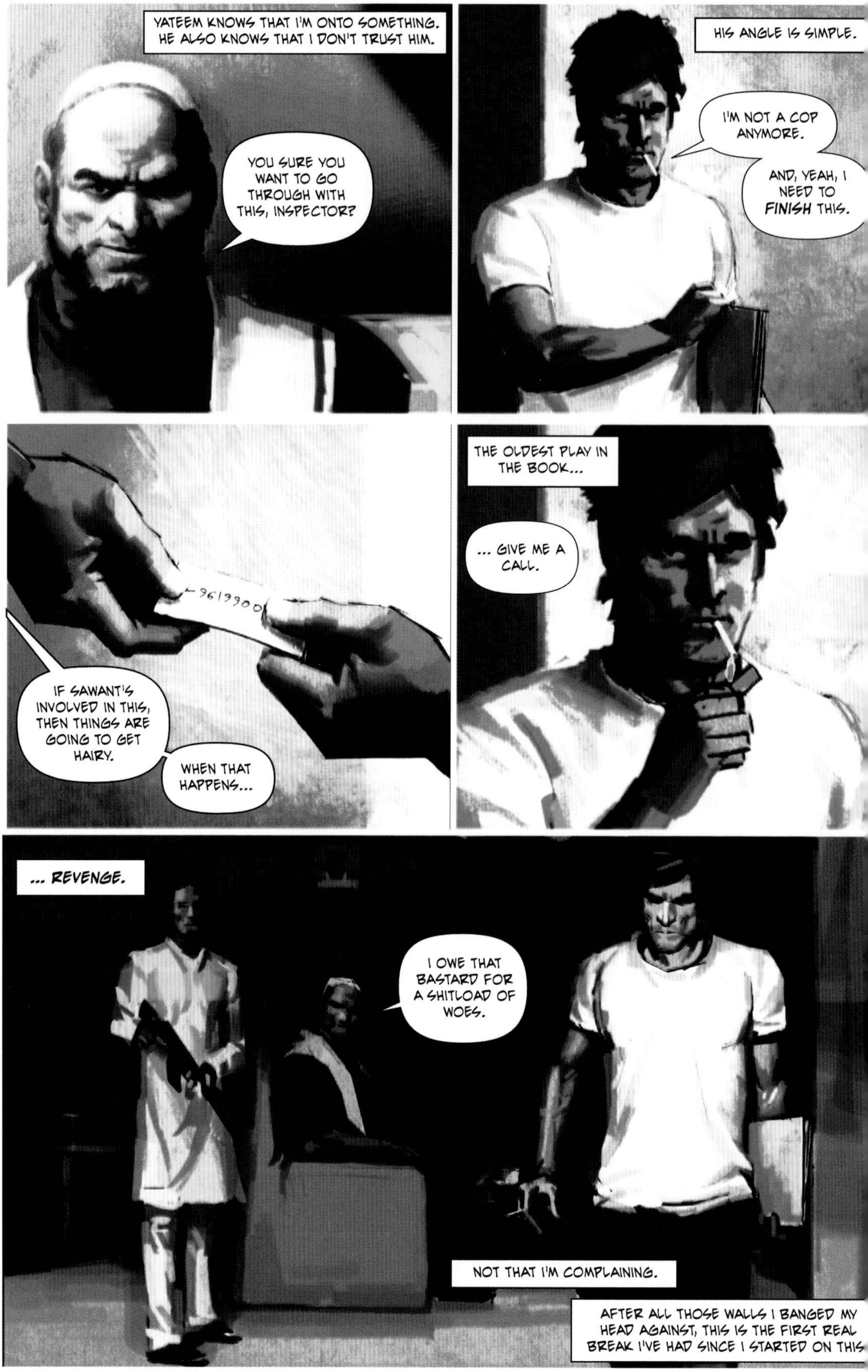
YATEEM KNOWS THAT I'M ONTO SOMETHING. HE ALSO KNOWS THAT I DON'T TRUST HIM.
YOU SURE YOU WANT TO GO THROUGH WITH THIS, INSPECTOR?
HIS ANGLE IS SIMPLE.
I'M NOT A COP ANYMORE.
AND, YEAH, I NEED TO FINISH THIS.
IF SAWANT'S INVOLVED IN THIS, THEN THINGS ARE GOING TO GET HAIRY.
WHEN THAT HAPPENS...
THE OLDEST PLAY IN THE BOOK...
... GIVE ME A CALL.
... REVENGE.
I OWE THAT BASTARD FOR A SHITLOAD OF WOES.
NOT THAT I'M COMPLAINING.
AFTER ALL THOSE WALLS I BANGED MY HEAD AGAINST, THIS IS THE FIRST REAL BREAK I'VE HAD SINCE I STARTED ON THIS

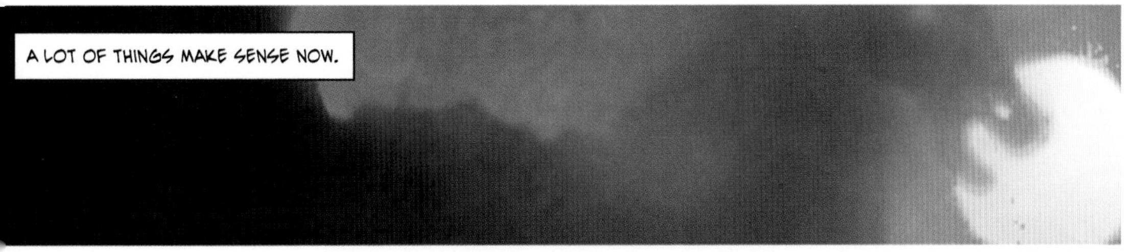
A LOT OF THINGS MAKE SENSE NOW.

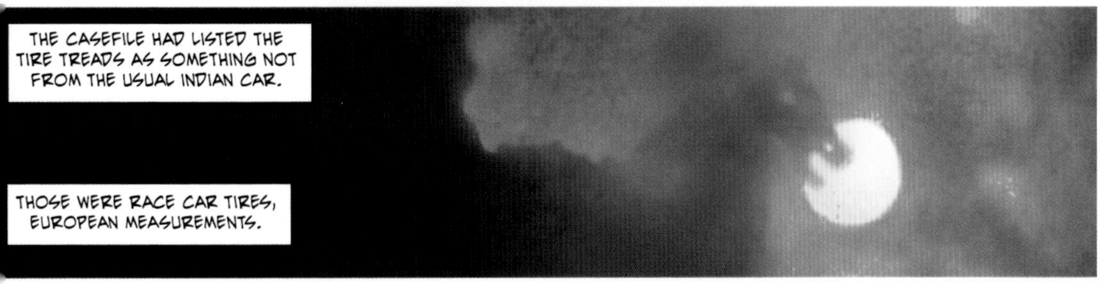
THE CASEFILE HAD LISTED THE TIRE TREADS AS SOMETHING NOT FROM THE USUAL INDIAN CAR.
THOSE WERE RACE CAR TIRES, EUROPEAN MEASUREMENTS.

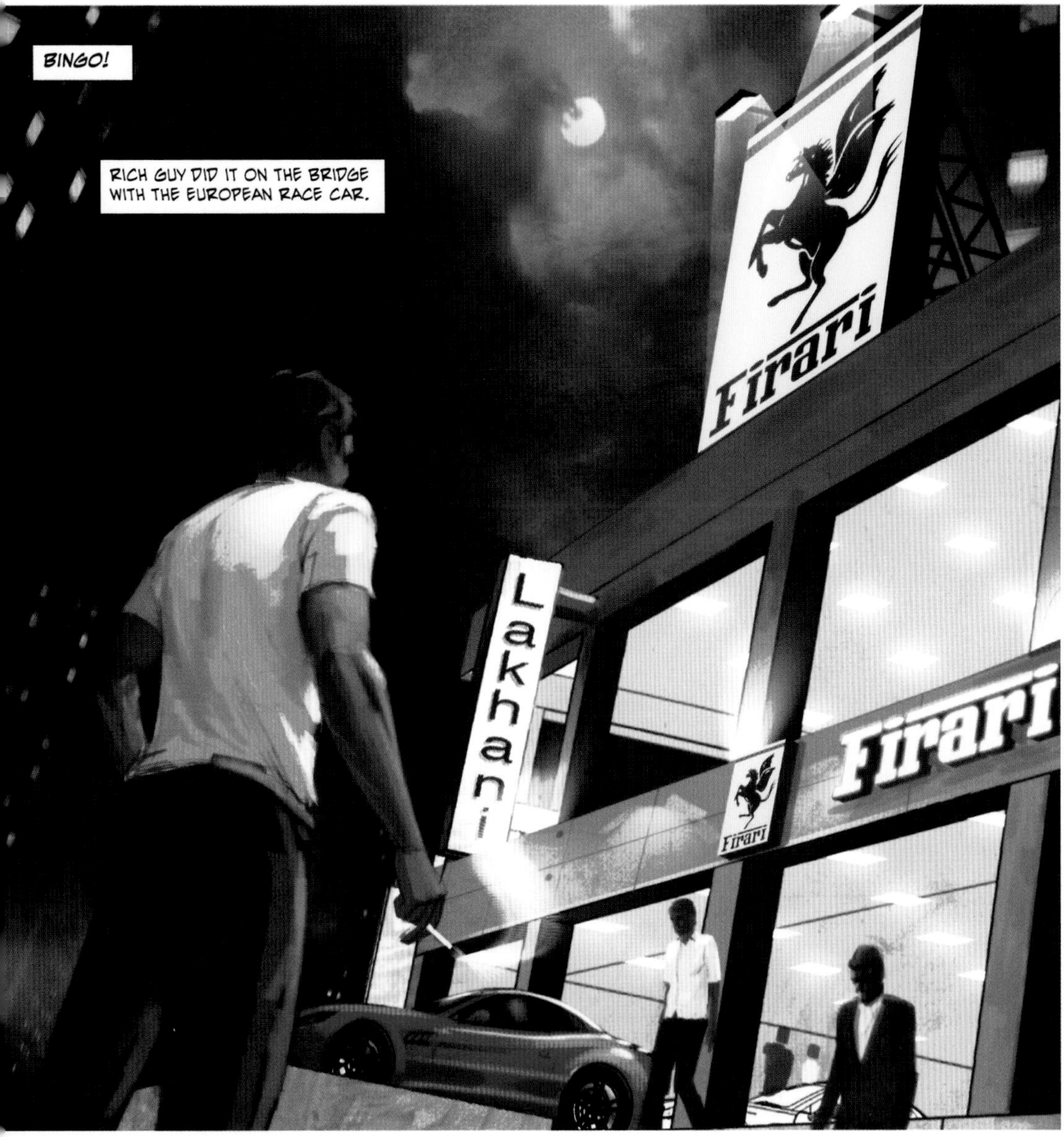
BINGO!
RICH GUY DID IT ON THE BRIDGE WITH THE EUROPEAN RACE CAR.
Firari
Lakhani
Firari
Firari

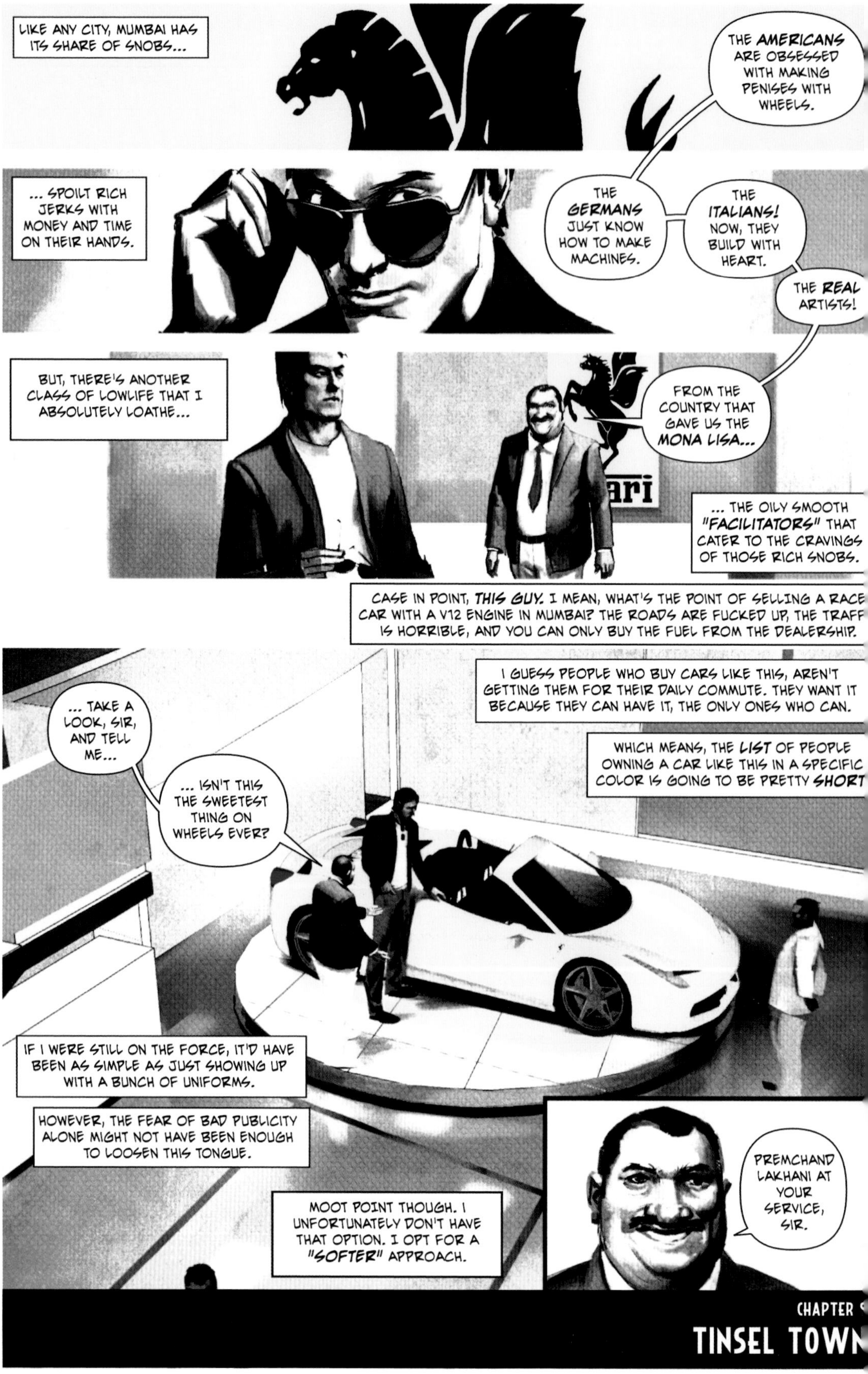
LIKE ANY CITY, MUMBAI HAS ITS SHARE OF SNOBS...
THE AMERICANS ARE OBSESSED WITH MAKING PENISES WITH WHEELS.
... SPOILT RICH JERKS WITH MONEY AND TIME ON THEIR HANDS.
THE GERMANS JUST KNOW HOW TO MAKE MACHINES.
THE ITALIANS! NOW, THEY BUILD WITH HEART.
THE REAL ARTISTS!
BUT, THERE'S ANOTHER CLASS OF LOWLIFE THAT I ABSOLUTELY LOATHE...
FROM THE COUNTRY THAT GAVE US THE MONA LISA...
... THE OILY SMOOTH "FACILITATORS" THAT CATER TO THE CRAVINGS OF THOSE RICH SNOBS.
CASE IN POINT, THIS GUY. I MEAN, WHAT'S THE POINT OF SELLING A RACE CAR WITH A V12 ENGINE IN MUMBAI? THE ROADS ARE FUCKED UP, THE TRAFF IS HORRIBLE, AND YOU CAN ONLY BUY THE FUEL FROM THE DEALERSHIP.
I GUESS PEOPLE WHO BUY CARS LIKE THIS, AREN'T GETTING THEM FOR THEIR DAILY COMMUTE. THEY WANT IT BECAUSE THEY CAN HAVE IT, THE ONLY ONES WHO CAN.
WHICH MEANS, THE LIST OF PEOPLE OWNING A CAR LIKE THIS IN A SPECIFIC COLOR IS GOING TO BE PRETTY SHORT
... TAKE A LOOK, SIR, AND TELL ME...
... ISN'T THIS THE SWEETEST THING ON WHEELS EVER?
IF I WERE STILL ON THE FORCE, IT'D HAVE BEEN AS SIMPLE AS JUST SHOWING UP WITH A BUNCH OF UNIFORMS.
HOWEVER, THE FEAR OF BAD PUBLICITY ALONE MIGHT NOT HAVE BEEN ENOUGH TO LOOSEN THIS TONGUE.
MOOT POINT THOUGH. I UNFORTUNATELY DON'T HAVE THAT OPTION. I OPT FOR A "SOFTER" APPROACH.
PREMCHAND LAKHANI AT YOUR SERVICE, SIR.
CHAPTER
TINSEL TOWN

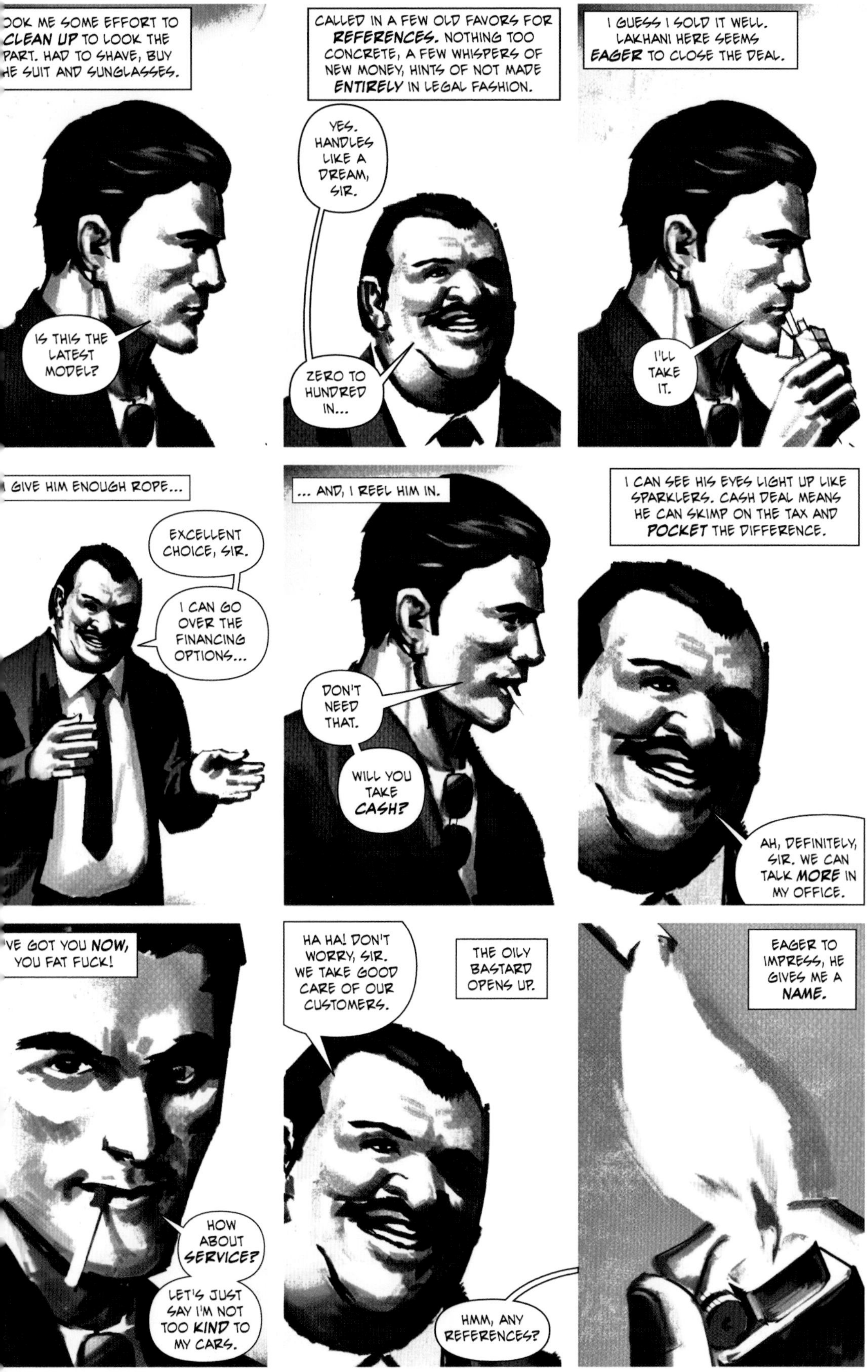
OOK ME SOME EFFORT TO CLEAN UP TO LOOK THE PART. HAD TO SHAVE, BUY HE SUIT AND SUNGLASSES.
IS THIS THE LATEST MODEL?
CALLED IN A FEW OLD FAVORS FOR REFERENCES. NOTHING TOO CONCRETE, A FEW WHISPERS OF NEW MONEY, HINTS OF NOT MADE ENTIRELY IN LEGAL FASHION.
YES. HANDLES LIKE A DREAM, SIR.
ZERO TO HUNDRED IN...
I GUESS I SOLD IT WELL. LAKHANI HERE SEEMS EAGER TO CLOSE THE DEAL.
I'LL TAKE IT.
GIVE HIM ENOUGH ROPE...
EXCELLENT CHOICE, SIR.
I CAN GO OVER THE FINANCING OPTIONS...
... AND, I REEL HIM IN.
DON'T NEED THAT.
WILL YOU TAKE CASH?
I CAN SEE HIS EYES LIGHT UP LIKE SPARKLERS. CASH DEAL MEANS HE CAN SKIMP ON THE TAX AND POCKET THE DIFFERENCE.
AH, DEFINITELY, SIR. WE CAN TALK MORE IN MY OFFICE.
VE GOT YOU NOW, YOU FAT FUCK!
HOW ABOUT SERVICE?
LET'S JUST SAY I'M NOT TOO KIND TO MY CARS.
HA HA! DON'T WORRY, SIR. WE TAKE GOOD CARE OF OUR CUSTOMERS.
THE OILY BASTARD OPENS UP.
HMM, ANY REFERENCES?
EAGER TO IMPRESS, HE GIVES ME A NAME.

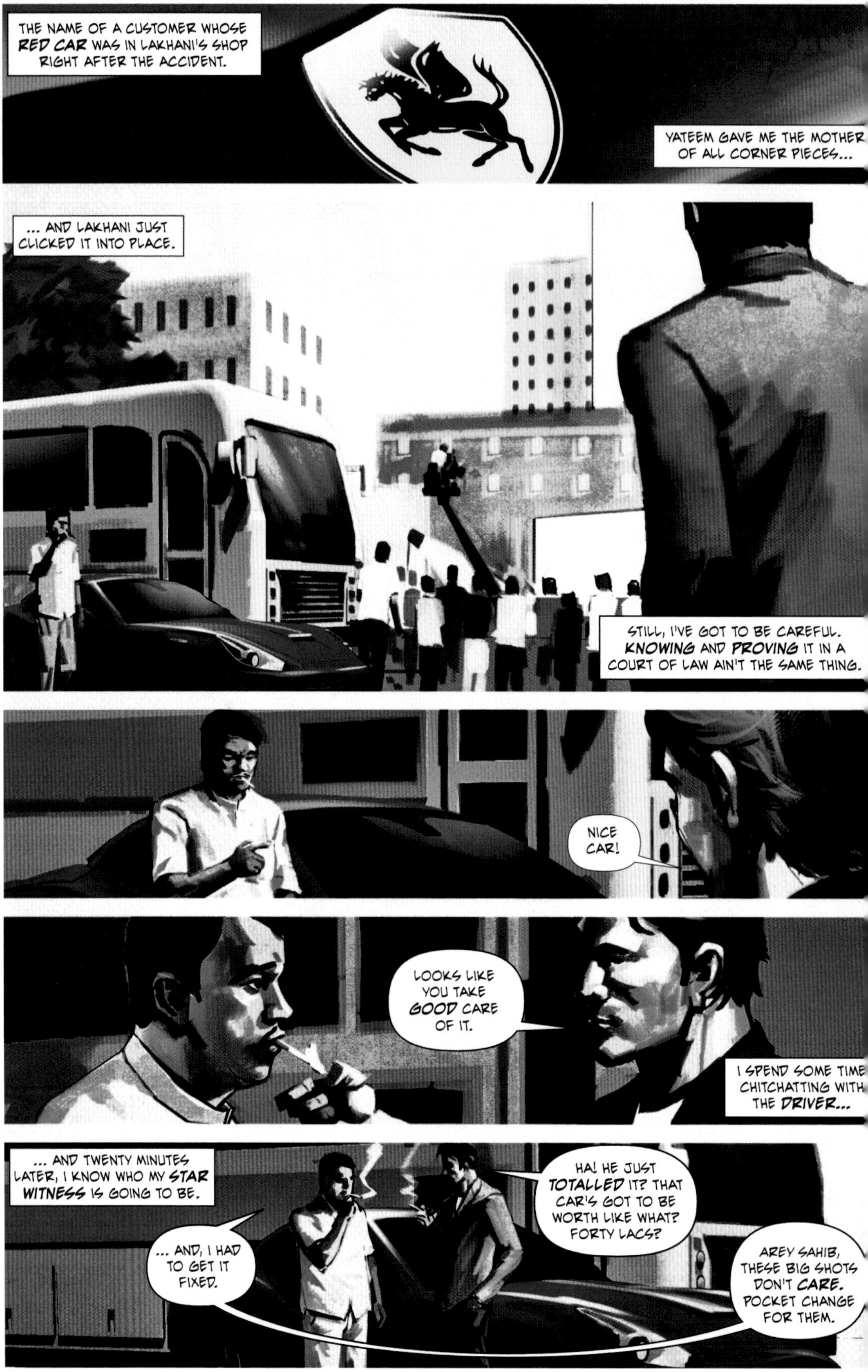
THE NAME OF A CUSTOMER WHOSE RED CAR WAS IN LAKHANI'S SHOP RIGHT AFTER THE ACCIDENT.
YATEEM GAVE ME THE MOTHER OF ALL CORNER PIECES...
... AND LAKHANI JUST CLICKED IT INTO PLACE.
STILL, I'VE GOT TO BE CAREFUL. KNOWING AND PROVING IT IN A COURT OF LAW AIN'T THE SAME THING.
NICE CAR!
LOOKS LIKE YOU TAKE GOOD CARE OF IT.
I SPEND SOME TIME CHITCHATTING WITH THE DRIVER...
... AND TWENTY MINUTES LATER, I KNOW WHO MY STAR WITNESS IS GOING TO BE.
... AND, I HAD TO GET IT FIXED.
HA! HE JUST TOTALLED IT? THAT CAR'S GOT TO BE WORTH LIKE WHAT? FORTY LACS?
AREY SAHIB, THESE BIG SHOTS DON'T CARE. POCKET CHANGE FOR THEM.

"SOMETIMES I THINK, JUST BECAUSE THEY CAN AFFORD IT..."

YOU KILLED MY FAMILY.

BURNED MY HOUSE.

I'VE TRIED TO HONOR THE LAW.

AS GOD'S MY WITNESS, I TRIED.

BUT, THE SYSTEM'S A JOKE TO YOU.

NO MORE! YOU ARE VERMIN...

"... DOESN'T MEAN THEY DESERVE IT."

KILL THEM, INSPECTOR!

THEY KILLED MY DAD.

KILL THEM DEAD!

THEY KILLED MY DADDY, TOO.

... AND I'M THE EXTERMINATOR!

JUSTICE HAS BEEN SERVED, INSPECTOR.

BALWAN KHAN. REAL NAME, ARMAN KHAN.

THERE'S NO JUSTICE, BABY...

... JUST US.

CUT! WRAP!

BURST ON TO THE SCENE FIFTEEN OR SO YEARS AGO.

ROMANCING DAMSELS AROUND THE TREES IN BUBBLEGUM, CANDY FLOSS ROMANCES.

AWESOME SHOT, BALWAN SAAB!

HAD A COUPLE OF HITS, THEN WOKE UP ON THE WRONG SIDE OF FORTY, WITH A RECEDING HAIRLINE.

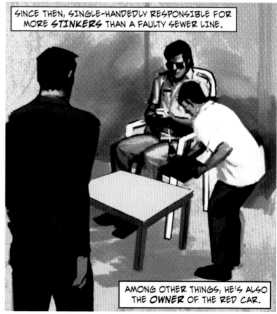

SINCE THEN, SINGLE-HANDEDLY RESPONSIBLE FOR MORE STINKERS THAN A FAULTY SEWER LINE.

AMONG OTHER THINGS, HE'S ALSO THE OWNER OF THE RED CAR.

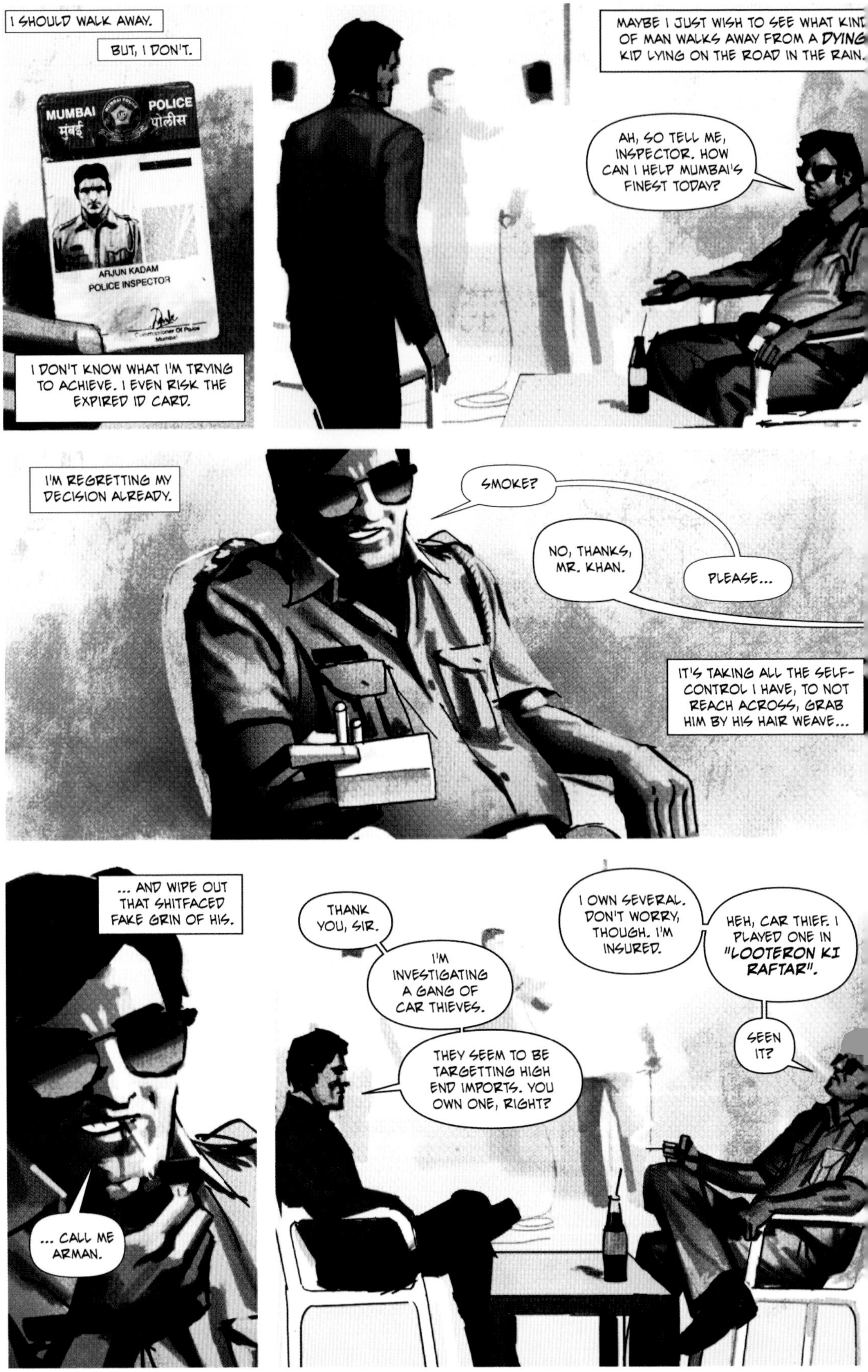
I SHOULD WALK AWAY.
BUT, I DON'T.
MUMBAI मुंबई POLICE पोलीस
ARJUN KADAM
POLICE INSPECTOR
I DON'T KNOW WHAT I'M TRYING TO ACHIEVE. I EVEN RISK THE EXPIRED ID CARD.
MAYBE I JUST WISH TO SEE WHAT KIND OF MAN WALKS AWAY FROM A DYING KID LYING ON THE ROAD IN THE RAIN.
AH, SO TELL ME, INSPECTOR. HOW CAN I HELP MUMBAI'S FINEST TODAY?
I'M REGRETTING MY DECISION ALREADY.
SMOKE?
NO, THANKS, MR. KHAN.
PLEASE...
IT'S TAKING ALL THE SELF-CONTROL I HAVE, TO NOT REACH ACROSS, GRAB HIM BY HIS HAIR WEAVE...
... AND WIPE OUT THAT SHITFACED FAKE GRIN OF HIS.
... CALL ME ARMAN.
THANK YOU, SIR.
I'M INVESTIGATING A GANG OF CAR THIEVES.
THEY SEEM TO BE TARGETTING HIGH END IMPORTS. YOU OWN ONE, RIGHT?
I OWN SEVERAL. DON'T WORRY, THOUGH. I'M INSURED.
HEH, CAR THIEF. I PLAYED ONE IN "LOOTERON KI RAFTAR".
SEEN IT?

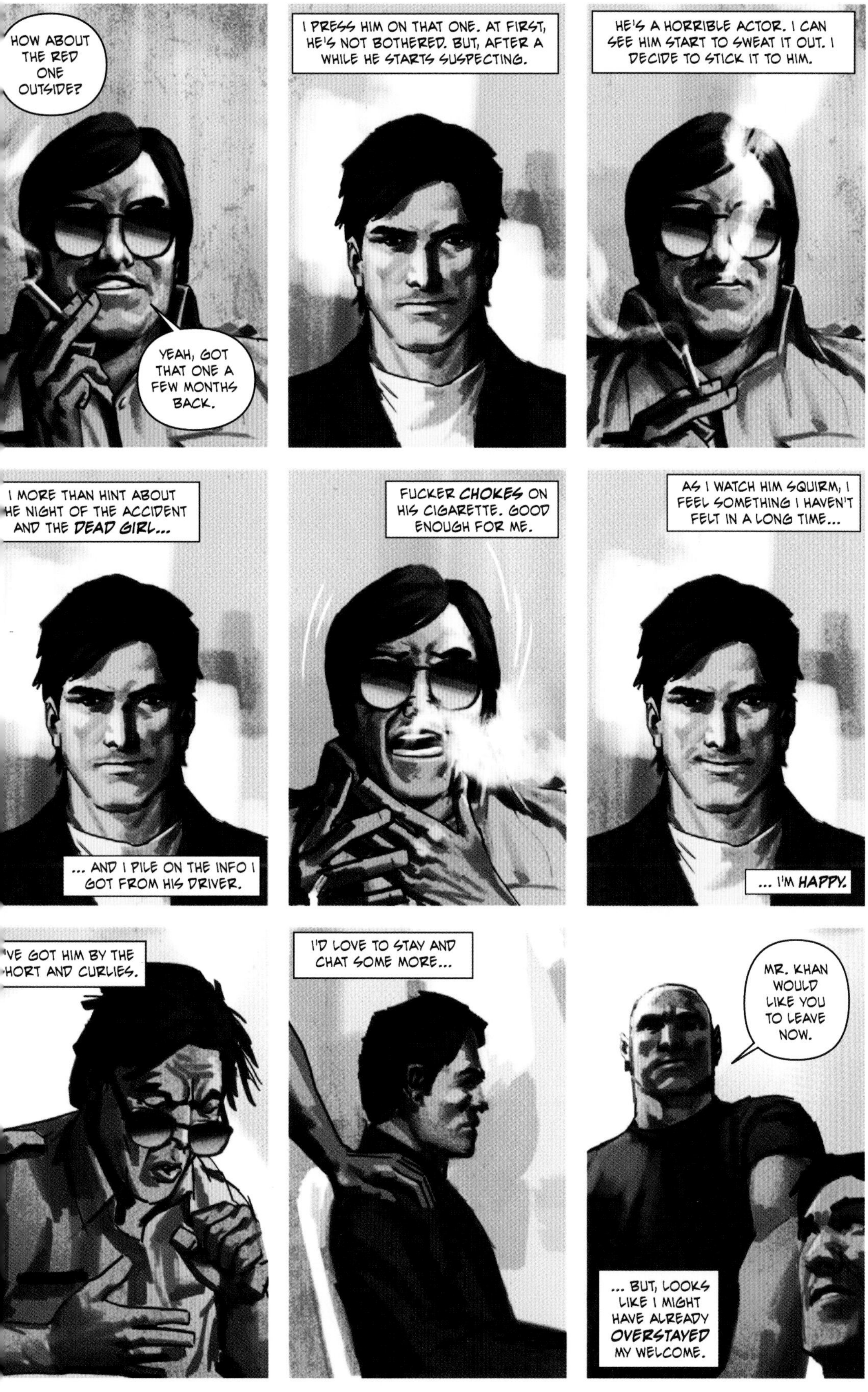
HOW ABOUT THE RED ONE OUTSIDE?
YEAH, GOT THAT ONE A FEW MONTHS BACK.
I PRESS HIM ON THAT ONE. AT FIRST, HE'S NOT BOTHERED. BUT, AFTER A WHILE HE STARTS SUSPECTING.
HE'S A HORRIBLE ACTOR. I CAN SEE HIM START TO SWEAT IT OUT. I DECIDE TO STICK IT TO HIM.
I MORE THAN HINT ABOUT HE NIGHT OF THE ACCIDENT AND THE DEAD GIRL...
... AND I PILE ON THE INFO I GOT FROM HIS DRIVER.
FUCKER CHOKES ON HIS CIGARETTE. GOOD ENOUGH FOR ME.
AS I WATCH HIM SQUIRM, I FEEL SOMETHING I HAVEN'T FELT IN A LONG TIME...
... I'M HAPPY.
'VE GOT HIM BY THE HORT AND CURLIES.
I'D LOVE TO STAY AND CHAT SOME MORE...
MR. KHAN WOULD LIKE YOU TO LEAVE NOW.
... BUT, LOOKS LIKE I MIGHT HAVE ALREADY OVERSTAYED MY WELCOME.

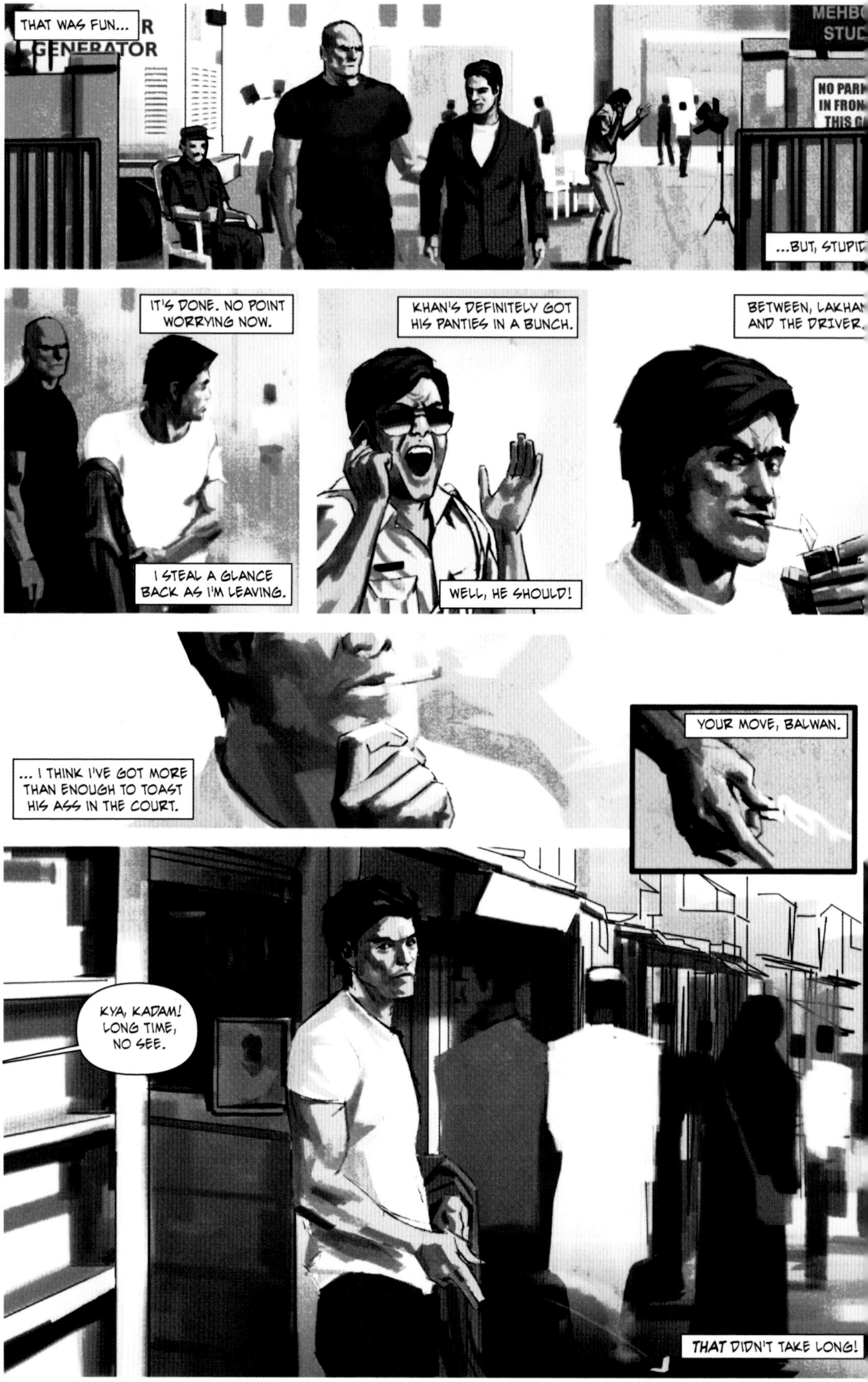
THAT WAS FUN...
GENERATOR
NO PARK
IN FRON
...BUT, STUPID
IT'S DONE. NO POINT WORRYING NOW.
I STEAL A GLANCE BACK AS I'M LEAVING.
KHAN'S DEFINITELY GOT HIS PANTIES IN A BUNCH.
WELL, HE SHOULD!
BETWEEN, LAKHAN AND THE DRIVER...
... I THINK I'VE GOT MORE THAN ENOUGH TO TOAST HIS ASS IN THE COURT.
YOUR MOVE, BALWAN.
KYA, KADAM! LONG TIME, NO SEE.
THAT DIDN'T TAKE LONG!

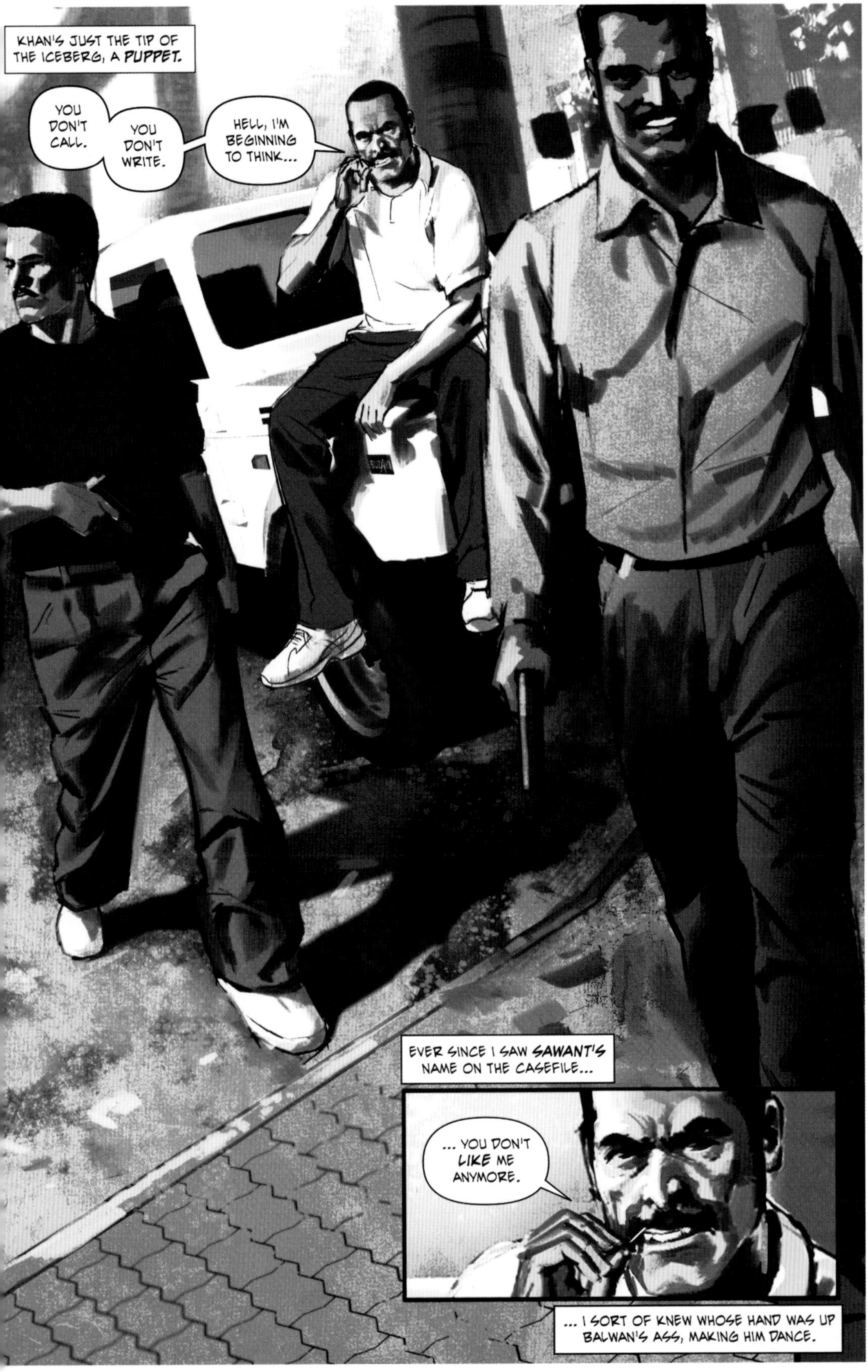
KHAN'S JUST THE TIP OF THE ICEBERG, A PUPPET.
YOU DON'T CALL.
YOU DON'T WRITE.
HELL, I'M BEGINNING TO THINK...
EVER SINCE I SAW SAWANT'S NAME ON THE CASEFILE...
... YOU DON'T LIKE ME ANYMORE.
... I SORT OF KNEW WHOSE HAND WAS UP BALWAN'S ASS, MAKING HIM DANCE.

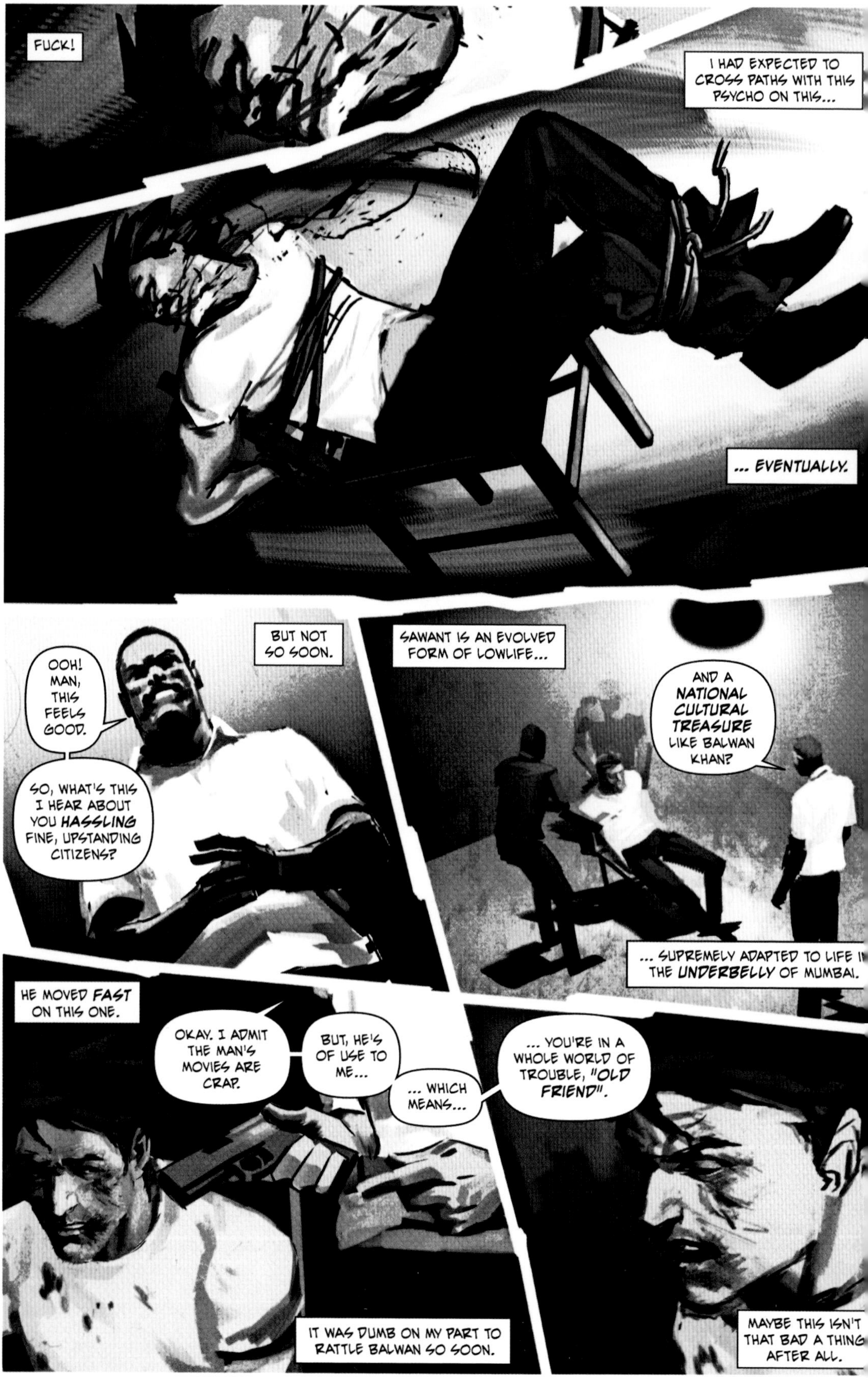
FUCK!
I HAD EXPECTED TO CROSS PATHS WITH THIS PSYCHO ON THIS...
... EVENTUALLY.
BUT NOT SO SOON.
OOH! MAN, THIS FEELS GOOD.
SO, WHAT'S THIS I HEAR ABOUT YOU HASSLING FINE, UPSTANDING CITIZENS?
SAWANT IS AN EVOLVED FORM OF LOWLIFE...
AND A NATIONAL CULTURAL TREASURE LIKE BALWAN KHAN?
... SUPREMELY ADAPTED TO LIFE IN THE UNDERBELLY OF MUMBAI.
HE MOVED FAST ON THIS ONE.
OKAY. I ADMIT THE MAN'S MOVIES ARE CRAP.
BUT, HE'S OF USE TO ME...
... WHICH MEANS...
... YOU'RE IN A WHOLE WORLD OF TROUBLE, "OLD FRIEND".
IT WAS DUMB ON MY PART TO RATTLE BALWAN SO SOON.
MAYBE THIS ISN'T THAT BAD A THING AFTER ALL.

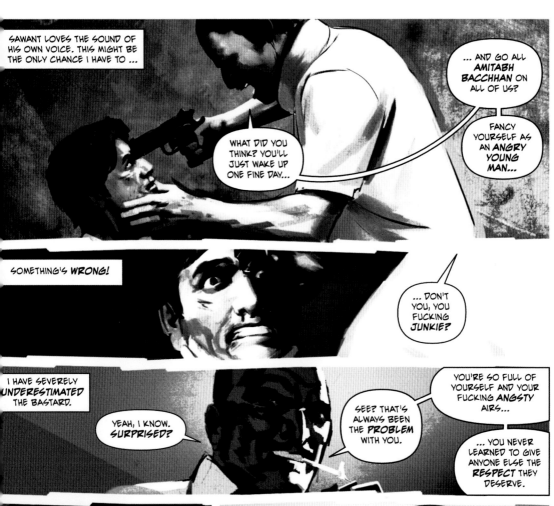

SAWANT LOVES THE SOUND OF HIS OWN VOICE. THIS MIGHT BE THE ONLY CHANCE I HAVE TO ...

... AND GO ALL *AMITABH BACCHHAN* ON ALL OF US?

FANCY YOURSELF AS AN *ANGRY YOUNG MAN...*

WHAT DID YOU THINK? YOU'LL JUST WAKE UP ONE FINE DAY...

SOMETHING'S *WRONG!*

... DON'T YOU, YOU *FUCKING JUNKIE?*

I HAVE SEVERELY *UNDERESTIMATED* THE BASTARD.

YEAH, I KNOW. *SURPRISED?*

SEE? THAT'S ALWAYS BEEN THE *PROBLEM* WITH YOU.

YOU'RE SO FULL OF YOURSELF AND YOUR FUCKING *ANGSTY AIRS...*

... YOU NEVER LEARNED TO GIVE ANYONE ELSE THE *RESPECT* THEY DESERVE.

"I'M *ARJUN FUCKING KADAM...*"

I'VE BEEN AN *IDIOT*, A SMUG LITTLE IDIOT GLOATING OVER CASTLES OF FANCY, WHILE SAWANT'S BEEN *BUSY.*

HE HAS ANTICIPATED MY *EVERY* MOVE.

"... EVERYONE ELSE SHOULD BOW DOWN AND JERK ME OFF."

THAT'S *BALWAN'S* DRIVER, IN SHORT, MY *WHOLE* CASE.

99

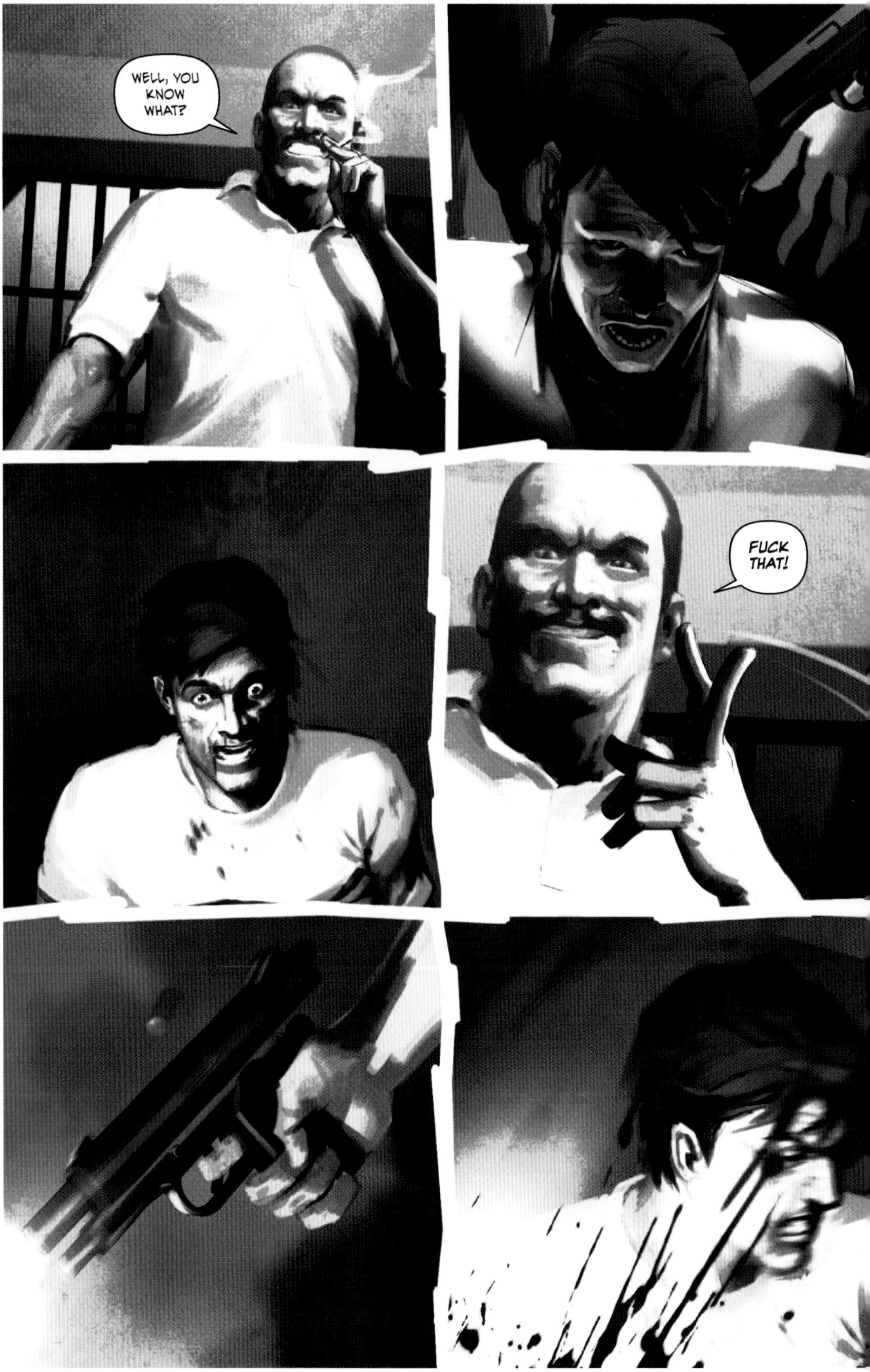
WELL, YOU KNOW WHAT?
FUCK THAT!

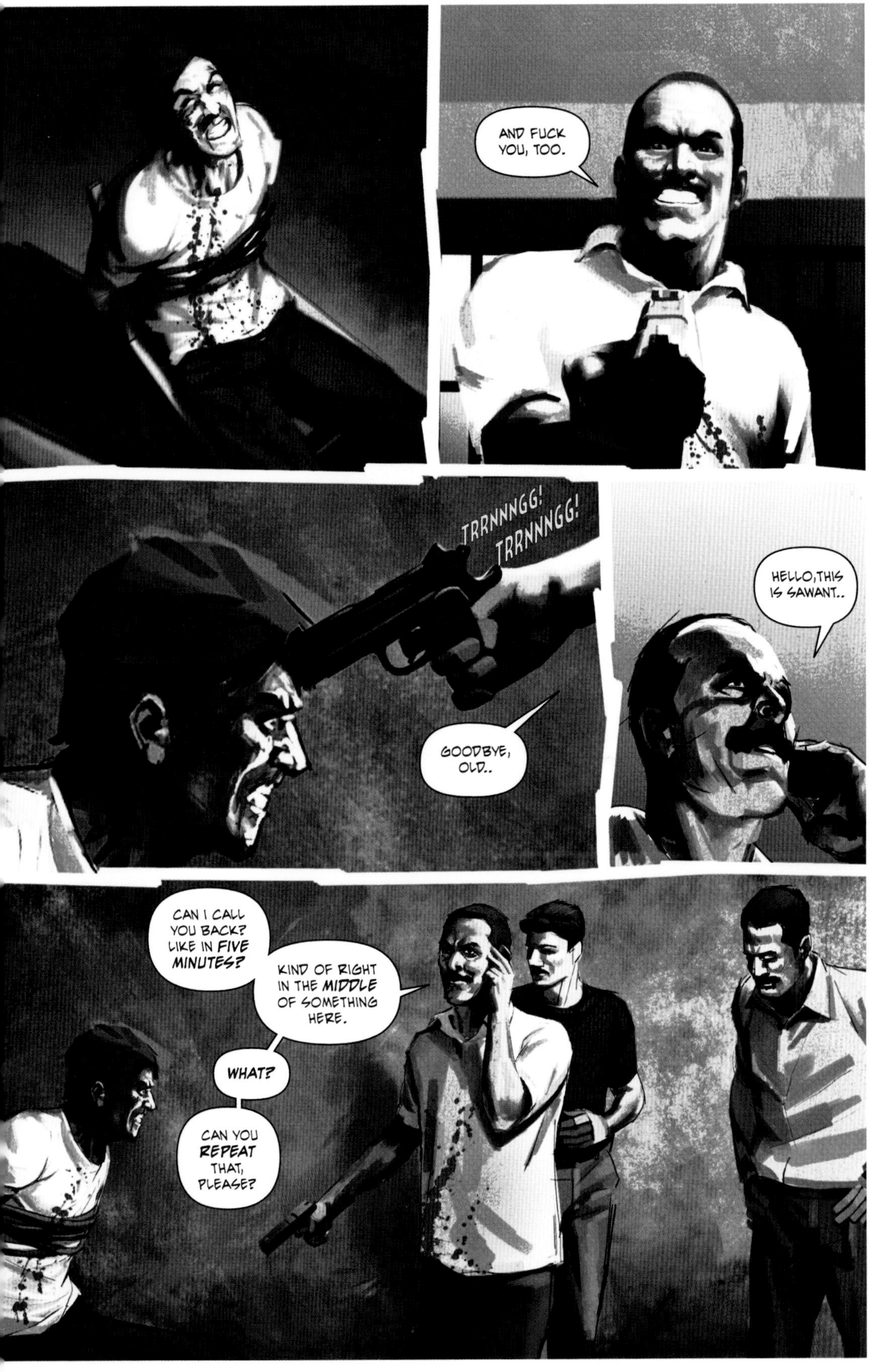
AND FUCK YOU, TOO.
TRRNNNGG! TRRNNNGG!
GOODBYE, OLD..
HELLO,THIS IS SAWANT..
CAN I CALL YOU BACK? LIKE IN FIVE MINUTES?
KIND OF RIGHT IN THE MIDDLE OF SOMETHING HERE.
WHAT?
CAN YOU REPEAT THAT, PLEASE?

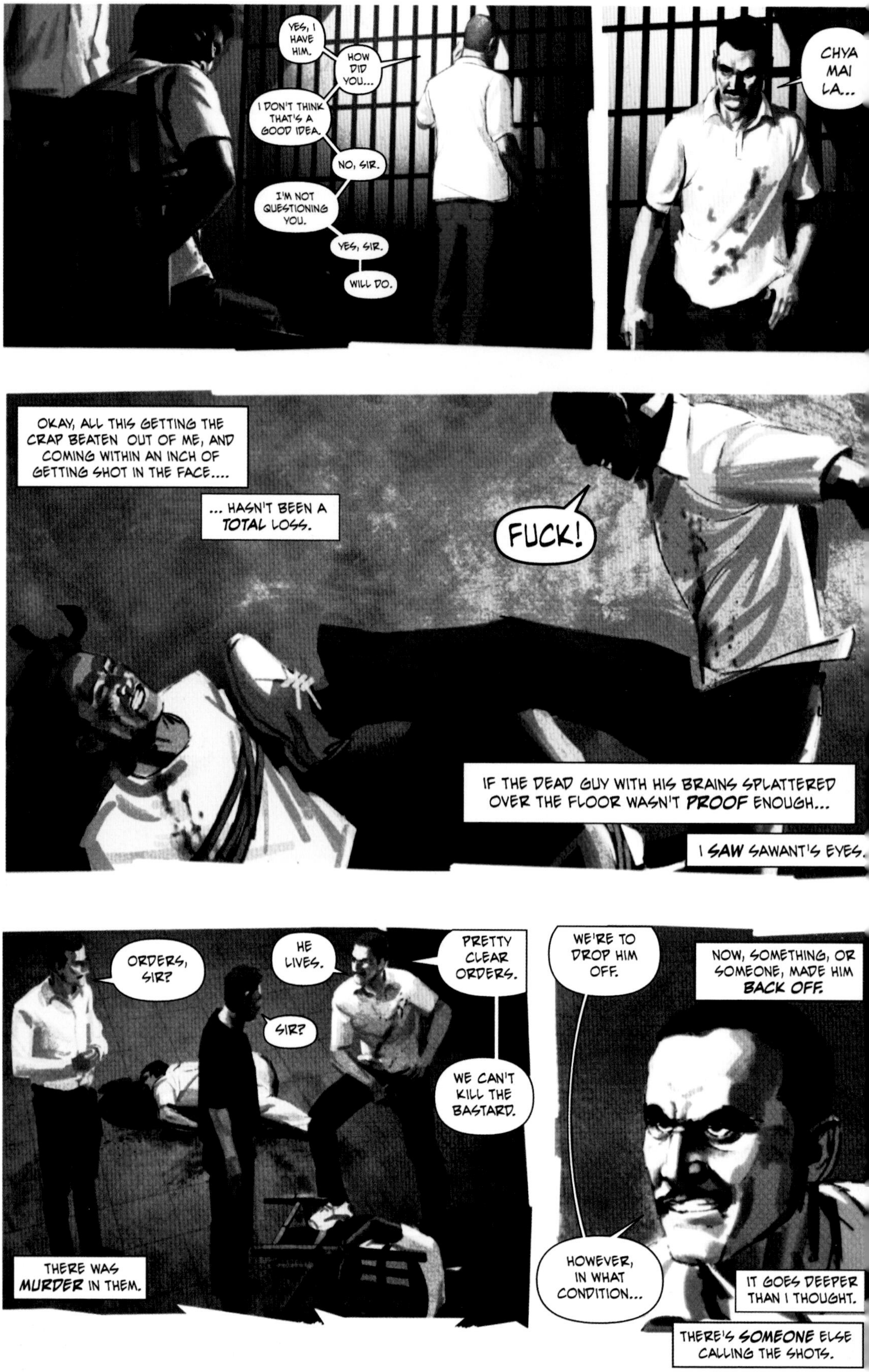
YES, I HAVE HIM.
HOW DID YOU...
I DON'T THINK THAT'S A GOOD IDEA.
NO, SIR.
I'M NOT QUESTIONING YOU.
YES, SIR.
WILL DO.
CHYA MAI LA...
OKAY, ALL THIS GETTING THE CRAP BEATEN OUT OF ME, AND COMING WITHIN AN INCH OF GETTING SHOT IN THE FACE....
... HASN'T BEEN A TOTAL LOSS.
FUCK!
IF THE DEAD GUY WITH HIS BRAINS SPLATTERED OVER THE FLOOR WASN'T PROOF ENOUGH...
I SAW SAWANT'S EYES.
ORDERS, SIR?
HE LIVES.
SIR?
PRETTY CLEAR ORDERS.
WE CAN'T KILL THE BASTARD.
THERE WAS MURDER IN THEM.
WE'RE TO DROP HIM OFF.
HOWEVER, IN WHAT CONDITION...
NOW, SOMETHING, OR SOMEONE, MADE HIM BACK OFF.
IT GOES DEEPER THAN I THOUGHT.
THERE'S SOMEONE ELSE CALLING THE SHOTS.

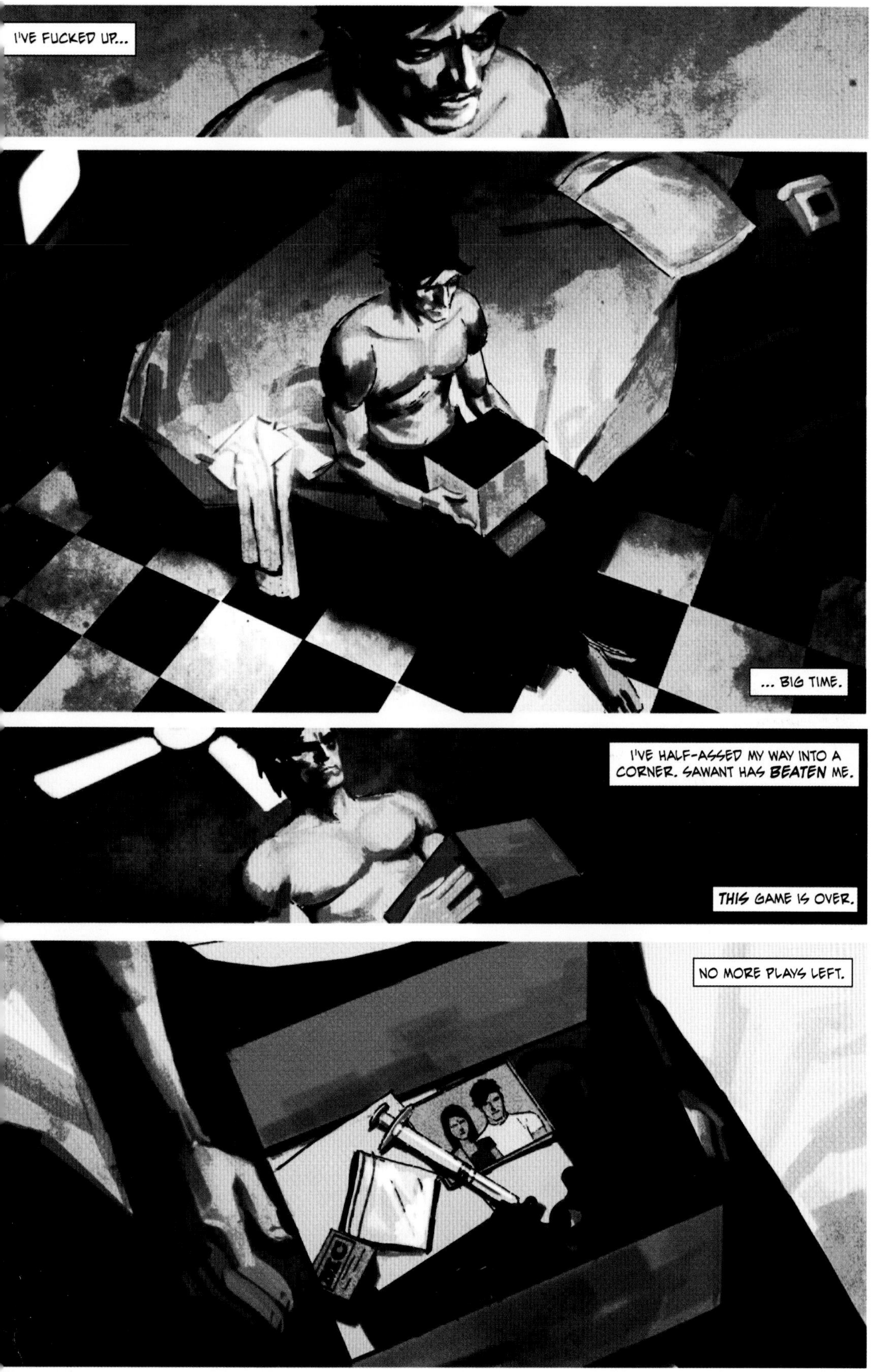
I'VE FUCKED UP...
... BIG TIME.
I'VE HALF-ASSED MY WAY INTO A CORNER. SAWANT HAS **BEATEN** ME.
THIS GAME IS OVER.
NO MORE PLAYS LEFT.

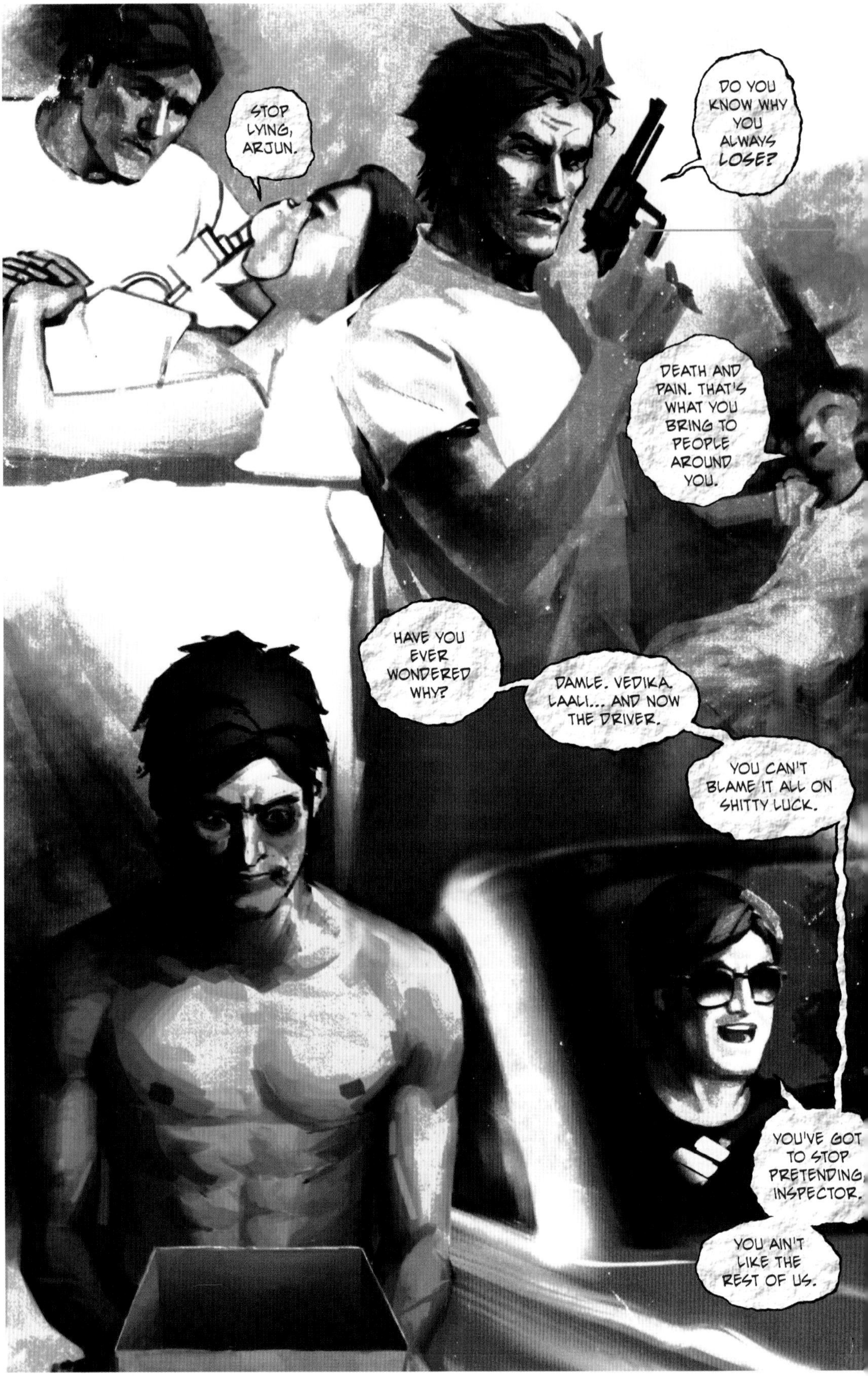
STOP LYING, ARJUN.
DO YOU KNOW WHY YOU ALWAYS LOSE?
DEATH AND PAIN. THAT'S WHAT YOU BRING TO PEOPLE AROUND YOU.
HAVE YOU EVER WONDERED WHY?
DAMLE. VEDIKA. LAALI... AND NOW THE DRIVER.
YOU CAN'T BLAME IT ALL ON SHITTY LUCK.
YOU'VE GOT TO STOP PRETENDING, INSPECTOR.
YOU AIN'T LIKE THE REST OF US.

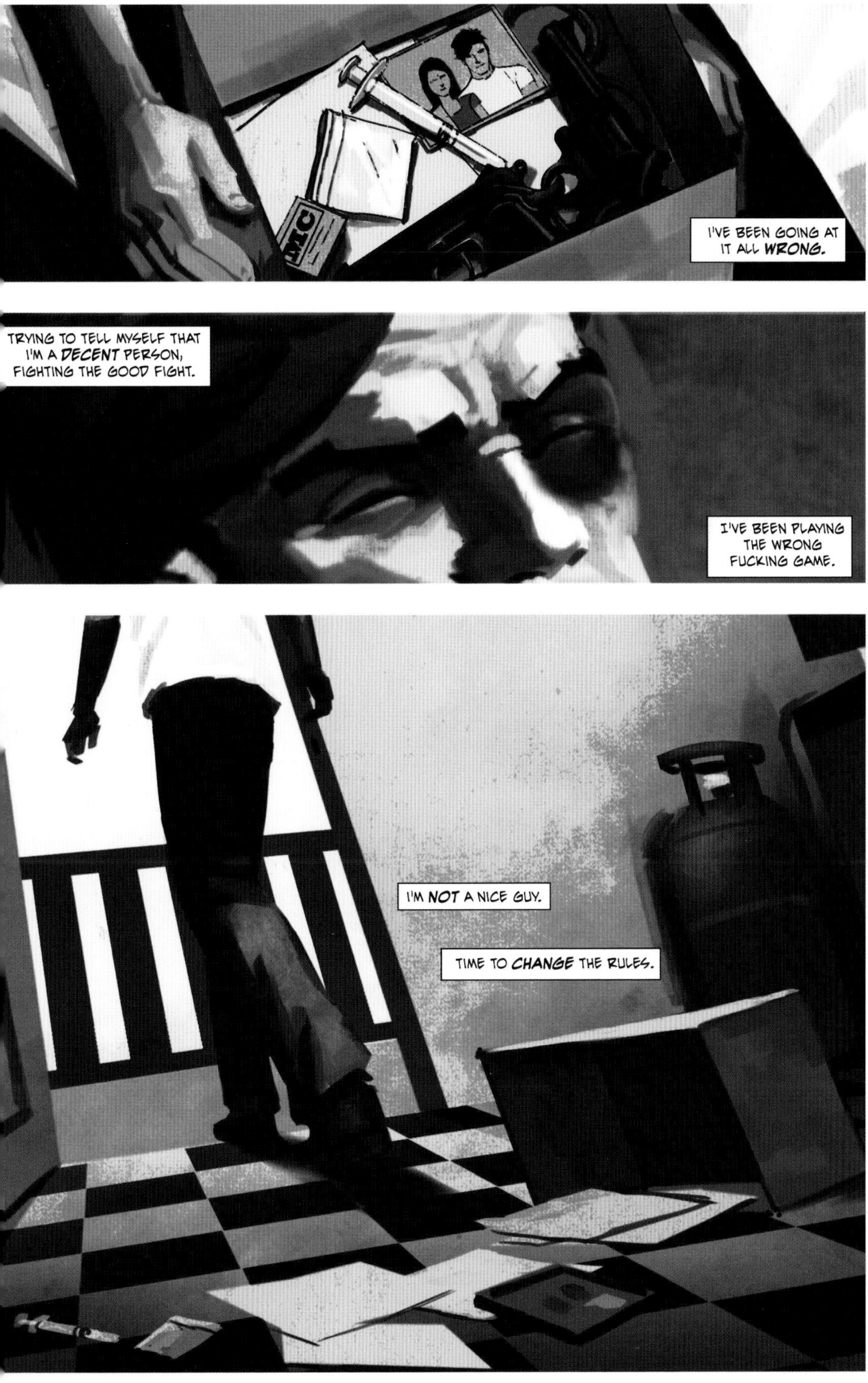
I'VE BEEN GOING AT IT ALL **WRONG.**
TRYING TO TELL MYSELF THAT I'M A *DECENT* PERSON, FIGHTING THE GOOD FIGHT.
I'VE BEEN PLAYING THE WRONG FUCKING GAME.
I'M **NOT** A NICE GUY.
TIME TO ***CHANGE*** THE RULES.

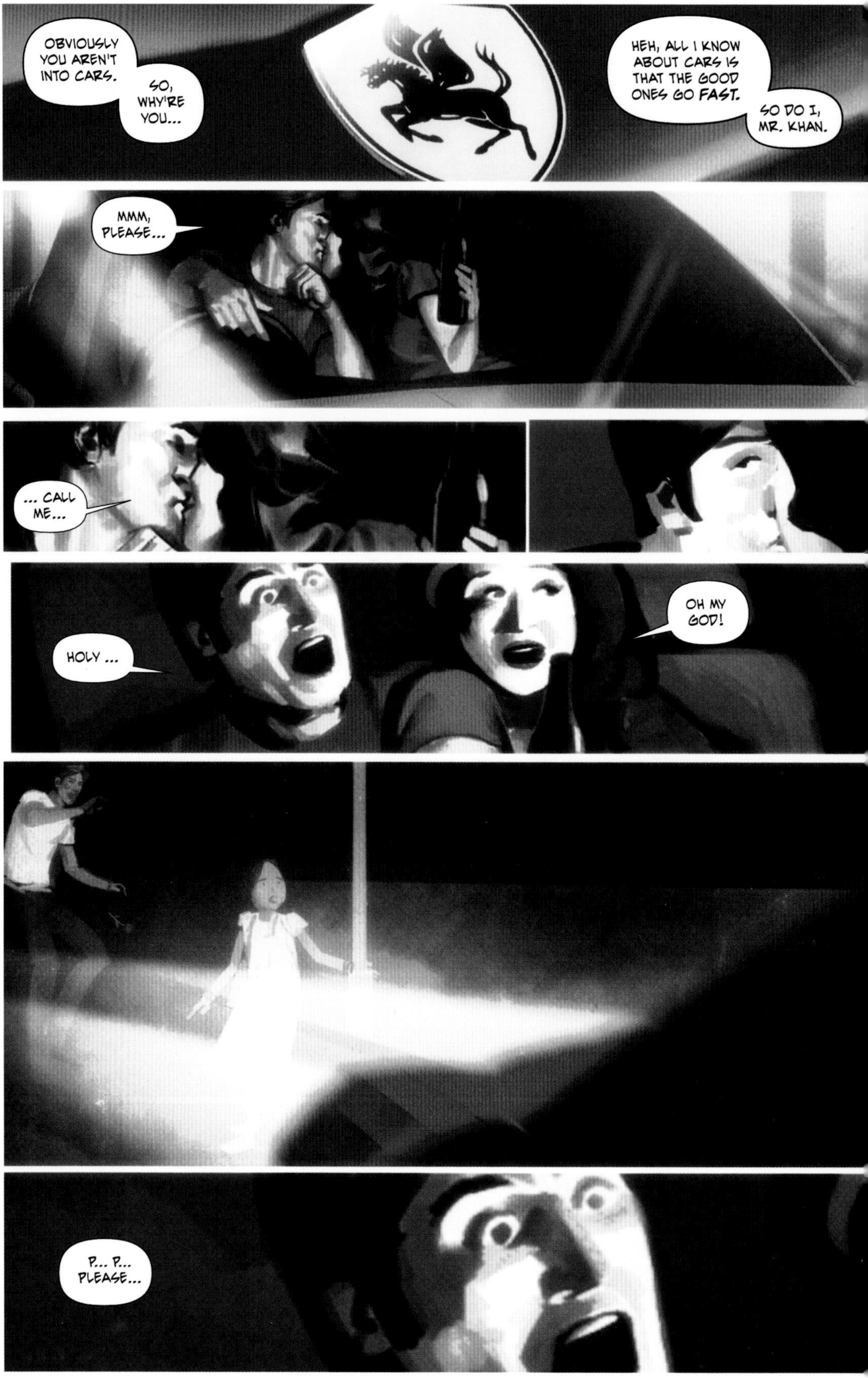
OBVIOUSLY YOU AREN'T INTO CARS.
SO, WHY'RE YOU...
HEH, ALL I KNOW ABOUT CARS IS THAT THE GOOD ONES GO **FAST.**
SO DO I, MR. KHAN.
MMM, PLEASE...
... CALL ME...
HOLY ...
OH MY GOD!
P... P... PLEASE...

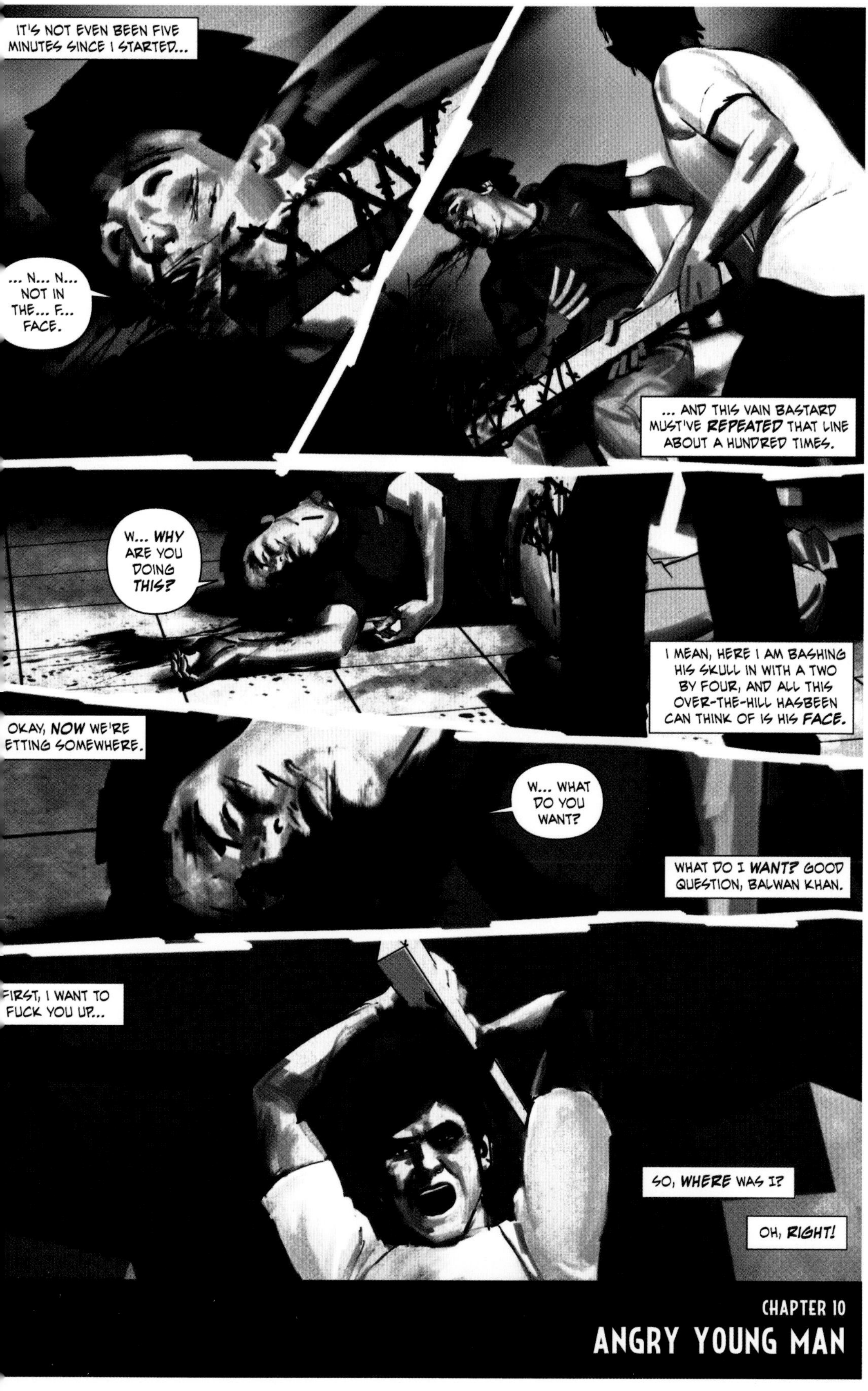
IT'S NOT EVEN BEEN FIVE MINUTES SINCE I STARTED...
... N... N... NOT IN THE... F... FACE.
... AND THIS VAIN BASTARD MUST'VE REPEATED THAT LINE ABOUT A HUNDRED TIMES.
W... WHY ARE YOU DOING THIS?
I MEAN, HERE I AM BASHING HIS SKULL IN WITH A TWO BY FOUR, AND ALL THIS OVER-THE-HILL HASBEEN CAN THINK OF IS HIS FACE.
OKAY, NOW WE'RE ETTING SOMEWHERE.
W... WHAT DO YOU WANT?
WHAT DO I WANT? GOOD QUESTION, BALWAN KHAN.
FIRST, I WANT TO FUCK YOU UP...
SO, WHERE WAS I?
OH, RIGHT!
CHAPTER 10
ANGRY YOUNG MAN

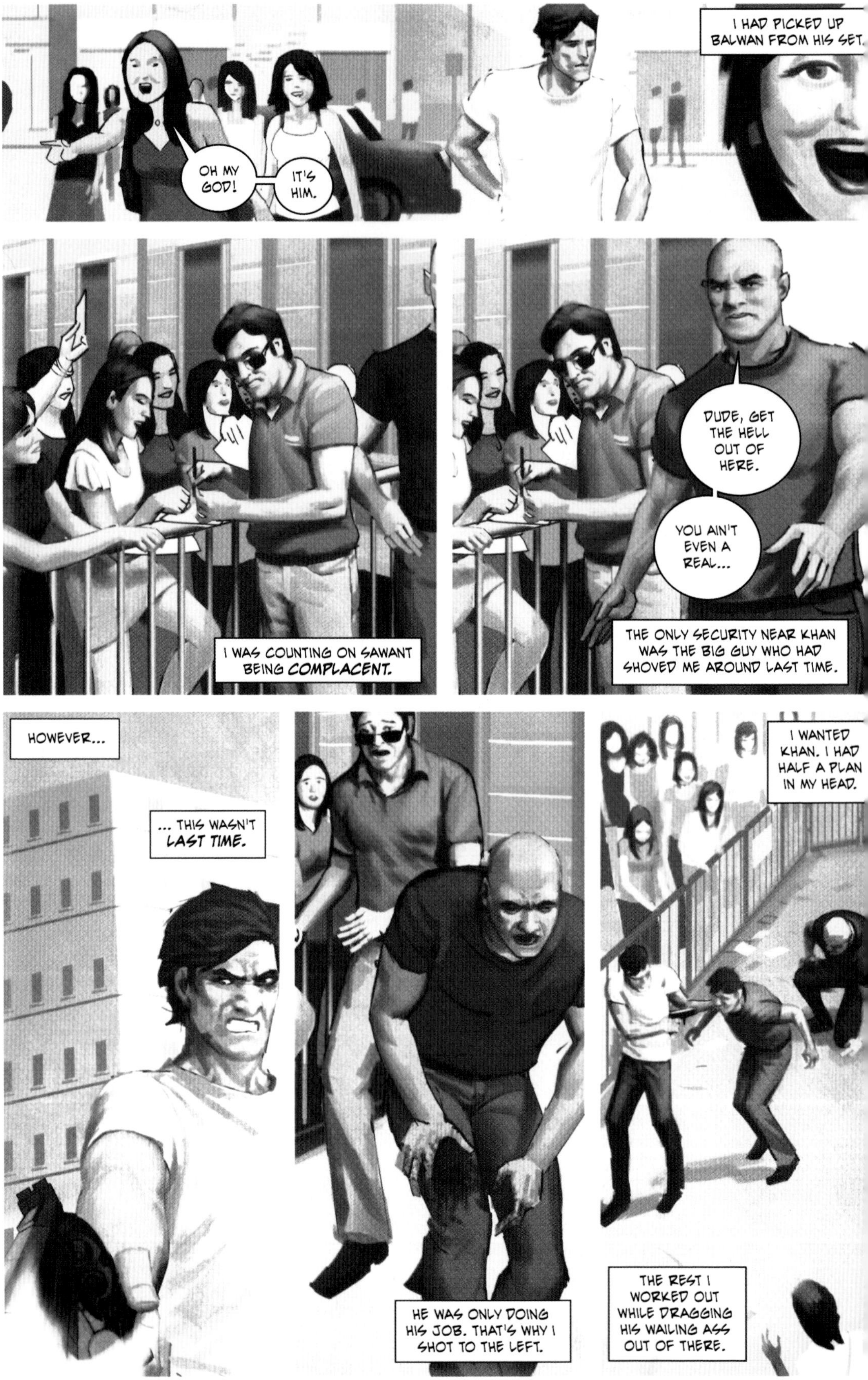
I HAD PICKED UP BALWAN FROM HIS SET.
OH MY GOD!
IT'S HIM.
I WAS COUNTING ON SAWANT BEING COMPLACENT.
DUDE, GET THE HELL OUT OF HERE.
YOU AIN'T EVEN A REAL...
THE ONLY SECURITY NEAR KHAN WAS THE BIG GUY WHO HAD SHOVED ME AROUND LAST TIME.
HOWEVER...
... THIS WASN'T LAST TIME.
HE WAS ONLY DOING HIS JOB. THAT'S WHY I SHOT TO THE LEFT.
I WANTED KHAN. I HAD HALF A PLAN IN MY HEAD.
THE REST I WORKED OUT WHILE DRAGGING HIS WAILING ASS OUT OF THERE.

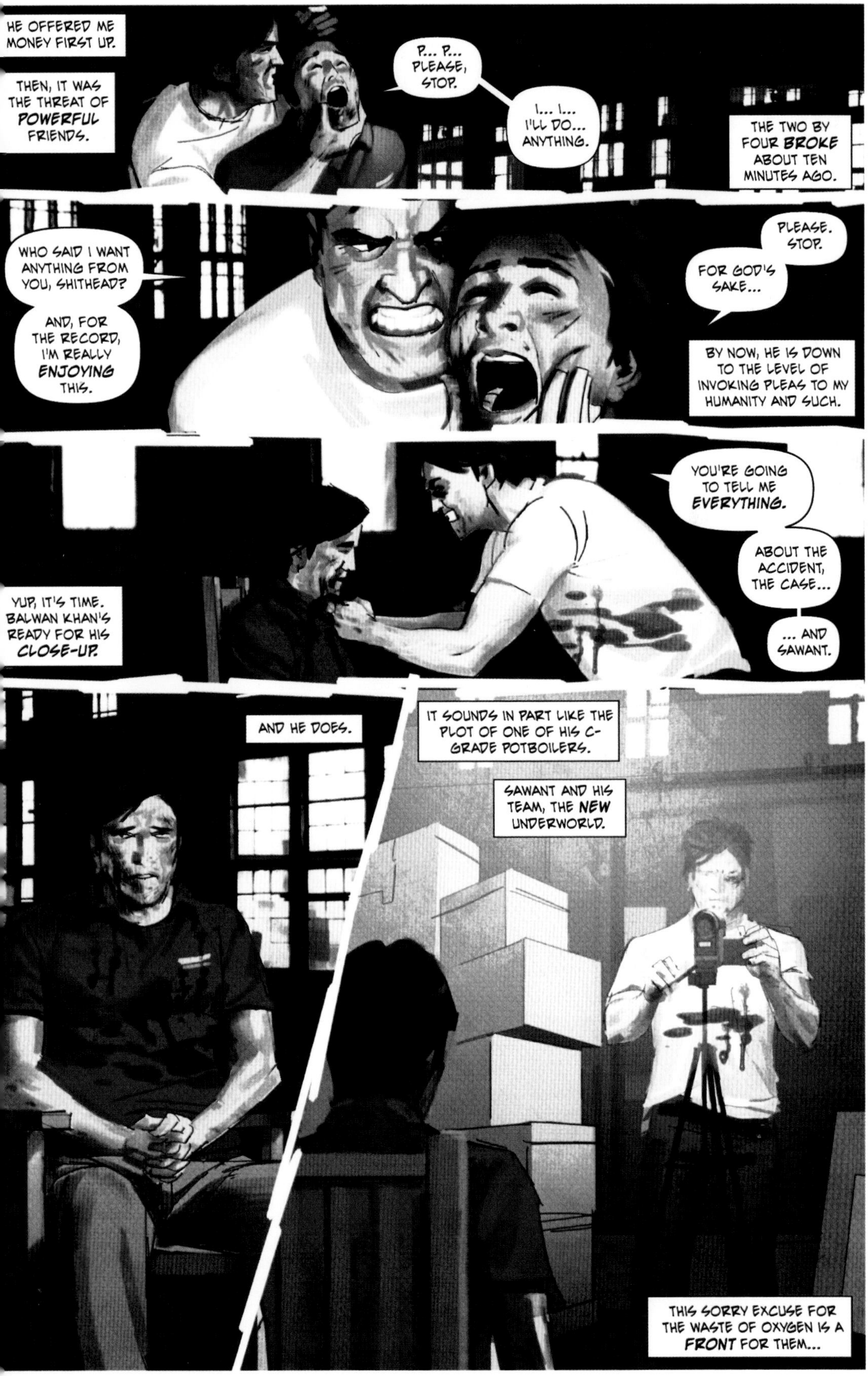
HE OFFERED ME MONEY FIRST UP.
THEN, IT WAS THE THREAT OF POWERFUL FRIENDS.
P... P... PLEASE, STOP.
I... I... I'LL DO... ANYTHING.
THE TWO BY FOUR BROKE ABOUT TEN MINUTES AGO.
WHO SAID I WANT ANYTHING FROM YOU, SHITHEAD?
AND, FOR THE RECORD, I'M REALLY ENJOYING THIS.
PLEASE. STOP.
FOR GOD'S SAKE...
BY NOW, HE IS DOWN TO THE LEVEL OF INVOKING PLEAS TO MY HUMANITY AND SUCH.
YOU'RE GOING TO TELL ME EVERYTHING.
ABOUT THE ACCIDENT, THE CASE...
... AND SAWANT.
YUP, IT'S TIME. BALWAN KHAN'S READY FOR HIS CLOSE-UP.
AND HE DOES.
IT SOUNDS IN PART LIKE THE PLOT OF ONE OF HIS C-GRADE POTBOILERS.
SAWANT AND HIS TEAM, THE NEW UNDERWORLD.
THIS SORRY EXCUSE FOR THE WASTE OF OXYGEN IS A FRONT FOR THEM...

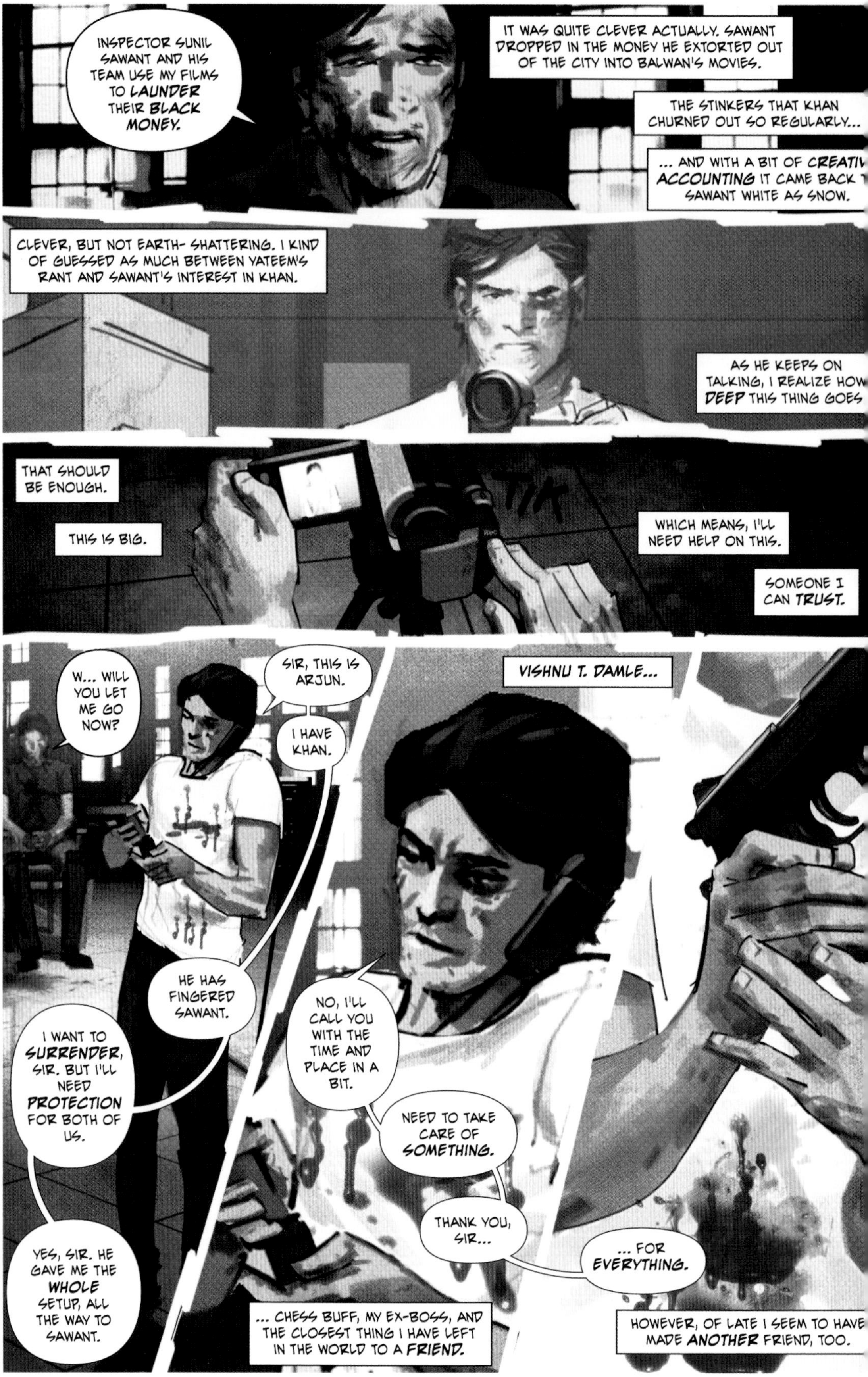
INSPECTOR SUNIL SAWANT AND HIS TEAM USE MY FILMS TO LAUNDER THEIR BLACK MONEY.
IT WAS QUITE CLEVER ACTUALLY. SAWANT DROPPED IN THE MONEY HE EXTORTED OUT OF THE CITY INTO BALWAN'S MOVIES.
THE STINKERS THAT KHAN CHURNED OUT SO REGULARLY...
... AND WITH A BIT OF CREATIV ACCOUNTING IT CAME BACK T SAWANT WHITE AS SNOW.
CLEVER, BUT NOT EARTH- SHATTERING. I KIND OF GUESSED AS MUCH BETWEEN YATEEM'S RANT AND SAWANT'S INTEREST IN KHAN.
AS HE KEEPS ON TALKING, I REALIZE HOW DEEP THIS THING GOES
THAT SHOULD BE ENOUGH.
THIS IS BIG.
TIK
WHICH MEANS, I'LL NEED HELP ON THIS.
SOMEONE I CAN TRUST.
W... WILL YOU LET ME GO NOW?
SIR, THIS IS ARJUN.
I HAVE KHAN.
HE HAS FINGERED SAWANT.
I WANT TO SURRENDER, SIR. BUT I'LL NEED PROTECTION FOR BOTH OF US.
YES, SIR. HE GAVE ME THE WHOLE SETUP, ALL THE WAY TO SAWANT.
VISHNU T. DAMLE...
NO, I'LL CALL YOU WITH THE TIME AND PLACE IN A BIT.
NEED TO TAKE CARE OF SOMETHING.
THANK YOU, SIR...
... FOR EVERYTHING.
... CHESS BUFF, MY EX-BOSS, AND THE CLOSEST THING I HAVE LEFT IN THE WORLD TO A FRIEND.
HOWEVER, OF LATE I SEEM TO HAVE MADE ANOTHER FRIEND, TOO.

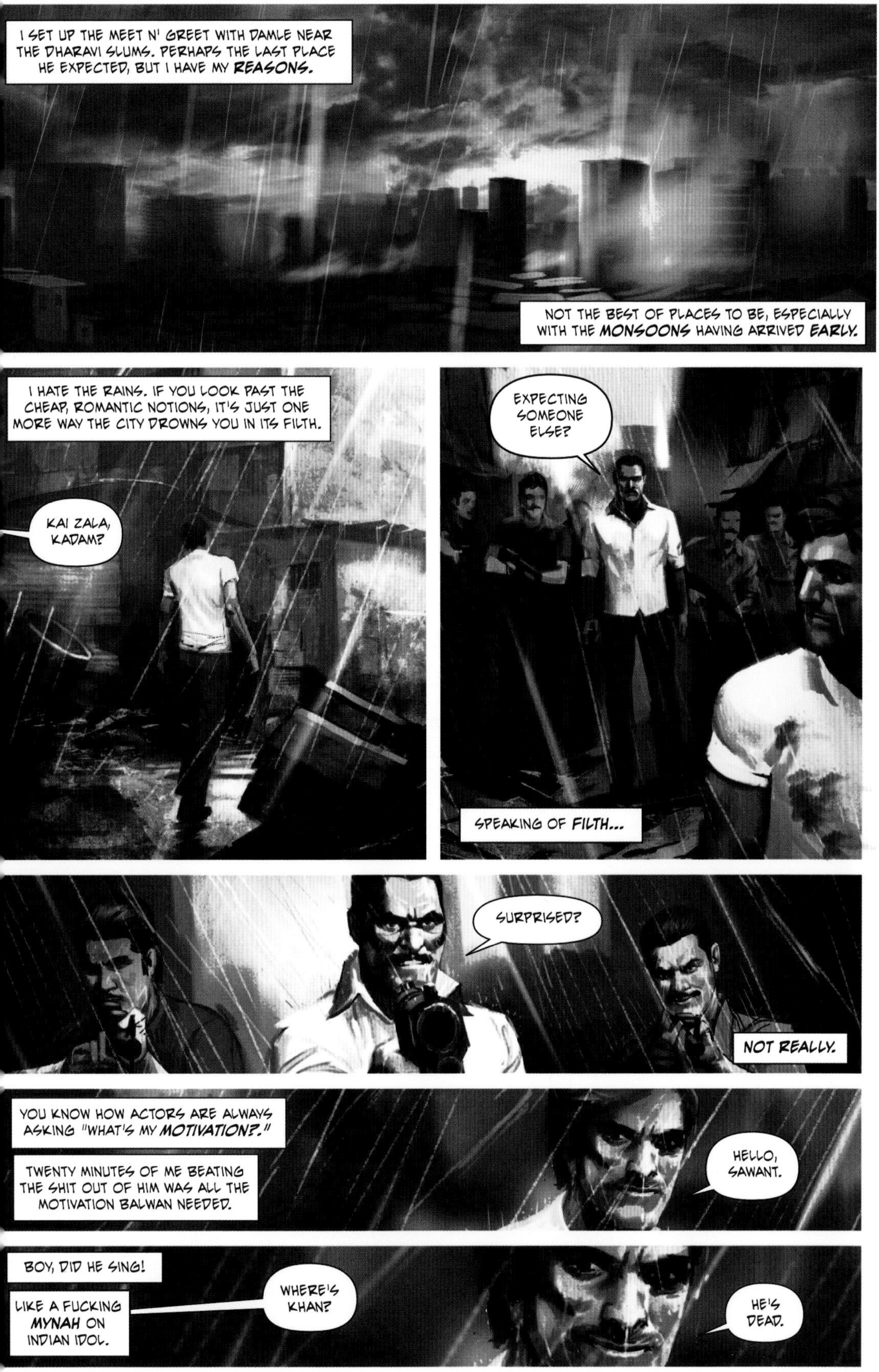
I SET UP THE MEET N' GREET WITH DAMLE NEAR THE DHARAVI SLUMS. PERHAPS THE LAST PLACE HE EXPECTED, BUT I HAVE MY REASONS.
NOT THE BEST OF PLACES TO BE, ESPECIALLY WITH THE MONSOONS HAVING ARRIVED EARLY.
I HATE THE RAINS. IF YOU LOOK PAST THE CHEAP, ROMANTIC NOTIONS, IT'S JUST ONE MORE WAY THE CITY DROWNS YOU IN ITS FILTH.
KAI ZALA, KADAM?
EXPECTING SOMEONE ELSE?
SPEAKING OF FILTH...
SURPRISED?
NOT REALLY.
YOU KNOW HOW ACTORS ARE ALWAYS ASKING "WHAT'S MY MOTIVATION?."
TWENTY MINUTES OF ME BEATING THE SHIT OUT OF HIM WAS ALL THE MOTIVATION BALWAN NEEDED.
HELLO, SAWANT.
BOY, DID HE SING!
LIKE A FUCKING MYNAH ON INDIAN IDOL.
WHERE'S KHAN?
HE'S DEAD.

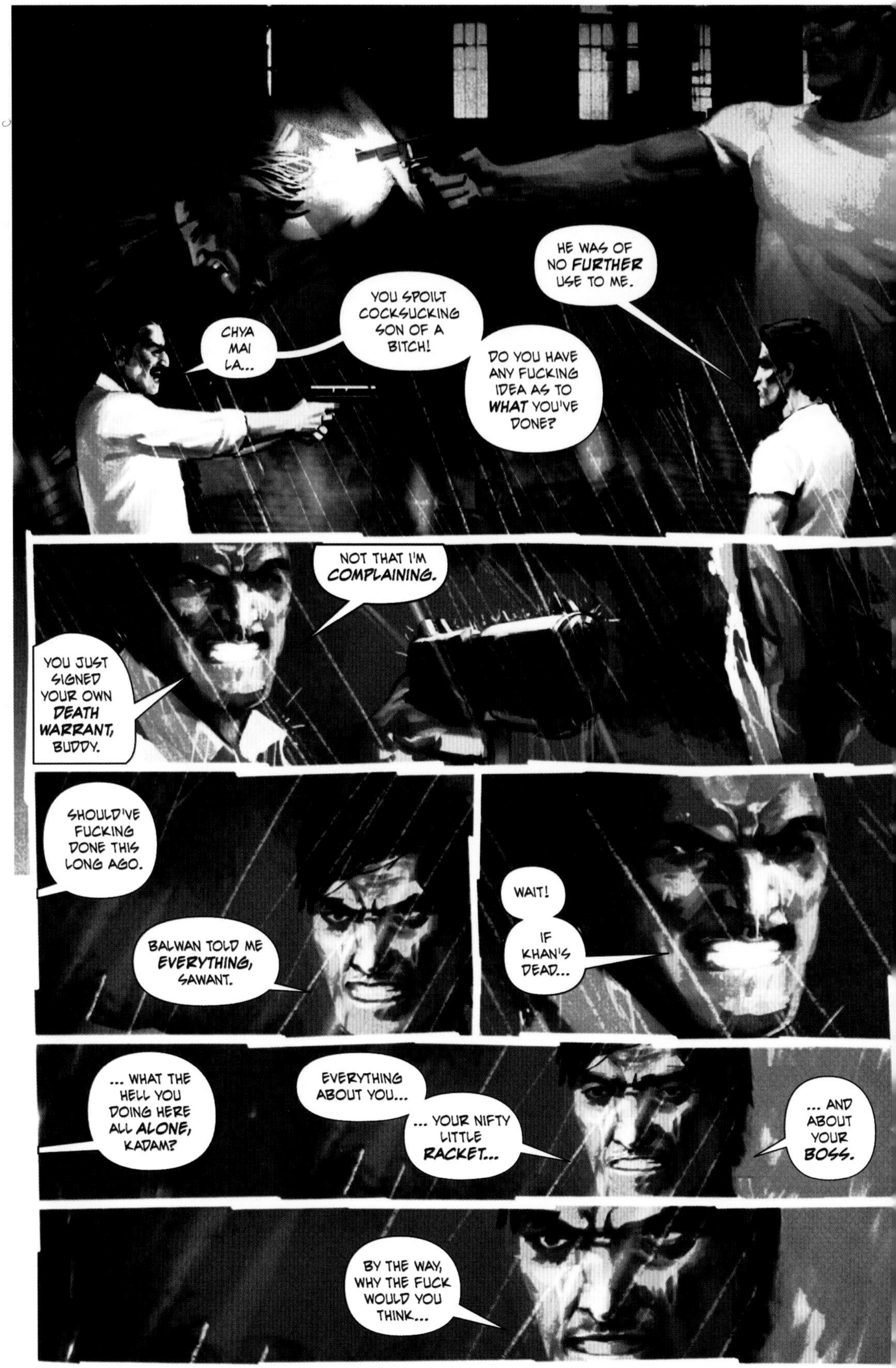
HE WAS OF NO FURTHER USE TO ME.
CHYA MAI LA...
YOU SPOILT COCKSUCKING SON OF A BITCH!
DO YOU HAVE ANY FUCKING IDEA AS TO WHAT YOU'VE DONE?
NOT THAT I'M COMPLAINING.
YOU JUST SIGNED YOUR OWN DEATH WARRANT, BUDDY.
SHOULD'VE FUCKING DONE THIS LONG AGO.
BALWAN TOLD ME EVERYTHING, SAWANT.
WAIT!
IF KHAN'S DEAD...
... WHAT THE HELL YOU DOING HERE ALL ALONE, KADAM?
EVERYTHING ABOUT YOU...
... YOUR NIFTY LITTLE RACKET...
... AND ABOUT YOUR BOSS.
BY THE WAY, WHY THE FUCK WOULD YOU THINK...

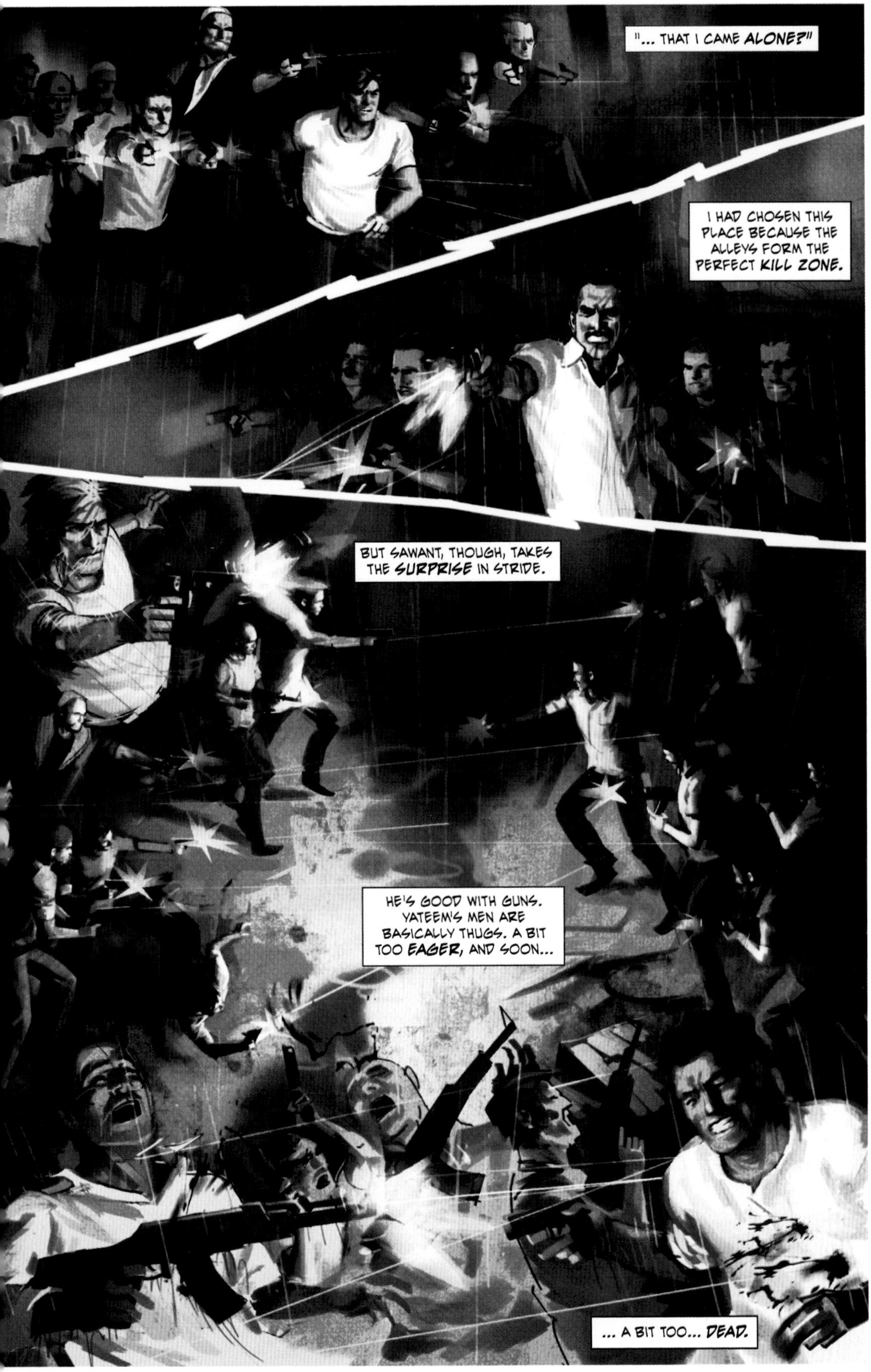
"... THAT I CAME ALONE?"
I HAD CHOSEN THIS PLACE BECAUSE THE ALLEYS FORM THE PERFECT KILL ZONE.
BUT SAWANT, THOUGH, TAKES THE SURPRISE IN STRIDE.
HE'S GOOD WITH GUNS. YATEEM'S MEN ARE BASICALLY THUGS. A BIT TOO EAGER, AND SOON...
... A BIT TOO... DEAD.

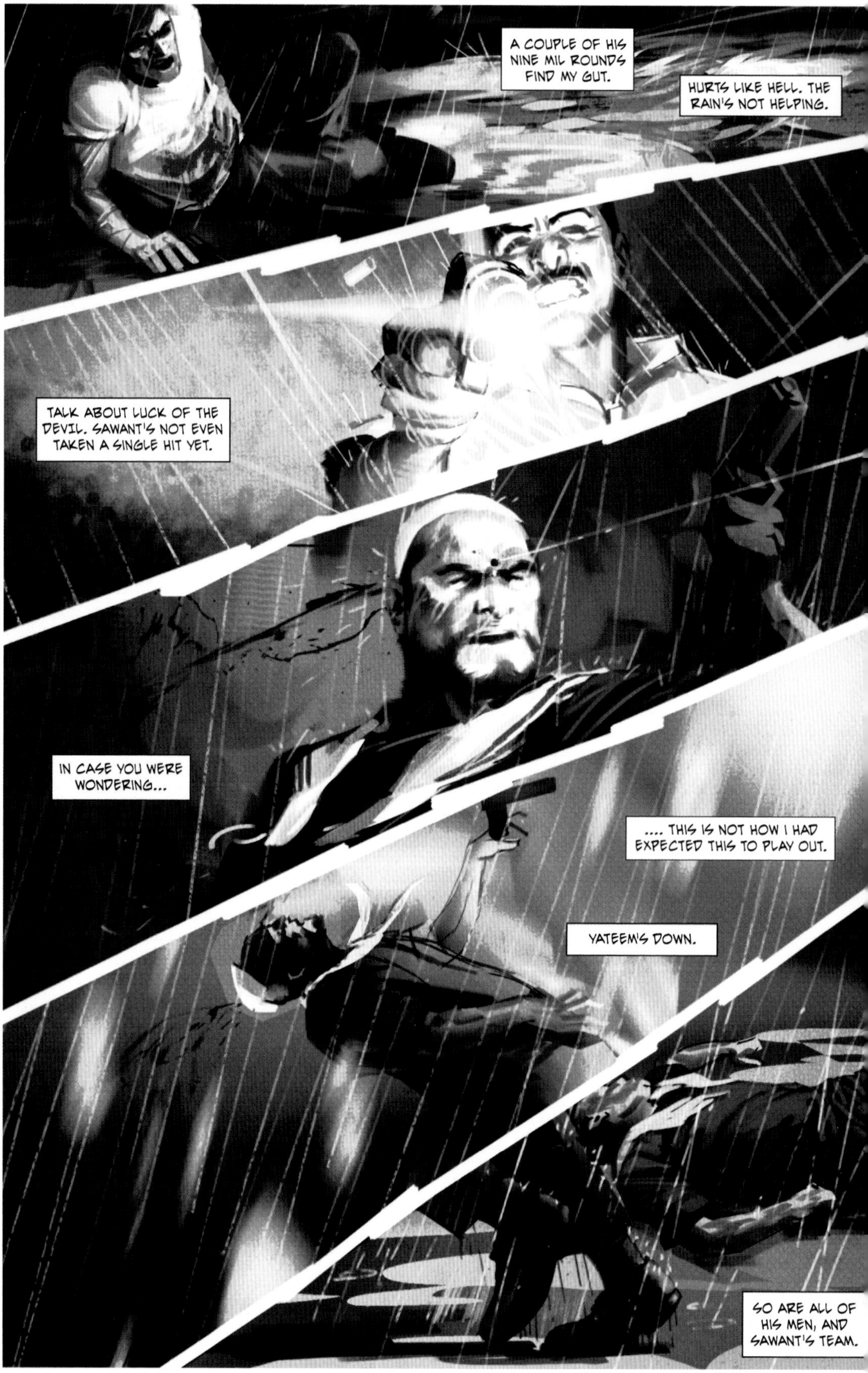
A COUPLE OF HIS NINE MIL ROUNDS FIND MY GUT.
HURTS LIKE HELL. THE RAIN'S NOT HELPING.
TALK ABOUT LUCK OF THE DEVIL. SAWANT'S NOT EVEN TAKEN A SINGLE HIT YET.
IN CASE YOU WERE WONDERING...
.... THIS IS NOT HOW I HAD EXPECTED THIS TO PLAY OUT.
YATEEM'S DOWN.
SO ARE ALL OF HIS MEN, AND SAWANT'S TEAM.

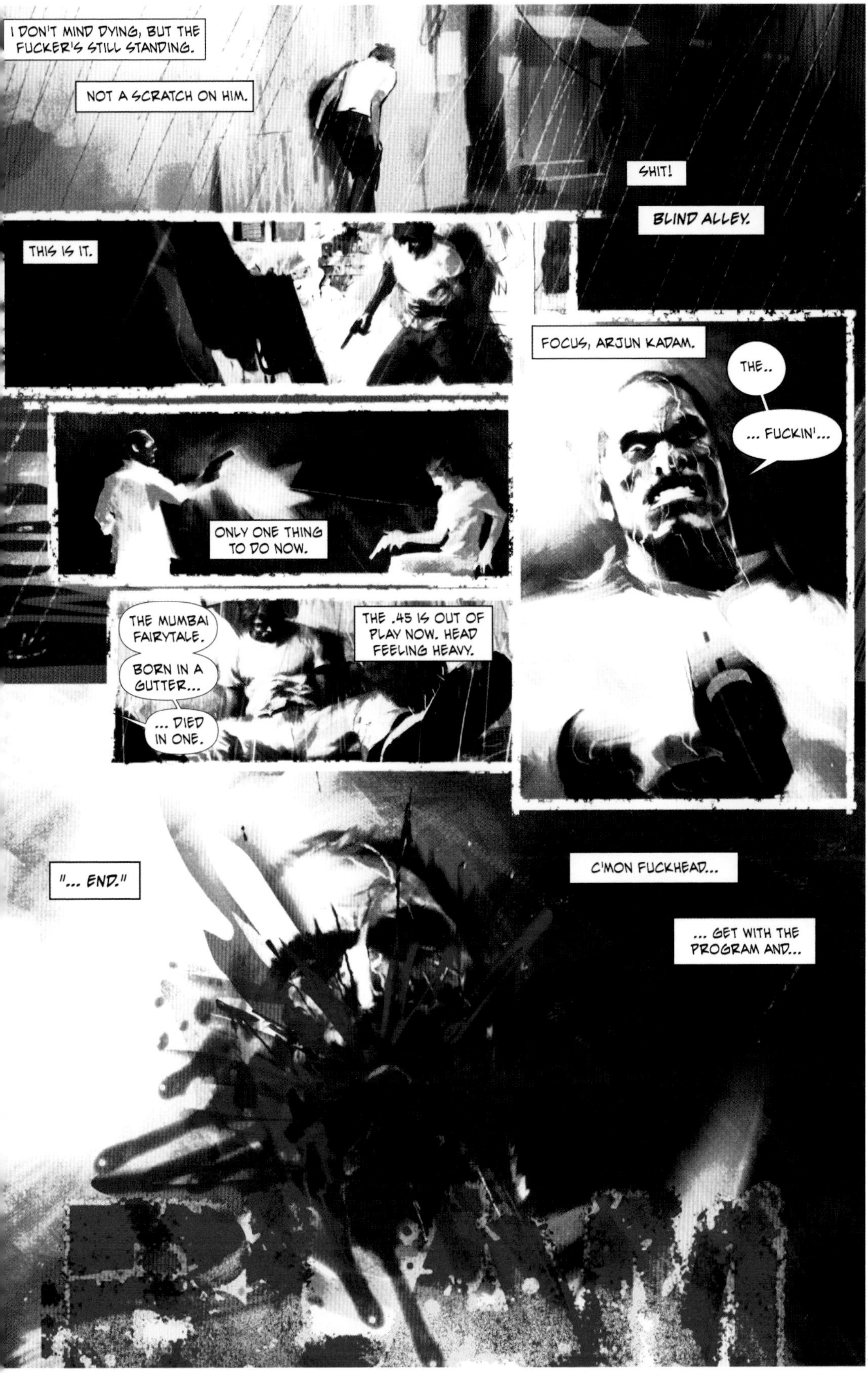
I DON'T MIND DYING, BUT THE FUCKER'S STILL STANDING.
NOT A SCRATCH ON HIM.
SHIT!
BLIND ALLEY.
THIS IS IT.
FOCUS, ARJUN KADAM.
THE..
... FUCKIN'...
ONLY ONE THING TO DO NOW.
THE MUMBAI FAIRYTALE.
BORN IN A GUTTER...
... DIED IN ONE.
THE .45 IS OUT OF PLAY NOW. HEAD FEELING HEAVY.
"... END."
C'MON FUCKHEAD...
... GET WITH THE PROGRAM AND...

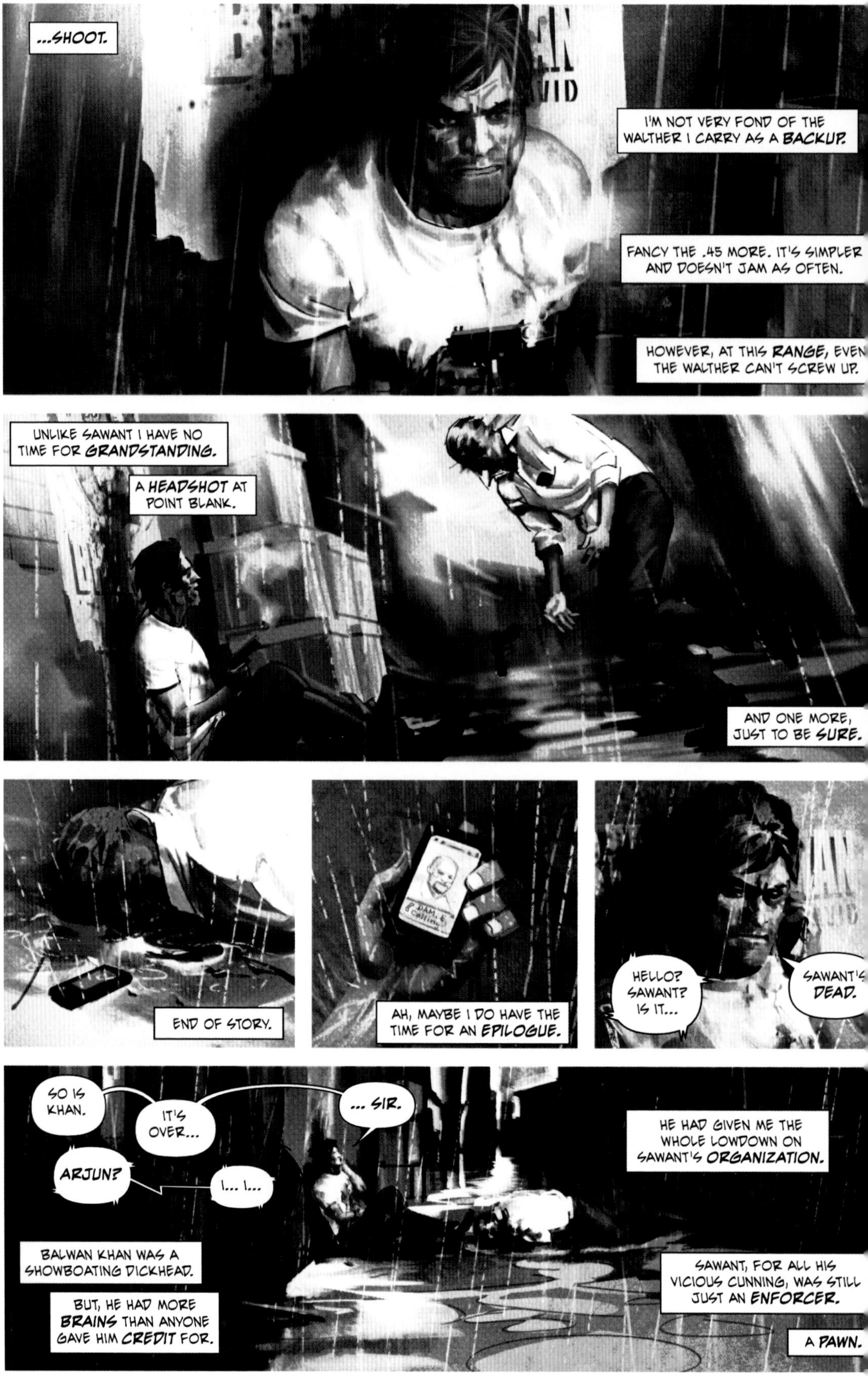
...SHOOT.
I'M NOT VERY FOND OF THE WALTHER I CARRY AS A BACKUP.
FANCY THE .45 MORE. IT'S SIMPLER AND DOESN'T JAM AS OFTEN.
HOWEVER, AT THIS RANGE, EVEN THE WALTHER CAN'T SCREW UP.
UNLIKE SAWANT I HAVE NO TIME FOR GRANDSTANDING.
A HEADSHOT AT POINT BLANK.
AND ONE MORE, JUST TO BE SURE.
END OF STORY.
AH, MAYBE I DO HAVE THE TIME FOR AN EPILOGUE.
HELLO? SAWANT? IS IT...
SAWANT'S DEAD.
SO IS KHAN.
IT'S OVER...
... SIR.
ARJUN?
I... I...
HE HAD GIVEN ME THE WHOLE LOWDOWN ON SAWANT'S ORGANIZATION.
BALWAN KHAN WAS A SHOWBOATING DICKHEAD.
BUT, HE HAD MORE BRAINS THAN ANYONE GAVE HIM CREDIT FOR.
SAWANT, FOR ALL HIS VICIOUS CUNNING, WAS STILL JUST AN ENFORCER.
A PAWN.

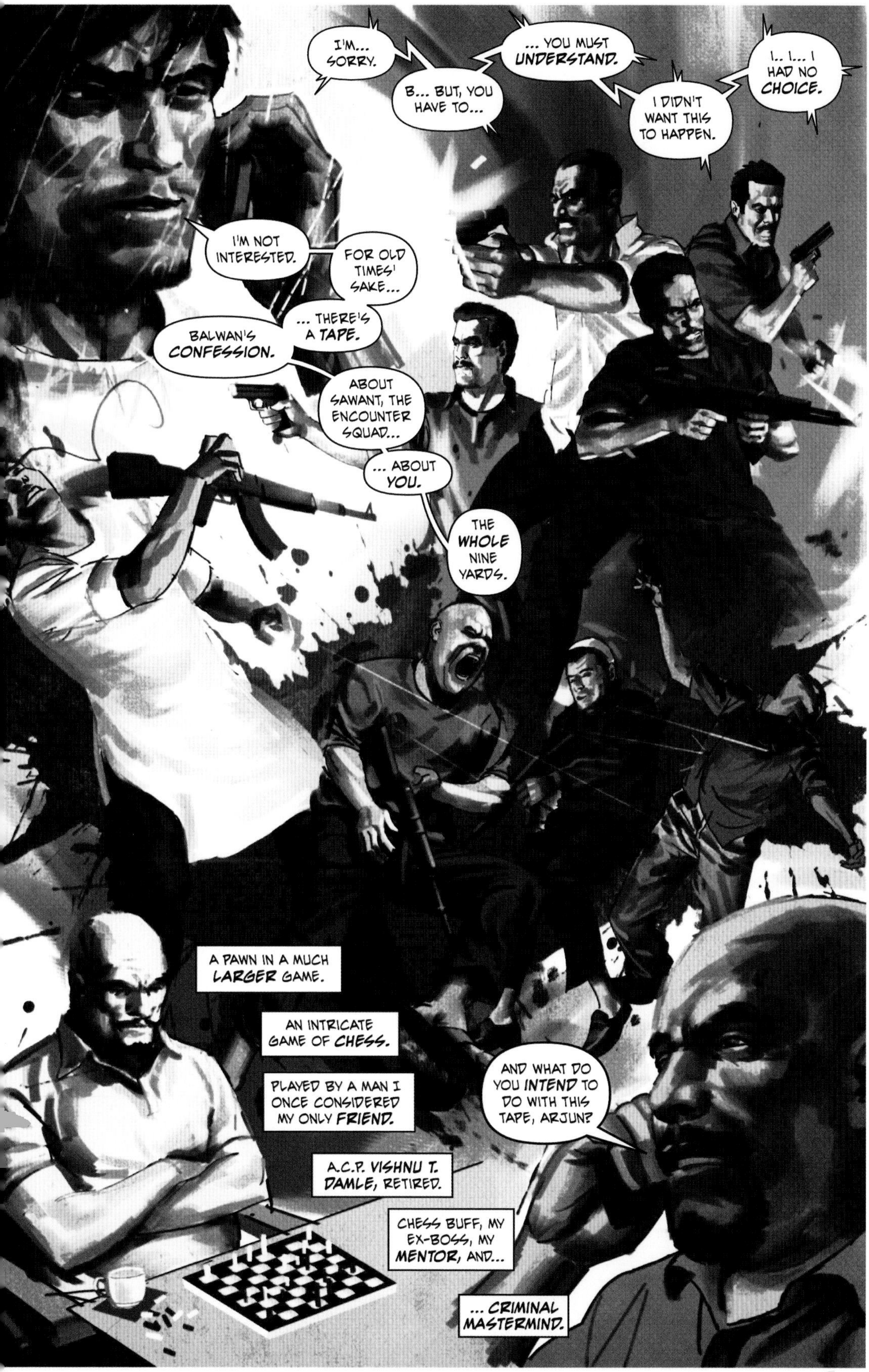
I'M... SORRY.
B... BUT, YOU HAVE TO...
... YOU MUST UNDERSTAND.
I DIDN'T WANT THIS TO HAPPEN.
I.. I... I HAD NO CHOICE.
I'M NOT INTERESTED.
FOR OLD TIMES' SAKE...
... THERE'S A TAPE.
BALWAN'S CONFESSION.
ABOUT SAWANT, THE ENCOUNTER SQUAD...
... ABOUT YOU.
THE WHOLE NINE YARDS.
A PAWN IN A MUCH LARGER GAME.
AN INTRICATE GAME OF CHESS.
PLAYED BY A MAN I ONCE CONSIDERED MY ONLY FRIEND.
A.C.P. VISHNU T. DAMLE, RETIRED.
CHESS BUFF, MY EX-BOSS, MY MENTOR, AND...
... CRIMINAL MASTERMIND.
AND WHAT DO YOU INTEND TO DO WITH THIS TAPE, ARJUN?

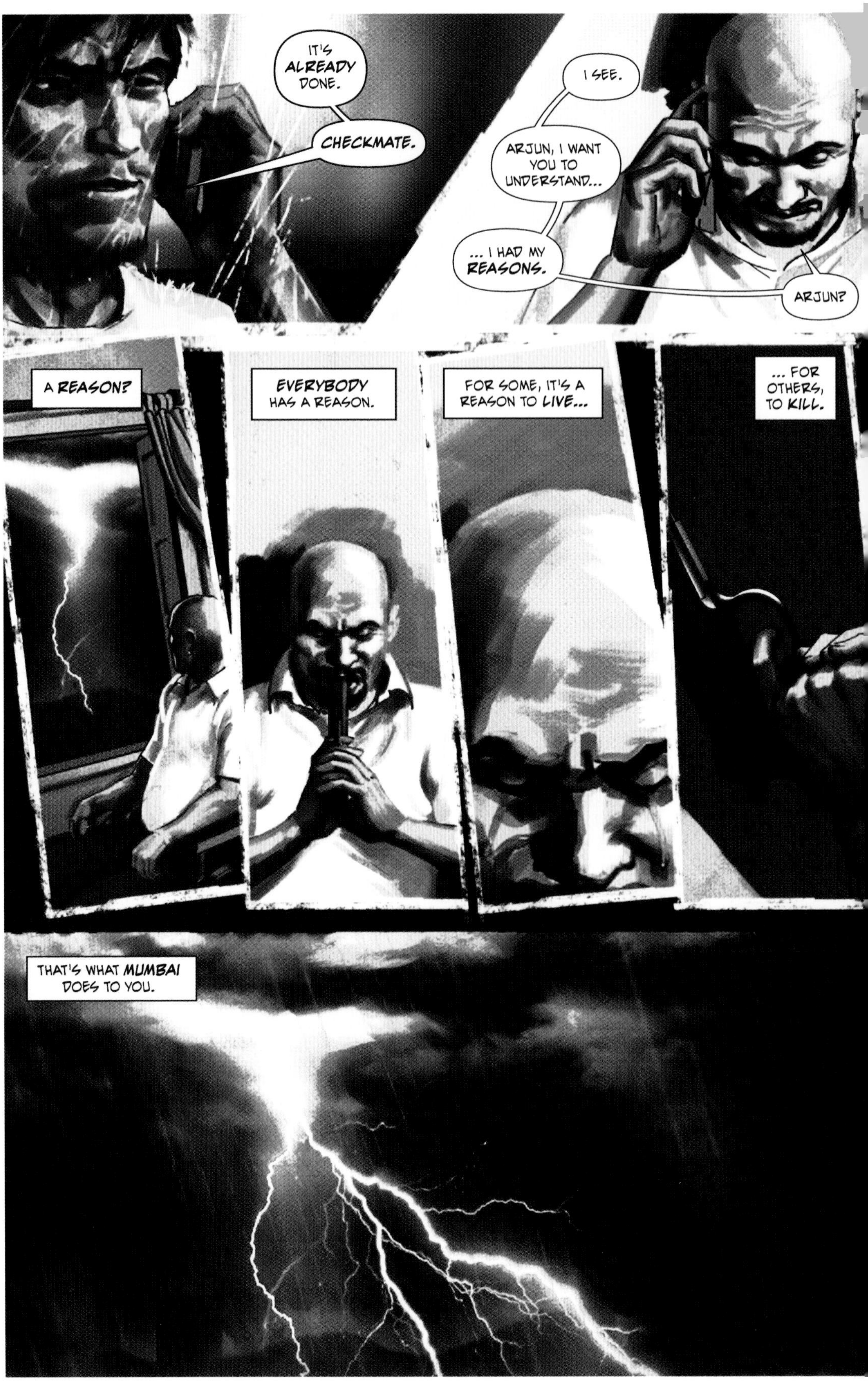
IT'S ALREADY DONE.
CHECKMATE.
I SEE.
ARJUN, I WANT YOU TO UNDERSTAND...
... I HAD MY REASONS.
ARJUN?
A REASON?
EVERYBODY HAS A REASON.
FOR SOME, IT'S A REASON TO LIVE...
... FOR OTHERS, TO KILL.
THAT'S WHAT MUMBAI DOES TO YOU.

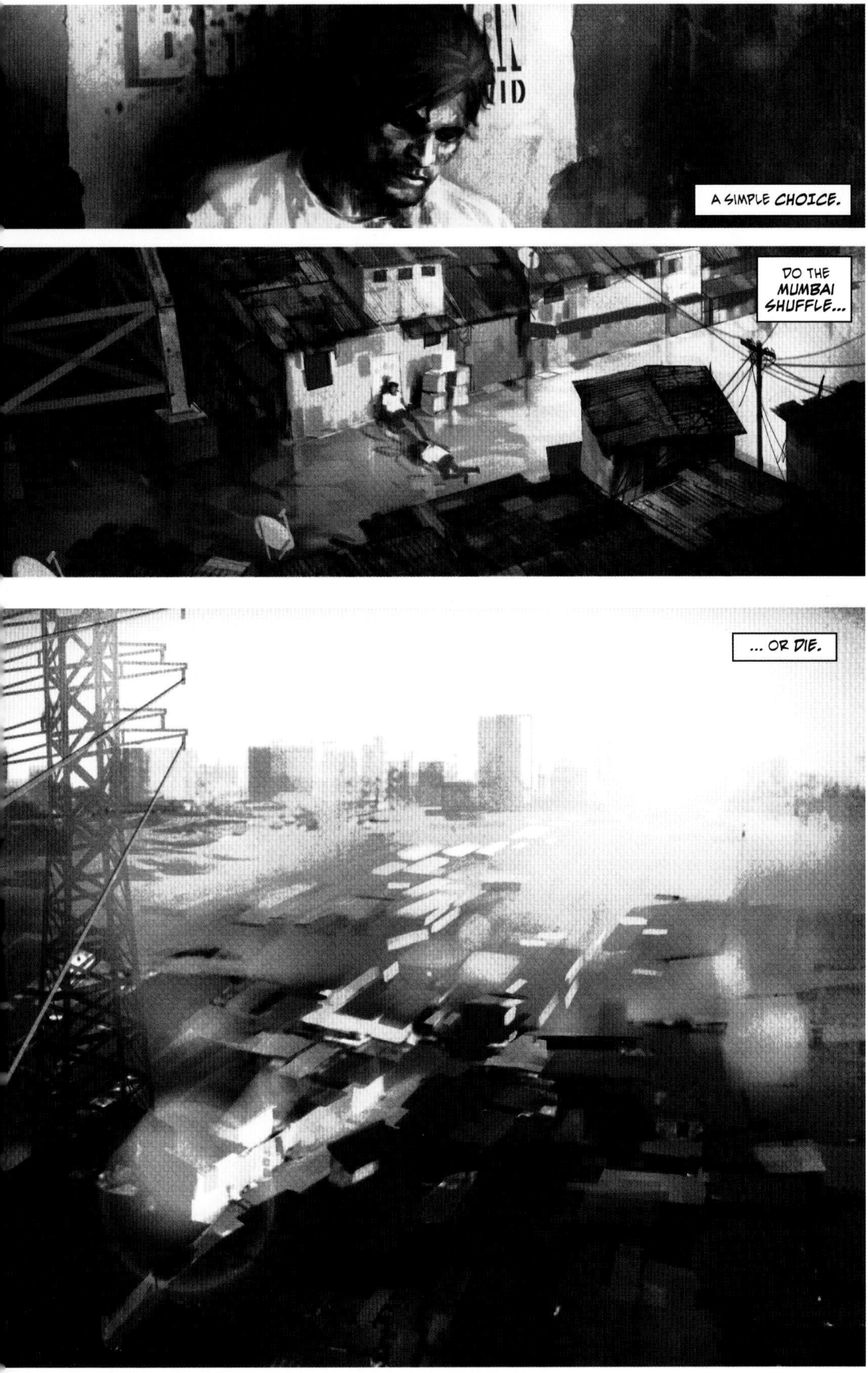
A SIMPLE CHOICE.
DO THE MUMBAI SHUFFLE...
... OR DIE.

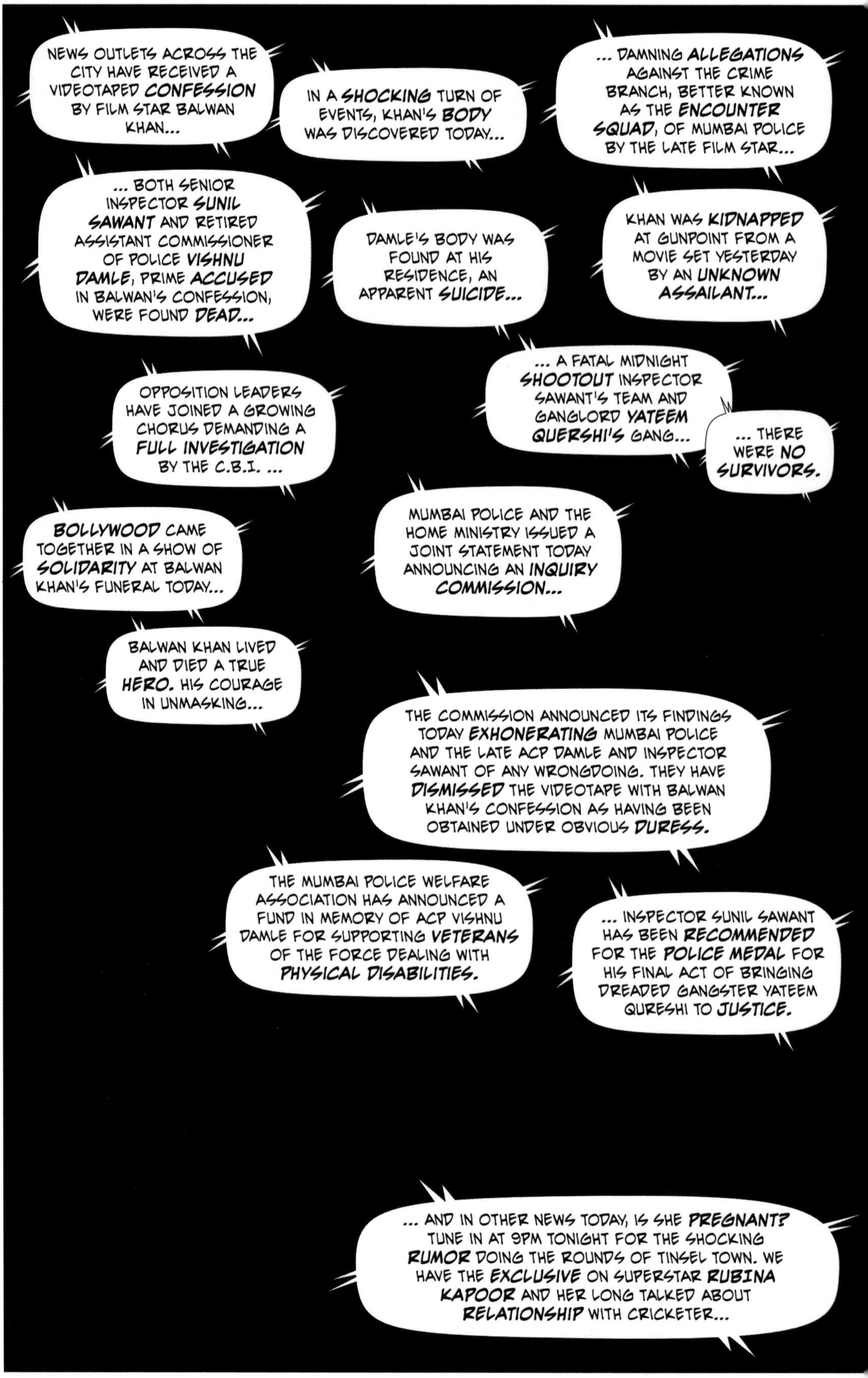
NEWS OUTLETS ACROSS THE CITY HAVE RECEIVED A VIDEOTAPED CONFESSION BY FILM STAR BALWAN KHAN...
IN A SHOCKING TURN OF EVENTS, KHAN'S BODY WAS DISCOVERED TODAY...
... DAMNING ALLEGATIONS AGAINST THE CRIME BRANCH, BETTER KNOWN AS THE ENCOUNTER SQUAD, OF MUMBAI POLICE BY THE LATE FILM STAR...
... BOTH SENIOR INSPECTOR SUNIL SAWANT AND RETIRED ASSISTANT COMMISSIONER OF POLICE VISHNU DAMLE, PRIME ACCUSED IN BALWAN'S CONFESSION, WERE FOUND DEAD...
DAMLE'S BODY WAS FOUND AT HIS RESIDENCE, AN APPARENT SUICIDE...
KHAN WAS KIDNAPPED AT GUNPOINT FROM A MOVIE SET YESTERDAY BY AN UNKNOWN ASSAILANT...
OPPOSITION LEADERS HAVE JOINED A GROWING CHORUS DEMANDING A FULL INVESTIGATION BY THE C.B.I. ...
... A FATAL MIDNIGHT SHOOTOUT INSPECTOR SAWANT'S TEAM AND GANGLORD YATEEM QUERSHI'S GANG...
... THERE WERE NO SURVIVORS.
BOLLYWOOD CAME TOGETHER IN A SHOW OF SOLIDARITY AT BALWAN KHAN'S FUNERAL TODAY...
MUMBAI POLICE AND THE HOME MINISTRY ISSUED A JOINT STATEMENT TODAY ANNOUNCING AN INQUIRY COMMISSION...
BALWAN KHAN LIVED AND DIED A TRUE HERO. HIS COURAGE IN UNMASKING...
THE COMMISSION ANNOUNCED ITS FINDINGS TODAY EXHONERATING MUMBAI POLICE AND THE LATE ACP DAMLE AND INSPECTOR SAWANT OF ANY WRONGDOING. THEY HAVE DISMISSED THE VIDEOTAPE WITH BALWAN KHAN'S CONFESSION AS HAVING BEEN OBTAINED UNDER OBVIOUS DURESS.
THE MUMBAI POLICE WELFARE ASSOCIATION HAS ANNOUNCED A FUND IN MEMORY OF ACP VISHNU DAMLE FOR SUPPORTING VETERANS OF THE FORCE DEALING WITH PHYSICAL DISABILITIES.
... INSPECTOR SUNIL SAWANT HAS BEEN RECOMMENDED FOR THE POLICE MEDAL FOR HIS FINAL ACT OF BRINGING DREADED GANGSTER YATEEM QURESHI TO JUSTICE.
... AND IN OTHER NEWS TODAY, IS SHE PREGNANT? TUNE IN AT 9PM TONIGHT FOR THE SHOCKING RUMOR DOING THE ROUNDS OF TINSEL TOWN. WE HAVE THE EXCLUSIVE ON SUPERSTAR RUBINA KAPOOR AND HER LONG TALKED ABOUT RELATIONSHIP WITH CRICKETER...

THE EN

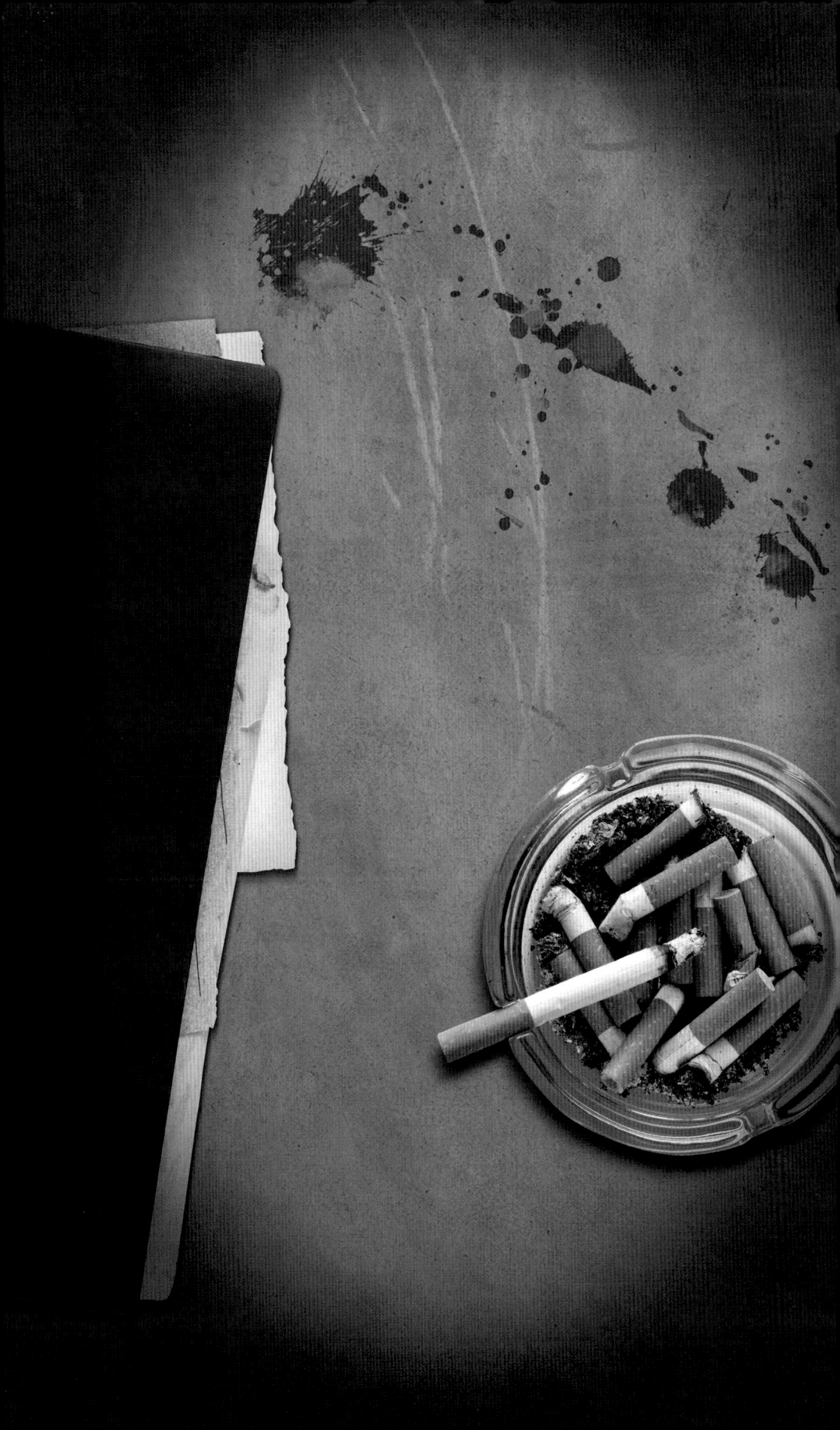

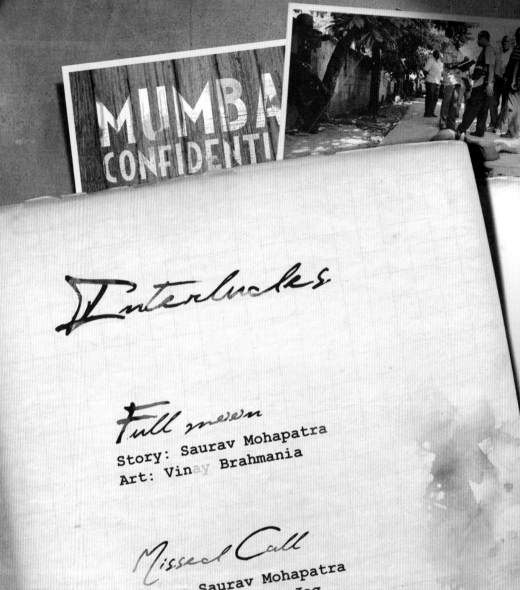

Interludes

Full moon

Story: Saurav Mohapatra
Art: Vinay Brahmania

Missed Call

Story: Saurav Mohapatra
Layouts: Shounak Jog
Art: Vinay Brahmania

Demand and supply

Story: Saurav Mohapatra
Art: Devaki Neogi

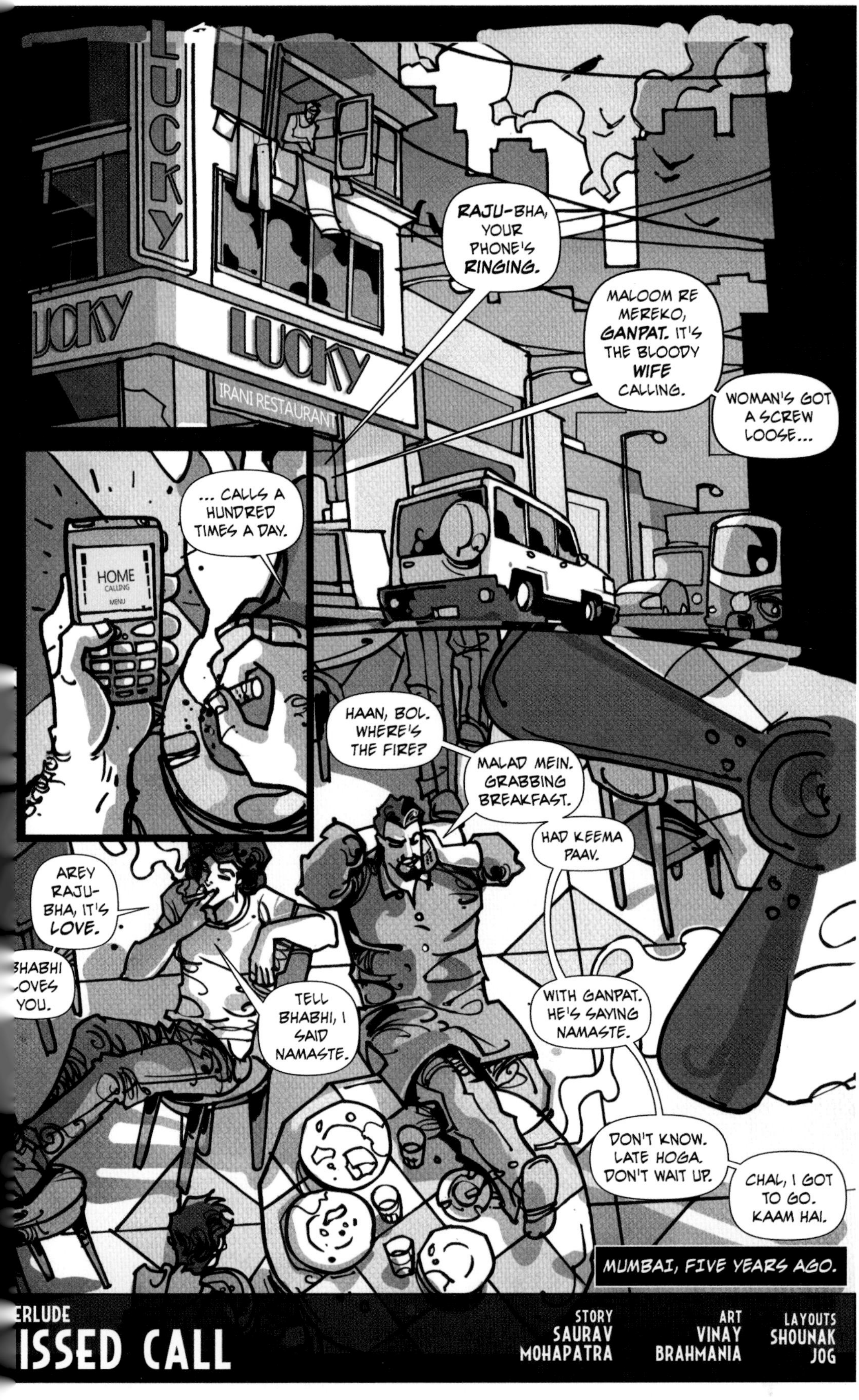
LUCKY
LUCKY
LUCKY
IRANI RESTAURANT
RAJU-BHA, YOUR PHONE'S RINGING.
MALOOM RE MEREKO, GANPAT. IT'S THE BLOODY WIFE CALLING.
WOMAN'S GOT A SCREW LOOSE...
HOME CALLING MENU
... CALLS A HUNDRED TIMES A DAY.
HAAN, BOL. WHERE'S THE FIRE?
MALAD MEIN. GRABBING BREAKFAST.
HAD KEEMA PAAV.
AREY RAJU-BHA, IT'S LOVE.
BHABHI LOVES YOU.
TELL BHABHI, I SAID NAMASTE.
WITH GANPAT. HE'S SAYING NAMASTE.
DON'T KNOW. LATE HOGA. DON'T WAIT UP.
CHAL, I GOT TO GO. KAAM HAI.
MUMBAI, FIVE YEARS AGO.
ERLUDE
ISSED CALL
STORY SAURAV MOHAPATRA
ART VINAY BRAHMANIA
LAYOUTS SHOUNAK JOG

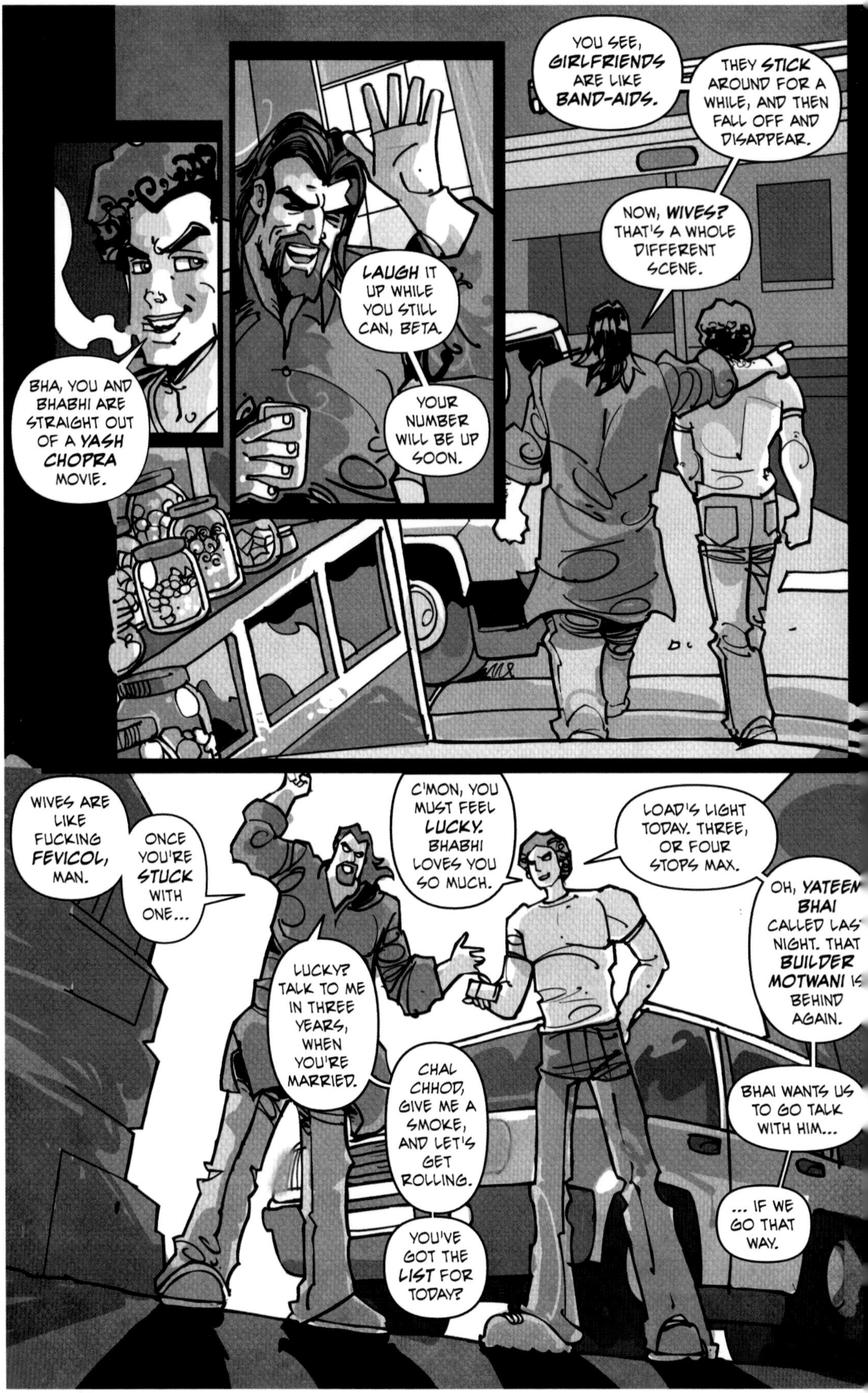
BHA, YOU AND BHABHI ARE STRAIGHT OUT OF A YASH CHOPRA MOVIE.
LAUGH IT UP WHILE YOU STILL CAN, BETA.
YOUR NUMBER WILL BE UP SOON.
YOU SEE, GIRLFRIENDS ARE LIKE BAND-AIDS.
THEY STICK AROUND FOR A WHILE, AND THEN FALL OFF AND DISAPPEAR.
NOW, WIVES? THAT'S A WHOLE DIFFERENT SCENE.
WIVES ARE LIKE FUCKING FEVICOL, MAN.
ONCE YOU'RE STUCK WITH ONE...
C'MON, YOU MUST FEEL LUCKY. BHABHI LOVES YOU SO MUCH.
LUCKY? TALK TO ME IN THREE YEARS, WHEN YOU'RE MARRIED.
CHAL CHHOD, GIVE ME A SMOKE, AND LET'S GET ROLLING.
YOU'VE GOT THE LIST FOR TODAY?
LOAD'S LIGHT TODAY. THREE, OR FOUR STOPS MAX.
OH, YATEEN BHAI CALLED LAST NIGHT. THAT BUILDER MOTWANI IS BEHIND AGAIN.
BHAI WANTS US TO GO TALK WITH HIM...
... IF WE GO THAT WAY.

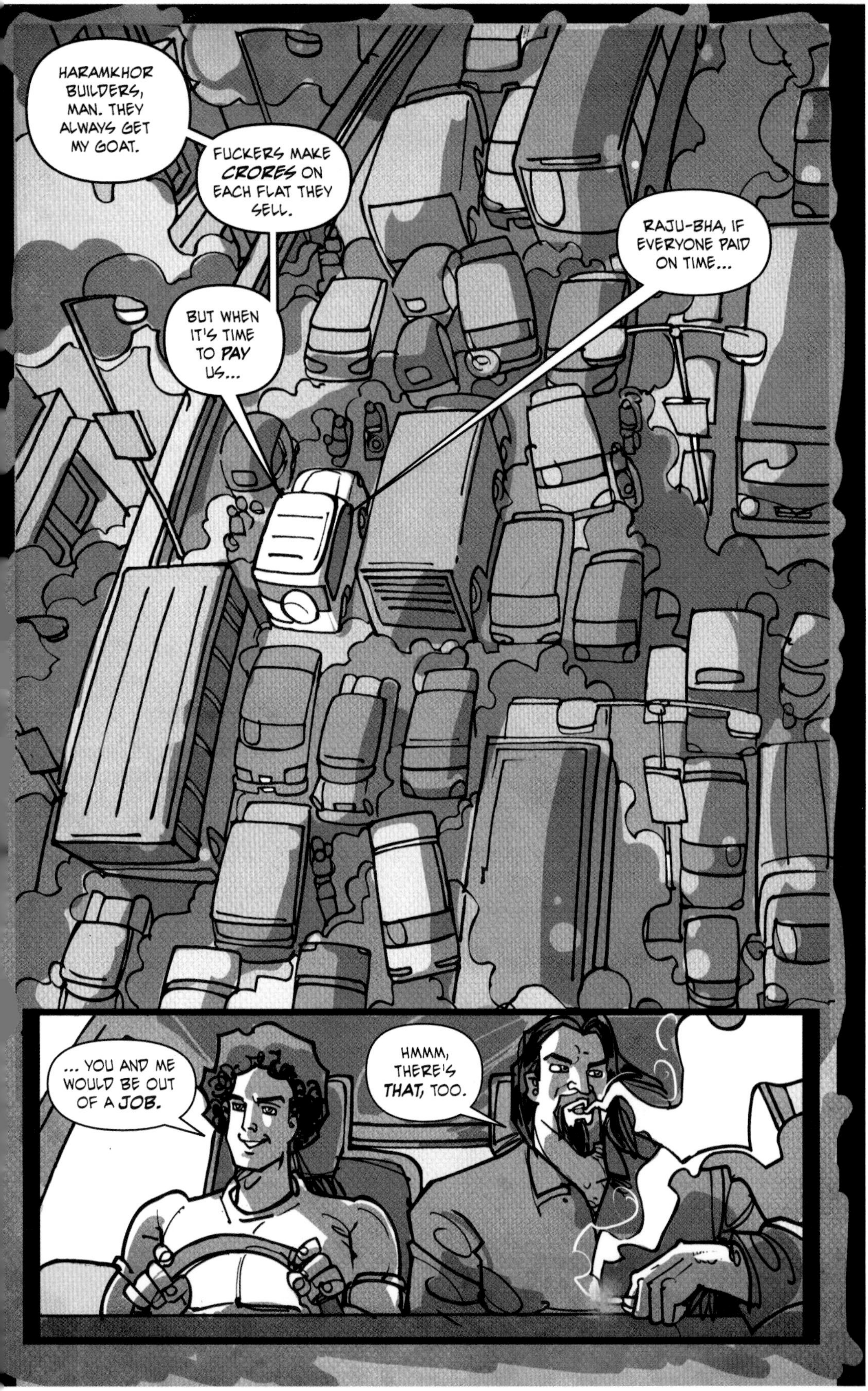
HARAMKHOR BUILDERS, MAN. THEY ALWAYS GET MY GOAT.
FUCKERS MAKE CRORES ON EACH FLAT THEY SELL.
BUT WHEN IT'S TIME TO PAY US...
RAJU-BHA, IF EVERYONE PAID ON TIME...
... YOU AND ME WOULD BE OUT OF A JOB.
HMMM, THERE'S THAT, TOO.

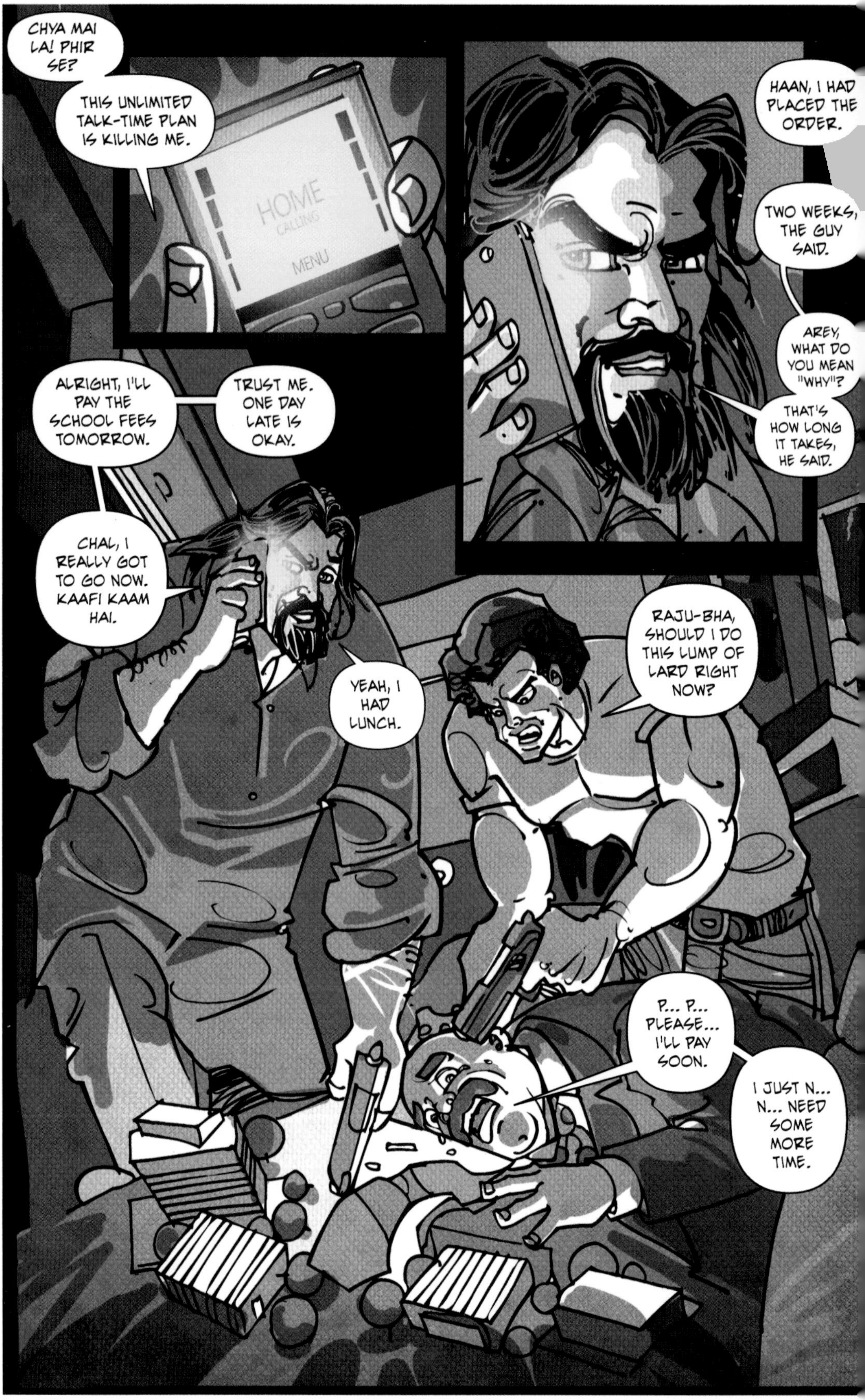
CHYA MAI LA! PHIR SE?
THIS UNLIMITED TALK-TIME PLAN IS KILLING ME.
HOME
CALLING
MENU
HAAN, I HAD PLACED THE ORDER.
TWO WEEKS, THE GUY SAID.
AREY, WHAT DO YOU MEAN "WHY"?
THAT'S HOW LONG IT TAKES, HE SAID.
ALRIGHT, I'LL PAY THE SCHOOL FEES TOMORROW.
TRUST ME. ONE DAY LATE IS OKAY.
CHAL, I REALLY GOT TO GO NOW. KAAFI KAAM HAI.
YEAH, I HAD LUNCH.
RAJU-BHA, SHOULD I DO THIS LUMP OF LARD RIGHT NOW?
P... P... PLEASE... I'LL PAY SOON.
I JUST N... N... NEED SOME MORE TIME.

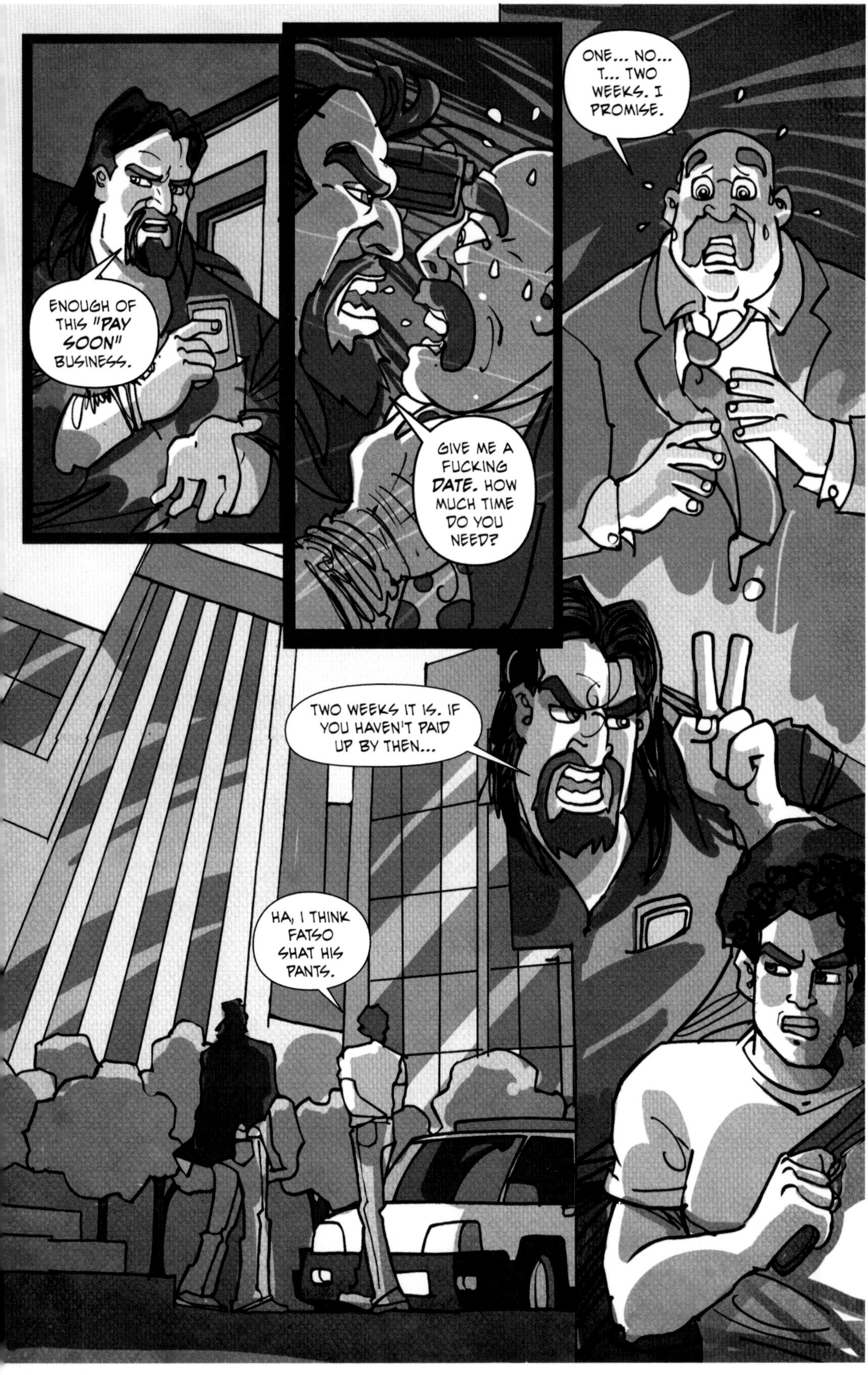
ENOUGH OF THIS "PAY SOON" BUSINESS.
GIVE ME A FUCKING DATE. HOW MUCH TIME DO YOU NEED?
ONE... NO... T... TWO WEEKS. I PROMISE.
TWO WEEKS IT IS. IF YOU HAVEN'T PAID UP BY THEN...
HA, I THINK FATSO SHAT HIS PANTS.

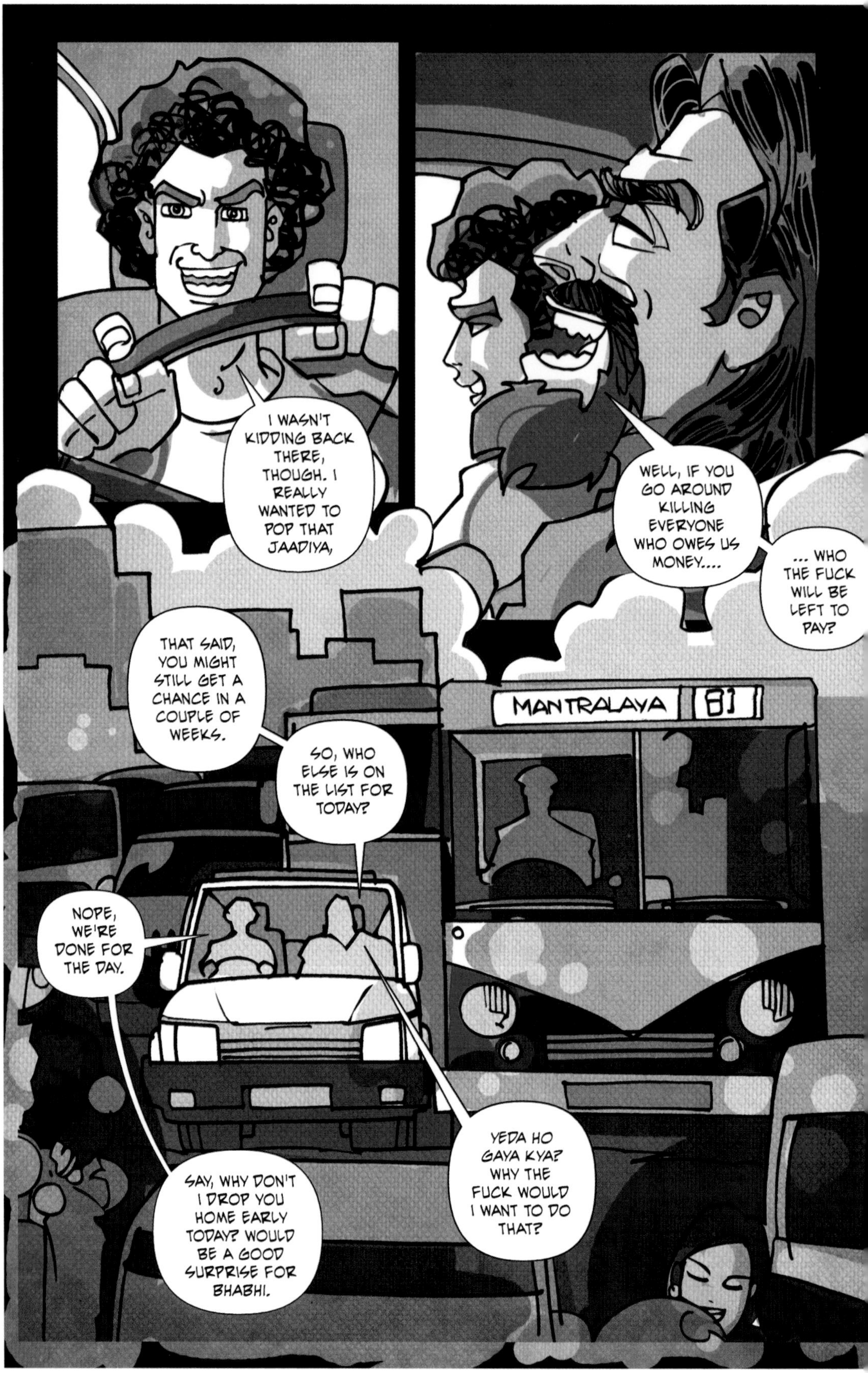
I WASN'T KIDDING BACK THERE, THOUGH. I REALLY WANTED TO POP THAT JAADIYA,
WELL, IF YOU GO AROUND KILLING EVERYONE WHO OWES US MONEY....
... WHO THE FUCK WILL BE LEFT TO PAY?
THAT SAID, YOU MIGHT STILL GET A CHANCE IN A COUPLE OF WEEKS.
SO, WHO ELSE IS ON THE LIST FOR TODAY?
MANTRALAYA 81
NOPE, WE'RE DONE FOR THE DAY.
SAY, WHY DON'T I DROP YOU HOME EARLY TODAY? WOULD BE A GOOD SURPRISE FOR BHABHI.
YEDA HO GAYA KYA? WHY THE FUCK WOULD I WANT TO DO THAT?

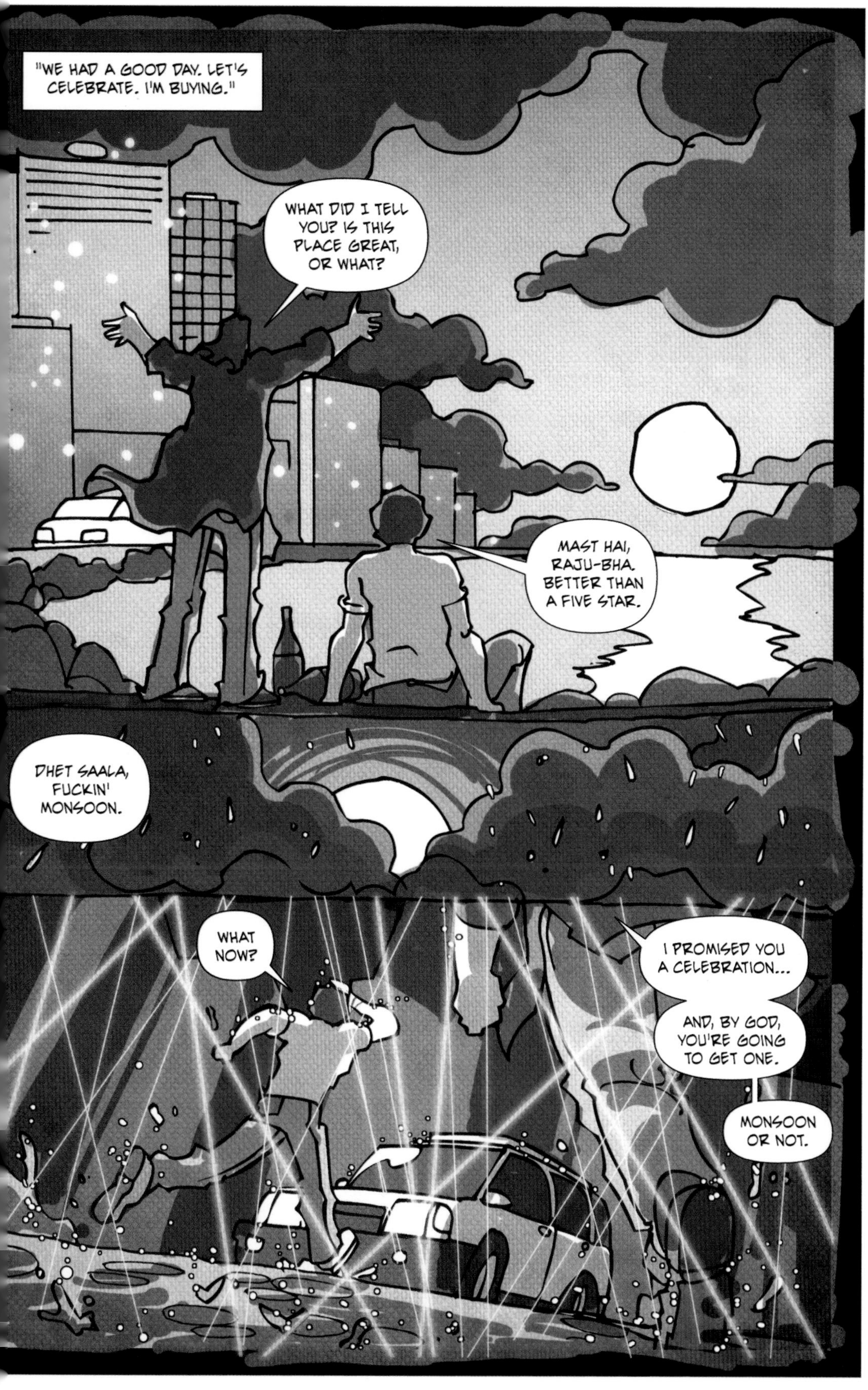
"WE HAD A GOOD DAY. LET'S CELEBRATE. I'M BUYING."
WHAT DID I TELL YOU? IS THIS PLACE GREAT, OR WHAT?
MAST HAI, RAJU-BHA. BETTER THAN A FIVE STAR.
DHET SAALA, FUCKIN' MONSOON.
WHAT NOW?
I PROMISED YOU A CELEBRATION...
AND, BY GOD, YOU'RE GOING TO GET ONE.
MONSOON OR NOT.

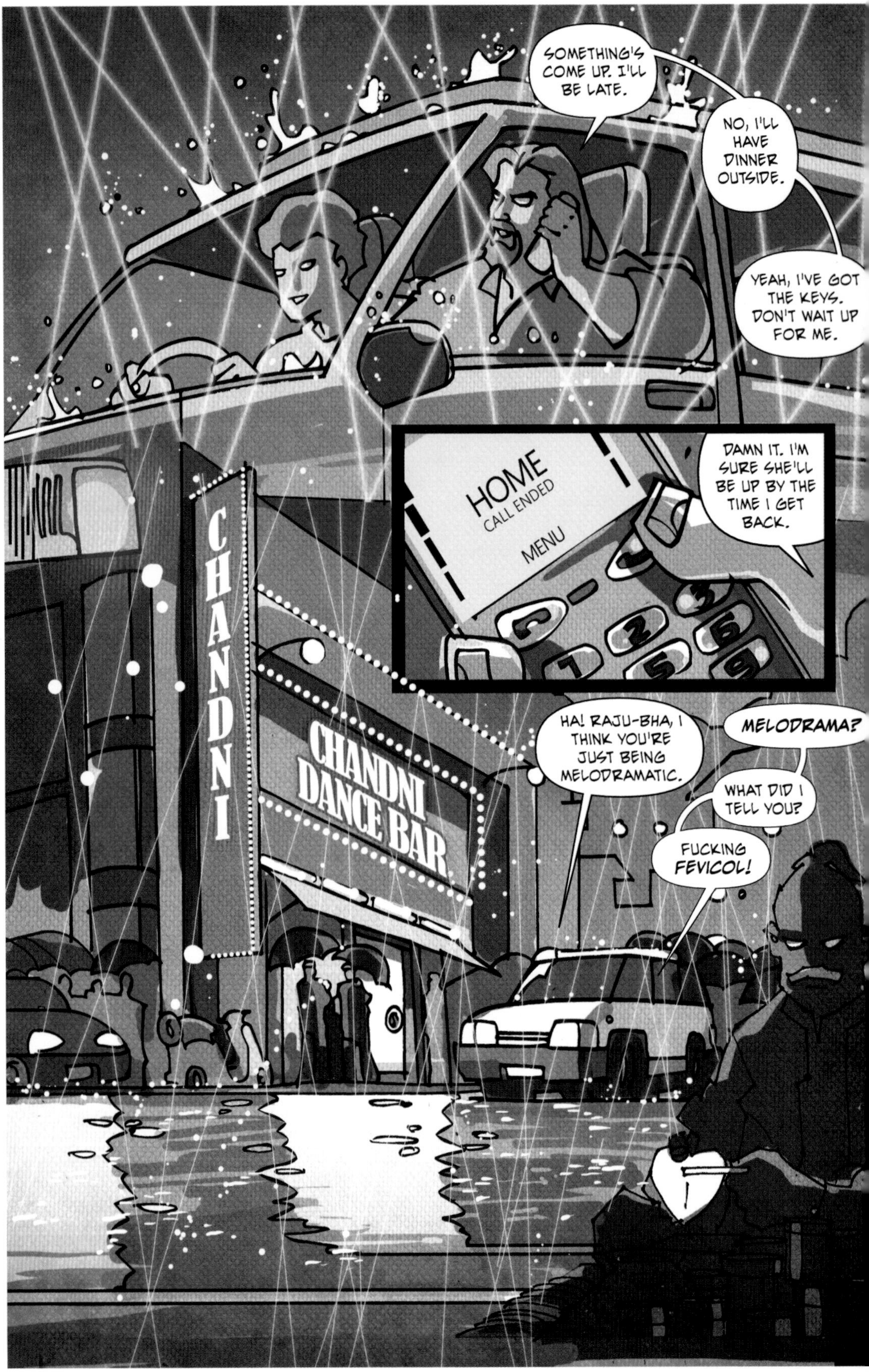
SOMETHING'S COME UP. I'LL BE LATE.
NO, I'LL HAVE DINNER OUTSIDE.
YEAH, I'VE GOT THE KEYS. DON'T WAIT UP FOR ME.
HOME
CALL ENDED
MENU
DAMN IT. I'M SURE SHE'LL BE UP BY THE TIME I GET BACK.
CHANDNI
CHANDNI DANCE BAR
HA! RAJU-BHA, I THINK YOU'RE JUST BEING MELODRAMATIC.
MELODRAMA?
WHAT DID I TELL YOU?
FUCKING FEVICOL!

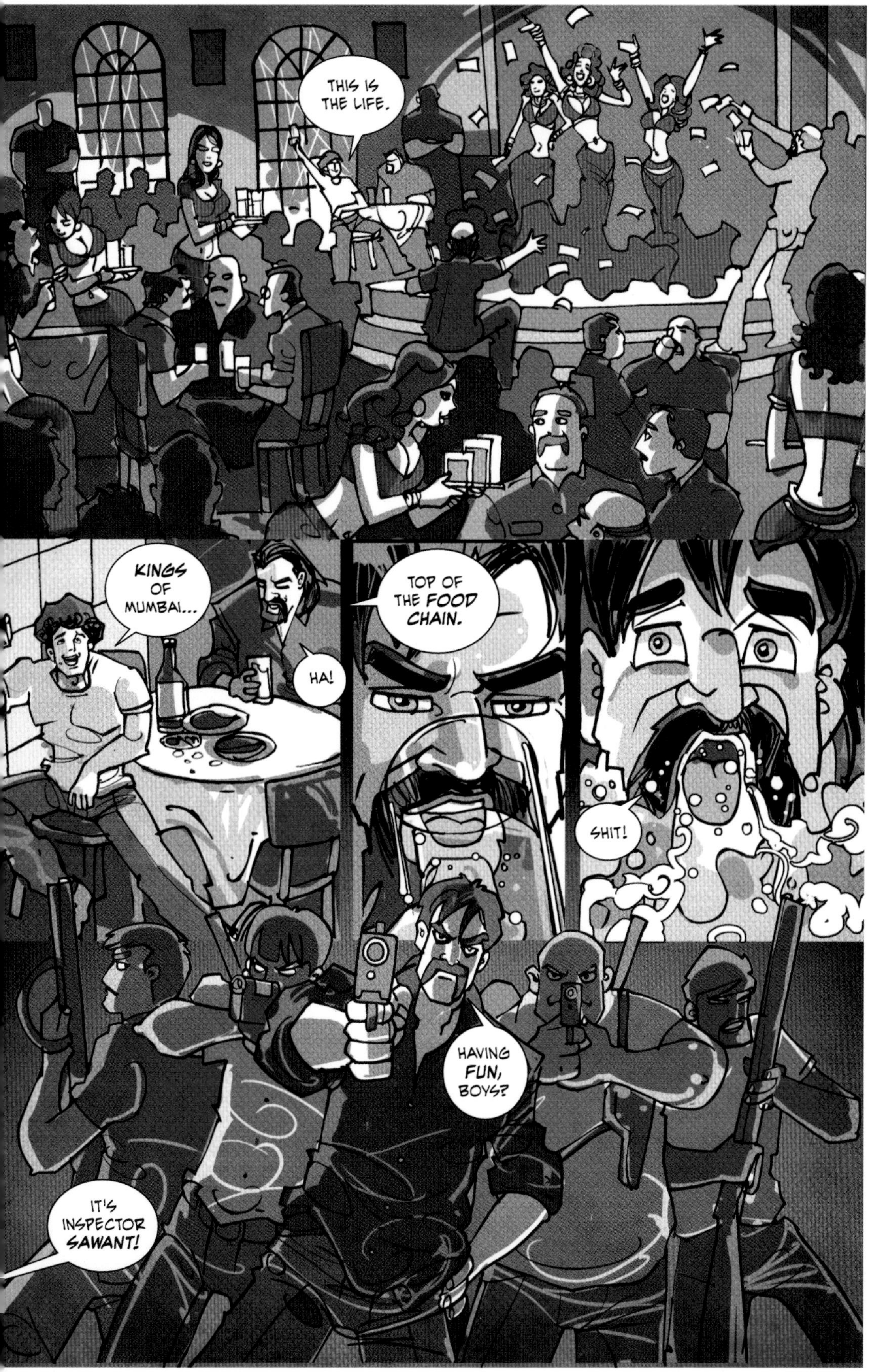
THIS IS THE LIFE.
KINGS OF MUMBAI...
HA!
TOP OF THE FOOD CHAIN.
SHIT!
HAVING FUN, BOYS?
IT'S INSPECTOR SAWANT!

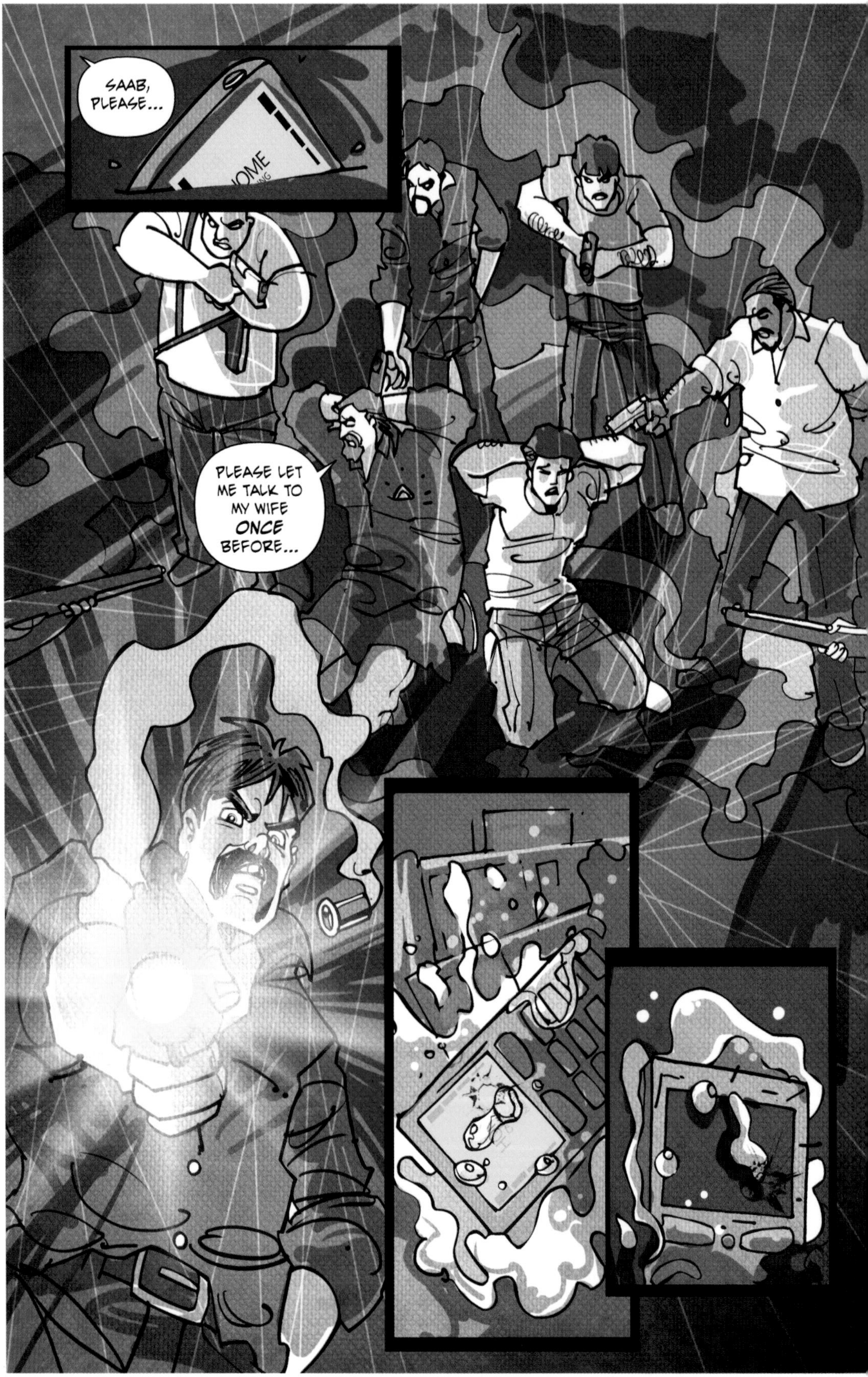
SAAB, PLEASE...
PLEASE LET ME TALK TO MY WIFE ONCE BEFORE...

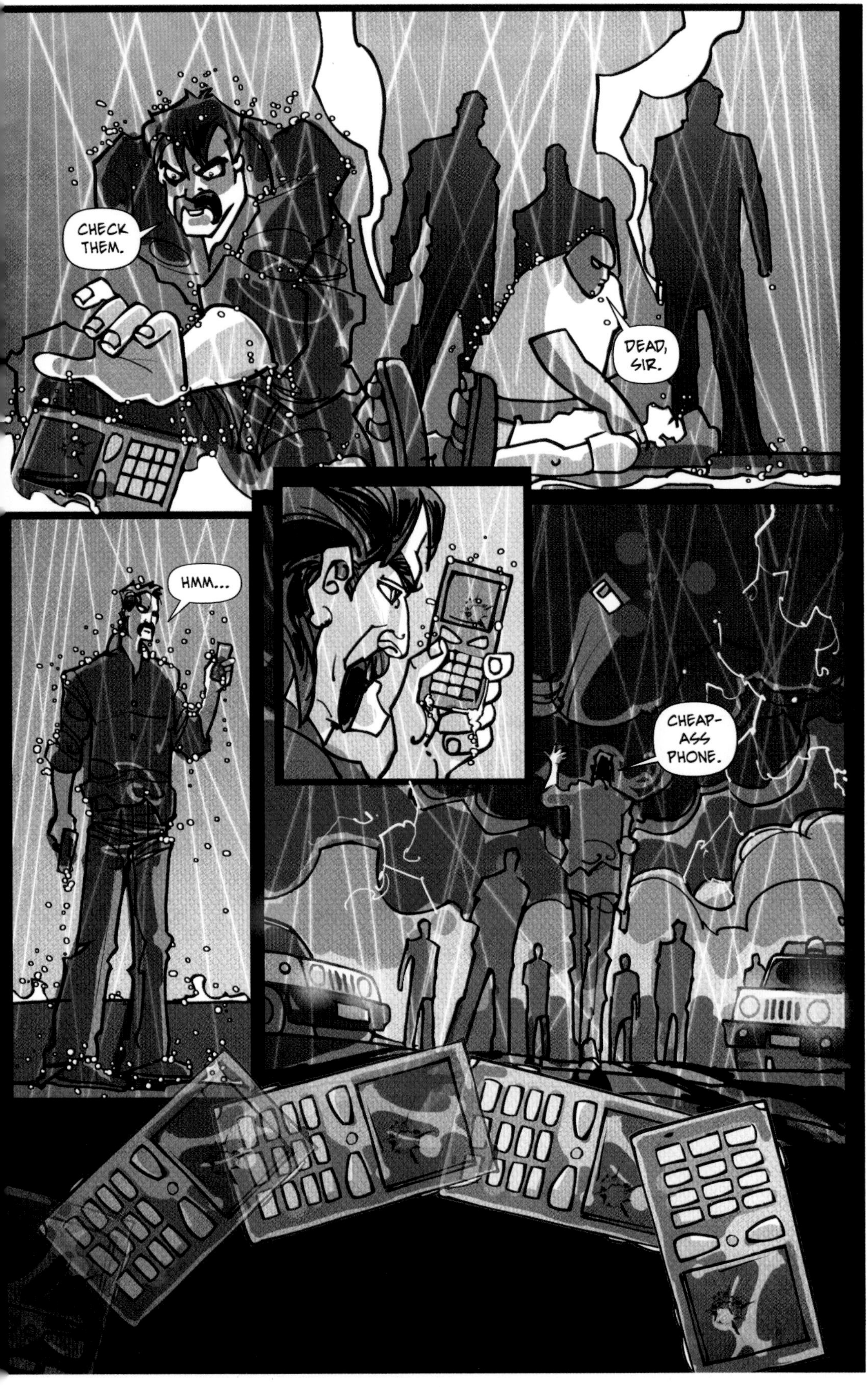
CHECK THEM.
DEAD, SIR.
HMM...
CHEAP-ASS PHONE.

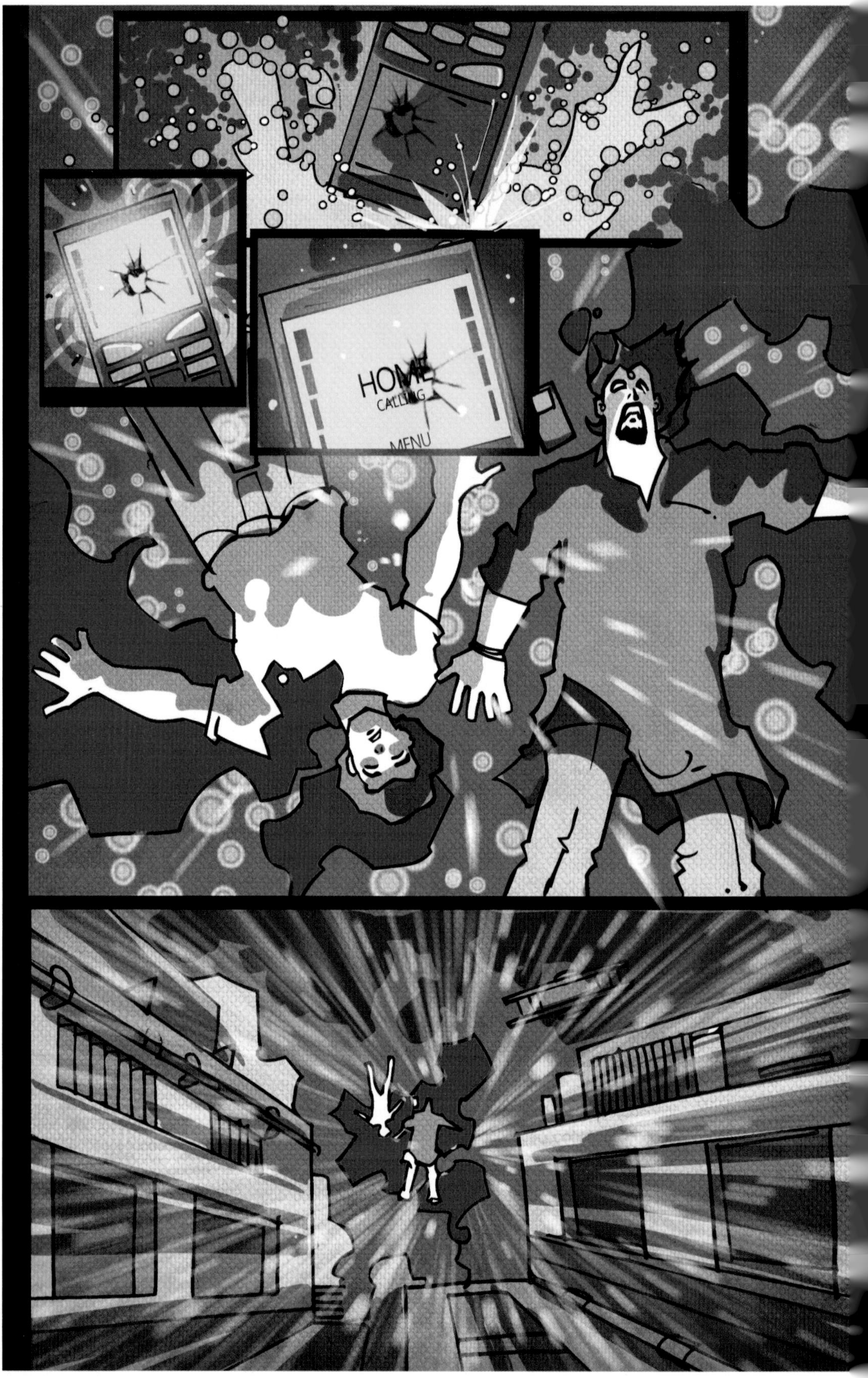
HOME
CALLING
MENU

FOR ANURAG, SHIMIT, AND RAM GOPAL - THANK YOU FOR SHOWING US A DARK AND GRUNGY WORLD BEYOND CHIFFON SAREES AND SONG & DANCE AT THE SWISS ALPS.

-- SAURAV & VI

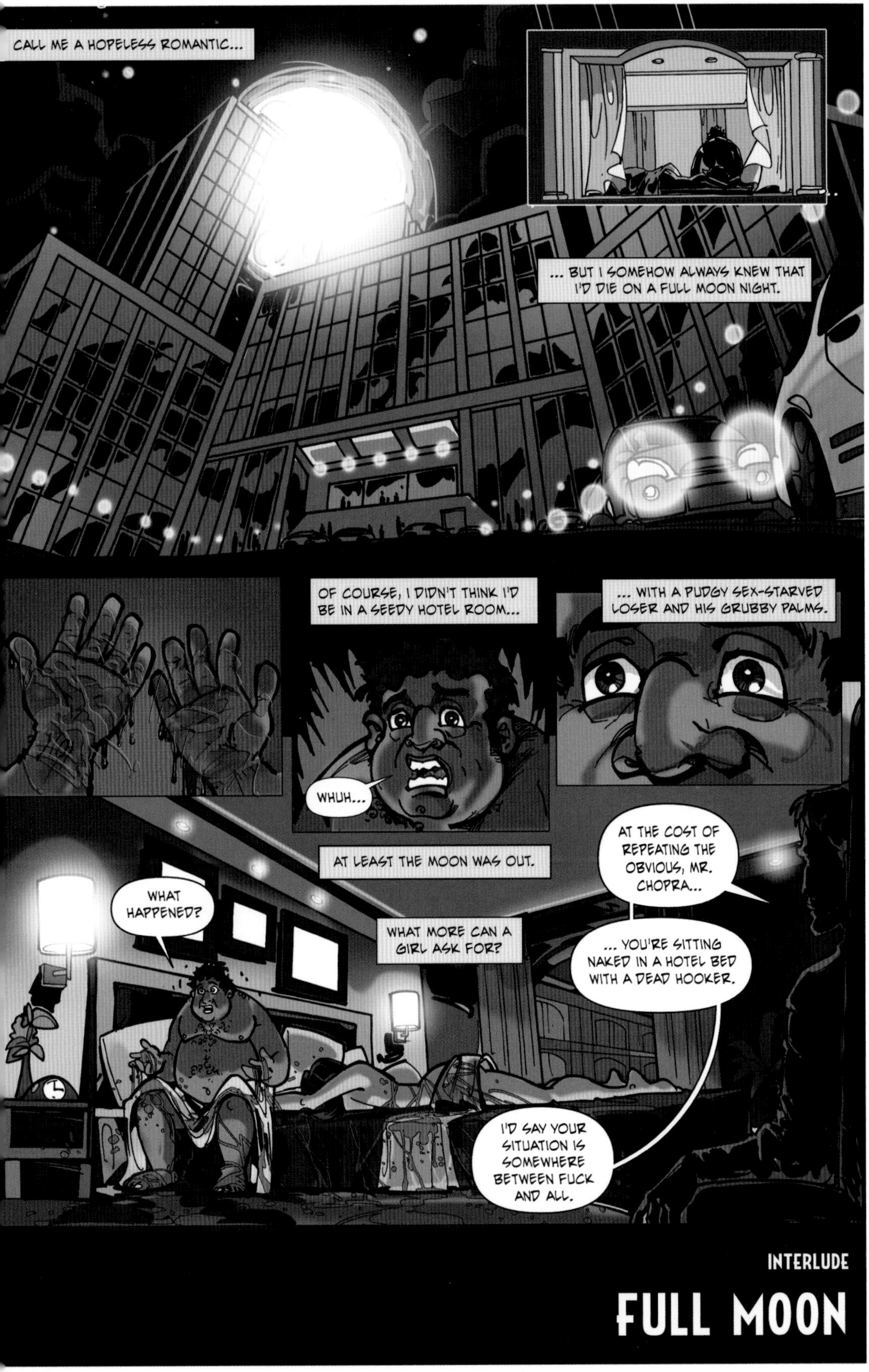
CALL ME A HOPELESS ROMANTIC...
... BUT I SOMEHOW ALWAYS KNEW THAT I'D DIE ON A FULL MOON NIGHT.
OF COURSE, I DIDN'T THINK I'D BE IN A SEEDY HOTEL ROOM...
WHUH...
... WITH A PUDGY SEX-STARVED LOSER AND HIS GRUBBY PALMS.
AT LEAST THE MOON WAS OUT.
WHAT HAPPENED?
WHAT MORE CAN A GIRL ASK FOR?
AT THE COST OF REPEATING THE OBVIOUS, MR. CHOPRA...
... YOU'RE SITTING NAKED IN A HOTEL BED WITH A DEAD HOOKER.
I'D SAY YOUR SITUATION IS SOMEWHERE BETWEEN FUCK AND ALL.

INTERLUDE

FULL MOON

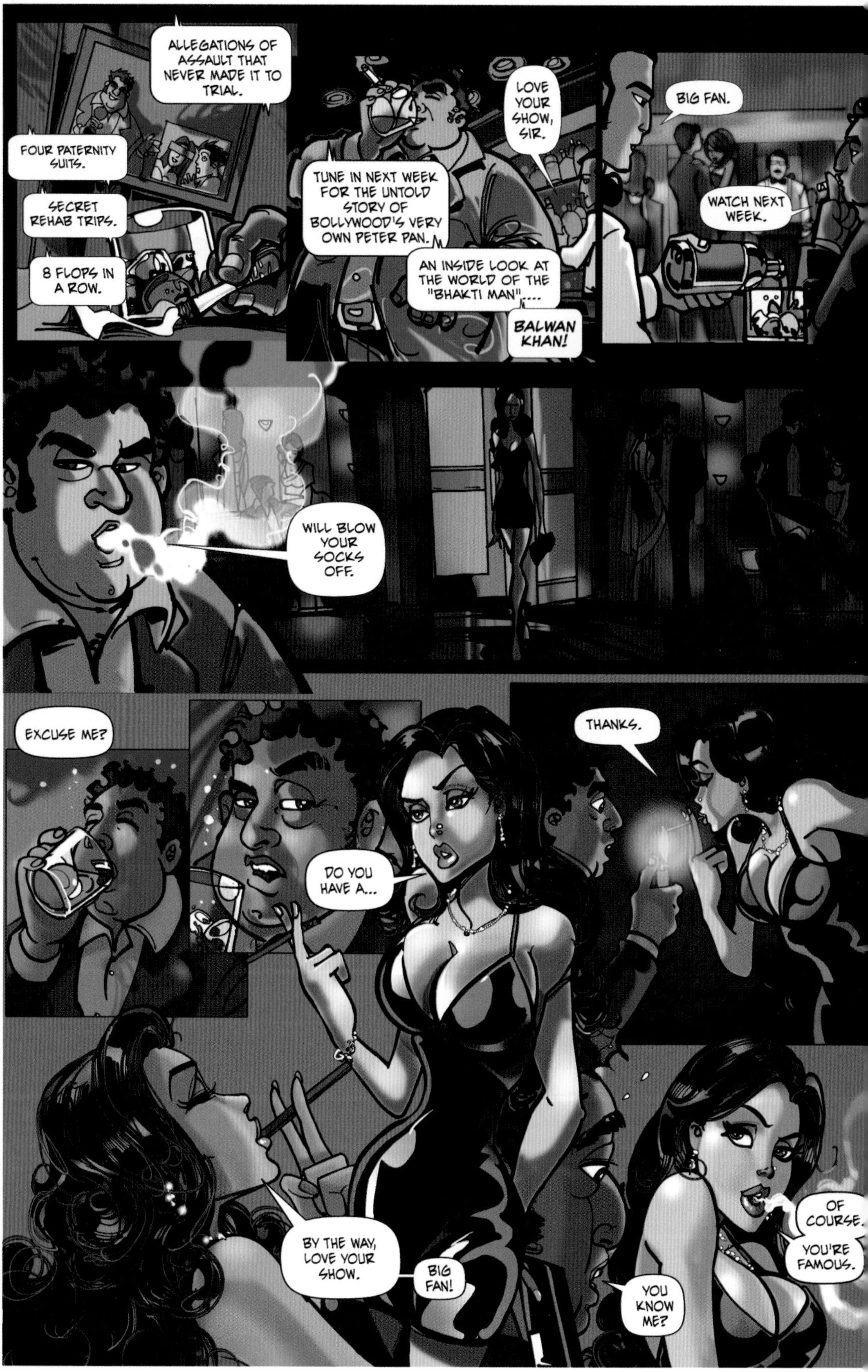
ALLEGATIONS OF ASSAULT THAT NEVER MADE IT TO TRIAL.
FOUR PATERNITY SUITS.
SECRET REHAB TRIPS.
8 FLOPS IN A ROW.
TUNE IN NEXT WEEK FOR THE UNTOLD STORY OF BOLLYWOOD'S VERY OWN PETER PAN.
LOVE YOUR SHOW, SIR.
AN INSIDE LOOK AT THE WORLD OF THE "BHAKTI MAN"....
BALWAN KHAN!
BIG FAN.
WATCH NEXT WEEK.
WILL BLOW YOUR SOCKS OFF.
EXCUSE ME?
DO YOU HAVE A...
THANKS.
BY THE WAY, LOVE YOUR SHOW.
BIG FAN!
YOU KNOW ME?
OF COURSE.
YOU'RE FAMOUS.

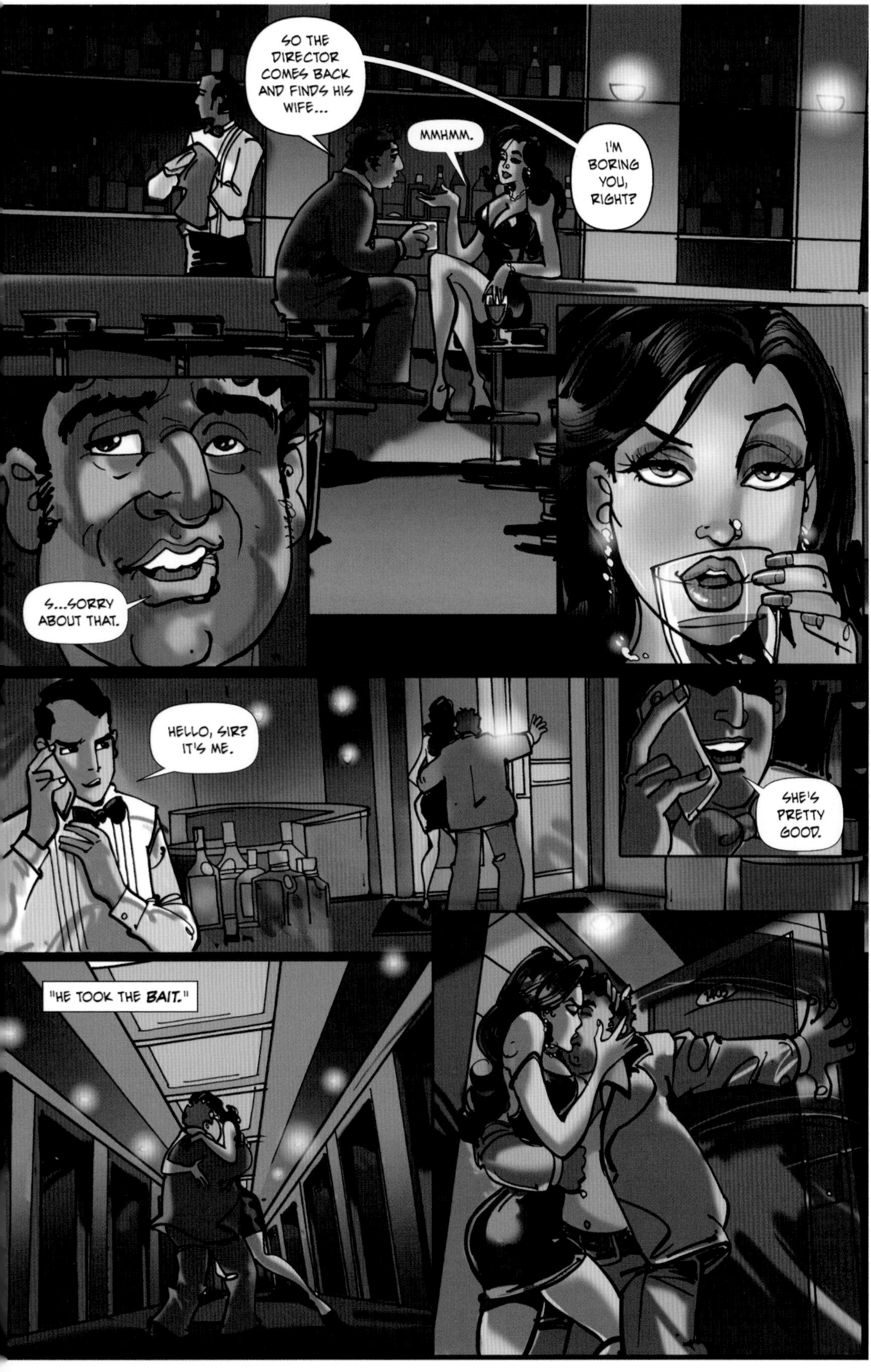
SO THE DIRECTOR COMES BACK AND FINDS HIS WIFE...
MMHMM.
I'M BORING YOU, RIGHT?
S...SORRY ABOUT THAT.
HELLO, SIR? IT'S ME.
SHE'S PRETTY GOOD.
"HE TOOK THE BAIT."

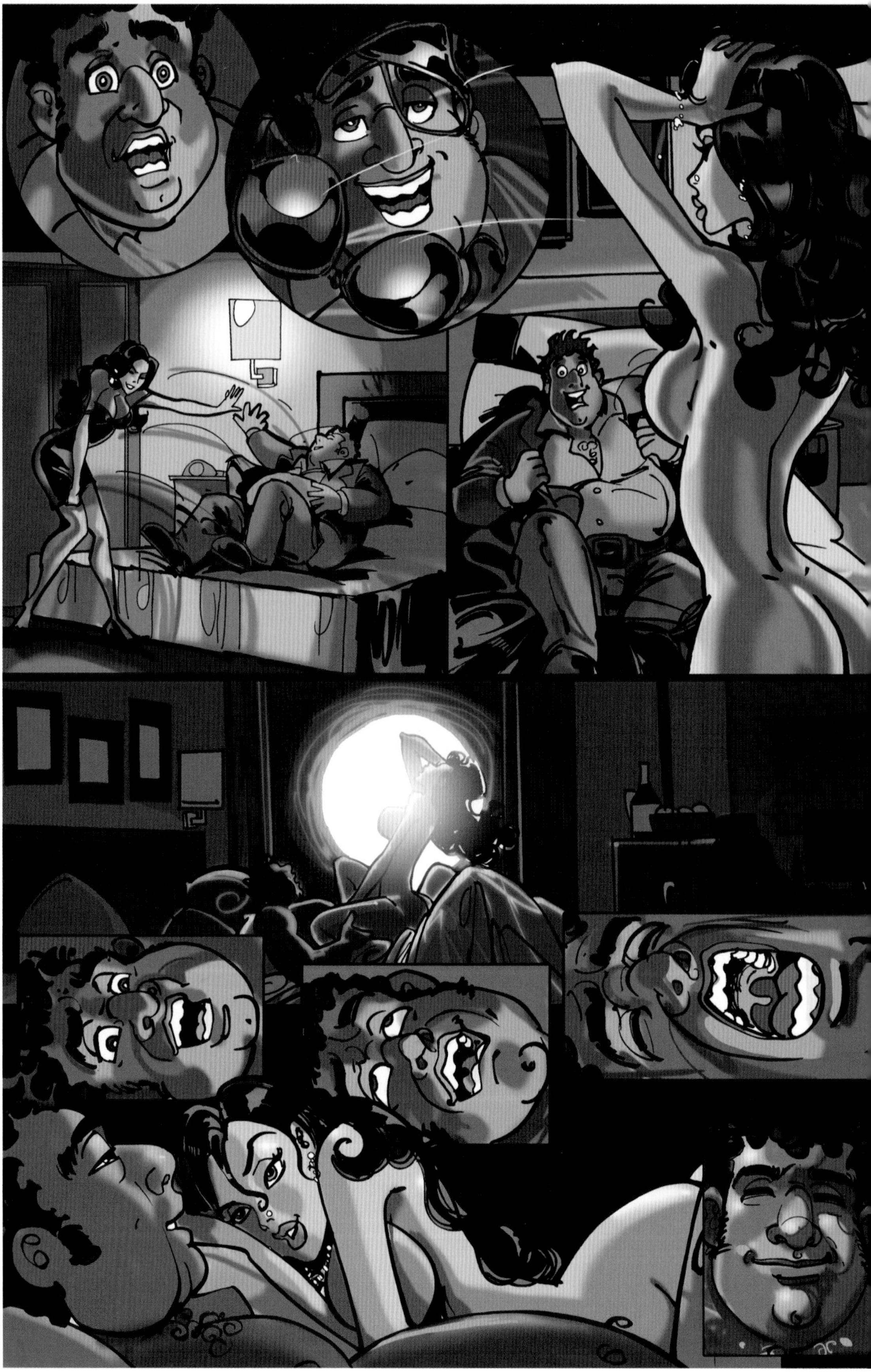

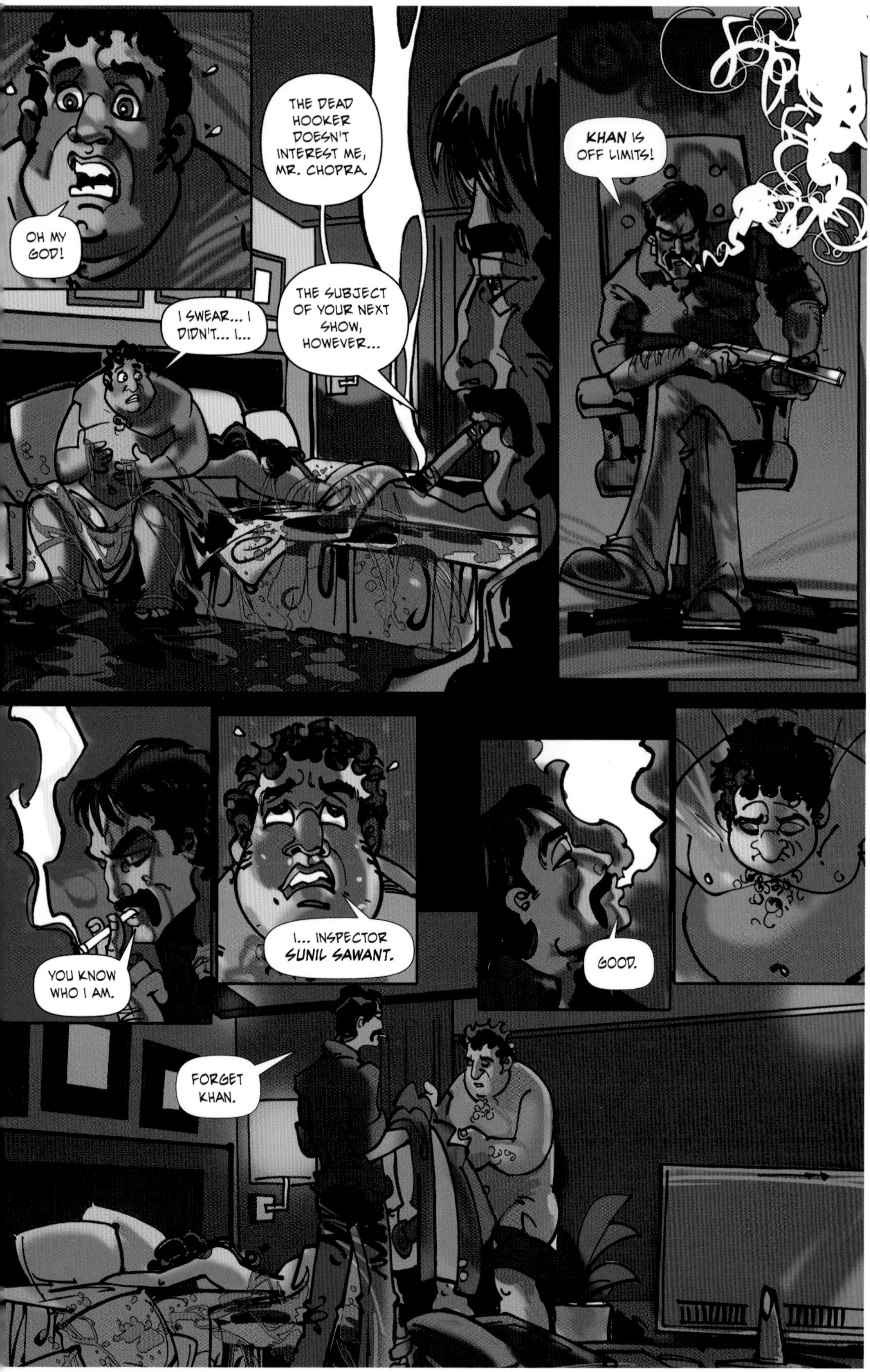
OH MY GOD!
THE DEAD HOOKER DOESN'T INTEREST ME, MR. CHOPRA.
I SWEAR... I DIDN'T... I...
THE SUBJECT OF YOUR NEXT SHOW, HOWEVER...
KHAN IS OFF LIMITS!
YOU KNOW WHO I AM.
I... INSPECTOR SUNIL SAWANT.
GOOD.
FORGET KHAN.

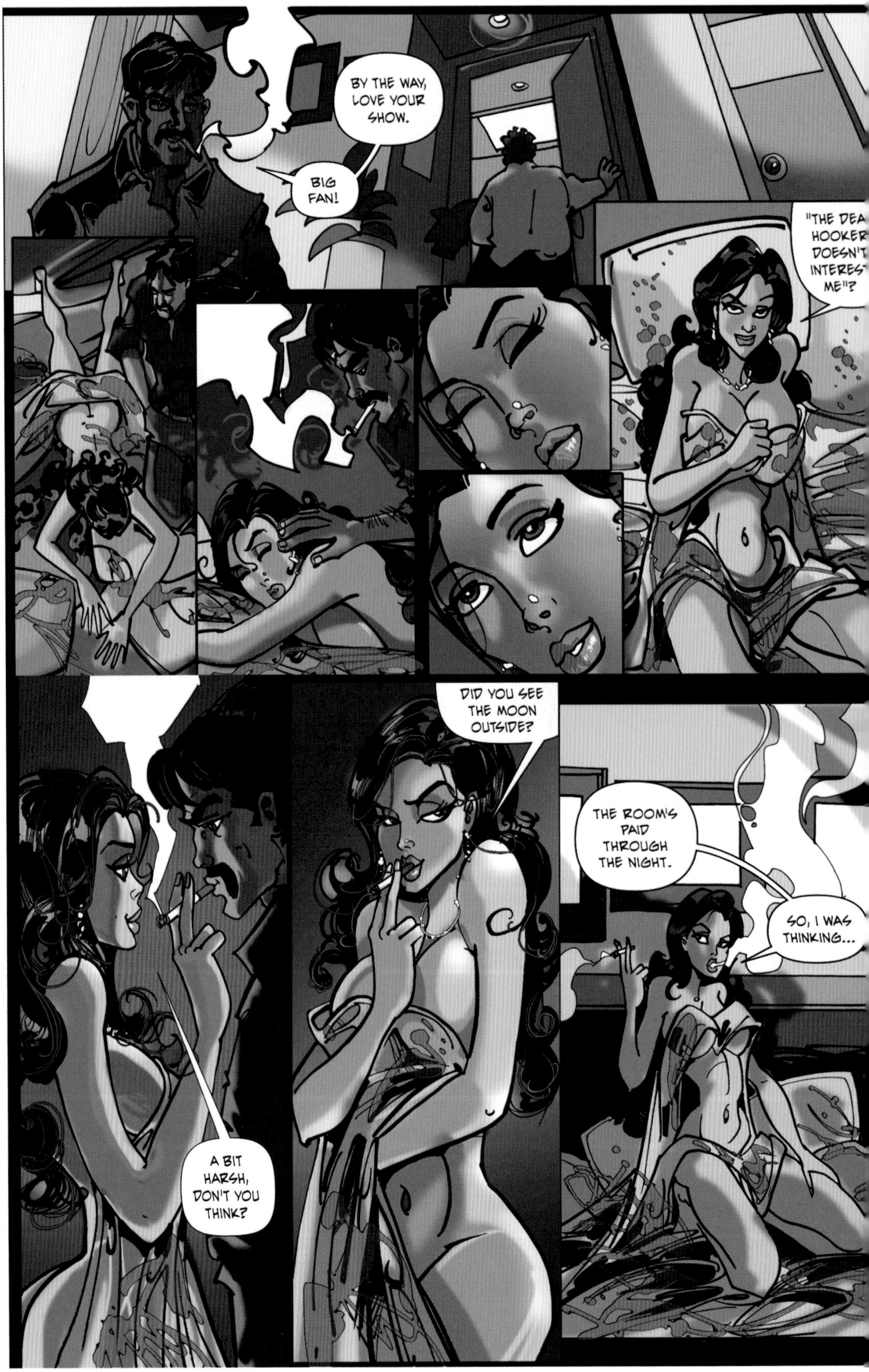
BY THE WAY, LOVE YOUR SHOW.
BIG FAN!
"THE DEA HOOKER DOESN'T INTERES ME"?
A BIT HARSH, DON'T YOU THINK?
DID YOU SEE THE MOON OUTSIDE?
THE ROOM'S PAID THROUGH THE NIGHT.
SO, I WAS THINKING...

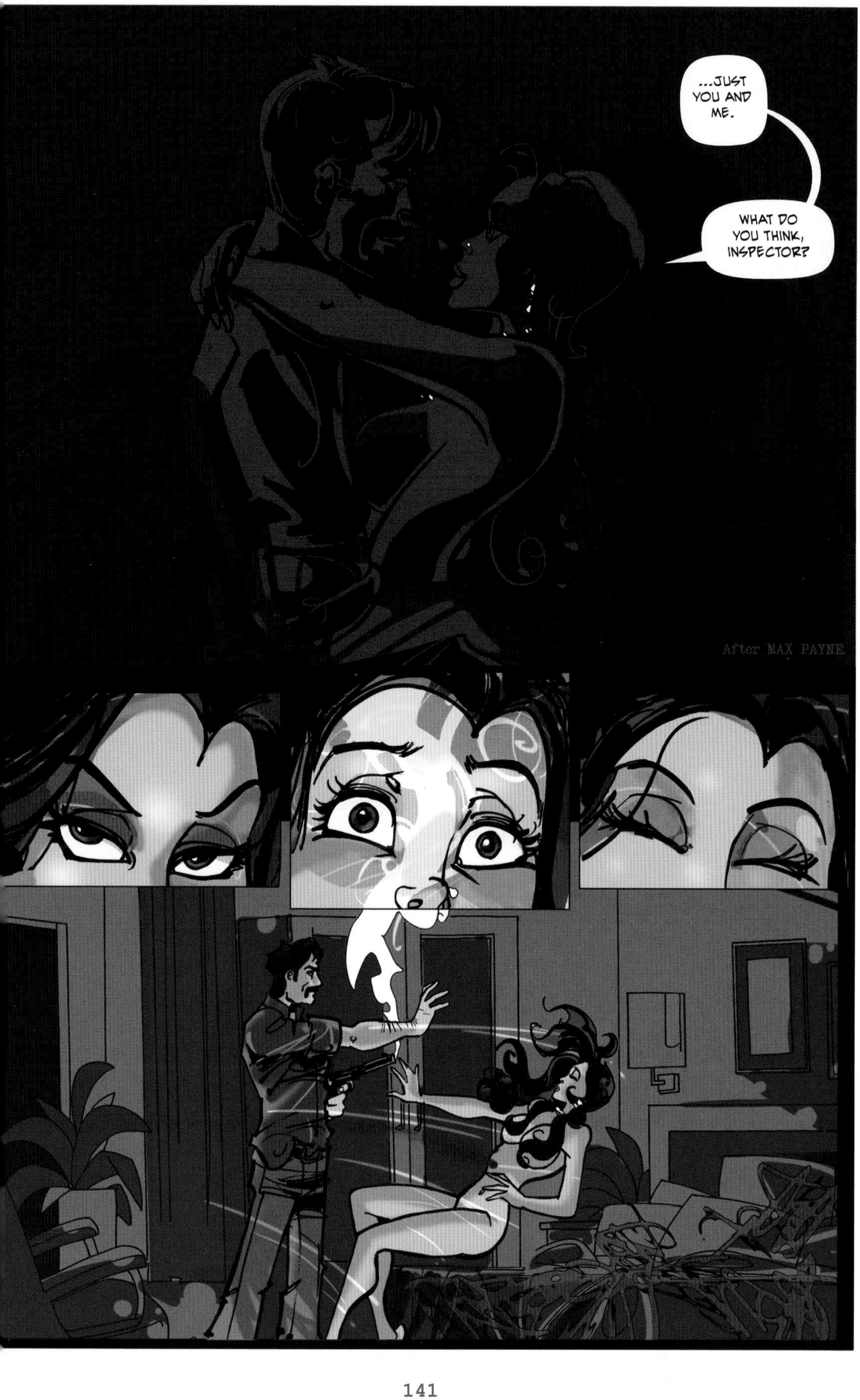
...JUST YOU AND ME.
WHAT DO YOU THINK, INSPECTOR?
After MAX PAYNE

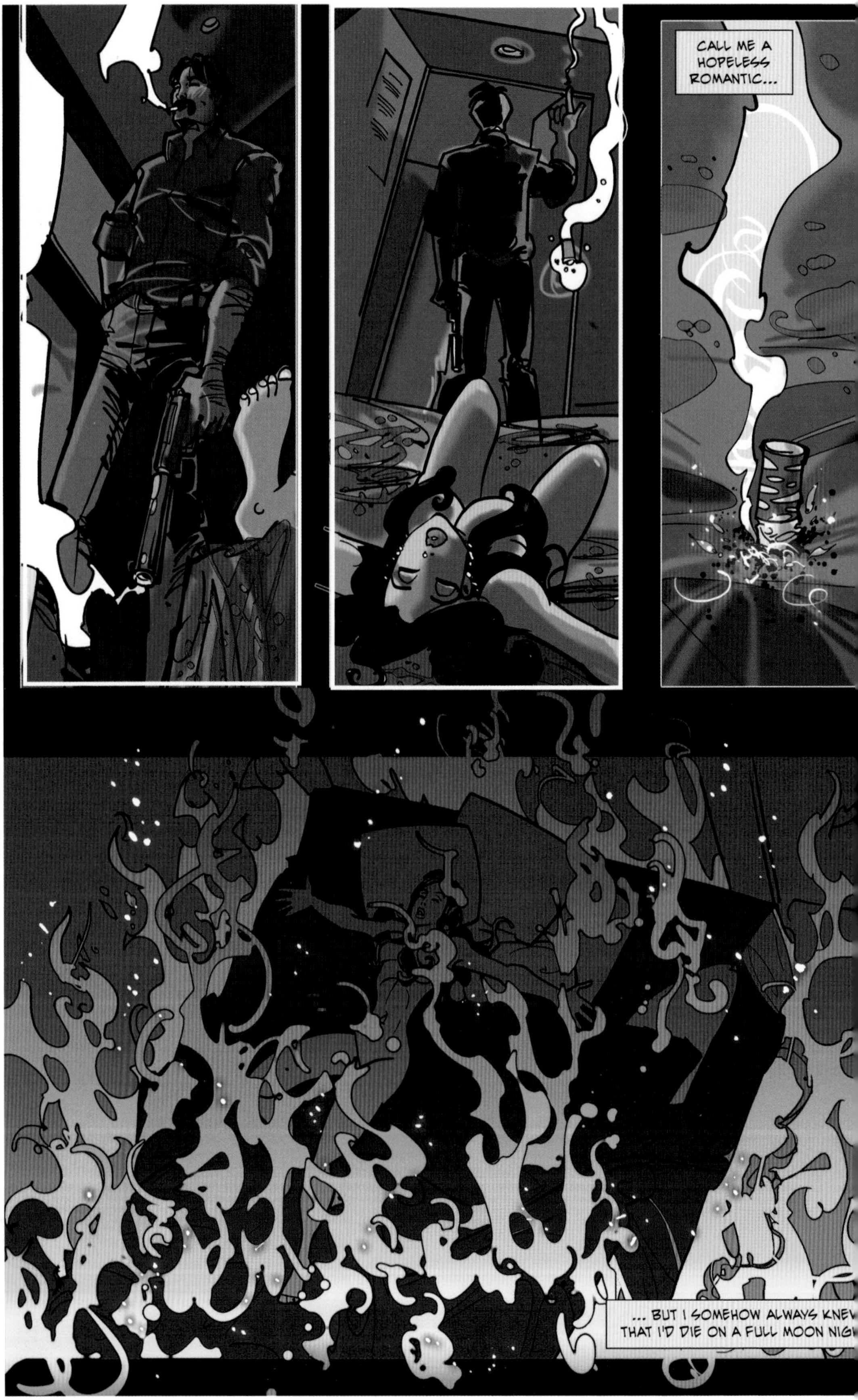
CALL ME A HOPELESS ROMANTIC...
... BUT I SOMEHOW ALWAYS KNEW
THAT I'D DIE ON A FULL MOON NIG

Dedicated to PARVEEN BABI (1954-2005)

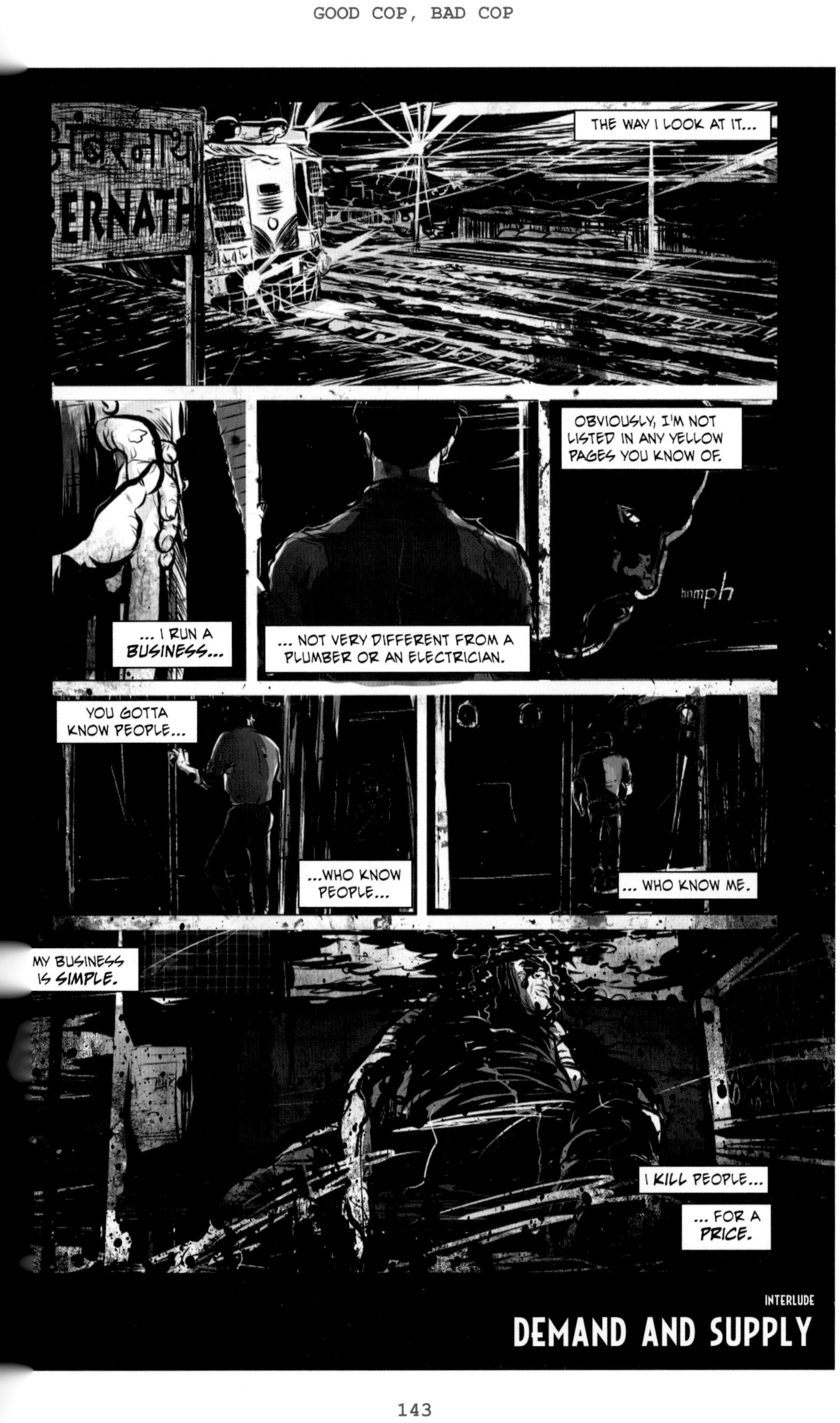
THE WAY I LOOK AT IT...
... I RUN A BUSINESS...
... NOT VERY DIFFERENT FROM A PLUMBER OR AN ELECTRICIAN.
OBVIOUSLY, I'M NOT LISTED IN ANY YELLOW PAGES YOU KNOW OF.
hnmph
YOU GOTTA KNOW PEOPLE...
...WHO KNOW PEOPLE...
... WHO KNOW ME.
MY BUSINESS IS SIMPLE.
I KILL PEOPLE...
... FOR A PRICE.

INTERLUDE

DEMAND AND SUPPLY

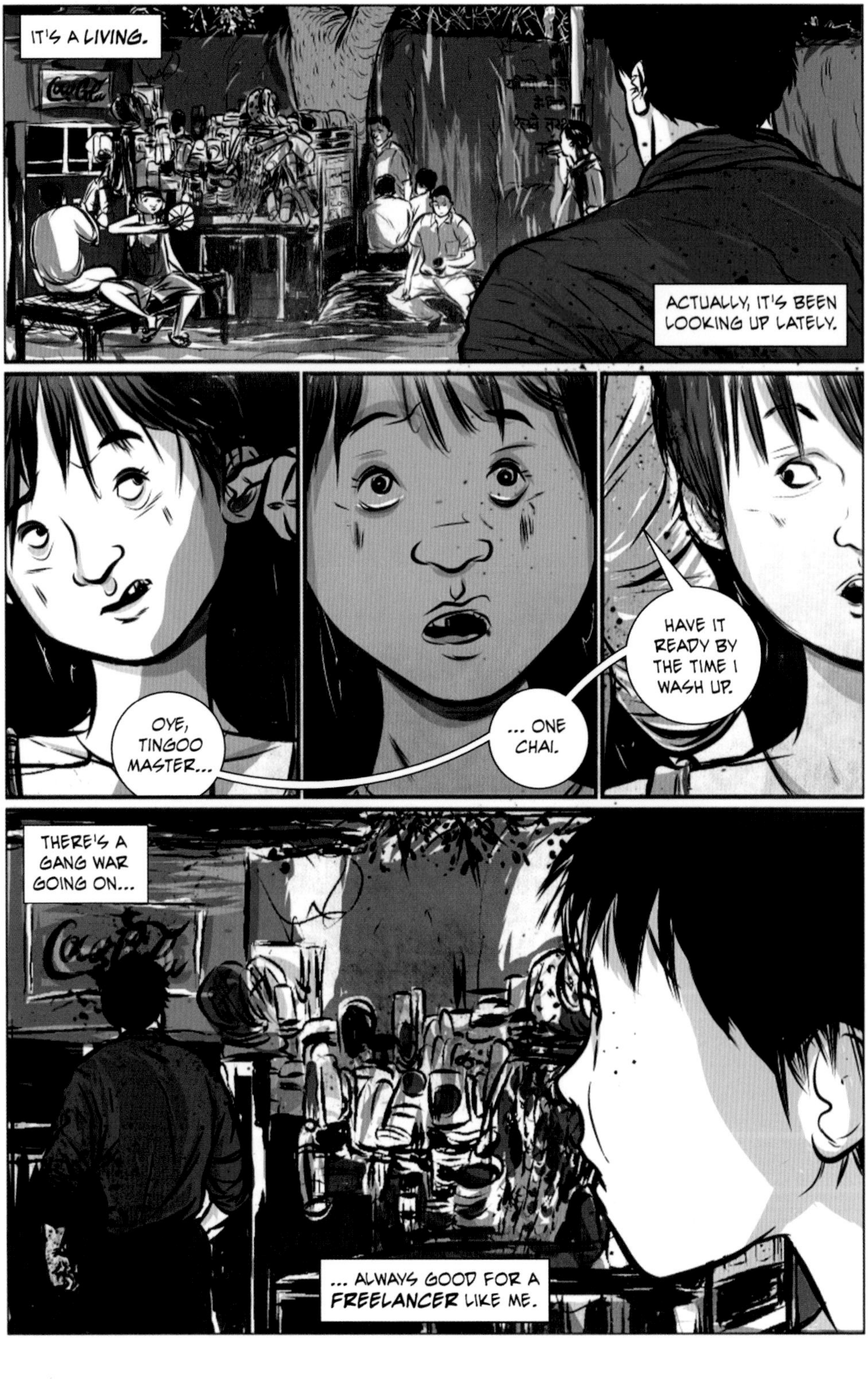
IT'S A LIVING.
ACTUALLY, IT'S BEEN LOOKING UP LATELY.
OYE, TINGOO MASTER...
... ONE CHAI.
HAVE IT READY BY THE TIME I WASH UP.
THERE'S A GANG WAR GOING ON...
... ALWAYS GOOD FOR A FREELANCER LIKE ME.

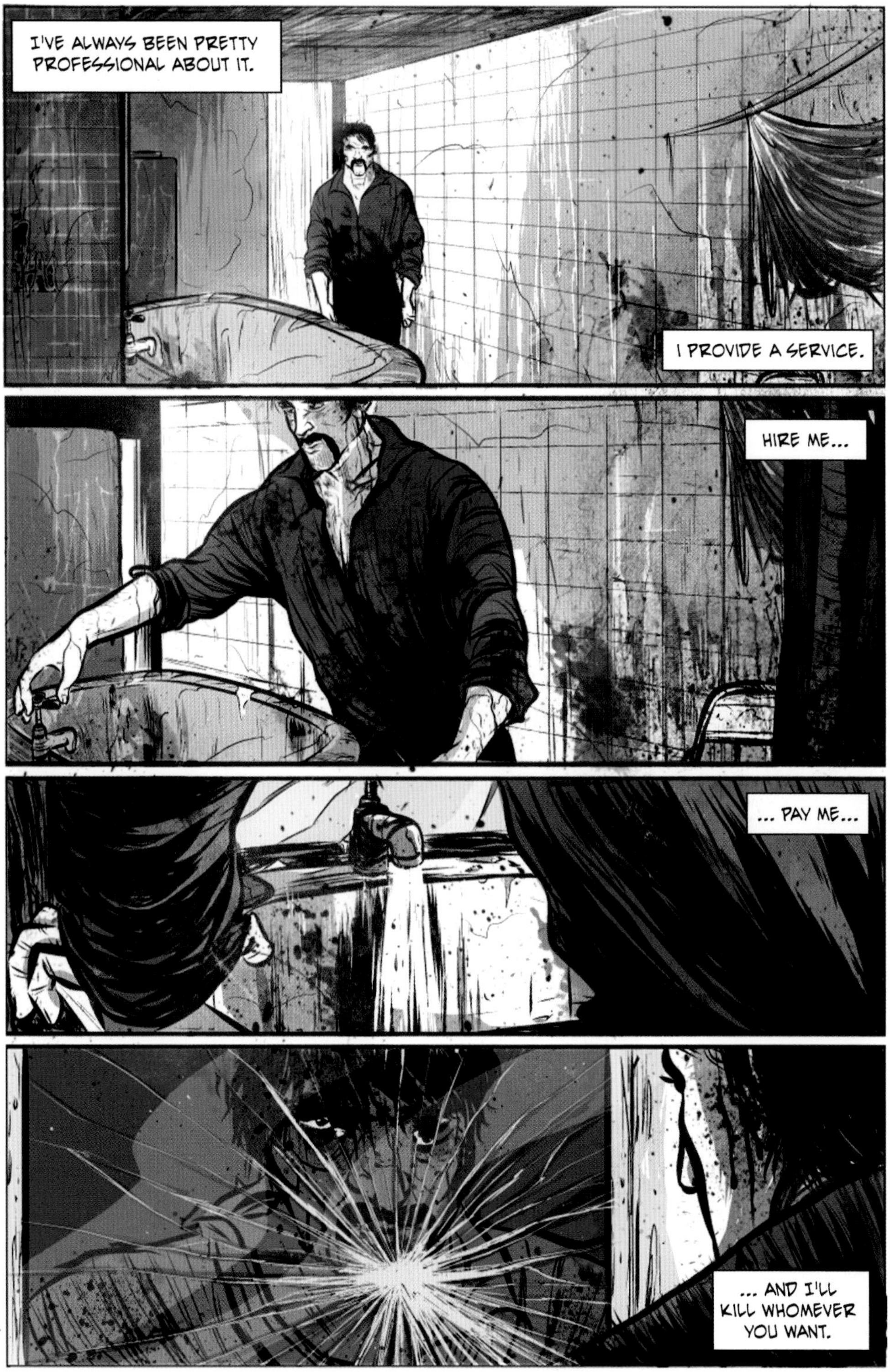
I'VE ALWAYS BEEN PRETTY PROFESSIONAL ABOUT IT.
I PROVIDE A SERVICE.
HIRE ME...
... PAY ME...
... AND I'LL KILL WHOMEVER YOU WANT.

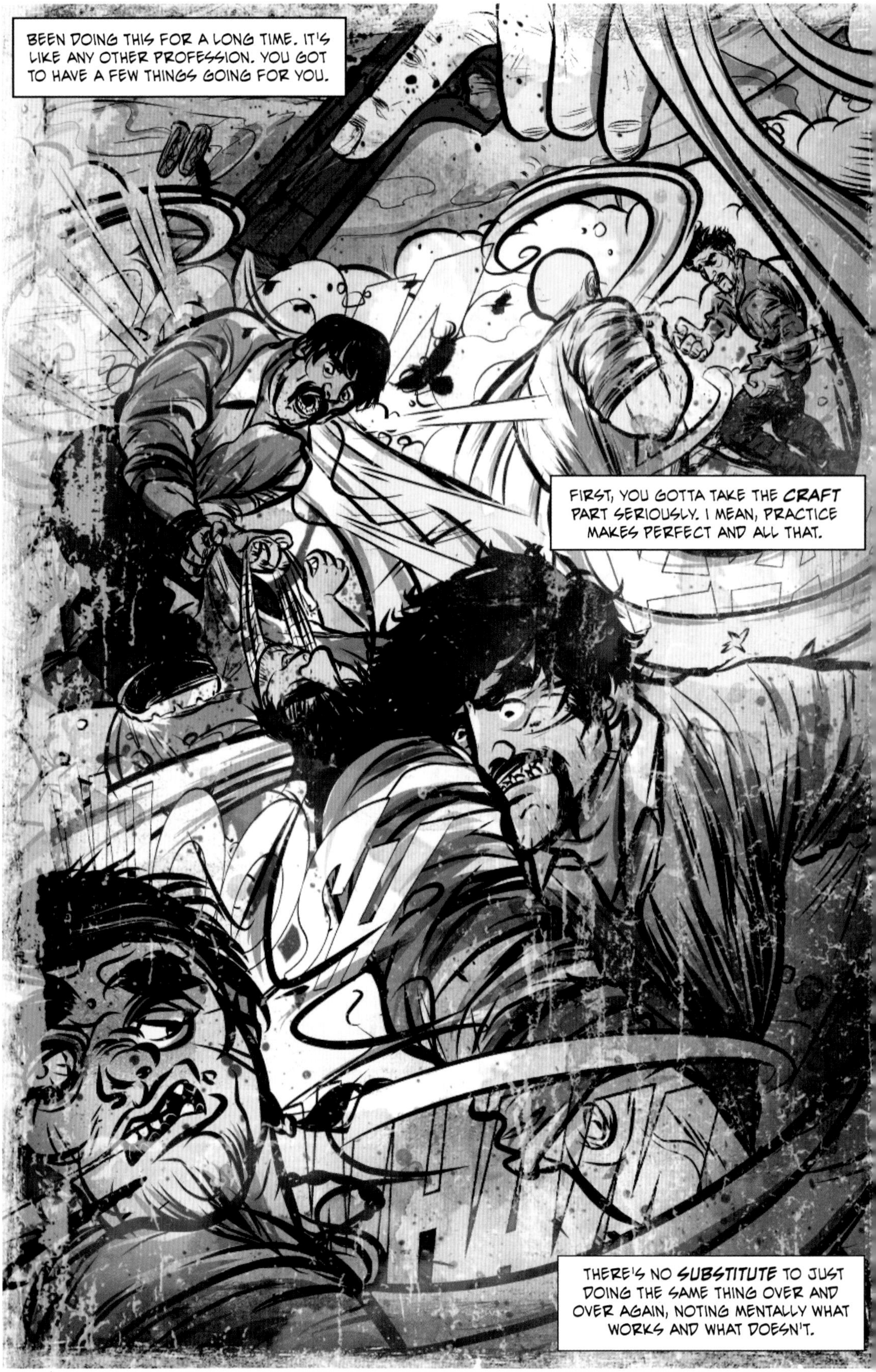
BEEN DOING THIS FOR A LONG TIME. IT'S LIKE ANY OTHER PROFESSION. YOU GOT TO HAVE A FEW THINGS GOING FOR YOU.
FIRST, YOU GOTTA TAKE THE CRAFT PART SERIOUSLY. I MEAN, PRACTICE MAKES PERFECT AND ALL THAT.
THERE'S NO SUBSTITUTE TO JUST DOING THE SAME THING OVER AND OVER AGAIN, NOTING MENTALLY WHAT WORKS AND WHAT DOESN'T.

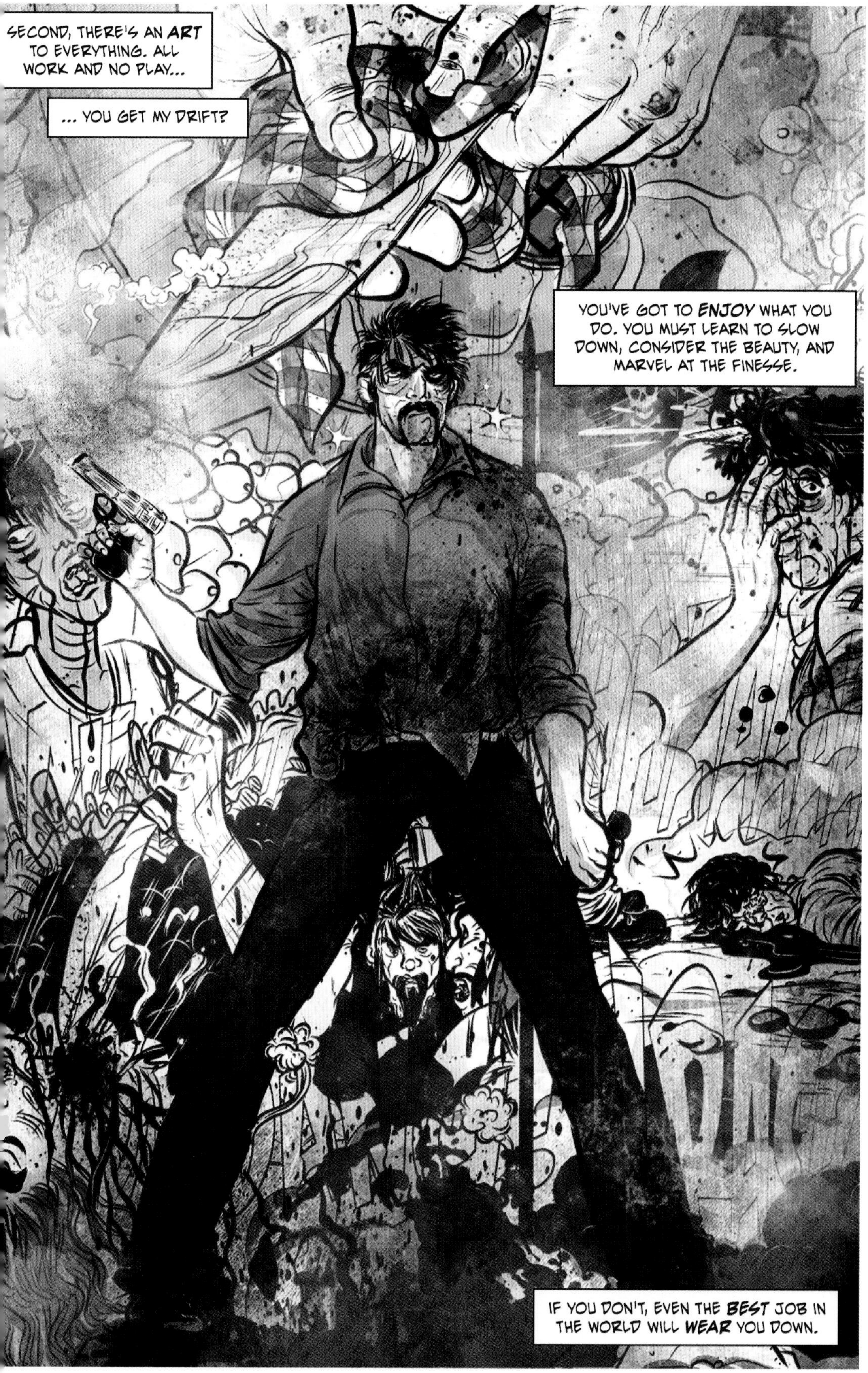
SECOND, THERE'S AN ART TO EVERYTHING. ALL WORK AND NO PLAY...
... YOU GET MY DRIFT?
YOU'VE GOT TO ENJOY WHAT YOU DO. YOU MUST LEARN TO SLOW DOWN, CONSIDER THE BEAUTY, AND MARVEL AT THE FINESSE.
IF YOU DON'T, EVEN THE BEST JOB IN THE WORLD WILL WEAR YOU DOWN.

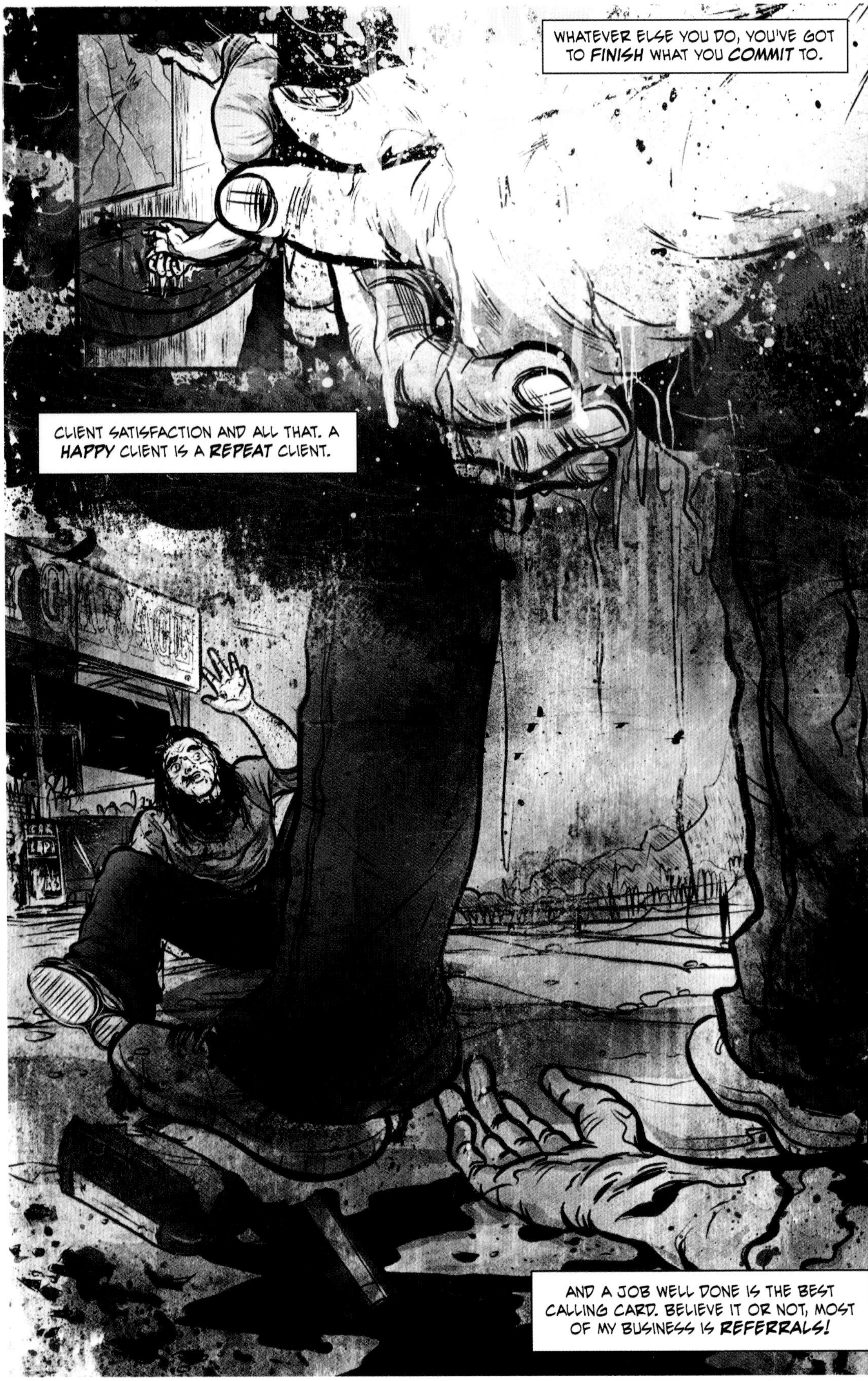
WHATEVER ELSE YOU DO, YOU'VE GOT TO FINISH WHAT YOU COMMIT TO.
CLIENT SATISFACTION AND ALL THAT. A HAPPY CLIENT IS A REPEAT CLIENT.
GARAGE
AND A JOB WELL DONE IS THE BEST CALLING CARD. BELIEVE IT OR NOT, MOST OF MY BUSINESS IS REFERRALS!

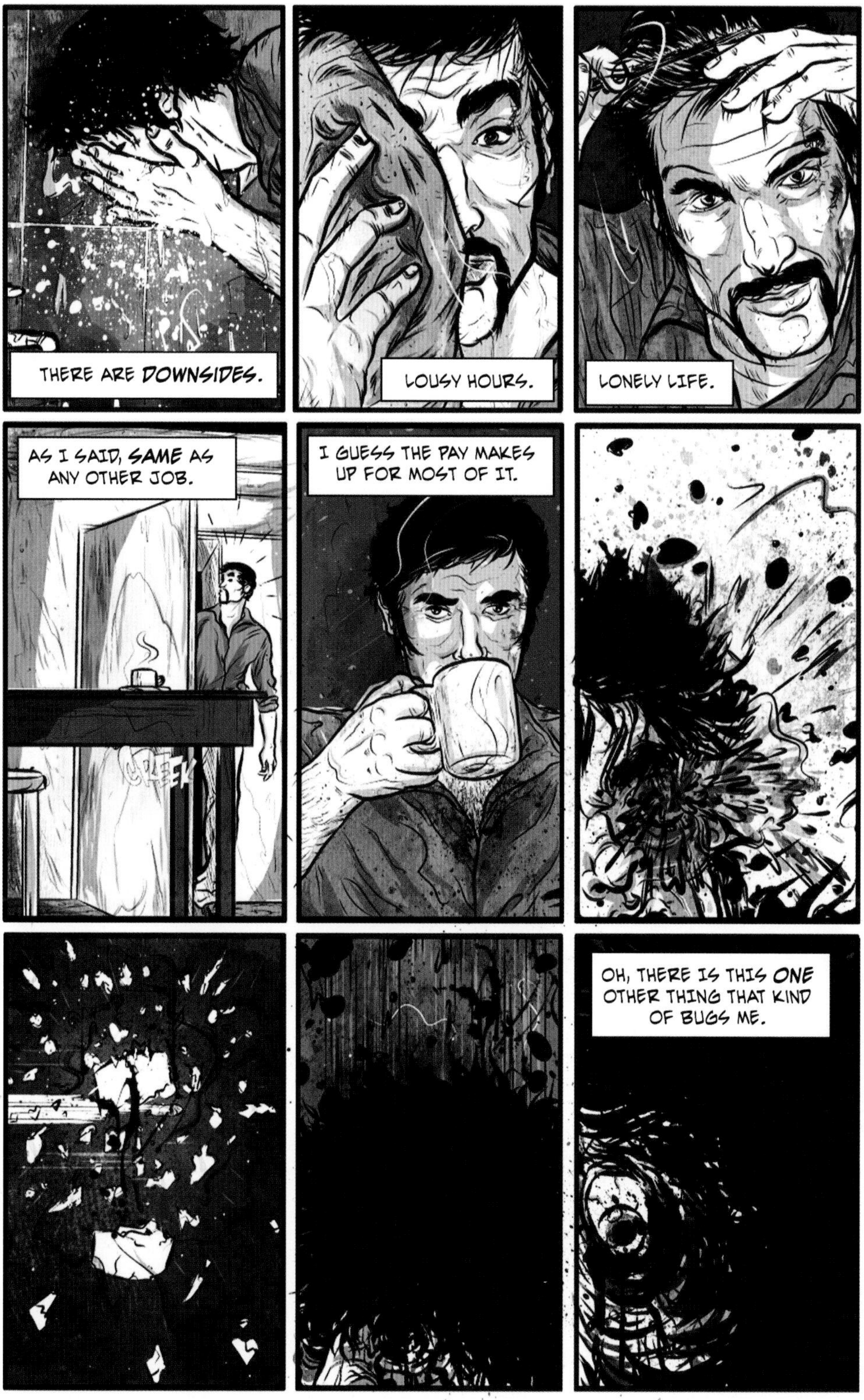
THERE ARE DOWNSIDES.
LOUSY HOURS.
LONELY LIFE.
AS I SAID, SAME AS ANY OTHER JOB.
CREEK
I GUESS THE PAY MAKES UP FOR MOST OF IT.
OH, THERE IS THIS ONE OTHER THING THAT KIND OF BUGS ME.

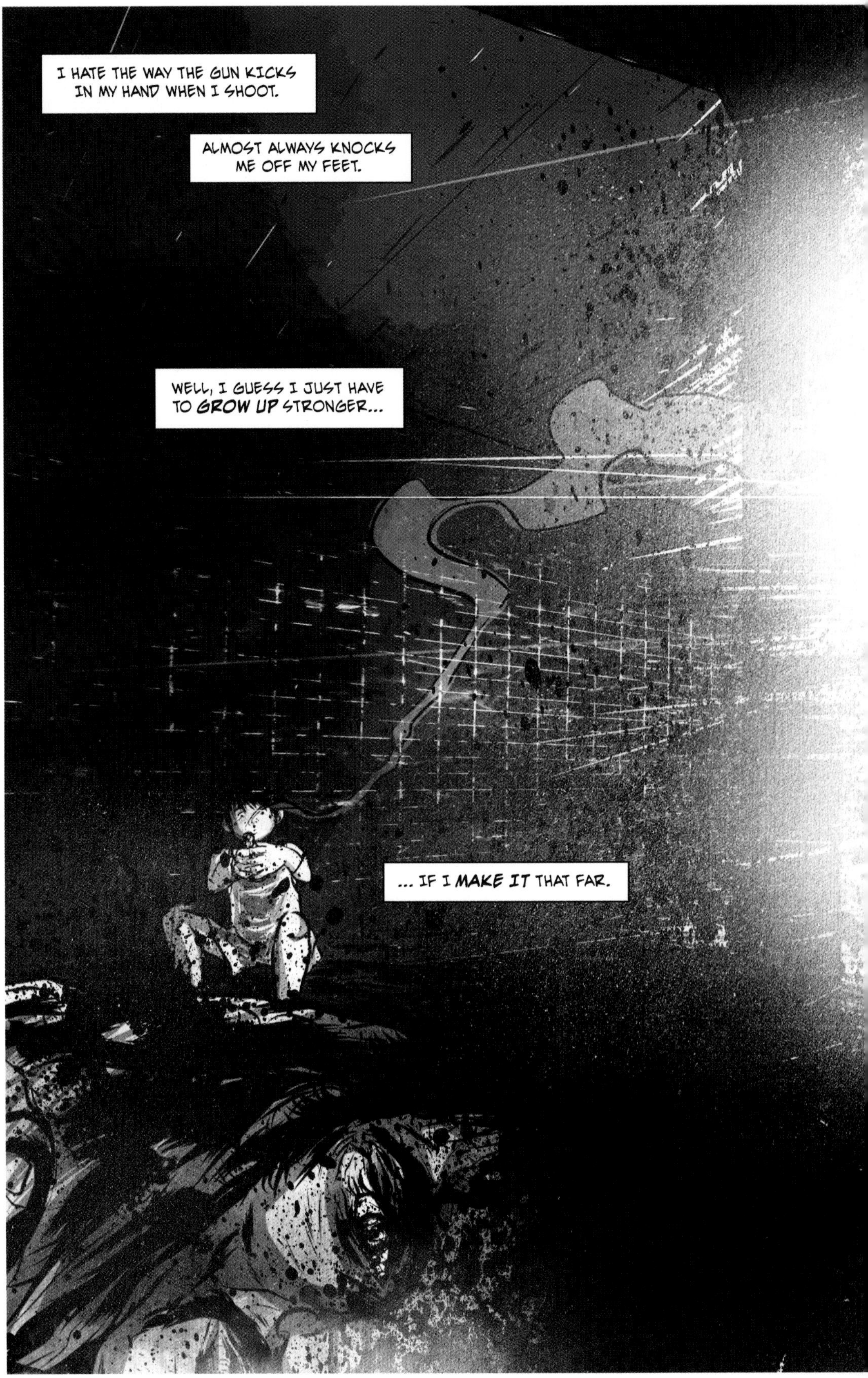
I HATE THE WAY THE GUN KICKS IN MY HAND WHEN I SHOOT.
ALMOST ALWAYS KNOCKS ME OFF MY FEET.
WELL, I GUESS I JUST HAVE TO **GROW UP** STRONGER...
... IF I **MAKE IT** THAT FAR.

Afterwords

The Mumbai Underworld has always been mentioned in hushed tones with respect to the Hindi film industry (Bollywood). Tales abound of star-struck mobsters cultivating friendships with Bollywood stars and movie makers, and of up-and-coming starlets becoming, in effect, what could be called Gangsters' Molls. Film financing by the underworld and money laundering allegations have been leveled time and again against the industry. The snazzy glamour of this tinsel town and the cold steel of the criminal universe have long enjoyed an alleged cozy honeymoon.

The heyday of the Mumbai Underworld was the eighties and the nineties. During this time period, the thriving city of Mumbai was plagued by rising crime, especially extortion of businessmen by gangsters. Desperate for a solution, the government took an unprecedented step. It sanctioned a band of elite cops to conduct extra-judicial executions of wanted criminals. The cops in question filed the paperwork, passing off these killings as Encounters, and the media picked up on it. The policemen involved earned notoriety as the Encounter Cops of Mumbai.

At first, as crime rates dropped and gang violence reached record lows, these policemen were the toast of the town. The press and the public alike declared them heroes and put them on a pedestal as the Saviors of Mumbai. Movies were made portraying their exploits, some real, some imaginary.

The honeymoon was not to last for long, however. In a way, the Encounter Cops were the victims of their own success. Once the gangsters' hold on Mumbai waned, there were hushed rumors of gross human rights violations and rampant abuse of authority and power. Perhaps it was the only way left for a cornered criminal underworld to retaliate, or maybe the allegations bore more than a kernel of truth. No one knows for certain.

What followed was a string of legal cases and investigations into these alleged excesses. The very same cops that were, until recently, fêted as heroes faced suspension from duty and transfers. Some were reinstated after due process, but the fall from grace didn't lessen the legend of the Encounter Cops of Mumbai.

The byways of Mumbai and in a way, the entire nation of India, speak in reverent whispers of a band of uniformed vigilantes who took on the criminals on their own terms, unleashing a righteous wave of retribution against the malcontents of the society, using methods the wrong-doers favored yet never expected to be facing in return.

But, there's a darker turn to the story.
One of the most disturbing allegations against the Encounter Cops is that they took money from the gangsters to either not shoot them or to kill their rivals, in effect becoming the very thing they set out to prevent, a protection racket.

The story you now hold in your hands is a fictionalized account of such a scenario, inspired by rumors, innuendos, and, in some cases, newspaper headlines. Perhaps all of it is true, perhaps none of it is.

It doesn't matter.
Whether you sit in a studio loft in Manhattan or a dingy bar in Mahim, it's a story worth telling.

We hope you like it.

Saurav & Vivek
July 2012

SPECIAL THANKS TO

Preeti Padhy, Aditi Kelkar-Shinde, Sid Kotian, Vinay Brahmania, Devaki Neogi, Samit Basu, Saumin Patel, Mukesh Singh, Mark Smylie, Pradipta Sarkar, Shounak Jog, Harshvardhan Kadam, Abhishek Malsuni, Paul "Well Regarded" Morrissey, David Lloyd, & Ron Marz.

Originally from India, **Saurav Mohapatra** currently lives in California and has written WITCHBLADE for Top Cow/Image Comics, and DEVI, SADHU, INDIA AUTHENTIC AND RIDERS for Virgin Comics. He co-created Mumbai MACGUFFIN and JIMMY ZHINGCHAK for Virgin Comics and has contributed to the second volume of THE PHANTOM CHRONICLES by Moonstone Books.

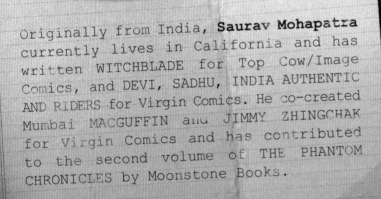

Vivek Shinde is a Mumbai-based artist who has worked on SNAKEWOMAN and PROJECT: KALKI for Virgin Comics. He co-created and drew the newspaper strip SPECIAL OFFICER SAWANT for MID-DAY, a Mumbai daily. He's also a freelance illustrator, concept/storyboard artist and a painter specializing in photorealistic renderings. His past clients include INX Networks, Oglivy & Mather and Leo Burnett.

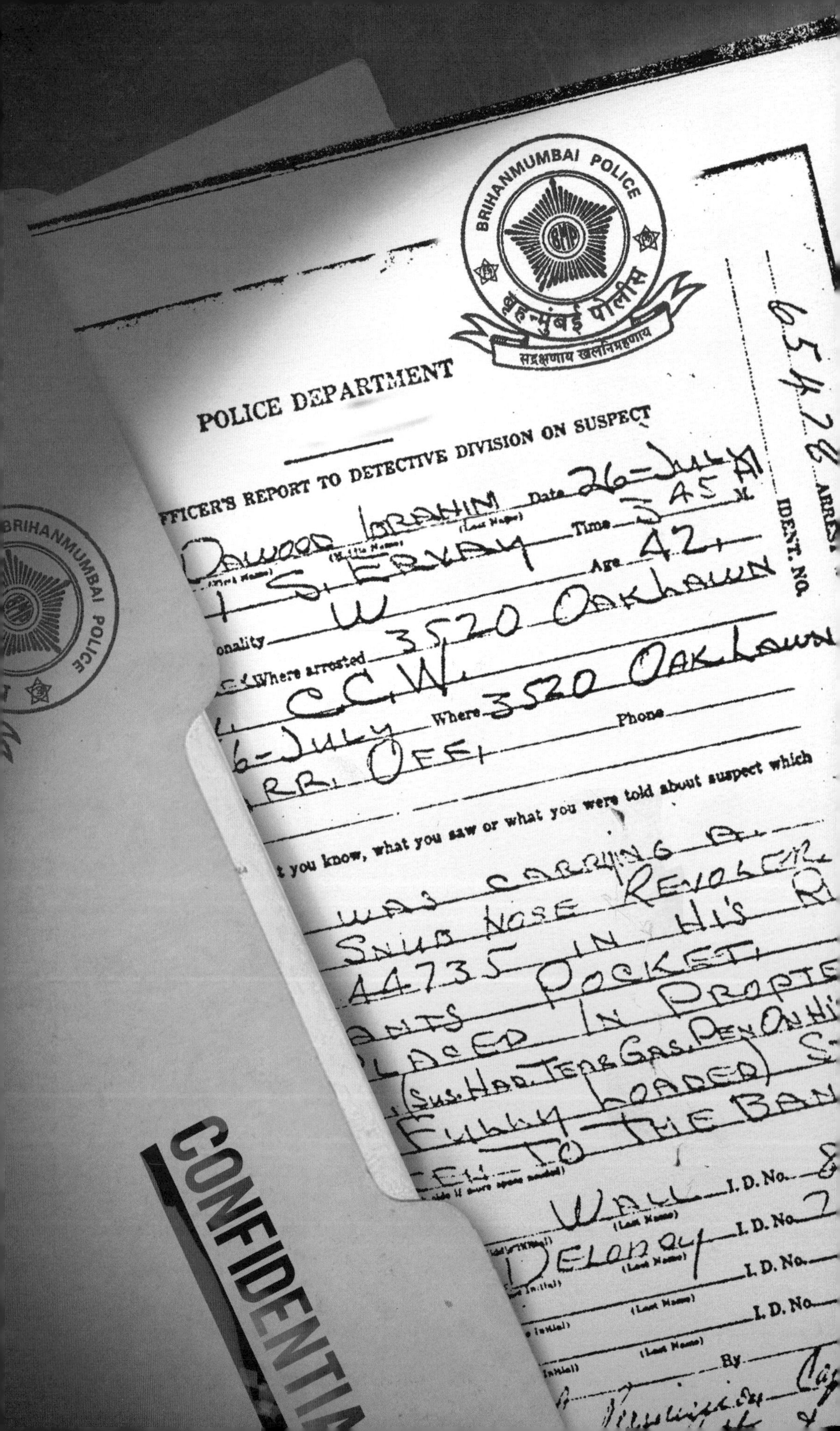

BRIHANMUMBAI POLICE

POLICE DEPARTMENT

FFICER'S REPORT TO DETECTIVE DIVISION ON SUSPECT

Dawood Ibrahim (Last Name) Date 26-July

S. ERVAY (Middle Name) Time 3 45 M

W Age 42

onality __ Where arrested 3520 Oaklawn

C.C.W. Where 3520 Oaklawn

6-July OFF Phone

RR.

t you know, what you saw or what you were told about suspect which

WAS CARRYING A

SNUB NOSE REVOLVER

44735 IN HIS R

ANTS POCKET

LACED IN PROPE

(SUS HAD TEAR GAS PEN ON HI

FULLY LOADED S

TO THE BAN

EL WALL (Last Name) I.D.No.

DELONEY (Last Name) I.D.No. 7

(Last Name) I.D.No.

(Initial) (Last Name) I.D.No.

(Initial) (Last Name)

By